Cultivating a Past

CULTIVATING A PAST *is a project of the Hadley Historical Commission in partnership with the Publications Committee of the 350th Celebration Steering Committee. It is gratefully dedicated to Katharine R. Nugent (1947–2007) in honor of her many years of service to the town and her generous support of this project.*

CULTIVATING A PAST

Essays on the History of Hadley, Massachusetts

EDITED BY

Marla R. Miller

University of Massachusetts Press

AMHERST

Printed in the United States of America

LC 2009006520

ISBN 978-1-55849-700-9

Designed by Steve Dyer

Set in Minion by Binghamton Valley Composition, Inc.

Printed and bound by Sheridan Books, Inc.

Library of Congress Cataloging-in-Publication Data

Cultivating a past : essays on the history of Hadley, Massachusetts / edited by Marla R. Miller.
p. cm.
Includes bibliographical references and index.
ISBN 978-1-55849-700-9 (cloth : alk. paper)
1. Hadley (Mass. : Town)—History. 2. Hadley (Mass. : Town)—Social life and customs.
I. Miller, Marla R.
F74.H14C85 2009
974.4'23—dc22

2009006520

British Library Cataloguing in Publication data are available.

Publication of this volume was aided by support from the Hadley Historical Commission and the Town of Hadley 350th Anniversary Celebration Committee.

HADLEY
1659-2009
350
YEARS

CONTENTS

ILLUSTRATIONS

ACKNOWLEDGMENTS

I thank Clark Dougan at the University of Massachusetts Press for his ever-cheerful support of local history, and also the anonymous readers whose valuable suggestions greatly strengthened the book. Doug Wilson passed away before the collection reached completion, but in some ways it was his well-timed query about the publication of his research on the Hadley regicides that spurred this volume's inception. More recently, my colleague David Glassberg generously read the introduction and other parts of the manuscript; his perceptive comments and practical advice are always welcome, and, as ever, I am grateful for his collegiality.

The book also owes a debt to the hardworking members of the Publications Committee of the 350th Celebration Steering Committee, Mary Thayer, Claire Carlson, and Jo-Ann Konieczny, and to Dave Martula, who co-chaired the 350th Celebration planning effort with Mary Thayer. Although the preparation of this book has often been a solitary endeavor, their commitment to the larger anniversary enterprise in many ways made it possible, and they were always quick to offer encouragement and advice along the way. Other supporters of Hadley history who have aided this effort include Eleanor Niedbala, who graciously provided the image of the Joseph Hooker celebration from the collections of the Hadley Historical Society, Miriam Pratt, who supplied the photo of her sister Dorothy Russell (and Rick Thayer, who nicely digitized it), and the family of Kate Nugent, who supplied the photograph of this much-missed friend and neighbor. Thanks are due the repositories and publishers who generously allowed us to reprint or publish material, waiving all or most of the customary fees.

I also thank each of the authors whose scholarship is represented here for making an enduring contribution to the history of our community. Some of them picked up work laid aside long ago to share their knowledge with new readers, and I am very grateful for their willingness to do so. Peter Hardin is to be particularly thanked for taking a cold call from a total stranger and agreeing to revise a thesis he thought he was done with more than thirty years ago. I also extend special thanks to James A. Freeman, who with his never-ending good cheer and wide-ranging curiosity embraced my request that he launch an entirely new project simply for the sake of this volume.

At the press, Mary Bellino deserves much more than mere gratitude for her careful attention and dedication to this project. Sally Nichols, Jack Harrison, Carol Betsch, and Carla Potts offered their usual patience and insight, for which I am also thankful.

Finally, this book would not have been possible without the encouragement and financial support of the Hadley Historical Commission. The commission had long ago earmarked funds toward a volume that would carry forward the story Sylvester Judd began to tell in the nineteenth century; when the planning for the town's 350th anniversary began, they agreed to put those funds toward this book. I am grateful to Margaret Freeman and Peg Tudryn (chair and secretary when this project began), for their enthusiasm for this enterprise, and for all their hard work through the years to preserve the resources—from manuscripts and ledgers to buildings and landscapes—that make such books possible. Selectboard member Kate Nugent likewise inspired us all, devoting her most precious hours to the betterment of the town. Her generous financial contribution to the Publications Committee made this volume possible. Her contribution to our community is too large to capture here. She will be remembered long and fondly.

The following chapters are reprinted by permission: Douglas C. Wilson, "Web of Secrecy: Goffe, Whalley, and the Legend of Hadley," *New England Quarterly* 60, no. 4 (December 1987): 515–48; Laurel Thatcher Ulrich, "Hannah Barnard's Cupboard," in *Through a Glass Darkly*, edited by Ronald Hoffman, Mechal Sobel, and Fredrika J. Teute (Chapel Hill: University of North Carolina Press for the Omohundro Institute for Early American History and Culture, 1997), 238–73; Karen Parsons, " 'We owe something more than prayers': Elizabeth Porter Phelps's Gift of Church Silver and Her Quest for Christian Fellowship," in *New England Silver and Silversmithing, 1620–1815*, edited by Gerald Ward and Jeannine Falino (Boston: Publications of the Colonial Society of Massachusetts, vol. 70, 2001), 91–112; Gregory H. Nobles, "Commerce and Community: A Case Study of the Rural Broommaking Business in Antebellum Massachusetts, *Journal of the Early Republic* 4 (Fall 1984): 287–308; Stephen W. Sears, "In Defense of Fighting Joe," from *Controversies and Commanders: Dispatches from the Army of the Potomac* (New York: Houghton Mifflin, 1999), 167–94; Ethan Carr, "Preserving Mt. Holyoke," in *Changing Prospects: The View from Mount Holyoke*, edited by Marianne Doezema (Ithaca: Cornell University Press, 2002), 63–76.

Cultivating a Past

Introduction

Pastkeeping in Another Small Place

Marla R. Miller

In the winter of 1827, in Plainville—a neighborhood in the northeast part of Hadley, Massachusetts—a half dozen or so men gathered together to talk about reading. Good books, they felt, were hard to come by in the small village. The group formed a social library, so that "all might thereby have a much greater chance for reading than they otherwise could have." Soon, some twenty subscribers—including members of the Cowls, Kellogg, and Hawley families, as well as Samuel Nash, John Strickland, Luther Miles, Sidney Smith, Dorus Green, Baxter Ayres, and other neighborhood men—expressed their desire to join. Each contributed a dollar toward the purchase of books that could circulate among the members. They chose to name their new organization the Historical Society, and the list of the first books they bought shows why: histories of Greece, England, and the United States; biographies of Martin Luther, George Washington, Benjamin Franklin, and Commodore Perry. They also obtained the memoirs of the missionary Mary H. Huntington and the Scottish theologian Claudius Buchanan, as well as Giles Gazer's historical novel *Frederick de Algeroy: The Hero of Camden Plains*. They bought a copy of the Koran and histories of the "Scottish chiefs"; a "history of the Indians" and a "history of the Pirates" filled out their initial collection.[1]

The Plainville Historical Society was interested, it seems, not in gathering and preserving local history but in reading about the history of the world, about men and women whose lives might inspire greatness in themselves. They sought instruction and edification, and horizons broader than their own. "If we look at the history of nations," an early officer wrote, "we shall [see] it to be universally true, that when the common people have the most learning that nation or people is the happiest." It was "for that very reason," he added, that "the people of New England are the happiest people on earth."[2]

The Plainville neighbors knew the value of history, and the pleasure of settling down for a good read. The Historical Society continued to meet for more than thirty years, until the eve of the Civil War. Their last annual report, from

1860, is brief, and it notes the purchase of just one volume: a life of John Brown. Perhaps the community had become too preoccupied with the immediate future to continue pondering the distant past. Just three years later, though, as the war raged on, Hadley readers' attention would turn (perhaps not coincidentally) to history once again; but now they traded global and national perspectives for local ones as they opened the cover of Sylvester Judd's *History of Hadley*.[3]

Judd's volume was one of more than sixty books of local history to appear in Massachusetts between 1825 and 1875, part of an emerging historical and literary tradition—the town history—that the Bay State led, and that has continued to flourish. "There is something so natural in enquiring into the history of those who have lived before us," wrote Alonzo Lewis in his 1829 history of Lynn (one of the first town histories to be published in Massachusetts), "and particularly of those with whom we have any connexion, either by ties of relation or place, that it is surprising anyone should be found by whom this subject is regarded with indifference." "To trace the settlement and progress of our native town," he continued, "to read the history of the play-place of our early hours, and which has been the scene of our maturer joys," and "to be informed of the people who were here before . . . now vanished like a dream of childhood . . . must certainly be objects of peculiar interest to every inquisitive mind."[4]

From Judd's day until the present, the history of Hadley has been similarly cherished by inquisitive minds. A town of just under five thousand residents on the bank of the Connecticut River in western Massachusetts and the native and adopted hometown of generations of residents over its three hundred and fifty years, it has generated its share of historians, both professional and avocational. Judd's narrative of Hadley's history, prompted in part by the town's bicentennial in 1859, has been joined by numerous efforts to probe corners of Hadley's past. The present volume, undertaken as part of a larger series of celebrations surrounding the 350th anniversary of the town's founding in 1659, marks our place in a timeline that stretches well before us and will continue long after us.

Inspired by Kerry Buckley's *A Place Called Paradise*, also published by the University of Massachusetts Press, this book likewise makes recent scholarship on a single New England town accessible to the local and regional community, as well as to readers whose lives are unfolding far from this bend in the Connecticut River.[5] In order to gain perspective on our roles as historians of Hadley and stewards of its heritage, this introduction contemplates the history of "past-keeping" (to borrow a useful term from the historian Michael Batinski) in Hadley, with particular attention to two of its most influential historians, the nineteenth-century antiquarian and author Sylvester Judd and the twentieth-century educator Dorothy Russell.[6] Judd and Russell were by no means the town's only historians of note: Clifton Johnson, James Lincoln Huntington, and the many other men and women who have preserved, curated, and written about the town's past have been essential to building and sustaining Hadley's sense of itself as a special place on the Massachusetts landscape. But Judd and Russell, as two of the town's most prominent pastkeepers—shaping even the essays gathered here—are worth pausing to remember as we observe our own moment in the history of our community.

Hadley's premier historian of the nineteenth century was never himself a resident of the town. Sylvester Judd Jr. was born in Westhampton, Massachusetts, in April 1789 to shopkeeper Sylvester Judd and his wife Hannah Burt Judd. At thirteen he began clerking in his father's store; two years later he moved to Boston, where he "fell in with persons of intelligence, whose influence was to stimulate him to an appreciation of knowledge, and to a determination to cultivate his own mind. . . . Whatever money he could now get was invested in books, and all the leisure moments intervening between the calls of customers, were given to their perusal."[7] Though Judd would briefly resume his career as a shopkeeper, the seeds had been sown for his rebirth as an antiquarian.

Judd returned to Westhampton, but now he would sit up until one or two o'clock in the morning, reading. He studied Latin and French, and "learned enough of Greek to understand the New Testament." He continued to gain a living through the store, and in January 1811 he married Apphia Hall and started a family of his own. But shopkeeping was not, as it turned out, Judd's strong suit; "his mind" (as his sister-in-law Arethusa Hall would later recall), "being always more bent upon the acquisition of knowledge than the accumulation of property, the matter of dealing with dollars and cents was irksome to him, and from a variety of causes, his pecuniary gains were small, and all his business operations proved very discouraging."[8] As Hall would note, "as time passed on, his love of study quite overbalanced his willingness to submit to the drudgery of exchanging pins, tape and snuff, . . . of measuring off calico and ribbons for their value in butter and cheese; or drawing molasses, rum, or brandy, for waiting customers."[9] Judd's distaste for business coupled with the economic disarray that followed the War of 1812 all but ended his mercantile career. As historians Gregory Nobles and Herbert Zarov more recently phrased it, the "bare outline" of Judd's career "reveals a series of disastrous business failures and a futile search for a viable vocation."[10]

Judd brought his disposition and his livelihood into closer correspondence when, in March 1822, he purchased the *Hampshire Gazette*, a weekly newspaper published in nearby Northampton. He found the paper to be "filled with stories, anecdotes, and other matter, fitted only to amuse for the passing moment," and he set about transforming it into "an educator of the people." According to Hall, he "occupied its columns with matter calculated to enlarge the boundaries of knowledge, and promote aspirations for further information concerning men and things." He printed abstracts and extracts from an array of scholarly texts; passages from the *Edinborough Encyclopedia* jockeyed for space alongside news articles, advertisements, and notices within the paper's columns.[11]

The *Gazette* under Judd's management was successful, doubling the number of its subscribers.[12] But in time Judd's career in journalism succumbed to the pressures of partisan politics. In the party strife attending Andrew Jackson's administration he found himself, as editor of what had been a Whig paper, "in a position so embarrassing" that he felt forced to sell the *Gazette* in 1834. Judd claimed that his aversion to extremism prevented him from remaining at the helm of a newspaper: "The truth is," he wrote, "I have become too skeptical in politics to be the conductor of a public press. I have but little confidence in politics, parties, and politicians. I dislike high whiggism and high Jacksonism, and cannot go with either."[13] His sister-in-law commented that "in the main, he had embraced Whig principles, yet, he had nothing of the partisan in his nature, and his mind was ever open to the influx of what he believed to be truth, coming from what quarter it might."

Now forty-six years old, Judd was disinclined to launch any new venture, choosing instead to "live on in a humble way, upon such means as he had, thus leaving himself free for such mental occupations as he might be drawn to."[14] The modest income generated by an inheritance enabled him to devote himself full-time to his antiquarian researches. Hall reports that at the age of seventeen he had begun filling blank volumes with "copious abstracts of Chronology, Biography, History, etc., with occasional entries by way of Private Journal, which had been kept up, with more or less continuity until this time." Now he "gave himself largely to Miscellaneous Collections, to a minute Diary, and to Genealogical, Historical, and Antiquarian researches, particularly with reference to the towns of Hampshire County, but extending also to the whole State of Massachusetts, and that of Connecticut." From 1835 until his death in 1860, Judd spent his days locating and transcribing documents from his community's past, recording extracts, and cross-referencing information. In the early 1840s he helped preserve, arrange, and index "old and valuable State documents" for the State of Connecticut. He was made an honorary member of both the Connecticut and Massachusetts Historical Societies, and of the American Antiquarian Society as well.

At first glance, Judd's *History of Hadley* would seem to be his greatest legacy to the town, but in fact he had already made a more important contribution to local history, in Hadley and through much of the Connecticut River Valley, long before he wrote its opening lines. Judd had begun pursuing a personal mission to capture a past he feared was vanishing completely, searching out documents, interviewing local citizens, and preserving papers and records he deemed historically significant. For twenty-first-century historians, the fruits of these labors—now preserved in the collection of the Forbes Library in Northampton—are simply stunning. Judd left more than sixty manuscript volumes, most running into the hundreds of pages, filled with crabbed handwriting. As Arethusa Hall would write, the volumes are "filled with an immense variety of little known, but curious matters, drawn from divers times and divers peoples, and gleaned from a wide range of miscellaneous reading."[15] Herbert Zarov and Gregory Nobles, who edited a selection of Judd's papers, once estimated that a complete transcription of the manuscript would run to some twenty thousand pages; they wrote that "several times we found ourselves wondering how one man could copy so much, even in a lifetime."[16]

The books are labeled according to topic. Five volumes are labeled "Massachusetts;" another series is titled "Connecticut." One volume is devoted to "Revolutionary Matters," another to the Congregational church in Northampton. Small subsets of volumes contain material specific to individual towns, including Northampton, Hatfield, and South Hadley, as well as, of course, Hadley. No fewer than nineteen carry the catch-all title "Miscellaneous." The volumes contain, again in Hall's words, "copious notices of our Indian tribes, vocabularies of their languages, and facts touching their domestic life; the varied experiences of the early settlers of this country; English and Scotch social life and manners, dress, furniture, etc.; prices of labor and merchandise, at different periods; . . . the history of woman in regard to social position, education, etc.; opinions concerning marriage, divorce, and the relations of man to woman generally; snatches of old song and quaint poetry, as well as the higher inspirations of the poet." As Hall further observes, the "above citations furnish but a mere hint, as to the multifarious and rare matter contained in these volumes."[17]

Indeed, scattered throughout the volumes are the minutiae of everyday life: pages are headed "Carpets," "Beds and materials for beds," "A girl's setting out," or "Coffee in New England," and then filled over time with anything he ran across, often cross-referenced to material elsewhere. Perhaps because of his time as a shopkeeper, Judd was particularly preoccupied with the prices of things: what people bought and what they paid for it, what work they did and how much they earned. Pages and pages are devoted to transcriptions and extracts from account books: the price of flax, the "price of board and value of eatables consumed," "wages of women," and so forth.

Judd was also interested in oral history. As early as August 1833, when he interviewed his seventy-six-year-old aunt, Charity Burt, he was seeking out aged residents of Hampshire County and soliciting their recollections. Twenty years later, Hatfield's Miriam Billings recounted local pirate legends, seventy-eight-year-old Jerusha Clark Sheldon described going to school at Pomeroy's meadow; and Sarah Amsden, also seventy-eight, related her memories of Independence and Election days, quiltings, and Thanksgiving.[18] In Hadley, John Cook reminisced about squirrel hunting, shooting turkeys below Goodman's tavern, and raising broom corn, while Abigail Dickinson Newton recalled for him the huskings of her youth.[19] South Hadley's Justin Alvord, Granby's Levi Moody—neighbor after neighbor sat down at Judd's request to serve up slices of everyday life from the past.

Judd's devotion to his antiquarian interests might seem eccentric, but he was also very much a product of his day. Among his friends was George Bancroft, who had moved to Northampton in 1823 to help found the Round Hill School.[20] Bancroft would leave his position at the school to devote his full energies to writing history, and he would become the premier historian of the nineteenth century; in 1834, just as Judd was moving toward his own decision to retire from business in favor of more academic concerns, the first volume of Bancroft's ten-volume *History of the United States* appeared.

At the same time, as Nobles and Zarov note, it may be "especially significant that Judd sold the *Gazette* and decided on a life of scholarship at precisely the moment that Ralph Waldo Emerson and the Transcendentalist movement he influenced came to prominence in Massachusetts."[21] Judd's connection to Transcendentalism is worth noting if only because it reminds us that his work was embedded in intellectual currents swirling far beyond Hampshire County. Judd's aversion to partisan politics—by 1845 he had even given up voting, except for antislavery candidates—reflects Transcendentalism's skepticism, its "distrust of authority and of formal institutions," and "paradoxical sense both that nineteenth-century American society was deplorably corrupt and that the celebration of native American subjects was the proper activity of native American scholars."[22] But he also embraced a Transcendentalist optimism, at least when it came to the potential of moral reform. A supporter of vegetarianism and utopian socialism, Judd was particularly passionate on the subjects of temperance and abolition; he served on the board of the Northampton Anti-Slavery Society and authored the group's constitution. He shared with Transcendentalists "a conviction that the country's greatness lay in the character of its common people and not in its institutions or great men," and his fascination with everyday life in Revolutionary New England and the early Republic was one outgrowth of those beliefs.[23]

Some of Judd's work found its way into print, if indirectly, in the writings of his son, also named Sylvester, a Harvard-trained Unitarian minister who drew on his father's antiquarian researches in his Transcendentalist novel, *Margaret: A Tale of the Real and the Ideal, Blight and Bloom*, published in 1845. The book was widely praised by leading figures of the Transcendentalist movement, including Nathaniel Hawthorne, Margaret Fuller, James Russell Lowell, and Theodore Parker, who called it the "most original and characteristic book that would appear here for twenty years to come."[24] The younger Judd, who was educated in part (during 1831 and 1832) at Hadley's Hopkins Academy, wrote the novel in Maine, where he lived for most of his adult life. But as he was revising *Margaret* for a new edition in 1851, he wrote to his father for help on some of the book's historical context. Interested especially in the years between 1783 and 1800, he asked his father to round up whatever he could on the "dress, literature, etc., the general costume of the time, what influences were upon it, its architecture, etc. . . . Also if you could lay hands on any old arms, or bits of dresses, and old furniture, etc."[25] The elder Judd was happy to comply.

In fact, Judd contemplated writing up his research in his own book, a history of Northampton and the towns around it, but in 1857 Sylvester Smith asked him to write a history of Hadley.[26] In the genealogies that Lucius Boltwood prepared to accompany Judd's narrative, Smith is identified as a deacon in the church, as well as "the person, by whose solicitations Mr. Judd was induced to commence the *History of Hadley*, and from whom he obtained ten-fold more information and assistance in the prosecution of the work, than from any one beside."[27] The two men were of the same generation (Smith, like Judd, was born in 1789); they both came of age together with the fledgling nation, and apparently shared an interest in the past. The occasion for the book was, like the present volume, an anniversary celebration: the town's bicentennial in 1859. The town meeting of March 30, 1857, voted that the selectmen appoint a committee to "take and adopt such measures as the case may require for a public celebration." Smith was asked, together with Giles Crouch Kellogg, Theodore Gregson Huntington, Eleazer Porter, Franklin Bonney, and other local notables, to help steer the events.[28]

Judd, as Smith knew, had already compiled a good deal of information about Northampton's eastern neighbor: three volumes of his notebook series are devoted to Hadley subjects. The third, in particular, teems with glimpses into everyday life in the town. Early pages contain close descriptions, often from the memories of past occupants or visitors, of seventeenth-century houses; Judd then turns his attention to wagons, geese, pastures, plowing, cheese, and other topics in the agricultural past. No item is too small for his notice: he recorded that rhubarb "came to Hartford first, then Hadley," and that "people didn't like the smell of them," that sand for floors came from the bank of the river, "opposite the Fort Meadow gate," and that tea was generally used sparingly in the years surrounding the Revolution, but often by women on wash day.

These extensive and meticulous records meant that Judd could take up Smith's charge with little difficulty. Soon a list of five hundred subscribers was assembled, guaranteeing sales upon publication, though the book would not be ready in time for the bicentennial events. Judd drafted a considerable amount of the manuscript—over four hundred of the planned six hundred pages—but then his health failed: "Paralysis seized upon a system, enfeebled by general debility, and accomplished its fatal work in a few days."[29] Judd died on April 18, 1860, with the work unfinished.

Amherst attorney Lucius M. Boltwood stepped in to complete the genealogical section, and the monumental volume, titled *History of Hadley, including the Early History of Hatfield, South Hadley, Amherst and Granby, Massachusetts*, appeared in the middle of 1863, at the height of the Civil War.[30] Judd's wife, Apphia, applied for the copyright, and his sister-in-law Arethusa Hall contributed a biographical sketch. It was, as Richard Hathaway has written, "one of the earliest and best of the fat volumes of local history appearing everywhere" as a generation of Americans—acutely aware that the nation's future was uncertain—rushed to capture the best of its past.[31]

Nobles and Zarov have argued that Judd's history represented a "new sort of American scholarship" that "not only explored native experience," but also "focused in a unique way on the details of everyday life for the common man."[32] To be sure, Judd's history covered in detail the history of the town's settlement. Early chapters traced the schism that sent members of the Hartford and Wethersfield churches north to Hadley, the first allocations of land there, and the building of the church and school. Judd was preoccupied, in his research and his writing alike, with the first fifty or sixty years of settlement. The first three-quarters of the text barely get out of those first few decades; the narrative never reaches Hadley's experience in the American Revolution (though one of his notebooks, "Revolutionary Matters," was ready should he have lived long enough to draft that narrative, and a late chapter in the *History of Hadley* covers events in South Hadley during the war years). But other chapters gather up thematically the information Judd recovered about daily life, and stand almost apart from the book's chronological narrative: one chapter, for instance, is devoted to "Highways – Bridges – Ferries – Grist-mills – Bolting-mills – Saw-mills and sawing boards by hand"; another to "Domestic Animals, &c.–Horses, Oxen – Fat Cattle – Butchers – Cows – Swine – Pork and Bacon – Puddings and Sausages – Sheep and Wool and trade to Newport–Domestic – Fowls – Geese – Bees and Honey – Tobacco – Butter and Cheese – Flaxseed and Oil – Berries – Nuts – Maple – Sugar – Soap – Lights – Timepieces – Blue Dyeing – Cotton – Rags – Sleighs – Carriages – Wagon to and from Boston Time of Planting, Harvesting, &c.–Statistics of four Towns, 1771."

Lucius Boltwood noted that is was with "not a little reluctance" that he agreed "to complete the work commenced by one, who has well been styled, 'the distinguished antiquary of Northampton.' "[33] In 1863, "distinguished antiquary" was not the oxymoron it would become. In the mid-nineteenth century, considerable respect was bestowed on people whose devotion to pastkeeping resulted in the collection of vast amounts of historical material, though in time "antiquarians" like Judd would become objects of derision among a rising historical profession, dismissed as unscholarly amateurs who couldn't see the forest for the trees. One contemporary historian, for instance, has called antiquarianism "an inability to distinguish what features of the past are historically insignificant; an indiscriminately romantic attitude to the past."[34] But one man's minutiae are another's gems. Judd's head was not buried in the sands along the Connecticut River; like his neighbors in the Plainville Historical Society he read widely and deeply in the history of the world. But he also became more and more curious about the past in his own back yard. He nourished both interests simultaneously, sustaining a commitment to the life of the mind in a culture he saw as increasingly and dangerously preoccupied with crass matters of commerce and politics. Frustrations with the excesses of his own society may have informed his work, but that is no less true of his twenty-first-century counterparts: historians have always been shaped by the events of their own times. For Sylvester Judd, the study of history offered something larger than himself, and perspectives longer than his own. "I resorted to books and read considerable this year," he wrote in 1820, two years before taking on editorship of the *Gazette*, "to prevent the recurrence of disagreeable thoughts occasioned by my own affairs."[35] The study of the past lifted his spirits, and in the end allowed him to become an invaluable member of his community. As Arethusa Hall wrote, Judd "was cheerful in temperament, and remarkably genial

FIGURE 1.1. *Dorothy Russell with Frank Zalot and Eleanor Niedbala*

in social intercourse, being a cherished companion for the young, as well as for the more advanced."

Sylvester Judd was not the last local historian to be beloved across generations, and most Hadley residents today point to Dorothy Russell as the town's premier historian of the twentieth century. Born in Hadley on the last day of May 1913 to Herbert and Madeleine Clark Russell, by the 1950s she had become the obvious heir to Judd's weighty mantle (she owned several editions and reprints of his book, but only really approved of the original version, before George Sheldon inserted an essay refuting the legend of the Angel of Hadley).[36] As one grateful recipient of Russell's scholarly generosity would later remark, "You had the *History of Hadley* tucked under your arm but it was evident to all of us that you could make every page of it come to life."[37]

Russell graduated from Hopkins Academy in 1931 and went on, as many women of her generation did, to a career in teaching. After graduating from the North Adams State Teachers College in 1935, she moved to Chesterfield, where she taught all six grades in a one-room schoolhouse. But she soon returned to

Hadley, and for almost forty years "Miss Russell" (as she was affectionately known) taught at the Russell School (named for John Russell, the town's founder and the brother of her ancestor Philip Russell).[38] Her retirement from the classroom in 1975 meant the close of only one chapter among many in an extraordinarily active life of service. For the next quarter century she remained the inimitable force behind innumerable asparagus suppers and church tag sales. A member of North Hadley Congregational Church for seventy years, she served as chairwoman of the church for more than fifty of them, and as secretary of the Ladies Aid Society from 1965 until 2001, the year of her death. She chaired the flower committee for nearly fifty years, and was a member of the choir for at least that long.

It is for her historical work, however, that Russell is best and most widely remembered. As a descendent of an important local family, Dorothy grew up with an acute sense of her family's past, inextricably bound up with the history of the town. Her contribution to Hadley history was very different from Sylvester Judd's. Though both spent innumerable hours poring over public and private records, trying to make sense of the town's past, Russell's contribution was not in tomes, but in action. Her emphasis was on people, on engaging others in an array of efforts aimed at documenting and appreciating the past. She maintained a staggering correspondence with genealogists across the country, supplying and confirming the small facts of which family histories are built. The hundreds of letters that survive among her papers at the Hadley Historical Society attest to her willingness to embrace their quests as though they were her own. "I only wish that everyone to whom I wrote would be so helpful," remarked one thankful correspondent, while another commented, "I feel like you are a friend."[39] Russell combed town records and church registers in search of the requested information, and if she could not find it carried the queries with her to Springfield and elsewhere. When she received two inquiries about the same surname, she often put the two correspondents—once strangers but now relatives—in touch so they could compare notes. But the heart of her work was really in building the institutions that continue to serve as stewards of Hadley's past. As a founder and longtime member of both the Hadley Historical Society and the Hadley Historical Commission, Russell arguably contributed more than any other member of the community to the preservation of local history in the last half of the twentieth century.

Today's Hadley Historical Society, like Judd's history, is in part a legacy of another centennial moment—the 1959 celebration of the three hundredth anniversary of the town's founding. But it has roots, too, in the local chapter of the Daughters of the American Revolution, founded in 1904.[40] Early on, D.A.R.

members identified the graves of Hadley's Revolutionary War veterans; they also placed the monument that stands today in the center of the common marking the original site of the Hadley meetinghouse.[41] For more than fifty years the D.A.R. met regularly to listen to papers on subjects of local interest, from the genealogies of their fellow members to Hadley in the Revolution to antique furniture. One hundred and thirty people turned out to celebrate the group's twentieth anniversary in 1924. At one particularly memorable meeting, members heard papers on samplers, handmade coverlets, and patchwork quilts before adjourning to an exhibit of some thirty quilts, twenty-four samplers, and eighteen coverlets assembled by the presenters.[42] In time the chapter came to accept donations of artifacts like these, as well as manuscripts, and they displayed many of them in a room on the ground floor of the public library.[43]

Among those eager to support the D.A.R.'s activities was Frank C. Reynolds, a key figure in the history of Hadley pastkeeping during these years. Interested in history at an early age, Reynolds spoke on at least one occasion before the membership. A selectman for more than twenty years, he was also the chairman of the Hadley Library Association. When preparations were being made for the town's tercentenary in 1959, Reynolds had been thinking about the town's historic materials housed there for some time, and he was eager to attend to their ongoing care.[44]

Already a beloved schoolteacher in the community, Dorothy Russell was an obvious choice for the committee formed in 1957 to begin planning the festivities that would surround the tercentenary—a highly successful occasion by all accounts. But that committee would take on a life far beyond the steering of the anniversary celebration. The D.A.R. membership was dwindling in the late 1950s; the group's aging members were struggling to maintain the artifacts and papers they had gathered over the years. Reynolds, Russell, and others overseeing the anniversary events seemed natural choices to help the D.A.R. chapter display its collections at the town-wide celebration, and after the chapter officially disbanded in 1961, the committee continued to help care for the assemblage of historical materials that had by now come to rest in the assembly room of the public library.[45]

The committee continued to meet through the 1960s, though with decreasing frequency. But efforts to curate the town's past were soon thereafter revived: the Hadley Historical Society formed in 1973, and it was incorporated in the year of the nation's bicentennial, 1976.[46] Dorothy Russell would hold a variety of leadership positions from that year until her advancing age made it difficult to continue; her sister Miriam Pratt served alongside her through those decades, and continues (now in her nineties) to be among the Historical Society's most valuable members.[47]

Unsurprisingly, when the Hadley Historical Commission was first organized in 1974 (at just around the same time that the Historical Society was getting on its organizational feet), Dorothy Russell was again among the first to be appointed, serving until 1998. The mission of the Historical Commission was different than that of the Historical Society; the commission was not concerned simply with Hadley history in general, but with the buildings and landscapes that together documented the town's past. Local historical commissions like Hadley's worked under the auspices of the Massachusetts Historical Commission, created in 1963 and charged with helping the Commonwealth to identify, document, and protect its historic buildings and landscapes. A statewide effort to form commissions at the municipal level soon followed, and at its spring 1974 town meeting the Town of Hadley authorized the selectmen to appoint a Historical Commission "to identify, inventory and record the historic assets of the town and to develop and implement a program for the preservation of Hadley's historical heritage."[48]

The commission's early years were spent documenting the histories of the buildings along West and Middle streets; members also attended a number of meetings about the future of the "mountain house atop Mt. Holyoke," the subject of Ethan Carr's essay in this volume. (Annual town reports from those years capture the intensity of that moment: "Three of the four proposals," they warned readers of the 1975 report, "begin with the word demolish. If the people of Hadley are truly interested in having the mountain house restored they must not wait until the bulldozers are ready for action. . . . Silence now could mean a cinderblock observation tower later.")[49] The Historical Commission surveyed dozens of properties throughout the town. In 1977, the Hadley Center Historic District was first nominated to the National Register of Historic Places, and in the mid-1980s a new initiative was launched to expand the boundaries of the earlier district to include some 2,500 acres and about 700 properties. (In connection with this work, the commission published in a walking tour of West Street, a resource that remains in demand today.) As that nomination made its way through the review process, work was undertaken to establish historic districts in Hockanum and North Hadley as well. The Hockanum district in particular was a pathbreaking effort, not only in Hadley but also in the Commonwealth, to recognize and document the significance of the town's agricultural landscapes.[50]

During Dorothy Russell's tenure the Historical Commission also worked closely with the town clerk to assure the survival of historic town documents, securing grant funds for the conservation and preservation of maps, broadsides, and other printed material.[51] By 1979 the commission had begun to consider the town's archaeological assets as well. In 1990 they undertook a particularly ambitious project when they supported an archaeological investigation into the site of Hadley's seventeenth-century fortifications, the only such structure in Massachusetts to be so documented.[52] (The essay in this volume by Ed Hood and Rita Reinke reports their work on that project.)

With Russell at the center of both the Historical Society and the Historical Commission, collaboration between the private and public organizations flourished. Their first cooperative effort took the form of a program that allowed residents to purchase small plaques for their homes stating the building's construction date. This project did not seek to acknowledge only the oldest buildings in town: anyone whose home's age could be documented no matter the date, was encouraged to participate, and by 1979 more than sixty Hadley houses sported plaques made by shop students at Hopkins Academy.[53] In the early 1980s, in anticipation of the town's 325th anniversary, the two groups collaborated again, this time on a town-wide genealogical survey aimed at updating the genealogies published in earlier editions of Judd's history.[54] Russell's complementary and simultaneous roles in both of these organizations have proven among her most cherished legacies. One appreciative fellow educator wrote to her: "Education should not end at the schoolroom door. Learning should involve the community. Certainly the Commission and Society have helped me to help students recognize those truths."[55]

Dorothy Russell's death in 2001 was met with much sadness, but her legacy, together with that of Sylvester Judd and other historians who came before, survives. Miss Russell had a hand in much of the scholarship assembled here, passing the baton on to a new generation of historians. Hadley's proximity to four of the nation's leading liberal arts colleges as well as the Commonwealth's flagship university campus has meant that dozens of scholars—students and faculty alike—have prowled among the town's records. Some of the resulting work has been published, but much of it has gained only limited circulation. Among the earliest student work is Ellen Elizabeth Callahan's 1930 Smith College thesis on the town's political history; more recently, Katherine Freedman's 2004 Hampshire College thesis explored relationships among women in the Porter-Phelps-Huntington family.[56] In fact, the large collection of artifacts and papers associated with the Porter-Phelps-Huntington house, Forty Acres, has generated its own subset of scholarly studies, including Elizabeth Pendergast Carlisle's biography of Elizabeth Porter Phelps, *Earthbound and Heavenbent*, as well as my own examination of women in Hampshire County's pre-industrial clothing trades, *The Needle's Eye*.[57]

The large body of scholarship grounded in the Porter-Phelps-Huntington family's papers reminds us of the close relationship between what has been written and what has been preserved—something of which both Sylvester Judd and Dorothy Russell were acutely aware. The Porter-Phelps-Huntington family has attracted more scholarly attention than others in Hadley because they preserved their family papers, as well as their 1752 home and hundreds of artifacts within it. In fact, Hadley boasts three private institutions dedicated to the preservation of the town's artifactual and archival records: the Hadley Farm Museum (a large and impressive collection of agricultural tools dating from the late eighteenth to the early twentieth century), the Hadley Historical Society (which collects both objects and archival material related to all eras of Hadley history), and the Porter-Phelps-Huntington Foundation (which preserves papers and objects associated with this extended family, from its founding generations in Hadley to the present day, no matter where history has taken them).[58]

Another of the largest and most significant collections documenting a Hadley family is curated by the Jones Library in Amherst, which holds the papers of Hadley photographer and author Clifton Johnson (1865–1940).[59] An author, folklorist, illustrator, and photographer of both local and national significance, Johnson amassed an impressive amount of material concerning the history of Hadley, particularly the Hockanum neighborhood where he and his family had lived for generations. In more than two thousand extant photographs, he documented and recreated scenes of rural life. Together with his brother Henry he helped found the Hadley Farm Museum (dedicated in May 1930), collecting farm implements and other artifacts of rural life (presciently, the Johnsons consciously elected not to "illustrate furniture, costumes, and the indoor household life of the old homes, for that was well and widely done already," but rather to begin their collecting "at the back door") and in time installing them in the barn from the Porter-Phelps-Huntington farm, which was moved to Russell Street (near the site of the First Congregational Church's onetime horse sheds) to house the collections and open them to the public.[60] He also recorded oral histories, folklore, and patterns of speech, inscribing them in dozens of small notebooks that today survive among his papers, creating an intriguing archive of nineteenth-century local history that remains largely untapped.[61]

Today's Hadley residents can take pride in the historical materials that one way or another have come to rest in area archives. But it has become increasingly apparent that if a community's full history is to be available for future generations, a proactive approach is necessary in order to help families, organizations, and institutions preserve their papers and records. The Historical

Commission, with Dorothy Russell's guidance, quickly encouraged residents to preserve their papers and artifacts: as early as 1979, their annual report noted that "commission members are hopeful that people in the community wanting to dispose of any historical material, books, maps, ledgers, account books, photographic albums, etc. will first offer their material to the commission [which is] anxious to keep Hadley memorabilia in Hadley for use by Hadley residents." Annual reports continued to urge residents to donate their papers and records, noting that "there are gaps in the official records of the Town and some material now stored in attics and basements might help to fill those gaps."[62] That mission was reinvigorated in the early 2000s, when the Historical Commission secured two grants designed to assess the current state of the town's historical records, to improve their care and enhance their scope.

In 2003 the commission, with funding from the Massachusetts Historical Records Advisory Board, began an ambitious two-year project to determine which areas of the town's history were already well documented, and whether any significant gaps might be remedied. With the help of consultants, commission members surveyed records preserved in public and private town repositories and worked with community groups and individuals anxious to preserve their own records for future generations. The survey revealed that a wealth of historical materials have been well cared for by a number of local organizations. For example, though few papers of Hadley women have been preserved from any era in the town's history, women's work in associations is well documented. The First Congregational Church preserves a marvelous run of records associated with women's groups through most of the nineteenth century that include societies to aid both foreign and home missions, as well as an outreach effort to the Onandogas. The records of the North Hadley Congregational Church, though smaller in size, are similarly rich. The Hadley Mother's Club (founded in 1946 and still one of Hadley's most active community groups) was among the earliest organizations to respond to the project's aims, and it was certainly the most enthusiastic; their records have been formally arranged and made available for study. Taken together, these materials will allow some future historian to write an important account of women's civic activism in Hadley over almost two centuries.

The project also revealed some important absences. For instance, there is very little material presently preserved that documents Hadley experiences during World War I either at home or abroad. Also surprising, and of equal concern, is the dearth of manuscript materials documenting the histories of Polish and other Eastern European families who moved to the community beginning in the late nineteenth century (and nothing yet preserved that represents the ethnic groups that would follow in later decades). The documentation project identified a number of records that remain in private hands and some oral histories that have been collected through the years, but no body of materials preserved in any local repository. Among the most exciting outcomes of that project, then, was the donation to the Hadley Historical Commission of four volumes of records and the published by-laws—all in Polish—of Hadley's St. Isadore Society, founded in the 1910s and continuing into the 1950s. These are exciting materials, which we hope will be joined in time by others.

In another effort to improve access to local history materials, and in the tradition of collaboration, the Historical Commission also secured grant funds—this time from the Bay State Historical League—to help the Hadley Historical Society inventory and arrange its manuscript materials, revealing other opportunities for future scholarship.[63] The society, for instance, holds an extraordinary set of letters from men in service during World War II that would support a fascinating study of how Hadley servicemen experienced life in camps across the United States as well as abroad. A large collection of scrapbooks—particularly two large series, compiled by Helen Nash and Sophie Mitchell—document many aspects of local history, as well as the art and craft of scrapbooking itself. When Hadley next celebrates a landmark anniversary, perhaps in 2059, studies based on these and other yet-to-be-collected materials may well have been written.

Cultivating the Past gathers together work that has been undertaken in recent years on a range of topics having to do with the town's history. Even a cursory glance at the table of contents confirms that most scholars working on Hadley subjects have concentrated on the town's history before the Civil War. (The series of booklets also planned in celebration of the town's 350th anniversary will take up some latter-day topics, including oral histories of agricultural history and of the Polish community, a study of the Civil War and citizens of that era, a history of the Common from 1659 to the present, and an essay examining the work of author, artist, and local historian Clifton Johnson.)

The core of the essays published here emerged from a day-long conference on Hadley during the era of the Renaissance, broadly conceived, an event generously hosted by Arthur Kinney and the University of Massachusetts Center for Renaissance Studies. (These talks have gained a second life on Hadley's local cable access channel, TV5.) Several of the papers presented at that conference have been developed into essays presented here for the first time in print. Bridget Marshall and Brian Ogilvie's chapter, on accused witch Mary Webster, grew from work Marshall first undertook for Historic Northampton, which built a Web exhibit interpreting the history of witchcraft in western Massachusetts.[64]

Alice Nash's chapter on Quanquan's mortgage is based on scholarship that grew out of her ongoing interdisciplinary collaboration with the linguist Roy Wright. Lynne Bassett, today among the leading historians of the region's clothing and textiles, presents research begun long ago, when she was still a student, on men's clothing in colonial Hadley. Martin Antonetti shares his work to authenticate the so-called Goffe Bible, a marvelous story of sleuthing and science.[65]

It is a pleasure to bring those pieces together here alongside other scholarship that has not yet been published, but deserves an equally wide readership. Joining Ed Hood and Rita Reinke's essay exploring the archaeological record of the fortifications (known locally as the "palisade") that surrounded the early village, Siobhan Hart, Elizabeth Chilton, and Christopher Donta's essay on Native communities and the archaeologists who have studied them is grounded in part in work they undertook as part of a University of Massachusetts Community Service Learning course that allowed students to catalog archaeological collections in the Hadley Historical Society. Peter Hardin contributes an essay drawn from his 1975 Hampshire College thesis on Hadley's Polish immigrants. Finally, one of the essays present here was solicited especially for this volume: James Freeman's look at the life and writings of Clarence Hawkes, known widely in Hadley as the community's "blind poet." Taking as his point of departure a large collection of Hawkes papers recently transferred from Northampton's Forbes Library to the Hadley Historical Society, Freeman reviews Hawkes's prolific career, with special attention to his nature writings—the work for which he was most celebrated during his life, although it is little appreciated today.

Lastly, the collection includes a number of essays that have been published previously or are in preparation for publication, but in venues that may not have come to the attention of the many Hadley and Connecticut Valley residents who might have an interest in them. Douglas Wilson's essay on the connection between Hadley and William Goffe and Edward Whalley, who were forced to flee England at the time of the Restoration because they had been among the signers of Charles I's execution order, won the Walter Muir Whitehill prize conferred by the Colonial Society of Massachusetts in partnership with the *New England Quarterly*. Greg Nobles's study of local broommaking, "Commerce and Community: A Case Study of the Rural Broommaking Business in Antebellum Massachusetts," originally appeared in the *Journal of the Early Republic*, among the most significant scholarly journals for historians interested in that era. Karen Parsons's study of the silver that Elizabeth Porter Phelps donated to the First Congregational Church originally appeared in the landmark volume *New England Silver and Silversmithing, 1620–1815*, while Laurel Thatcher Ulrich's invaluable consideration of the so-called Hadley chests was published in the collection *Through a Glass Darkly: Reflections on Personal Identity in Early America.* Stephen W. Sears's reappraisal of the leadership of Civil War general Joseph Hooker appeared in his book *Controversies and Commanders: Dispatches from the Army of the Potomac*; musicologist Andrea Olmstead draws from her biography of celebrated American composer Roger Sessions to contribute an essay contemplating possible influences of heritage and hometown on Sessions's work; and Ethan Carr offers an analysis of the local, state, and national forces that have shaped efforts to preserve what is arguably Hadley's most notable natural feature—Mt. Holyoke—in an essay that appeared in the catalog accompanying the 2002 exhibition *Changing Prospects: The View from Mount Holyoke* at the Mount Holyoke College Art Museum.

When he was "reading a history," Sylvester Judd mused, he was "for the time being happy." All thoughts of his "embarrassed circumstances" and "perplexed affairs" were "driven out by the magic wand of the historian."[66] More than simply a diversion from the pressures of contemporary life, as Hadley historian Alice Morehouse Walker wrote in 1906, the "love of one's own town" is also one of the "dominant motives underlying good citizenship."[67] Members of the Plainville Historical Society knew that: they read history in order to make themselves better citizens of their own place and time. They also took pleasure in the fact that, though their effort was "not now large, we may still comfort ourselves by reflecting that the greatest libraries which have ever adorned our world, like the brightest stars in heavens, have appeared dim at their rising."[68] *Cultivating the Past*, likewise, is meant to add some small radiance to the study of Hadley's history. Like the readers of the Plainville Historical Society, we read about the past so that we might think in new ways about the present. I will give the Plainville Historical Society the last word, because, as they write, "it is needless to proceed farther to illustrate the benefits of learning: you all know its benefits & none present we presume would be willing to be deprived of the privilege of reading."[69]

Notes

1. First annual report of the Plainville Historical Society, March 1827, Hadley Historical Society, Hadley, Mass. (hereafter cited as HHS).
2. Ibid. Another early library organization, the Hadley Young Men's Library Association, formed in March 1856 and led more directly to the creation of the current Goodwin Memorial Library. Its membership pressed for a town-wide public library, and the townspeople began to move in that direction in 1888, when they appointed the first Board of Library Trustees in 1888. That group shepherded the creation of the Goodwin Memorial Library, which was dedicated in 1903.

3. Sylvester Judd, *History of Hadley, including the Early History of Hatfield, South Hadley, Amherst and Granby, Massachusetts* (Northampton, Mass: Metcalf & Company, 1863). A second edition was issued in 1905 by the H. R. Huntting Co. of Springfield, Mass.; it includes, apart from minor changes in punctuation and pagination, an introduction by Deerfield historian George Sheldon on the regicides Goffe and Whalley and the Angel of Hadley story, and a number of additions to Lucius Boltwood's genealogical appendix. The second edition is the one most often cited in this volume, because it is available in several photographic reprint editions.
4. Alonzo Lewis, *The History of Lynn* (Boston: J. H. Eastburn, 1829), 3. For more on this work and the blossoming of local history as a genre, see David J. Russo, *Keepers of Our Past: Local Historical Writing in the United States, 1820s–1930s* (New York: Greenwood Press, 1988).
5. Kerry W. Buckley, ed., *A Place Called Paradise: Culture and Community in Northampton, Massachusetts, 1654–2004* (Amherst: University of Massachusetts Press, 2004).
6. Michael C. Batinski, *Pastkeepers in a Small Place: Five Centuries in Deerfield, Massachusetts* (Amherst: University of Massachusetts Press, 2004).
7. Arethusa Hall, "Biographical Notes," in Judd, *History of Hadley*, 5. Hall drew this sketch in part from the book she published on Transcendentalist author Sylvester Judd III. See her *Life and Character of the Rev. Sylvester Judd* (Boston: Crosby, Nichols; New York: C. S. Francis, 1854), 6–14. See also her *Memorabilia of Sylvester Judd, Sr.* (Northampton, Mass: privately printed, 1882).
8. Hall, "Biographical Notes," 6.
9. Hall, *Life and Character*, 13.
10. Gregory H. Nobles and Herbert L. Zarov, *Selected Papers from the Sylvester Judd Manuscript* (Northampton, Mass.: Forbes Library, 1976), 12. This discussion of Judd is deeply indebted to Nobles and Zarov's analysis.
11. Hall, "Biographical Notes," 6.
12. Ibid.
13. Ibid.; Nobles and Zarov, *Selected Papers*, 13. Judd was not unfamiliar with the political arena: his father had served as a member of the convention that framed the 1779 Massachusetts Constitution, and Judd himself was elected a representative to the 1817 General Court.
14. Quotes in this paragraph are taken from Hall, "Biographical Notes," 6–7.
15. Ibid., 7.
16. Nobles and Zarov, *Selected Papers*, 3. Nobles's essay in this volume draws partly on Judd's notes.
17. Hall, "Biographical Notes," 7. Judd's personal diary, "continued with regularity from 1833 to within a week of his death," also survives. Hall notes that "besides much that serves as auto-biography, and an exponent of his feelings, principles, and opinions, he recorded, with scrupulous regard to exactness, the tri-daily state of the thermometer; the changes of wind and weather; the different stages of vegetation; the appearance and disappearance of birds, frogs, and different kinds of insects, their habits, and so forth" (ibid.).
18. See the following entries in the volumes of the Sylvester Judd Manuscript, Forbes Library, Northampton, Mass. (hereafter cited as Judd Manuscript): "Northampton," vol. 1, 472; "Hatfield-Deerfield," vol. 2, 93; "Northampton with Westfield," vol. 2, 16; "Miscellaneous," vol. 15, 423–24; see also "Miscellaneous," vol. 15, 350.
19. Judd Manuscript, "Hadley," vol. 3, 54, 13; "Miscellaneous," vol. 16, 273.
20. Recently returned from Europe, Bancroft was among a handful of men who, as literary critic Richard Hathaway has observed, formed the "first wave of scholars bringing

new ideas back from German universities, ideas that were the foundation of the romantic movement in literature, religion, philosophy and history." Richard D. Hathaway, *Sylvester Judd's New England* (University Park: Pennsylvania State University Press, 1981), 119.

21. Nobles and Zarov, *Selected Papers*, 14. The discussion in this paragraph is based on ibid., 14–17.
22. Ibid., 14–15.
23. Ibid., 17.
24. Quoted in Gavin Jones, "The Paradise of Aesthetics: Sylvester Judd's *Margaret* and Antebellum American Literature," *New England Quarterly* 71, no. 3 (September 1998): 449. See also C. Grant Loomis, "Sylvester Judd's New England Lore," *Journal of American Folklore* 60, no. 236 (April 1947): 151–58; Hathaway, *Sylvester Judd's New England*; Philip Judd Brockway, *Sylvester Judd (1813–1853): Novelist of Transcendentalism* (Orono, Maine: Printed at the University Press, 1941); and Bruce Rhonda, "Sylvester Judd's *Margaret*: Open Spirits and Hidden Hearts," *American Transcendental Quarterly* 39 (Summer 1978): 217–30. An annotated edition of *Margaret*, with an introduction by Gavin Jones, will be published in 2009 by University of Massachusetts Press.
25. Hall, *Life and Character*, 350.
26. Smith appears among Judd's informants on matters historical; see Judd Manuscript, "Miscellaneous," vol. 18, 81 (on fruit growing); and "Miscellaneous," vol. 19, 386 (on beekeeping).
27. Judd, *History of Hadley*, 576.
28. Ibid., 610. Curiously, Judd is not listed among those invited to speak at the celebration ceremonies; Frederic Dan Huntington delivered the historical address. On the events of the bicentennial, see Frederic Dan Huntington and Edward Clarke Porter, *Bi-centennial Celebration at Hadley, June 8, 1859* (Northampton, Mass.: Bridgman & Childs, 1859).
29. Hall, "Biographical Notes," 7.
30. Hadley lost thirty-six of its citizens to the Civil War, nine of them in 1863. See Eric Freeman, "They March to See the Elephant: Hadley's Participation in the Civil War," typescript, 1991, HHS.
31. Hathaway, *Sylvester Judd's New England*, 26. Other local histories tended to come much later in the nineteenth century: J. H. Temple's *History of the Town of Northfield, Massachusetts* (with George Sheldon) appeared in 1875; Sheldon's *History of Deerfield, Massachusetts* followed in 1895. The turn of the century saw Charles Oscar Parmenter's *History of Pelham. Mass., from 1738 to 1898* (Amherst, Mass.: Carpenter and Morehouse, 1898) and James Russell Trumbull's *History of Northampton, Massachusetts, from Its Settlement in 1654*, 2 vols. (Northampton, Mass.: Press of the Gazette Printing Co., 1898–1902). The early twentieth century added Daniel White Wells and Reuben Field Wells's *History of Hatfield, Massachusetts* (Springfield, Mass.: F. C. H. Gibbons, 1910). A valuable study of history writing for general audiences in the nineteenth century is Gregory M. Pfitzer, *Popular History and the Literary Marketplace, 1840–1920* (Amherst: University of Massachusetts Press, 2008).
32. Nobles and Zarov, *Selected Papers*, 18.
33. L. M. Boltwood, "Preface," in Judd, *History of Hadley*, 4.
34. J. D. Marshall, *The Tyranny of the Discrete* (Aldershot, England: Scolar Press, 1997), 46, quoted in Carol Kammen and Norma Prendergast, eds., *Encyclopedia of Local History* (Walnut Creek, Calif.: AltaMira Press, 2000), 22.
35. Quoted in Nobles and Zarov, *Selected Papers*, 19.
36. Miriam Russell Pratt, interview by author, 2 January 2007.

37. Eleanor Reid (President, Five Colleges Learning in Retirement) to Dorothy M. Russell, 2 July 1994, Dorothy M. Russell Papers, HHS (hereafter cited as Russell Papers).
38. *Daily Hampshire Gazette*, 2 August 2001; Pratt, interview.
39. M. Ruth Norton to Dorothy M. Russell, 9 February 1990; and Margot [ ] to Dorothy M. Russell, 10 March 1998, Russell Papers.
40. *Daily Hampshire Gazette*, 13 October 1904. The organizational meeting was held in the home of Mrs. H. S. Shipman.
41. Another monument was also probably erected about this time; located at the northeast corner of Russell and West streets, it commemorates the harboring of the regicides (see Douglas Wilson's essay in this volume) in the home of the Reverend John Russell, which once stood near that site.
42. Bertha Montague, "Review . . . 1925–30," D.A.R. papers, series VI, box 1, HHS.
43. Helen B. McQueston, "History of Goodwin Memorial Library," typescript, 1983, Goodwin Memorial Library.
44. Frank C. Reynolds obituary, undated clipping [*Daily Hampshire Gazette*, 1975], HHS.
45. Key members included Frank Reynolds, Doheny Sessions, Ruth Scott, and Dorothy Russell; Pratt, interview.
46. Penny Humphrey, "Years Blur History on Hadley," undated clipping, Russell Papers; and Dorothy M. Russell, "Timeline of events for historical room," ibid.
47. Miriam Pratt also served on the board of directors of the Porter-Phelps-Huntington Foundation (where she and Dorothy worked as volunteer guides), and her husband, George Pratt, was active in local history circles as well, acting as the curator of the Farm Museum between 1980 and 1997; Pratt, interview.
48. Town of Hadley Annual Report, 1974, 55–56. The original members were Dorothy Russell, Margaret Dwyer, Esther Barstow, Mac Gress, and John Clough.
49. Town of Hadley Annual Report, 1975, 45.
50. Town of Hadley Annual Report, 1991, 117. The nomination is misnamed and misconstrued in the Hadley Town Report; the Hockanum Rural Historic District, as it is correctly called, was not the first such district in the nation, but was indeed among the first efforts in Massachusetts to implement the guidelines published in the National Park Service's Bulletin 30, on the nomination of rural districts; personal communication, Betsy Friedberg, Massachusetts Historical Commission, January 2007.
51. Town of Hadley Annual Report 1979, 41; 1980, 41; 1982, 24.
52. Town of Hadley Annual Report, 1979, 41.
53. Ibid.
54. Town of Hadley Annual Report, 1981, 25.
55. Kathleen Woods Masalski to Dorothy M. Russell, 9 June 1989, Russell Papers.
56. Ellen Elizabeth Callahan, "Hadley: A Study of the Political Development of a Typical New England Town from the Official Records (1659–1930)" (thesis, Smith College, 1931); Katherine K. Freedman, "I Am My Mother's Daughter: The Role of the Mother-Daughter Relationship in the Development of Feminine Identity in the Early Republic, as Illustrated through the Personal Writings of Elizabeth Porter Phelps and Elizabeth Whiting Phelps Huntington" (thesis, Hampshire College, 2004). Other theses include Sarah P. Helyar, "Degree of Patriarchy: Land Inheritance in the First Three Generations of Hadley, Massachusetts" (Hampshire College, 1978); Peter Hardin, "Poles and Puritans in Hadley, Massachusetts: An Historical Study of Hadley's Polish Population (Hampshire College, 1975); and Andrea L. Vannelli, "The Establishment of a Township: Natural and Cultural Influences That Shaped the Settlement of Hadley, Massachusetts" (University of Massachusetts Amherst, 2000).

57. Elizabeth Pendergast Carlisle, *Earthbound and Heavenbent: Elizabeth Porter Phelps and Life at Forty Acres, 1747–1817* (New York: Scribner's, 2004); Marla R. Miller, *The Needle's Eye: Women and Work in the Age of Revolution* (Amherst: University of Massachusetts Press, 2006). Theses and dissertations based on the Porter-Phelps-Huntington materials include Elisabeth Briggs Nichols, " 'Pray Don't Tell Any Body That I Write Politics': Public Expressions and Private Admonitions in the New Republic" (PhD diss., University of New Hampshire, 1997); Tara Louise Gleason, "The Porter-Phelps-Huntington Family: The Social Position and Material Wealth of an Elite Family in Eighteenth-Century Hadley, Massachusetts (thesis, Amherst College, 1994); and Regina Leonard, "The Porter-Phelps-Huntington Property, 1659–1955: History of the Vernacular Landscape in Context" (thesis, University of Massachusetts Amherst, 2000). The Porter-Phelps-Huntington Family Papers, owned by the Porter-Phelps-Huntington Foundation, are on deposit at the Amherst College Archives and Special Collections.
58. For more information on the Hadley Farm Museum, see www.hadleyonline.com/farm museum/; on the Porter-Phelps-Huntington Foundation, see www.pphmuseum.org/.
59. Pockets of archival material related to Hadley history reside in other regional libraries as well. The Massachusetts Historical Society, for instance, holds the papers of Giles Kellogg and Elisha Porter, materials that document the town's military and political history in the late eighteenth and early nineteenth centuries. Old Sturbridge Village preserves records (1785–1847) from William Porter's shop on the Hadley common, as well as the papers and financial records (1813–1870) of Royal Woodward, a peddler and silk merchant based in North Hadley after 1840. The Baker Library at Harvard University's business school holds papers and records (1805–1858) of Charles Porter Phelps, as well as the fascinating R. G. Dun & Co. credit reports on nineteenth-century Hadley businesses; Harvard's medical school preserves the diaries and school notebooks of physician William Workman, who attended Hopkins Academy in the first quarter of the nineteenth century. Collections of the Pocumtuck Valley Memorial Association in Deerfield, Massachusetts, include the papers (1746–1892) of Hadley's Dickinson family and the account book of eighteenth-century Hadley woodworker Samuel Gaylord. The University of Massachusetts Amherst Special Collections and Archives holds the Civil War–era letters of North Hadley's Ellen and Mary Ware.
60. See Clifton Johnson, "The Tribulations of Founding a Farm Museum," *Old-Time New England: Bulletin of the Society for the Preservation of New England Antiquities* 23 (July 1932): 3–16. The museum was deeded briefly to the Massachusetts Society for the Promotion of Agriculture, and deeded back to the Hadley Farm Museum Association in 1963.
61. Of course, the papers include Johnson family materials as well that are invaluable; these include the school-age diaries of Roger Johnson, scrapbooks, and correspondence. Related materials donated by the Johnson family to the Connecticut Valley Historical Museum include a "Record of that part of Hockanum Meadow which lies easterly of the new channel recently cut through by Connecticut River, 1840–1872"; the "Commonwealth of Massachusetts instructions to Samuel Russell, Collector for the Proprietors of Hockanum Meadow" (1866), which includes a list of taxpayers; Chester Johnson's journals from 1854 and 1856; and Stephen Johnson's papers, including about forty deeds and other legal instruments.
62. Town of Hadley Annual Reports, 1979, 1981.
63. Kathleen Nutter and Marla Miller, Inventory to the Collections of the Hadley Historical Society, 2002, HHS.
64. The exhibit may be viewed at ccbit.cs.umass.edu/parsons/hnmockup/.

65. Other papers delivered at this conference but not developed into article-length essays here include Joshua Lane, "Seated in the Past: A Carved Joined Hadley Settle"; and James Freeman, "The Angel of Hadley: How the Myth Grew."
66. Quoted in Nobles and Zarov, *Selected Papers*, 19.
67. Alice Morehouse Walker, *Historic Hadley* (New York: Grafton Press, 1906).
68. First annual report of the Plainville Historical Society, March 1827, HHS.
69. Ibid.

1

Alice Nash's interest in the history of Hadley is both personal and professional: she descends from the Nash family that helped launch the seventeenth-century colonial town of Hadley, and herself moved to the Pioneer Valley in 1999, when she joined the faculty at the University of Massachusetts Amherst. Among other things, she found here opportunities to extend her long-standing interest in the Native Americans of New England to the town of her ancestors. The community of scholars engaged in Native American studies around the university is substantial and thriving, and Nash's essay is closely related to the two that follow: Siobhan Hart, Elizabeth Chilton, and Chris Donta's survey of the pre-contact era, and Ed Hood and Rita Reinke's report on the town's fortifications. As all of these authors note, they are indebted to archaeologist Dena Dincauze, whose research has influenced many scholars in the region.

Like many of the essays in this volume, Nash's begins with a moment of pastkeeping, when longtime local historian Dorothy Russell introduced her to an iconic document in Hadley's history, one that immediately engaged her curiosity. Her study of Quanquan's mortgage contributes to a larger conversation in the study of that first period of contact between English and Dutch migrants and the Native communities already settled in the area. Historians have focused attention on competing conceptions of property ownership and land use; Nash's close attention to the language of the document reveals a far more complex exchange than popular historical imagination, and even some scholarly inquiries, generally admit, and opens a view on those early, tentative encounters between two very different peoples.

Quanquan's Mortgage of 1663

Alice Nash

SOMETIME IN THE FALL OF 1999 I sat drinking tea in the home of Dorothy Russell of Hadley, an old family friend and the locally acknowledged expert on all aspects of Hadley history. Dot, as I knew her, was pleased to hear that I had recently been hired as a faculty member in the History Department at the University of Massachusetts in Amherst. In a sense, I was coming home to a place where I had never actually lived. The Nashes, like the Russells, go back to the original settlement of Hadley. Although I hated history in school, whenever I visited Hadley I loved digging through the attic of the old family homestead on Mt. Warner Road, where my paternal grandfather, Herman B. Nash, was born and where his younger sister, my great-aunt Helen E. Nash, lived until the mid-1980s. Aunt Helen's attic shaped my abiding belief that the stuff of history persists in private hands as much as in museums and archives. But even I was surprised by what came out of Dorothy Russell's closet.

After dispensing with family news, I talked about my interest in seventeenth-century Indian deeds. These documents from early New England are a rich source of information on the process through which English colonists acquired land and the indigenous inhabitants lost title in the English sense, although many continued to live on and around their original homelands. Because they record the names of the men and women who signed away land and the relationships between them, and they include careful descriptions of physical landmarks that often use Native terms and place-names, Indian deeds open up a window through which we can glimpse a world in the midst of far-reaching change. Dot listened and asked a few questions, then said, "You might be interested in seeing this." She went to a closet, rummaged around, and brought out something framed under glass. I gasped. It appeared to be a genuine seventeenth-century deed, complete with a red wax seal. On closer inspection it turned out to be a mortgage, not a deed per se—a significant detail that will be discussed below—dating from 1663. It recorded a transaction in which Quanquan, one of the sachems of the land that came to be known as Hadley, mortgaged the place he called Mattabaoug to Zachariah Field for the sum of twenty-two pounds. This debt, secured by the land, was to be repaid in a period of time variously noted in the document as either thirty or three hundred years. Quanquan's mortgage now resides in the vault of the Hadley Historical Society.[1]

The document (shown in figure 1.1) is difficult to read in several ways. The handwriting is unfamiliar to modern eyes, as is the spelling. Curlicues and flourishes abound, and words are abbreviated with superscripted letters. A number of corrections have been added, with crossed-out text amended by tiny script squeezed in between the lines. Beyond these technical matters, however, the content and context of the mortgage require a certain amount of explanation.

Let us begin by reading the text in its entirety. The following is lightly edited for easier reading: abbreviations are spelled out in full, spelling is modernized, and minimal punctuation has been added.

> This present testifies that I, Quanquan, being the true, right and proper owner of a place and piece of land commonly called and named by the

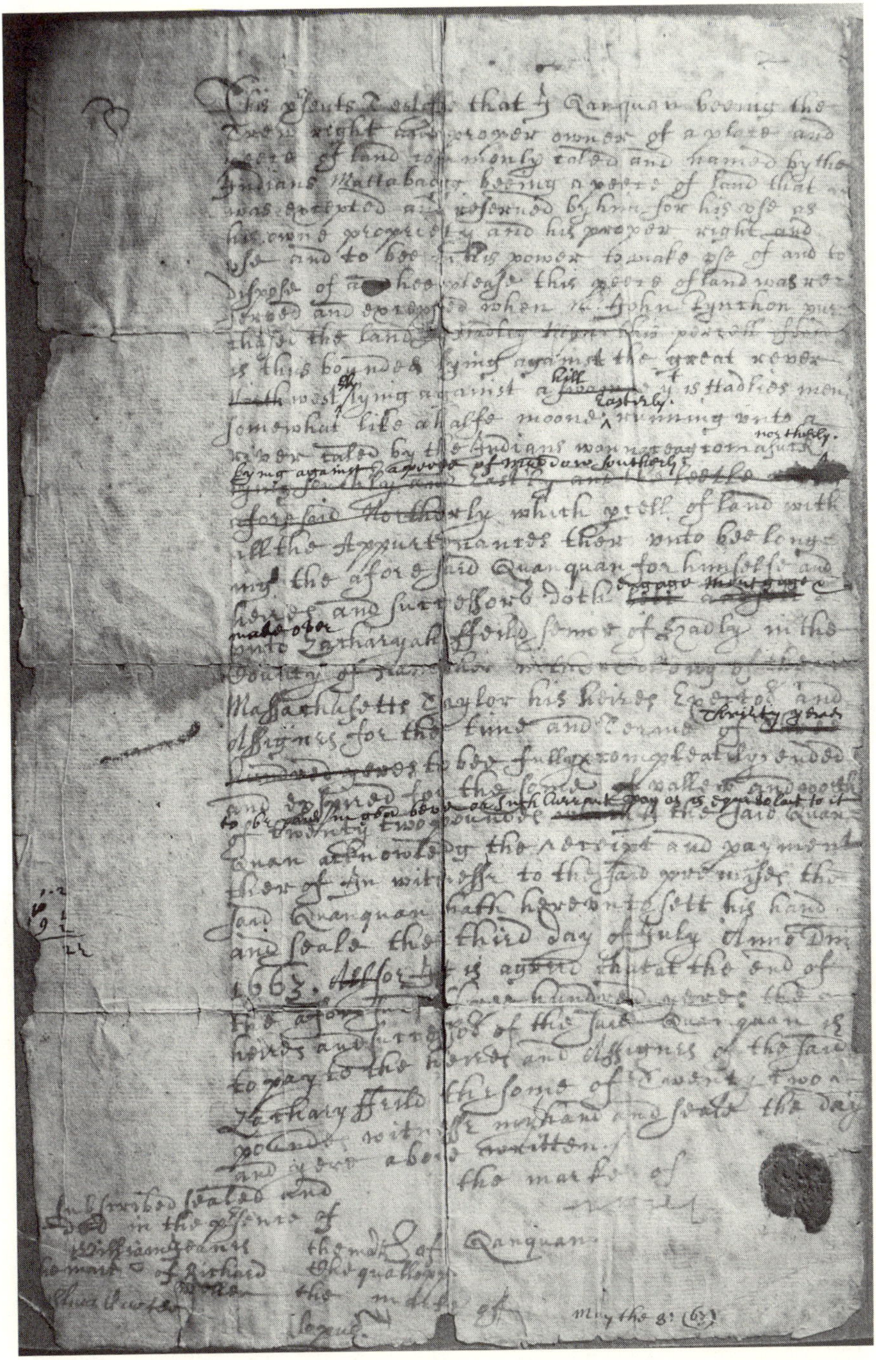

FIGURE 1.1. *Quanquan's mortgage to Zachariah Field, 1663. Courtesy of the Hadley Historical Society. Photo by Richard Thayer.*

Indians Mattabaoug, being a piece of land that was excepted and reserved by him for his use as his own property and his proper right and use and to be in his power to make use of and to dispose of [if] he please, this piece of land was reserved and excepted when Mr. John Pynchon purchased the land for Hadley men. This parcel of land is thus bounded lying against the great river westerly lying against a hill that is Hadlies men somewhat like a half moon easterly running into a river called by the Indians *Won nac eag comasuck* northerly lying against a piece of meadow southerly. Which parcel of land with all the appurtenances thereunto belonging the aforesaid Quanquan for himself and heirs and successors doth engage, mortgage and make over unto Zachariah Field, Senior, of Hadley in the County of Hampshire in the Colony of this Massachusetts Bay for his heirs, executors and assigns for the time and term of ~~three hundred years~~ thirty years, to be fully & completely ended and expired for the sum, value and worth to be paid in good beaver or such current pay as is equivalent to it of twenty-two pounds. I, the said Quanquan, acknowledge the receipt and payment thereof. In witness to the said promises the said Quanquan hath hereunto set his hand and seal the third day of July Anno Domini 1663. So it is agreed that at the end of the aforesaid three hundred years the heirs and successors of the said Quanquan are to pay to the heirs and assigns of the said Zachary Field the sum of twenty-two pounds. Witness my hand and seal this day and year above written.

Subscribed, sealed and recorded
in the presence of
William Jeanes
the mark of Richard Weller
Joshua Carter

the mark of Quanquan
the mark of Chickwallop[2]
the mark of Soxus

May 8, 1663

To summarize: this document is a mortgage, not an outright sale of land. Quanquan is the "true, right and proper owner" of a place called Mattabaoug that he held back when he sold the rest of his land on the east side of the Connecticut River to John Pynchon "for Hadley men," that is, for the town of Hadley. He is borrowing or receiving credit from Zachariah Field, Senior, of Hadley to the value of twenty-two pounds, which he promises to pay "in good beaver" or other currency equal to that amount. The loan period is unclear. The first mention of a repayment period says "three hundred years," which is crossed out and amended to thirty years. The second mention specifies that "at the end of the aforesaid three hundred years," the heirs and successors (that is, descendants) of Quanquan will pay the sum of twenty-two pounds to the heirs and successors of

Zachariah Field. Quanquan placed his mark on the document. On the original, it looks like an EKG line, zigzagging in an echo of script. Curiously, there is no mark or signature for Field. The transaction is witnessed by William Jeanes and Joshua Carter, who sign, and by Richard Weller, Chickwallop, and Soxus, who make their marks.

The documents known as Indian deeds are English legal forms adapted to a New World context.[3] They mark the uneasy recognition by New England colonists that imperial assertions of land ownership had little meaning to the people who already lived there. European nations such as England, France, and Spain based their claims to colonial empires in the New World on the Doctrine of Discovery, a legacy of the Crusades, which held that vacant lands could be claimed by the Christian nations that discovered them. Significantly, "vacant" encompassed all lands inhabited by non-Christian peoples. Other recognized ways to acquire territory were by purchase, by conquest, and by cession. Colonists in New England quickly realized, however, that they needed to stay on friendly terms with the local inhabitants, and that waving a piece of paper from the king of England was not a convincing argument. On April 17, 1629, the New England Company sent these instructions to the governor and council of Massachusetts Bay: "If any of the salvages pretend right of inheritance to all or any part of the lands granted in our pattent, we pray you endeavor to purchase their tytle, that wee may avoyde the least scruple of intrusion."[4] Five years later, the General Court at Boston modified that statement, requiring that the purchase of Indian lands be approved by the Court and that every town (and later, every county) keep a record book. In the Nolwottog (accent on the second syllable) homeland, John Pynchon and his agents were the ones authorized to negotiate the purchase of land from local sachems.

The historian Francis Jennings dubbed these efforts to establish legal title to lands in New England "the deed game," a great swindle in which hapless indigenous people were systematically deprived of land, subsistence, and sovereignty.[5] Jennings made the important point that English colonists were more concerned with a performance of legitimate title that would be respected by both English neighbors and other European nations than with justice in the sense of fairness. More recently, scholars such as Emerson W. Baker, Peter A. Thomas, and Jean M. O'Brien have added important clarifications to Jennings's insight. Baker, who studied Indian deeds in early Maine, argued persuasively that deeds are a critical source of ethnohistoric data because they document a face-to-face negotiation between the parties and illuminate how each understood the terms of the resulting agreement.[6] While the indigenous peoples of New England did not have the same conception of property ownership as the English, they quickly figured out what the English meant. This is reflected in the many deeds both in Maine and in the Connecticut River Valley in which the Indian sellers retain the right to hunt, fish, gather nuts, plant corn, and even erect their wigwams on the lands being sold. In Baker's capable hands, deeds become a window into seventeenth-century social relations, political and physical landscapes, the dynamics of family leadership, and gender relations. The Indian grantors named in them are people recognized by the tribe or family group as having a right to speak for others. To avoid later problems, the deeds were often witnessed by siblings who shared a claim in the land, or by neighboring sachems or sagamores whose territories bordered on the land being sold, to signify their approval and consent.

It is clear from the work of Peter A. Thomas that several factors affected the willingness of indigenous peoples to sell land. In some cases epidemics, such as the smallpox that swept through the Connecticut River Valley in 1635, had a devastating effect. The extremely high mortality rate meant that there was more room for newcomers.[7] The people of Agawam (Springfield), Woronoco (Westfield), and Nolwottog welcomed the English as allies against their enemies and as a direct source of trade goods. The fur trade flourished from the 1630s to about 1660, and Native leaders enhanced their prestige by acquiring and redistributing items such as cloth, metal pots and tools, and wampum. All too soon, however, it became clear that the English were coming in increasing numbers, and that land sales meant imminent if not immediate dispossession for themselves and for future generations. The beaver population declined after 1660, making it harder to pay off debts. Pynchon and his agents circumvented the laws regulating land purchases by issuing credit, secured by a deed of mortgage, then claiming the land as a just forfeit. Jean M. O'Brien's study of Natick, in eastern Massachusetts, makes it clear that this pattern was common across New England.[8] There is a qualitative difference between the early deeds based on relative equality and the later deeds that represent forced sales by Native peoples drawn into a burgeoning global market. Quanquan's mortgage of 1663 is a good example of the link between the fur trade and land loss. To understand it more fully, however, it is important to know a bit more about what it meant for Quanquan to be described as a sachem of Nolwottog.

The Nolwottog homeland encompasses land on both sides of the Connecticut River. Ethnohistorian Gordon M. Day describes the region as a "linguistic and ethnographic no-man's-land" because of the scarcity of written source materials to document lifeways during the early contact period.[9] It stretches north from Springfield, its boundary roughly corresponding to the break between Hampden and Hampshire counties, and includes the present-day towns of Northampton, Hadley, South Hadley, and Hatfield. The earliest Nolwottog deed, dated 1653, is for land on the west side of the river, purchased for Northampton. It is signed by three men described as sachems, or leaders: Nenessahalant, Nassicohe, and Chickwallop, who is also known as Wawhillowa. The first two names do not appear on later deeds, although it is possible that the same men may have signed under other names.[10] The third sachem, Chickwallop alias Wawhillowa, continues to appear on deeds, and I will say more about him below. Four other people are named as "proper owners," that is, people with a claim to the land recognized by both the Indians and the English as legitimate, although they are not sachems. They are Kiunks, Paquahalant, and Assellaquompas, all men, and Awonunske, the wife of Wulluther. Awonunske herself is listed as an owner, rather than her husband; it is not clear whether she inherited this status from her mother or her father, as both situations appear in deeds from this region.

Nolwottog is also known in the literature as Norwottock and Nonotuck, with orthographic variations on the three names. The 1653 deed calls the place Nonotuck.[11] This is not a misspelling. The Algonkian languages spoken by indigenous peoples in New England have three major forms, or reflexes.[12] The most obvious difference to the nonspecialist is that one uses *n* where the others use *l* or *r*. John Eliot, the Protestant missionary, wrote, "We in [eastern] *Massachusetts* pronounce the N; the *Nipmuck* Indians pronounce L; and the *Northern* Indians pronounce R."[13] Similarly, the endings *–ogg* or *–og*, *–ock*, and *–uck* are all variants of a locative ending, indicating that the word refers to a place. When documents were written by Englishmen who knew the land and its people well, such as John Pynchon and the fur traders who worked for him, they wrote *Nolwottogg*, because that was what they heard.[14] Nonotuck, the *n* form used in the 1653 deed, is an historical remnant, reflecting a kind of internal colonialism. When Englishmen such as John Pynchon and his father, William, first began to buy inland tracts in the Connecticut River Valley, they often hired the services of Native men from eastern Massachusetts as interpreters and to aid in the negotiations. The earliest interpreter, a Wampanoag man named William Ahhaton,[15] understood the dialect spoken by the people of Nolwottog, but he pronounced their name as Nonotuck. The name was written as Ahhaton pronounced it. Although John Pynchon later recorded the name as Nolwottog, the alternate spelling persists to this day. Ironically, the Nolwottog have been better known by what others called them than by what they called themselves.

In December 1658, "the Indians of Nolwotogg" sold a second large tract of land, this time on the east side of the Connecticut River, to John Pynchon, who was acting as agent for the inhabitants of Hadley. There is an obvious tension in the deed as Pynchon tried to reconcile the reality of collective ownership by "the Indians of Nolwotogg" with the need to create a legal fiction of individual ownership, or of individuals with the authority to sell land on behalf of everyone else. He identified three men as sachems of Nolwottog, "ye sole and proper owners" of the land: Chickwallop alias Wawhillowa, Umpanchela alias Wonscom, and Quanquan alias Wompshaw, in that order. As payment, the deed specified that Pynchon gave them 220 fathoms of wampum, a large coat worth 8 fathoms of wampum for Chickwallop, and other gifts and considerations. The coat suggests that Chickwallop was the senior statesman in the group; heavy cloth coats in red or blue were sought-after markers of status among Algonkian leaders. The 1658 deed clearly says that Quanquan retains ownership of "one corne field about twelve, sixteene or twenty acres of Ground," and gives a careful description of its location and boundaries.[16] Quanquan seems to be claiming this land as an individual, but Peter Thomas calculates that the reserved land would have supported sixty to a hundred people for eight to ten years.[17]

These terms suggest a more complex understanding of land and boundaries than one might expect, given the prevailing modern belief that Native people had no concept of individual land ownership at this time. Clearly, deeds such as the 1658 sale of Nolwottog land by three sachems speaking on behalf of a larger group exhibit the principle of collective ownership. But Algonkians also had a concept of individual property based on use. The land belonged to everyone, or, more accurately, everyone belonged to the land, but some people had a greater stake in one place over another because of their relationship to the land through use. This held true even if people were not living on the land at a particular moment. The Nolwottog, like other Algonkian peoples in the Northeast, followed a seasonal round of movements within a defined area. They might leave for a while, or even for a generation, after some kind of trauma, but other Native peoples knew that this did not constitute emigration in the European sense. Within the larger Nolwottog homeland, certain places were associated with particular people. The cornfields at Mattabaoug were one such place. Quanquan was also recognized as having a claim to land on the west side of the Connecticut River in present-day Hatfield (which was part of Hadley until 1670), bounded by lands belonging to Umpanchela and his people.

Why, then, did Quanquan agree to mortgage these cornfields to Zachariah Field in 1663, especially when he still owned a tract of land on the west side of the river that was not sold until after his death?[18] There is little data about Quanquan's participation in the fur trade and how exactly he became indebted to Field, although we know that Field was active as one of Pynchon's agents from 1661 to 1666. During this five-year period Field brought in 343 pounds of beaver pelts. Compare this to the 2,903 pounds of beaver brought in by David Wilton over seven years (1663–1670), or the 3,662 pounds brought in by Joseph Parsons between 1654 and 1667.[19] Field was such a minor player that in lieu of purchasing a license he paid a fee of three shillings per skin.[20] Still, Field must have started with bigger dreams. In 1661 he was awarded seventeen pounds owed to him by John Webb of Northampton, probably for trade goods, as Webb was even less successful in the business.[21] There is no record of what goods Quanquan (and likely his relatives) bought in racking up his debt of twenty-two pounds. After Zachariah Field's death in 1663, the Probate Court tried to examine his account books, which were "Soe badly written, and the accounts therein Soe doubtfull," that they gave up.[22]

Other records shed light on how Quanquan might have acquired this debt and why he chose to mortgage the land to Field in particular. There were two ways for Indians to be trapped by debt during this period: to accept goods on credit in anticipation of a successful season of hunting and trapping, or to become enmeshed in the English legal system by breaking English laws, for which the punishment might include jail time, whipping, fines, or all three. For example, in 1636 Cuttonis, the "owner" of lands at Agawam (Springfield), together with his mother, Kewenusk, and others, sold land on both sides of the Connecticut River to William Pynchon, reserving for themselves the right to plant corn in their own fields, to hunt and fish, and to gather nuts. In exchange they received wampum, coats, hoes, hatchets, and knives—all in all a positive, reciprocal transaction. Cuttonis and his people continued to live in the area, but their situation changed as the English population increased. As we will see, in 1661 Cuttonis and five other men mortgaged their remaining land at Agawam to Samuel Marshfield in exchange for goods already received, but they could not produce the necessary pelts on time and Marshfield took possession of their land.[23]

A second example hits even closer to home because it concerns Umpanchela, another sachem of Nolwottog. Umpanchela was a man who seemed comfortable with his new English neighbors. A deed shows that in July 1657 he, as an individual, sold a piece of land to the town of Northampton in exchange for the sum of thirty shillings, paid by John Webb. As noted above, Webb was one of the least successful agents working for Pynchon. A year later, in September 1658, "The Indian Sachem Umpanchela" complained to the court at Northampton that he had been cheated. He acknowledged making his mark on the deed but insisted that he understood the price to be fifty shillings, not the thirty-six he had actually received. The court decided in his favor.[24] This successful resolution may have encouraged Umpanchela to engage in further transactions with the English, as he was the first to sign the Hadley deed of December 1658.[25]

John Pynchon's account books tell us that during the fifteen-month period from September 1659 to December 1660 Umpanchela incurred substantial debts. On twenty occasions he bought cloth, mainly red shag cotton but some blue cloth as well as a single purchase of white. He also bought clothing: one pair of stockings, a blue waistcoat, two shirts, two pairs of breeches, and seventeen coats. Other purchases—all on credit—included a kettle, two guns, and seven knives. Umpanchela's account includes a small fine for drinking alcohol.[26] As a sachem, part of his status and prestige among his own people came from his ability to take care of others and to demonstrate his ability to act in the world. Trade goods allowed him to do that, whether he was wearing them, trading them, or giving them away.

On September 14, 1660, Pynchon made a notation in his account book that Umpanchela owed him three hundred fathoms of wampum for all of these goods received, and "So much I Ingaged to him for his land at Nalwotogg." This land on the west side of the Connecticut River was purchased for Hadley, and Pynchon immediately applied for reimbursement.[27] The actual transaction had taken place two months earlier, on July 10. The price paid for the land is given in the deed as "three Hunderd ffatham of Wampam in hand pd Besides severll other small gifts." Umpanchela specifically held back his planting ground, together with the right to hunt, fish, gather wood, and set wigwams on the commons. Pynchon was perhaps hoping to limit these rights to Umpanchela himself and not his people, for the deed specifies that all of the cornfields would belong to the English after Umpanchela's death, except that "ye Indians" would continue to enjoy the use of "ye old planted Ground in Wequetayyage and Down to ye Brook Cappowongseate alias Mattoolanick."[28] The last place-name, Mattoolanick, is intriguing because it is a variant of the word for a ritual specialist, imperfectly translated as "shaman," together with a locative ending. There may have been more than cornfields at stake. Further evidence that this was not solely an individual transaction for individual debts is the fact that the deed is cosigned by Umpanchela's brother, Etowomp, with a statement that he recognizes, approves, and witnesses the sale. The land did not belong to Umpanchela as an individual, even though his name was on the debt and the deed.

However much Umpanchela wanted to retain these planting grounds, he continued to accumulate debt in Pynchon's account books, which made his land vulnerable under English property law. Near the end of September 1660, Pynchon "trusted" Umpanchela for a fancy coat worth five fathoms of wampum, for which Umpanchela pledged "4 or 5 little Indian fields" or else "some of his old Indian Corne fields" from the land set aside. Two weeks later, and once again in December, Umpanchela incurred a debt for expensive coats, although this time Pynchon noted that the actual purchaser was Etowomp. The pressure mounted through

December as Umpanchela bought four more red coats, four knives, and a gun, and agreed to be responsible for two coats purchased on credit by "an Indian called Wuteallatssun."[29] This was a period of tension between the Nolwottogs and their neighbors, the Mohawks to the west and the Narragansett and Mohegan to the south, and it may be that Umpanchela was engaged in diplomacy and needed these items as gifts. By the end of December, without even a minimal period allowed for possible repayment, Pynchon noted in his account book that he had purchased all of Umpanchela's reserved land for Hadley.[30] The formal deed is dated January 17, 1660/1, and is signed by Umpanchela and Etowomp. With their title safely in hand, the inhabitants of Hadley agreed to give Umpanchela five acres of land within the boundaries of his formerly reserved lands. They also agreed to fence it and plow it if needed for the first year.[31]

Indians could get into debt even without buying trade goods by being fined for a wide range of behaviors if they were within the jurisdiction of an English town. This became an increasing problem after 1660. For example, in 1662 two men, Pagamunt of Pocomtuck and Awasshaws, were fined ten shillings each for being drunk, a behavior not criminalized in Native society.[32] In 1674 a man named Wellawas found himself in a similar situation. Since he was a "knowne Indian," as opposed to being a stranger, the Court granted him the favor of eight days in which to pay the fine. If he defaulted, he would be whipped ten times.[33] Sachems sometimes took responsibility for these debts. In 1674 Nowattassome and Wepuck were arrested for stealing a trap from Timothy Cooper. John Pynchon ordered them to return the trap and pay a fine of twelve fathoms of wampum. Three men, including Wequagen alias Wulluther, the husband of Awonunske of Nolwottog, came forward to guarantee that this would be done, and the men were released.[34] By 1663, when Quanquan mortgaged his cornfield, he must have known that owing money to the English, and especially to John Pynchon, could lead to the loss of his land under English law. Perhaps he hoped to do better when he chose to do business with Zachariah Field.

Zachariah or Zechariah Field was born in Yorkshire, England, in 1596. He arrived in Boston in 1629 and lived for seven years in Dorchester. In 1636 he moved to Hartford, then a new town on the Connecticut River. He fought with other Hartford men against the Pequots in 1637. A few years later Field married Mary Stanley, and in 1659 they moved up the river to Northampton. There, according to one biographer, he "had a large trade with the Indians," a doubtful statement given the evidence from Pynchon's account books.[35] By 1663 he was living in Hatfield, then still part of Hadley.[36] There is nothing about his life, from what remains in the historical record, that suggests any reason why Field and Quanquan should have any type of relationship whatsoever, positive or negative. Nothing sheds light on the strangest and most puzzling element in the 1663 mortgage: the clause that gives Quanquan and his descendents the right to redeem the mortgaged land by repaying the debt of twenty-two pounds in full within three hundred years. Even a period of thirty years, as corrected, is remarkable.

Other mortgages from this period specify limited repayment terms. For example, in September 1660 Amoakussen alias Nacogewallant of Woronoco mortgaged a parcel of land to Ensign Thomas Cooper of Springfield, one of Pynchon's top agents, as surety for his debts in the amount of twelve pounds. Amoakussen and his wife, who also put her mark on the document, agreed to repay the debt within twelve months or forfeit their land.[37] In April 1661 Samuel Marshfield, another of Pynchon's subtraders, acquired a mortgage from Cuttonis, Coo, Mattaquallanant, Menis, Wallny, and Tagnalloush of Springfield, who promised to repay their debts in beaver, if they could get it during the summer, or corn, or in wampum at a rate of six fathoms paid for every five fathoms owed. If these resources failed, they might pay him with moose, otter, or deer skins at a reasonable rate of exchange, or, as a last resort, he might keep their guns. They promised to repay the debt by "Michelmas next ensuing the date hereof," that is, by the end of September that same year. In May 1662 Joseph Parsons of Northampton acquired a mortgage on Hockanum, a part of Hadley, from Wequagon (also known as Wulluther), his wife Awonunske, and their son Squompe. They owed him eighty beaver skins in exchange for coats and wampum and other goods that they had already received and promised to pay the debt by September 5 or forfeit the land. In each of these cases, the Indians lost their land. When the mortgages became deeds of sale, the amount paid might be given in vague terms such as "for good & valluable considerations," as noted in Amoakussen's deed of 1664.

It is possible—just possible—that Zachariah Field and Quanquan negotiated the terms of this mortgage as a strategy to help Quanquan hold onto the land. We know that Quanquan also had land on the west side of the Connecticut River in present-day Hatfield, and they may have already known each other, even traded with each other. There is no evidence that Field made an effort to take the land, as did his peers Thomas Cooper, Samuel Marshfield, and Joseph Parsons in the cases cited above. In truth, Field could have used the income. He collected a debt of seventeen pounds owed to him by John Webb in 1661.[38] He sold land to William Olcott in 1661, to Richard Goodman in 1662, to James Pringridays in 1664, and to Goodman again in 1665.[39] When he died on June 30, 1666, Field left so many debts that his creditors received only a portion of what they were owed and his widow, Mary, had to make do with "a bed & Some other

Small necessarys for her Livelyhood" valued at just under £10.[40] The largest creditor, John Pynchon, received the biggest portion because he held a mortgage signed by Field that gave him the house, barn, and homelot, as well as "severall other tracts of land," worth about £178.[41]

The mortgage is also unusual among the group cited above for the 1660s because it is witnessed by Chickwallop, one of the other sachems of Nolwottog. As Baker has demonstrated for deeds from Maine, these additional signatures generally indicate that the person in question—in this case, Chickwallop—has some right or interest in the disposition of land. In some but not all cases this means that the signer is entitled to a portion of the payment.[42] Chickwallop's presence adds gravitas to this transaction.

I have not been able to identify Soxus, the third Indian to sign the deed, although it is likely that he is somehow connected to the land. William Jeanes of Northampton, the first of the English signers, was a Clerk of the Court and therefore present in an official capacity.[43] Richard Weller, who signs with a mark, is a marginal figure from Windsor, Connecticut, who, like Field, made his way up the Connecticut River. They may have been friends. Weller and Field were both made freemen at Northampton on January 31, 1663.[44] The last signer, Joshua Carter, was engaged to Zachariah Field's oldest daughter, Mary. They were married in Northampton on October 6, 1663.[45]

Two absences among the signers are worth noting. The first is Zachariah Field himself. One can only speculate as to what this might mean. The second is that no one from Quanquan's family is mentioned. If Field had formally taken possession of the land, it is quite likely that others would have been brought in to add their confirmation and approval, as when Umpanchela's brother Etowomp added his mark to Umpanchela's individual land sales of 1660 and 1661.

We know of Quanquan's family because they came forward after his death to sell his remaining land in Hatfield. That deed, dated October 19, 1672, describes the sellers as "Sarah ye wife of Quanquan Sachem late deceased & Pocunohouse ye Son of Quanquan ye Indian Sachem & Mattabauge Squa & Majessett daughter of ye sd Sachem & Momecouse Indians."[46] As is typical of this period, the document contains little punctuation, making it difficult to decipher the family relationships. In one reading, Quanquan leaves three children: a son, Pocunohouse, and two daughters, Mattabauge Squa and Majesset. The daughters may be the children of a second wife named Momecouse, or Momecouse may be a husband or other interested party. Another possible interpretation is that Quanquan had three *wives* rather than three children. In this reading, Sarah is recognized by the English as Quanquan's legal (legitimate) wife, perhaps because she is the oldest and presumably the first; she may have been a Christian, or someone who had close relationships with the English and therefore used an English name. Pocunohouse is the son of Quanquan and a woman named Mattabauge Squa. Majesset (also written as Muessett) is the daughter of Quanquan and Momecouse, also known as Memewatts. The existence of these three wives would of course have posed a dilemma for the English, who came from a legal tradition that emphasized the transmission of property through a man's "legitimate" heirs, defined through a specific legal paradigm of patrilineal inheritance and serial monogamy.

The possibility that Mattabauge Squa was Quanquan's wife rather than his daughter is heightened when we go back to the mortgage and see that the land in question is "commonly called and named by the Indians Mattabaoug." Allowing for differences in transliteration, this is the same word. *Squa* (**skw*) is actually a suffix that indicates that a person is female. It is part of the name, which should be written as one word: Mattabaugesqua, or woman from Mattabaoug. She would have had other names for other contexts, but in this instance it suggests that she may be more closely tied to this particular piece of land than Quanquan, and that his status as "true, right and proper owner" of it is a result of their marital alliance. Algonkian-speaking peoples sometimes identify women by the name of their husband with the **skw* suffix attached to the man's name. We see this at the end of the 1672 deed: Sarah makes her mark as Sarah Quanquan Squa (Quanquansqua), meaning "Sarah, Quanquan's wife" rather than "Sarah Quanquan, [a] squaw." This suffix is the origin of the English word *squaw*, meaning "woman" or "wife" in regard to Native women.[47] Writing her name in this way underscores Sarah's position as Quanquan's (legitimate, by English law) wife.

The confirmation of the deed offers further information. Hatfield paid fifty fathoms of wampum for Quanquan's land on October 19, 1672. About five weeks later, on November 25, Sarah "and her Son Pacanohouse" acknowledged the receipt of additional goods, mainly cotton cloth, equivalent to twenty-seven fathoms of wampum.[48] Although they are described as mother and son, it may be that this was a convenient fiction for either or both parties to the transaction. The English needed a wife and legitimate heir to complete the deal; Sarah and her family needed the goods or perhaps the goodwill that they gained from the sale. Where were they in 1663, when Quanquan signed his mortgage with Zachariah Field?

Whether or not Field intended to honor the terms of the mortgage, or whether he claimed the land but failed to register the deed, the executors of his estate counted the land as part of his worldly goods after his death in 1666. Hadley paid the estate of Zachariah Field ten pounds in 1667 for "ye land yt Zach. ffeild bought of ye Indians." This is the land mortgaged by Quanquan in 1663. Less than a decade after Quanquan signed his first deed with the English, Hadley claimed it all. What did Hadley do with the land?

When Dorothy Russell first showed me the Quanquan mortgage, she said that it was a deed for the land near her home on River Road in North Hadley, and that it was originally used to support Hopkins Academy, the public school in Hadley that was founded in 1664.[49] I began to look for more information and found that Sylvester Judd, in his *History of Hadley*, agreed. In his discussion of the 1658 Hadley deed he wrote: "The corn-field of 12, 16 or 20 acres, reserved in the foregoing deed, was sold to Hadley in a few years. It seems to have been a part of the upper School Meadow."[50] Indeed, on January 14, 1666/7, six months after Zachariah Field died, the land specified in Quanquan's mortgage became part of the "School Meadows," or land granted by the town of Hadley to support a grammar school. A note by Peter Tilton in the margin of the original record says: "These 2 meadows—one the round neck of land; and the little long meadow that was reserved by the Indians in the first sale, and afterwards purchased by itself."[51] In subsequent decades, part of the land was leased to the miller at Mill Brook and the remainder was leased or harvested for income to support the school. The corn mill on this site was burned by Indians in 1677, during King Philip's War.[52]

Over time, the land passed into private hands, although the site of the original corn mill still belonged to Hopkins Academy as of 1964, on the 300th anniversary of the school and the Hopkins Trust.[53] During the spring of 1904 Lyman P. Bullard, a farmer plowing his tobacco field in North Hadley, turned up some bones. Shortly thereafter the site was excavated by Charles Willoughby, archaeologist and director of the Peabody Museum of Harvard University, who found skeletons of two adults and a child of six or seven years old. Harris Hawthorne Wilder, a professor at Smith College in Northampton (discussed, together with other local archaeologists, in an essay by Hart, Chilton, and Donta in this volume), identified the site as the place where Quanquan had his cornfields and presumably a village. Wilder soon made his own arrangement with the owner of the field and spent two weeks in October 1904 digging up two more skeletons.[54] He returned in November 1915 to try his luck again. This time he used a new technique for excavating the skeletons, which were buried in fetal position rather than laid out on their backs. He cut into the earth around the skeletons and moved everything intact to his laboratory at Smith. He then carefully cleared the dirt and took photographs.[55] The remains of seven to eight Nolwottog people excavated from Quanquan's land by Wilder were never returned to the earth. They were part of Wilder's collection at Smith College until they were moved to the University of Massachusettes Amherst sometime between 1960 and 1980, where they remain in storage, classified as "Nonotuck."[56]

Quanquan's mortgage is a jewel in the collection of the Hadley Historical Society. It embodies, in a single page, the layered reality where history and the present intersect, reminding us that what we can see with our own eyes, dig up from our fields, or store in our closets and archives may be just the starting point for uncovering a much more complex history—one that began long ago and reverberates to this day. The document raises more questions than it answers. We learn that men like Quanquan and Zachariah Field participated in the fur trade, but neither got rich, and in fact both lost more than they gained. What brought them together and what did they hope to achieve? We see Quanquan as part of an extended family and community, but did he have one wife or three, and where did they go after selling their lands? Where is Quanquan buried? What responsibility do we, in the present, bear to the people whose bodies have been dug up from the lands we live on, and to their descent communities? Quanquan's mortgage of 1663 reminds us that Hadley's history begins, and continues, in Nolwottog.

Notes

1. Mortgage, Quanquan to Zachariah Field, 1663. Hadley Historical Society, Hadley, Mass.
2. The name is spelled "Chequallopp" in the manuscript but standardized herein as Chickwallop.
3. Roy Wright, "The Quanquan Deed as Artifact," *Massachusetts Center for Renaissance Studies Newsletter*, Autumn 2003, 8.
4. Quoted in Harry Andrew Wright, ed., *Indian Deeds of Hampden County* (Springfield, Mass.: [n.p.], 1905), 7.
5. Francis Jennings, *The Invasion of America: Indians, Colonialism, and the Cant of Conquest* (Chapel Hill: University of North Carolina Press, 1975), 128–45.
6. Emerson W. Baker, " 'A Scratch with a Bear's Paw': Anglo-Indian Land Deeds in Early Maine," *Ethnohistory* 36 (1989): 235–56.
7. Peter A. Thomas, *In the Maelstrom of Change: The Indian Trade and Cultural Process in the Middle Connecticut River Valley, 1635–1665* (New York: Garland, 1990).
8. Jean M. O'Brien, *Dispossession by Degrees: Indian Land and Identity in Natick, Massachusetts, 1650–1790* (Cambridge: Cambridge Unversity Press, 1997).
9. Gordon M. Day, "Historical Notes on New England Languages," in *In Search of New England's Native Past: Selected Essays by Gordon M. Day*, ed. Michael K. Foster and William Cowan (Amherst: University of Massachusetts Press, 1998), 103.
10. The people of Nolwottog, like other Algonkian-speaking peoples in the region, were commonly referred to by multiple names during their lives. In some cases these are proper names, perhaps given to honor life passages or significant milestones. Others may be either nicknames or descriptive terms, such as "so-and-so's wife" or "my son," that denote personal relationships.

11. Wright, *Indian Deeds*, 26–28.
12. Ives Goddard, "Introduction," in *Languages*, ed. Ives Goddard, vol. 17 of *Handbook of North American Indians* (Washington, D.C.: Smithsonian Institution, 1996), 4.
13. John Pickering, ed., "A Dictionary of the Abenaki Language in North America," *Memoirs of the American Academy of Arts and Sciences*, n.s., 1 (1833): 571.
14. Harry Andrew Wright, "Some Vagaries in Connecticut Valley Indian Place-Names," *New England Quarterly* 12, no. 3 (September 1939): 536. In modernizing spelling, I write *Nolwottog* instead of *Nolwottogg*, as it is written in the 1663 document, because the *–ogg* ending is archaic (much as we would write *dog* today, even though Pynchon and his contemporaries would have written *dogg* or *dogge*).
15. Ahhaton, a Christianized Wampanoag Indian from southeastern Massachusetts, was the interpreter for the first Springfield deed of 1636. He is listed there as "Ahaughton an Indian of the Massachusetts [people]." Wright, *Indian Deeds*, 12.
16. Ibid., 33–35.
17. Thomas, *In the Maelstrom of Change*, 322.
18. This land is mentioned as a boundary for land sold by Umpanchela in Hatfield in January 1661 (Wright, *Indian Deeds*, 44); it was sold by Quanquan's family in 1672 (ibid., 76–77).
19. Thomas, *In the Maelstrom of Change*, 281–85.
20. Carl Bridenbaugh and Juliette Tomlinson, eds., *The Pynchon Papers*, vol. 2, *Selections from the Account Books of John Pynchon, 1651–1697*, Publications of the Colonial Society of Massachusetts, vol. 61 (Boston: The Colonial Society of Massachusetts, 1985) 120.
21. Joseph H. Smith, ed., *Colonial Justice in Western Massachusetts, 1639–1702: The Pynchon Court Record* (Cambridge, Mass.: Harvard University Press, 1961), 249.
22. Hampshire County (Mass.) Probate Court Records (microfilm, Holyoke, Mass.: New England Archives Center for the Connecticut Valley Historical Museum), reel 1 (vols. 1–4, 1660–1780), 87.
23. Wright, *Indian Deeds*, 11–12, 46–47.
24. Ibid., 31–32.
25. Ibid., 34–35.
26. Bridenbaugh and Tomlinson, *Pynchon Account Books*, 283–88.
27. Ibid., 286.
28. Wright, *Indian Deeds*, 37–38.
29. Bridenbaugh and Tomlinson, *Pynchon Account Books*, 286–88.
30. Ibid., 288.
31. Wright, *Indian Deeds*, 44–45.
32. Smith, *Colonial Justice*, 263.
33. Ibid., 281–82.
34. Ibid., 282. During the time of King Philip's War (1675–76) the Indian resistance near Springfield was led by "their old sachem Wequogon (in whom as much confidence was put as in any of their Indians)," according to the Reverend John Russell of Hadley, quoted in Sylvester Judd, *History of Hadley, including the Early History of Hatfield, South Hadley, Amherst and Granby Massachusetts*, 2nd ed. (Springfield, Mass.: H. R. Huntting, 1905; repr., Camden, Maine: Picton Press, 1993, 1999), 144 (see also 143).
35. Frederick Clifton Pierce, *Field Genealogy, being the record of all the Field family in America, whose ancestors were in this country prior to 1700*, 2 vols. (Chicago: Hammond Press/ W. B. Conkey Company: 1901), 1:97.
36. Lucius M. Boltwood, "Genealogies of Hadley Families, embracing the early settlers of the towns of Hatfield, South Hadley, Amherst and Granby," in Judd, *History of Hadley*, 50.
37. The examples in this paragraph are taken from Wright, *Indian Deeds*, 40–48.

38. Smith, *Colonial Justice*, 249.
39. Hampden County (Mass.) Registry of Deeds, Liber A, folios 16, 19, 29, and 57.
40. Date of Field's death: Pierce, *Field Genealogy*, 97. Field's estate was valued at some £320. He owed £322, of which more than half (£178) was claimed by Pynchon even before the estate was settled. Zechariah Field inventory, March 1667, Hampshire County Probate Court Records, vol. 1, 86–87.
41. Hampshire County Probate Court Records, vol. 1, 79–80.
42. Baker, "A Scratch with a Bear's Paw," 249–52.
43. Smith, *Colonial Justice*, 248.
44. Ibid., 257; Linda Auwers Bissell, "From One Generation to Another: Mobility in Seventeenth-Century Windsor, Connecticut," *William and Mary Quarterly*, 3rd ser., 31, no. 1 (January 1974): 83.
45. Pierce, *Field Genealogy*, 1:100.
46. Wright, *Indian Deeds*, 76.
47. For further discussion of the word *squaw*, see Marge Bruchac, "Reclaiming the Word 'Squaw' in the Name of the Ancestors," November 1999, www.nativeweb.org/pages/legal/squaw.html (accessed 28 July 2008).
48. Wright, *Indian Deeds*, 77.
49. For further information on Hadley schools see Judd, *History of Hadley*, 48–62. Margaret Clifford Dwyer, in her history of Hopkins Academy, seems unaware of the previous history of this land (*Hopkins Academy and the Hopkins Fund, 1664–1964* [Hadley, Mass.: The Trustees of Hopkins Academy, 1964], 53–55).
50. Judd, *History of Hadley*, 107.
51. Sylvester Judd Manuscripts, Forbes Library, Northampton, Mass., vol. 5 (Hadley), 44.
52. Ibid., 44–45.
53. Dwyer, *Hopkins Academy*, 180.
54. Harris Hawthorne Wilder, "Excavation of Indian Graves in Western Massachusetts," *American Anthropologist*, n.s., 7, no. 2 (April–June 1905): 295–300.
55. Harris Hawthorne Wilder and Ralph Wheaton Whipple, "The Position of the Body in Aboriginal Interments in Western Massachusetts," *American Anthropologist*, n.s., 19, no. 3 (July–September 1917): 374.
56. A list of the human remains at the University of Massachusetts Amherst may be found online through the National NAGPRA Culturally Unidentifiable Native American Inventories Database maintained by the National Park Service, U.S. Department of the Interior, at 64.241.25.6/CUI/index.cfm. At present, the Five College Repatriation Committee is working toward the reburial of these remains in consultation with several Native American communities in the region, both because these people should be buried in a culturally appropriate manner and to comply with the Federal Native American Graves Protecton and Repatriation Act of 1990. See the chapter by Hart, Chilton, and Donta in this volume for further discussion of NAGPRA.

2

While historian Alice Nash enters the story of colonization through a single legal document that illuminates complex relationships among individuals at a moment in time, archaeologists Siobhan Hart, Elizabeth Chilton, and Christopher Donta look below ground to glimpse centuries of change. Their essay has its origins in a study, funded in part by the University of Massachusetts Office of Community Service Learning, of artifacts today curated by the Hadley Historical Society. They begin by by considering how Hadley residents at another anniversary moment thought about the native history of this place, and then sweep backward in time thousands of years, tracking the story of indigenous occupation from the retreat of Lake Hitchcock to the era of Quanquan and beyond. Along the way, they illuminate the role nineteenth- and early twentieth-century pastkeepers have played in the preservation, and sometimes the destruction, of that history. They also trace the professionalization of archaeology as a discipline, and—like Ethan Carr's essay elsewhere in this volume—have something to teach us about the present generation's work as stewards of our cultural resources.

Before Hadley

Archaeology and Native History, 10,000 BC to 1700 AD

Siobhan M. Hart, Elizabeth S. Chilton, and Christopher Donta

Popular representations of Native Americans have played a central role in the commemorations of the founding of Hadley. A perusal of the volume commemorating Hadley's 250th anniversary in August 1909, *Old Hadley Quarter Millennial Celebration*, offers several rich examples.[1] In the many speeches given over the course of the four-day celebration, Native Americans are mentioned only in the context of land transfers and violence. In fact, there is no substantive mention of Native Americans until the evening of the third day, in a speech delivered by Judge Francis M. Thompson, which recounted the violent encounters and wars among Native American groups and English settlers in the seventeenth and eighteenth centuries.[2] Thompson began by noting that "the history of the people whom our ancestors found occupying this broad and beautiful valley . . . the people who hunted in the primeval forest which then covered the waste places, with whom our ancestors lived, with whom they fought, and whom they finally blotted out—or drove, a scanty remnant, into the western wilds—is closely interwoven with our own."[3] Thompson's narrative is one of English loss and courage in the face of Indian hostilities, but it also points to the deep history of Native peoples in the region.

Photographs and descriptions of the floats that paraded up Middle Street, North Lane, West Street, and Russell Street on Wednesday, August 4, contrast with the record of the spoken word. They clearly show that Native Americans were crucial to the making and remaking of the identities of the town and its citizens taking place through these commemorative events. Clifton Johnson reported that this parade was the climax of the celebration, and he estimated that at least 25,000 people witnessed or participated in it.[4] In his view the floats were "remarkably realistic presentations of the events and life which they were intended to portray."[5] Of the twenty-four floats in the parade, ten included representations of Native Americans or invoked them in some way; most of these consisted of what might be described as white Hadley residents playing Indian. One particularly evocative float called "Opposing Races: Red Man or White?" was the second in the parade. It juxtaposed a log cabin with two white settlers (woman seated and knitting; man standing with gun at the ready) with a wigwam and two Indians (no description given of what they were doing). Red and white bunting decorated the float and the horses that pulled it, further emphasizing the racial and cultural dichotomy. Representations of Native Americans appeared in other floats as well; one commemorated the signing of the 1659 land deed, another the famous Angel of Hadley story. The Northampton float called "Perils of Our Ancestors" depicted "Puritan men, women and children in a clearing and armed Indians skulking behind rocks and bushes at the edge of the woods." Missing from these brief, ethnocentric glimpses of Native American presence is any acknowledgement of the deep history of Native peoples in the area, or any awareness that European colonialism did not erase or entirely sever Native Americans' relationship to their homelands in the Connecticut River Valley.

Ironically, while preparations for these festivities were under way, local residents, farmers, antiquarians, and archaeologists were amassing collections of Native American artifacts that attest to the long and complex history of Native American life in Hadley. Indeed, such artifacts have been collected since at least the time of Hadley's bicentennial in 1859. Today, these collections, along with the Native American archaeological sites in the area, offer the opportunity for cross-cultural collaboration and stewardship, creating space for discourses and multiple perspectives on the past. Material culture collected from archaeological and ethnographic contexts offers clear evidence that Native peoples have occupied the valley for thousands of years, traveling established paths and water routes, hunting in the uplands, fishing in the rivers and streams, farming the fertile soil, and performing the mundane tasks of daily life.[6]

Hadley is rich in archaeological sites that record a long and diverse history of human experiences, and evidence recovered from them demonstrates that people have lived in the area for at least twelve thousand years. Like the rest of New England, Hadley was first inhabited by the ancestors of the Algonkian-speaking peoples encountered by Europeans in the sixteenth and seventeenth centuries. In this chapter we trace the Native American history of Hadley, from about 10,000 BC through the pre-contact era (prior to the arrival of Europeans) and the early Contact period, defined here as 1600–1700 AD. We begin by discussing the continuity and transformations of Native American lifeways in the middle Connecticut River Valley, using archaeological sites and artifacts from Hadley to illustrate these trends.[7] Next, we turn to the different kinds of archaeology practiced in Hadley, including the work of nineteenth-century collectors and twentieth-century professional archaeologists. Their collections form the basis of our archaeological interpretations, and the collecting activities themselves provide insights into Euroamerican–Native relations, past and present.[8] We also address the preservation and governmental compliance issues that have affected the archaeological investigations that have taken place here. We conclude by noting the role that people today—including landowners, town citizens, and descendant communities, along with archaeologists—play as stewards of the past, as well as the importance of collaborative planning for the preservation and stewardship of archaeological sites.

Good Places to Live

Present-day Hadley comprises diverse natural environments, ranging from fertile floodplains to rugged uplands, which for thousands of years have made it an attractive place to hunter-gatherers and farmers alike. The archaeological record attests to this appeal: pre-contact archaeological sites in Hadley are among the densest in Massachusetts, spanning the range of known human occupation in New England.[9] More than ninety pre-contact sites have been documented in the town to date.[10]

The distribution of pre-contact sites over the landscape is not uniform. Rather, the sites we know about are clustered according to soils, landforms, and water availability, and are reflected in present-day land use patterns.[11] Archaeological evidence suggests that pre-contact Native peoples strongly favored the terraces and floodplains of the Connecticut River and its major tributaries.[12] They left a notable material imprint in these places, although it is likely that materially "empty" places also had meaning to past peoples, who may well have had oral histories, beliefs, or knowledge systems grounded in an extensive physical landscape. Areas in which no material traces have been preserved may have been used for resource-gathering, or even inhabited. It is also important to note that many archaeological sites may yet remain buried under the ever-changing Connecticut River floodplain.

The range of raw materials available in the area also helped to attract Native peoples, whose technologies focused on stone, clay, and animal and vegetal products. Quartz and quartzite cobbles, central to lithic (stone) tool manufacture, were plentiful in the small brooks and along the banks of the Connecticut River. Other lithic raw materials could be found in cobbles and outcrops in Massachusetts and New Hampshire, as well as in the nearby Hudson and Champlain valleys. Glacial lake deposits throughout the Connecticut River Valley supplied clays for use in pottery manufacture. A variety of plant and animal species provided food as well as raw materials for tools, clothing, and shelter.

Pioneer Sites (Paleo-Indian and Early Archaic Periods)

There is no archaeological evidence for human habitation in the Connecticut River Valley prior to the last glacial period, which lasted from about 100,000 to 17,000 years ago. At the height of the last glaciation, ice covered Northern Europe, Asia, and a large portion of North America. New England lay under a continental ice sheet, with the terminal moraine (edge of the glacier) forming Long Island, Cape Cod, and the islands off southern New England. In the area of Hadley, the ice would have been up to one mile thick. When it retreated, the ice left a huge amount of debris and numerous bodies of water, including Glacial Lake Hitchcock. Between 15,500 BC and 11,500 BC this lake rested in the basin of the Connecticut River Valley, stretching from Rocky Hill, Connecticut, to near Burke, Vermont—a length of about 350 miles. Eventually, around 14,000 BC, the southernmost of the sediment dams that held it in place collapsed, and the lake slowly started to drain. In the Hadley area, this process began around 13,400 BC, and the entire lake was gone by 11,500 BC.[13]

To date, we have no archaeological evidence suggesting that people were living in the area when the glacial lake filled the valley, though the earliest inhabitants certainly recognized the remnant beaches and shoreline features.[14] Oral tradition suggests that Algonkian people may have observed the dams that had formed the lake and encoded these observations in a narrative that describes a large, powerful force—a "Great Beaver"—that dammed and flooded the valley.[15] The large amounts of mineral sediment deposited by the retreating glacier filled river valleys and streams and, as a consequence of this and a higher water table overall, area rivers flowed up to two hundred feet higher than they do today. Thus many of the earliest archaeological sites have been buried or destroyed by post-glacial river down-cutting.

The first clear evidence of human activity in the middle Connecticut Valley dates to about 10,000 BC. Prior to that time, the area was a tundra landscape, "with only a few shrubs and dwarf trees to break the monotony of the lichens and mosses."[16] Animal populations during this period were dynamic in response to deglaciation and relatively rapid climate change, as was plant life. The forests were dominated by northern conifer species such as spruce and fir, and were interspersed with areas of patchy tundra.[17] Climatic warming allowed white pine, spruce, fir, and temperate deciduous trees to migrate into southern New England at the time humans were arriving in the region.[18]

At around this time, a site in Hadley was established on a terrace of the Connecticut River, a surface cut into the old lakebed. Windblown sand from the former lake bottom created dunes that had good drainage and offered warm, dry campsites. Archaeological evidence for these first Paleo-Indians indicates that they were hunter-gatherers living in fairly small family groups of about twenty to fifty people, moving their encampments to exploit seasonally available resources. The old lakebed was "very lightly inhabited," and forests were likely used for hunting and gathering plants, but not for habitation.[19] Poor site preservation makes it difficult to estimate population, but it is likely that there was a fairly rapid colonization of the area. Initially there were probably about 250 individuals located in a few different settlements.[20]

Paleo-Indians subsisted on a wide variety of plants and animals, including hawthorn seeds, wild grapes, caribou, giant beaver, and migratory birds.[21] They relied on stone tools for tasks such as hunting, plant processing, hide scraping, and the manufacture of clothing, tools, and ornaments. The predominance of stone artifacts in the archaeological record for this period results from the poor preservation of organic remains in acidic soils and the freeze/thaw cycles typical of New England. Moreover, because of a 300-foot increase in sea level after about 9000 BC, many Paleo-Indian sites are likely submerged offshore.

We know that people were in Hadley during this time because of the discovery of spear points (fluted projectile points and bifurcate-base points) that are known to date from this time period.[22] Although we have good information about this period for southern New England generally, we know very little of the lifeways of these early inhabitants of Hadley specifically. Archaeological evidence suggests that they were probably mobile groups of hunters and gatherers. It is likely that most of the sites that date to this era were either destroyed or are now deeply buried under flood deposits.[23]

Settler Sites (Middle Archaic to Middle Woodland Periods)

After about 5000 BC the environment began to stabilize and diversify. The climate became temperate, and the boreal forests were replaced first by white pine and oak forests and then by a diverse forest of broad-leafed and conifer species.[24] Archaeological evidence indicates that people were establishing camps near rich food sources and gathering places, moving less often, and increasing in numbers. In southern New England, Archaic-era people clearly exploited the rich deciduous forests through the harvesting and storage of acorns, hickory nuts, beechnuts, and chestnuts. Heavy woodworking tools, such as stone gouges, axes, and adzes, were used primarily for making wooden dugout canoes. There is evidence of fishing in interior rivers and lakes (particularly in the spring and fall), shellfish collecting on the coast and some interior rivers, the hunting of deer and other land animals throughout the year, and the collecting of hundreds of plant species for food as well as medicinal and other purposes.[25] In Hadley, the favored areas were on the high and mid-level terraces of the Connecticut River and around the stream networks of its tributaries.[26]

Native peoples used local diabase (an ancient volcanic rock also called traprock) found on the Holyoke Range to make heavy stone tools for woodworking and the pounding and grinding of plant foods.[27] They also used other local raw materials, such as quartz, and traded for such materials as chert (a type of rock) from the Hudson and Champlain valleys to the west and north and steatite (soapstone) from quarries in central Massachusetts and elsewhere in the middle Connecticut River Valley.[28] Woodworking tools as well as chipped stone tools, such as scrapers, drills, and knives, are frequently found on sites of this period. These objects were used for such tasks as building canoes and processing animal products for food and clothing. Many other domestic artifacts, including ground stone pestles, used to process seeds, nuts, and other edible plant materials, have been recovered from sites in Hadley. Several types of spear points

FIGURE 2.1. *A variety of projectile points from North Hadley. Photographed with permission of UMass Archaeological Services.*

from this period are also frequent finds.[29] Made of local and nonlocal materials, they include a variety of stemmed and notched projectile points, such as those seen in figure 2.1.

The introduction of carved stone bowls indicates a revolution in cooking technology. Steatite conducts heat well and can withstand high temperatures and long cooking times. The collection of the Hadley Historical Society includes two steatite bowl fragments that likely date to around 1500 BC.[30] Fired clay vessels dating from around 1000 BC, also found in diverse forms all over New England, indicate another significant change in cooking and storage technology. Because clay is locally available and pottery vessels are much more portable than heavy stone bowls, pottery replaced steatite vessels; pottery sherds recovered from many sites in Hadley illustrate this shift in technology (see figure 2.2).

The change in cooking technology likely accompanied a change in diet. At about 1000 BC, archaeological evidence across eastern North America indicates intensive exploitation of weedy plants that grow in disturbed soils, particularly goosefoot (*Chenopodium berlandieri*), sumpweed (*Iva annua*), and sunflower (*Helianthus annuus*).[31] The oily, starchy seeds of these plants were boiled into porridge to make them palatable and digestible, and the species were apparently modified genetically through selective breeding, representing the earliest phase of horticulture. Soapstone bowls and ceramic pots made superior cooking vessels for the boiling of nuts as well as starchy seeds.

While the domestication of these weeds has been well documented in the Midwest and Southeast beginning about 1000 BC, similar conclusive evidence is lacking in the Northeast.[32] Nevertheless, a wide range of plant species have been recovered from Late Archaic and Woodland period sites: goosefoot and many other weed seeds, grass seeds, berries and other fleshy fruits, tubers, and several kinds of nuts.[33] All of our evidence for this period supports the interpretation of diverse hunting, fishing, and foraging bases for New England Native peoples.[34]

Mobile Farmer Sites (Late Woodland Period)

The most common and best documented sites in the Connecticut River Valley are those from the Late Woodland period (around 1000–1500 AD). Increasing artifact frequencies and site sizes after 1000 AD have been thought to reflect an increase in population density in southern New England, and may correlate with the introduction of cultivated plants such as corn (maize), beans, and squash. More recent data suggest that Late Woodland period site densities in New England are on par with those from the Late Archaic period,[35] however, so this apparent increase may simply be the result of better preservation of later sites. During the Late Woodland period, two important innovations arrived in New England: bow and arrow technology, and tropical cultigens (maize, beans, and squash, which were originally domesticated in Mexico 5,000 years ago). While a few sites with maize date to 1000 AD, many more radiocarbon dates for maize are in the range of 1300 to 1500.[36] Since maize decomposes rapidly except under unusual conditions such as charring (that is, being burned in a fire), these dates represent a conservative estimate for introduction.

Some archaeologists believe that Native peoples in the Connecticut River Valley were not reliant on maize as a subsistence staple.[37] Rather, the evidence suggests that their diet was diverse and included maize along with a number of other food resources such as nuts, seeds, berries, small mammals, fish, and shellfish. Recent scholarship suggests that Late Woodland peoples in the middle Connecticut River Valley were "mobile farmers" living in short-term seasonal encampments.[38] Highly dispersed and mobile settlement patterns served to "maintain the environmental diversity and sociopolitical fluidity upon which these communities depended."[39]

In Hadley, small-scale cultivation took place on or near the floodplains of the Connecticut River, where soils were light and easily hoed.[40] Again, the diabase of the slopes of Mt. Holyoke served as a critical resource, providing the raw material for stone hoes. Archaeological sites that date to this era are also present along the major tributaries of the Connecticut River, and these may have been seasonal camps for special activities: harvesting fish runs, gathering plants, and social gatherings.[41] A temporary campsite or remnant of a larger site dating to approximately 1000 AD was encountered in an archaeological survey in Hadley, and the artifacts recovered included a thin, stamped ceramic sherd along with chipping debris and a biface (stone tool flaked on two sides) fragment.[42] Triangular points for arrows, agricultural tools such as stone hoes, and a number of thin-walled, collared pottery sherds (figure 2.2), have been recovered from

FIGURE 2.2. *Native American pottery sherds from an archaeological site in North Hadley. Photographed with permission of UMass Archaeological Services.*

other archaeological projects on sites of this period and are present in the collection of the Hadley Historical Society.[43]

The Early Contact Era

Native people in the middle Connecticut River Valley encountered Dutch and English explorers traveling up the Connecticut River as early as 1614, but had infrequent contact with European colonists and traders until the late 1650s.[44] Colonial records provide relatively sparse information about Native communities in the Connecticut River Valley. Indeed, one of the problems of relying on historical documents to interpret Native life during the Contact period, particularly subsistence and settlement patterns, is that Europeans' perceptions of Native settlements were based on the notion of "improvement" and "ownership" of land predicated on intensive farming. They did not understand the concepts of mobile farming, Native homelands, or Native territories.

Colonial sources do suggest that present-day Hadley and its neighbor Northampton (on the western banks of the Connecticut River) were central locations of a Native community cluster referred to as "Nolwotogg," "Nonotuck," "Norrotuck," or "Norwottuck" (see Alice Nash's essay in this volume).[45] Europeans often attached Native place names, particularly Algonkian locative words that referred to geography rather than tribal identity, to the people who lived in these communities, and these place names have since become conflated with tribal names.[46] Abenaki storyteller and scholar Margaret Bruchac notes that the region around the oxbow of the Connecticut River was called Nonotuck, "a term which has been roughly translated to mean 'the middle of the river' (Noah-tuk), or the 'far away land' (Nauwut-ucke) in the Massachusetts dialect."[47] It is likely that the Nonotuck or Norwottuck, as well as other Connecticut Valley Native "tribes" such as Pocumtuck, Woronoco, and Agawam, were more akin to village polities comprised of politically autonomous but related mobile communities than to fixed identities or nationalities.[48]

Native settlements appear to be larger and more densely packed than in the pre-contact era (year-round in some places, while in others seasonal encampments are more common), and there is an increase in more permanent, consistently shaped architecture. Palisaded villages and locales become more common for Native sites in the Connecticut River Valley, as they did for English settlements (see Hood and Reinke in this volume for a discussion of the late seventeenth-century palisade in Hadley). Fortified settlements were well known to Europeans at the time, but they were a new phenomenon for Native peoples of the New England interior, as there is no evidence for fortifications—or warfare—on Native sites prior to European contact. In Hadley, Contact-period settlement appears to have been heaviest on the fertile Connecticut, Mill, and Fort River floodplains. The two most likely focal points were in southern Hadley, in the general vicinity of the confluence of the Connecticut and Fort rivers, and adjacent to Mt. Warner in North Hadley.[49] As Sylvester Judd notes in his *History of Hadley*, there were probably several fortified village sites during this period.[50]

Archaeological evidence illustrates a continuation of the mobile farming trend that began around 1000 AD, though horticulture became increasingly important, perhaps because it provided a valuable trade good and because the range of movement for Native peoples became more constrained throughout the seventeenth century. Historical records indicate that the people living in and around Norwottuck and their neighbors around Pocumtuck (present-day Deerfield) grew maize with occasional surpluses. At the same time, Native peoples retained traditional methods of subsistence and continued to pursue seasonal rounds, although in a somewhat smaller area as colonial settlements began to encroach on their homelands.

Local Native people were involved in the seventeenth-century fur trade centered in Springfield.[51] The trade system that existed among Native groups in New England for millennia was transformed, and Native economies, which had been based on reciprocity and redistribution, shifted to a market-focused system. The Connecticut River and its tributaries continued to be used as trade routes throughout the seventeenth century in both Native–Native and Native–European trade networks. The introduction of new kinds of material culture into Native societies can be seen in the artifacts recovered from sites that date to this period. Many of the trade goods obtained by Native peoples were used as raw materials rather than for their intended purposes. For example, the metal of copper or brass kettles was used to create arrowheads, effigies, knives, and ornaments, because Native clay pots were superior cooking and storage vessels. Though to date there has been little documented archaeological evidence of early Contact period sites in Hadley, some trade materials have been recovered from sites along the town's waterways.

Native history and presence in Hadley did not end in the seventeenth century. Though there does not appear to have been a large Native community in Hadley or the surrounding towns, substantial research by Margaret Bruchac clearly demonstrates Native presence in the Connecticut River Valley through the eighteenth and nineteenth centuries.[52] Bruchac notes that "a number of local Native families and individuals continued to circulate within their traditional homelands, marketing baskets and brooms, hiring out as day labor, and dispensing traditional Native medicines to their white neighbors."[53] In fact, historian Sylvester Judd, writing in 1863, learned from a Mrs. Newton of Hadley that "Indians and squaws peddled brooms and baskets in Hadley when she was young and after."[54]

Archaeology in Hadley

The evidence that supports the story of Hadley's Native history we have related was deposited by Native people over millennia, and then gathered in collections over the course of the last two centuries. Before turning to how these collections have been accumulated, we must note several potential biases in the archaeological record of Hadley. First, archaeological sites in the town have been preserved, revealed, or destroyed by both natural and cultural processes. The intensive farming that provided the basis for the town's economic life during the eighteenth, nineteenth, and twentieth centuries has revealed archaeological sites, but it has also had detrimental effects. Plowing has destroyed the vertical context of many sites. More serious destruction has resulted from generations of collecting from plowed fields as well as the construction of houses, stores, roads, and pipelines. The substantial flooding that the area experienced in 1896, 1936, and 1938 also took a toll on archaeological sites, exposing and destroying some and likely deeply burying others.[55]

Second, it is important to note again that some materials do not preserve well over long periods of time. As we have seen, Native peoples in New England used a wide range of materials for utilitarian and nonutilitarian purposes. While archaeologists in New England often recover objects made of stone and clay, such as the stone flakes and pottery sherd shown in figure 2.3, it is less common to recover artifacts made of such materials as shell, bone, fibers, feathers, grasses, leather, seeds, nuts, wood, and antler, which do not preserve in New England's acidic soil. The collections of Hadley artifacts are undoubtedly missing everyday objects such as fish hooks, perforators, ornaments, combs, animal and plant remains, shell beads, cooking utensils, tool handles, nets, baskets, clothing, and building materials. These artifacts are not found as often as those made of stone, but they played equally significant roles in the material world of Native peoples in New England.

FIGURE 2.3. *Stone flakes, the byproduct of stone tool manufacture, and a pottery sherd recovered from an archaeological site in Hockanum, Hadley. Photographed with permission of UMass Archaeological Services.*

COLLECTORS AND COLLECTIONS

Archaeological research in Hadley began in the nineteenth century with the collection of artifacts by local people interested in the history of the area and curious about ancient objects and peoples.[56] Hadley native Reverend Frederic Dan Huntington, then Plummer Professor of Christian Morals at Harvard College, noted the archaeological evidence of local Native Americans in his address at the town's bicentennial celebration in 1859:

> I shall always deem it mutually to the interest of the spot and its red master, that he lingered about its meadows, wet his canoe in its waters, built his wigwam under its woods, lit his council-fires by its hills, and made his chosen grave in its loveliness. That he did so, we have visible and material proofs enough left, in the relics of his rude skill and taste, in the mouldering bones that have been found bleaching on the surface or decaying in the loam; in the populous grave-yard on the ridge between the two "School-meadows." . . . [O]ther proofs we have in forts that are still partly discernible, in half-leveled mounds and embankments . . . and others yet in the flinty arrow heads, stone pestles, hatchets, hoes and mortars, which click against

> your ploughshares or reward the eager eyes of boyish teamsters, in your homelots.[57]

Not long after Huntington's address, the town's first historian, Sylvester Judd, wrote about local antiquities and Native American history in his *History of Hadley*, though his work reveals the ethnocentrism common at the time.[58] "The Indian men were fond of fighting, hunting and fishing, and disdained other pursuits," he writes. "All agricultural labor and all kinds of drudgery were thrown upon the women, who, with hoes of shells, wood or iron, cultivated small pieces of land."[59] Here, Judd characterized the lives of the local Native peoples in generalized and oversimplified ways that mirror both the gendered division of labor common in Euroamerican society at the time and colonial perceptions of Native American life. Nonetheless, Huntington and Judd offer the earliest published accounts of visual surveys of several Native American sites in Hadley.

The earliest era of collecting in New England, during the mid- to late nineteenth century, was shaped by the interests and intentions of the collectors themselves and motivated largely by the antiquarian idea of gathering curiosities for their own sake and for aesthetic satisfaction. In an extensive discussion of the collecting practices in the Connecticut River Valley, Margaret Bruchac writes:

> Farmers might pick up (and set back down) lithics, bone fragments, and pottery shards overturned by the plow; hobbyists would visit favorite spots repeatedly over a period of years, searching for unknown finds; looters would seek out valuable items to keep or sell; children might stumble over (and pocket) arrowheads; scientists would excavate, mix, and match skeletal elements from different individuals to create "perfect" specimens for display; students working an archaeological site for the first time might mistake human remains for animal bones (and vice versa); homeowners, surprised to discover skeletal remains in their backyard, might call the authorities, rebury them, hide the evidence, or even select a good-looking skull for the mantelpiece. Few local collectors kept precise data about the locations of their finds. . . . Few had first-hand knowledge of the cultural beliefs and practices of Native people. I would also venture to suggest that few (if any) were willing to consider the possibility that the Native remains they unearthed were people who might have living descendants.[60]

A number of renowned artifact collectors and archaeologists were active in Hadley during the nineteenth and early twentieth centuries, including Charles Willoughby (1857–1943; archaeologist and director of Harvard University's Peabody Museum), Harry Andrew Wright (1872–1950; amateur linguist, historian, and member of the American Antiquarian Society, well known locally for his historical research of Native American sites), William J. Howes (born ca. 1866; architect and avid student of archaeology in the 1940s), Harris Hawthorne Wilder (1864–1928; professor of zoology, Smith College), William Fowler (1893–1983; founder of the Connecticut Valley chapter of the Massachusetts Archaeological Society), and Walter Rodimon (1885–1972; railroad worker, avocational archaeologist, and local historian who collected extensively throughout the area).[61] In many ways, these collectors were part of a broader national movement to document the "vanishing" Native American cultures of North America and reinforce (white) American identity. They cultivated relationships with local residents as well as fellow collectors throughout Massachusetts who knew the locations of Native sites in the town through oral tradition, written histories, or personal observation.

During the early and mid-twentieth century, many of these collectors began to incorporate information on local artifact collections into more scientific analyses. Examples include Willoughby's *Antiquities of the New England Indians* and Wright's *The Story of Western Massachusetts*.[62] Howes, a resident of Holyoke who had served as vice president of the Massachusetts Archaeological Society, spent a significant amount of time in Hadley, documenting sites and artifacts.[63] Fowler and Rodimon recorded many sites in the Connecticut River Valley and western Massachusetts and contributed to a number of local museum collections and displays.[64]

At around the same time, Harris Hawthorne Wilder conducted the first scientific archaeological investigations in Hadley. Wilder was interested in the precontact Native Americans of New England, particularly their burial customs, and he explored several sites in the area.[65] He often worked in concert with Edward ("Doc") Hitchcock Jr., professor of hygiene and physical education and college physician at Amherst College, and he was assisted in fieldwork by his wife, Inez Whipple Wilder (also a professor at Smith College), and Smith students. Wilder pursued research on anthropometry (the measurement of living individuals in order to understand human physical variation, though at the time it played a central role in the theory of biological races), facial reconstructions and craniometry (measuring the skull), and the burial positions of New England Native peoples.[66] Wilder sought out Native American burial grounds and excavated many Native American graves to pursue his research.[67] Today, both Native and non-Native people are still grappling with Wilder's legacy, as many of the materials he collected, including human remains and burial items, are now subject to a federal law (the Native American Graves Protection and Repatriation Act, or NAGPRA, enacted in 1990) aimed at restoring Native American human remains and burial items to contemporary descendant groups.[68]

Few collectors, even among the early "scientific" archaeologists, kept detailed records of where artifacts were recovered, beyond noting the town and a general description of a find spot. In this way, some of the fine detail of Hadley's prehistory has been lost, at least in regard to a handful of sites that were heavily collected during this period. Nonetheless, the collections of materials from different locales in Hadley held by museums can still shed light on the antiquity and complexity of Native American life in the millennia before English settlement.

The majority of collections of archaeological materials from Hadley are curated by local institutions. The Hadley Historical Society holds sixty-four Native American objects, and the Department of Anthropology at the University of Massachusetts Amherst curates approximately two hundred objects from Hadley. The collections of the Springfield Science Museum and the Amherst College Museum of Natural History each include a hundred or more objects from various Hadley sites. The Peabody Museum of Archaeology and Ethnology at Harvard has forty-six objects identified from Hadley. These collections, typically dominated by an assortment of stone tools, were assembled through gifts from collectors, purchases, and direct research, and the quality of the records accompanying them varies widely.

In particular, the Native American artifacts held by the Hadley Historical Society (founded in the 1970s, but the inheritor of collections assembled earlier) span a period of at least ten thousand years. The society's collection was amassed largely through gifts from Hadley residents to a number of local organizations, such as Hopkins Academy, that eventually gave the material to the present Historical Society. Most of the recorded donations occurred between 1896 and 1912, around the time of Hadley's 250th commemoration, but many acquisition dates are unknown. Local collectors who contributed to the Historical Society's holdings include Norman Barstow (1919–2006; lifelong Hadley resident),[69] Emory Cooke (born 1848; farmer in Hadley), Clifton Johnson (1865–1940; an author born in the village of Hockanum), and Edwin Kennedy (1890–1970; of Chicopee), among others. Many of the society's donors lived in Hadley, and the artifacts they collected were recovered near their homes.

The Historical Society's pre-contact collection is largely comprised of stone tools and projectile points (many mounted in cases, as seen in figure 2.4), but it also includes pottery sherds, stone vessel fragments, and other ground stone objects. Much of the information accompanying the displays focuses on the collectors themselves, rather than on precisely where the objects were found. The collection represents a wide range of time, from as early as 10,000 BC to 1500 AD. The majority of the material probably dates to the last six to seven thousand years and includes projectile points (figure 2.4), ground stone tools (such as pestles, axes, and gouges), steatite bowl fragments, bifaces, drills and perforators,

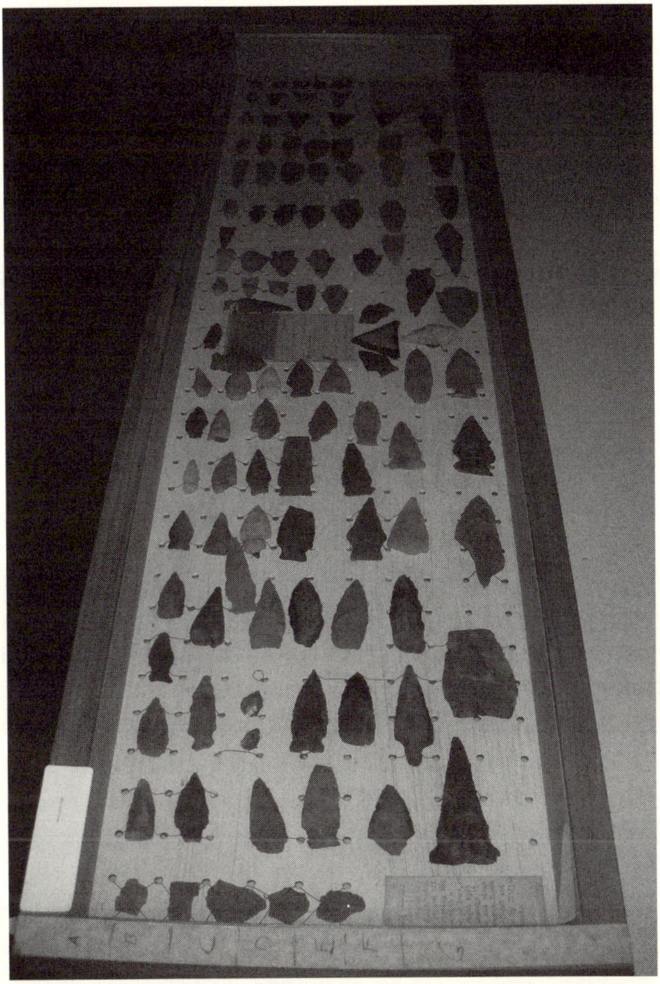

FIGURE 2.4. *Projectile point display at the Hadley Historical Society. Photographed with permission of the Hadley Historical Society.*

and pottery sherds. A number of local and nonlocal lithic material types are represented, such as rhyolite, basalt, hornfels, quartzite, and varieties of quartz and chert. As a whole, this collection tells us about several aspects of Native lifeways in Hadley over thousands of years, including trade and the movements of materials, styles, and people; activities of daily life such as flintknapping, woodworking, and food processing; and diet and resources such as plants, fish, shellfish, nuts, berries, seeds, and animals.

Professional Archaeology

The second half of the twentieth century saw a shift in the archaeological research conducted in Hadley, as archaeology continued to develop as a professional discipline at the national level, cultural resource management and site protection legislation was introduced in the 1960s and 1970s, and an archaeological fieldwork program was established at the University of Massachusetts Amherst. Cultural resource management is the practice of archaeology in response to federal and state laws aimed at protecting and documenting archaeological sites and historic buildings in advance of construction or other destructive forces. Section 106 of the National Historic Preservation Act (1966) requires that projects on public lands or receiving public funding undertake assessments to determine if cultural resources will be affected. The process involves several stages, from the identification of sites to the evaluation of the resources and, ultimately, mitigating the impact of development projects. Consulting firms such as UMass Archaeological Services (part of the Department of Anthropology at the university) are contracted to conduct the archaeological surveys and report on the assessed effects. The act also established state historic preservation offices to maintain inventories of historic places and archaeological sites, grant permits for archaeological projects, and nominate places to the National Register of Historic Places. In Massachusetts, this office is part of the Massachusetts Historical Commission, which was established by the legislature in 1963 to identify, evaluate, and protect important historical and archaeological assets of the Commonwealth. Other legislation, including the Archaeological Resources Protection Act (1979), provides criminal and civil penalties for looting or damaging sites on public and Native American lands. State laws, such as the Massachusetts Unmarked Burial Law, protect gravesites and outline procedures in the case of inadvertent discovery of human remains. These state and federal laws have informed, and in some cases required, the recent archaeology that has taken place in Hadley.

To date, seven professional archaeological investigations have taken place in the town. Most of these were cultural resource management studies conducted by UMass Archaeological Services, including work for pumping stations, road reconstruction, sewerage, canal work, soil conservation, and school renovations (figure 2.5).[70] These projects located and documented several archaeological sites in Hadley, and the resulting reports and data are recorded with the Massachusetts Historical Commission. In contrast to the objects collected and excavated in the nineteenth and early twentieth centuries, there are detailed context records for materials recovered from these excavations, and these reports are crucial to making archaeological interpretations.

FIGURE 2.5. *Professional archaeologists from UMass Archaeological Services working on the Hockanum School Stabilization Project (UM-261) in April 1998. Photo courtesy of UMass Archaeological Services.*

Two other research projects in Hadley have been associated with archaeologists from the University of Massachusetts. In 1975, professor of anthropology Dena F. Dincauze directed the UMass Archaeological Field School, which conducted an archaeological survey of diverse environments in the town, from the slopes of Mt. Holyoke to the floodplains of North Hadley and Hockanum, in order to document pre-contact and early Contact period Native American sites. The fieldwork and extensive research resulted in a summary of Hadley's archaeological resources.[71] These efforts, and the subsequent efforts of Dincauze and graduate students from the university, generated the bulk of the data presented here. More recently, Ed Hood and Rita Reinke directed an investigation into the location of the town's seventeenth-century colonial palisade[72] (see their essay in this volume).

Stewardship Today

Archaeologists, Native Americans, and citizens in New England are increasingly becoming allies and working in consultation with one another to support and implement legislation to protect archaeological sites and Native American heritage.[73] One of the primary causes of this shift has been the implementation of the federal Native American Graves Protection and Repatriation Act (NAGPRA), which protects Native American graves, provides for inventories and in some cases repatriation of Native American human remains, grave goods, sacred objects, and objects of cultural patrimony. The law requires that institutions inventory their Native American collections and consult with Native American tribes, lineal descendants, or traditional religious leaders. In many cases, these consultations have led to increased communication between archaeologists and Native Americans, laying the groundwork for further collaboration outside of repatriation efforts. NAGPRA, along with a heightened sensitivity to ethics in the discipline of archaeology, has increased the social and political power of Native American groups, and a growing demand from both descendant and local communities to make archaeology relevant to people today has brought about new ways of approaching archaeological research and interpretation.

While professional ethical codes and legislation have opened formal channels of communication among archaeologists and descendant communities, some archaeologists have chosen to go beyond baseline consultation requirements and are participating in archaeological projects designed for, by, and with communities. Many such partnerships have been established among descendant/nondescendant local communities and archaeologists.[74] Community-based approaches are fundamentally changing the practice of archaeology here in New England—a region in which there are many stakeholders with varying interests and claims to the past and varying amounts of political and social power in the present. There would be much to gain from community-based partnerships focusing on archaeological sites in Hadley.

Present-day Hadley has a deep and complex human history that predates European contact by several thousand years and is still continuing. Now, at the 350th anniversary of the town's founding, it is important to recognize that Hadley's Native American history contributes significantly to its richness and diversity, past, present, and future. The town's archaeological resources span twelve thousand years of human activity, but they are finite, and it is crucial to protect and preserve them. While the collections discussed here are those that have been donated to institutions and thus are accessible to the public, no doubt many artifacts are in the possession of landowners and collectors, and it is likely that some collections have been broken up and traded or sold. These collections are valuable for the information they can contribute to our understanding of Native history in Hadley and human history in the Connecticut River Valley as a whole.

Archaeologists, historians, local institutions, descendant communities, and contemporary local communities throughout the country must work together to plan for the protection, preservation, and stewardship of archaeological sites and the long-term curation of archaeological collections.

Notes

The authors are indebted to Dena F. Dincauze for her significant contribution to understanding the archaeology and Native American history of Hadley and, more broadly, New England, as well as for her substantive comments on a draft of this chapter. We thank Marla Miller for her keen interest in including archaeology and Native American history in this volume and for many comments that improved this chapter. We also thank Eleanor Niedbala of the Hadley Historical Society for graciously facilitating several visits to the society's collections.

1. Clifton Johnson, ed., *Old Hadley Quarter Millennial Celebration* (Springfield, Mass.: F. A. Bassette Company, 1909).
2. Francis M. Thompson, "Hadley in the Colonial Wars," in Johnson, *Hadley Quarter Millennial*, 43–49.
3. Ibid., 43.
4. Johnson, *Hadley Quarter Millennial*, 54. It is not clear how Johnson arrived at this figure.
5. Ibid., 55. The descriptions of the floats that follow are based on Johnson's account, 56–64. See also the volume produced for Hadley's bicentennial in 1859, *Bicentennial Celebration of Hadley* (Northampton, Mass.: Bridgman & Childs, 1859), which recounts, among other things, a "surprise" Indian attack staged during the parade: "This scene was capitally enacted, the Indians were most completely equipped with bows, arrows, spears and tomahawks, clothed in blankets and skins, and with head dresses of feathers, and ornaments dangling from ears and nose, and faces painted and stained. It afforded much amusement to the spectators and whenever the Indians appeared during the rest of the day, they were the 'observed of all observers.' "
6. Christopher L. Donta and Jennifer Wendt, "Archaeological Reconnaissance Survey for the Northstar Natural Gas Pipeline, Northampton, Hatfield, and Hadley, Massachusetts" (report on file at the Massachusetts Historical Commission, Office of the Secretary of State, Boston [hereafter cited as MHC], 2006), 29.
7. The organization of these sections follows the chronological and cultural framework suggested by archaeologist Dena F. Dincauze in "A Capsule Prehistory of Southern New England," in *The Pequots in Southern New England*, ed. Laurence M. Hauptman and James D. Wherry (Norman: University Oklahoma Press, 1990), 19–38. Dincauze's treatment is comprehensive, yet accessible to a general audience. We find her framework useful for conceptualizing both the chronology and lifeways of Native peoples in the New England interior, but realize that, like the standard archaeological period names also included for ease of reference (e.g., Paleo-Indian, Archaic, Woodland), these terms are contemporary constructs and do not reflect how people in the past saw themselves. Rather, we employ them here as a heuristic for talking about the antiquity and complexity of Native peoples in Hadley and the middle Connecticut River Valley.
8. For an extensive discussion of collecting practices in the middle Connecticut River Valley, see Margaret M. Bruchac, "Historical Erasure and Cultural Recovery: Indigenous People in the Connecticut River Valley" (PhD diss., Department of Anthropology, University of Massachusetts Amherst, 2007).

9. Dena F. Dincauze, "Prehistoric Archaeological Resources in Hadley, Massachusetts: A 1978 Assessment with Recommendations for Protection" (report, MHC, 1978).
10. Christopher L. Donta, "Archaeological Intensive (Locational) Survey for the Proposed Hockanum School Stabilization Project, Hadley, Massachusetts" (report, MHC, 1998).
11. Dincauze, "Prehistoric Archaeological Resources," 4.
12. Ibid., 5, 31; Donta, "Hockanum School Project."
13. Tammy Rittenour, Michael E. Mann, and Julie Brigham-Grette, "Drainage History of Glacial Lake Hitchcock and Paleoclimatic Implications of Late Quaternary Sediments and Terraces in the Central Connecticut Valley, New England," *Geological Society of America* 33 (2000): 14.
14. Dincauze, "Prehistoric Archaeological Resources," 21.
15. Margaret M. Bruchac, "Earthshapers and Placemakers: Algonkian Indian Stories and the Landscape," in *Indigenous Archaeologies: Decolonizing Theory and Practice*, ed. C. Smith and H. M. Wobst (London: Routledge, 2005), 56–80.
16. Dincauze, "Prehistoric Archaeological Resources," 27.
17. Dincauze, "Capsule Prehistory," 19; D. R. Foster and T. M. Zebryk, "Long-Term Vegetation Dynamics and Disturbance History of a *Tsuga*-Dominated Forest in New England," *Ecology* 74 (1993): 982–998; Denise C. Gaudreau, "The Distribution of Late Quaternary Forest Regions in the Northeast: Pollen Data, Physiography, and the Prehistoric Record," in *Holocene Human Ecology in Northeastern North America*, ed. George P. Nicholas (New York: Plenum, 1988), 215–56; Denise C. Gaudreau and Thompson Webb III, "Late Quaternary Pollen Stratigraphy and Isochrone Maps for the Northeastern United States," in *Pollen Records of Late-Quaternary North American Sediments*, ed. V. M. Bryant Jr. and R. Holloway (Dallas: American Association of Stratigraphic Palynologists Foundation, 1985), 247–80; and M. Lindbladh, W. W. Oswald, D. R. Foster, and E. Faison, "A Late-Glacial Transition from *Picea glauca* to *Picea mariana* in Southern New England," *Quaternary Research* 67, no. 3 (2007): 502–8.
18. Lucinda McWeeney, "Cultural and Ecological Continuities and Discontinuities in Coastal New England: Landscape Manipulation," *Northeast Anthropology* 64 (2003): 75–84.
19. Dincauze, "Prehistoric Archaeological Resources," 35, 31, 5.
20. Brian D. Jones, "Paleoindian Population Dynamics in New England: Possible Typological Consequences," in *Hunters and Gatherers in Theory and Archaeology*, ed. George M. Crothers (Carbondale: Center for Archaeological Investigations, Southern Illinois University, 2004), 48–67.
21. Elizabeth S. Chilton, "Beyond 'Big': Gender, Age, and Subsistence Diversity in Paleo-Indian Societies," in *The Settlement of the American Continents: A Multidisciplinary Approach to Human Biogeography*, ed. C. M. Barton, G. A. Clark, D. Yesner, and G. Pearson (Tucson: University of Arizona Press, 2004), 162–72; Dincauze, "Capsule Prehistory," 20–21; and Dena F. Dincauze and V. Jacobson, "The Birds of Summer: Lakeside Routes into Late Pleistocene New England," *Canadian Journal of Archaeology* 25 (2001): 121–26.
22. Dincauze, "Prehistoric Archaeological Resources," 36.
23. Donta, "Hockanum School Project," 9.
24. Dincauze, "Capsule Prehistory," 23–24; Foster and Zebryk, "Long-Term Vegetation Dynamics."
25. Dincauze, "Capsule Prehistory," 23–25.
26. Dincauze, "Prehistoric Archaeological Resources," 37.
27. Ibid.
28. William R. Young, "A Survey of the Available Knowledge on the Middle Connecticut Valley Indians—Prehistoric and Historic," in *An Introduction to the Archaeology and History*

of the Connecticut Valley Indian, ed. William R. Young (Springfield, Mass.: Springfield Museum of Science, 1969), 47–48.

29. Mitchell T. Mulholland and Ellen-Rose Savulis, "Archaeological Locational Survey of Stockbridge Road and Vicinity, Hadley, Massachusetts" (report, MHC, 1985), 37–43.
30. It is very likely that Native peoples used bowls made from wood or textiles prior to stone and pottery bowls, but these stone bowls are the earliest that have survived.
31. For a discussion of the domestication process and archaeological evidence, see Bruce D. Smith, *Rivers of Change: Essays on Early Agriculture in Eastern North America* (Washington, D.C.: Smithsonian Institution Press, 1992).
32. For the Midwest and Southeast, see Smith, *Rivers of Change*. On the Northeast, see David George and Robert E. Dewar, "Chenopodium in Connecticut Prehistory: Wild, Weedy, Cultivated, or Domesticated?" in *Current Northeast Paleoethnobotany*, ed. John P. Hart (Albany: University of the State of New York, State Education Department, 1999), 121–32.
33. For further discussion see David J. Bernstein, "Prehistoric Use of Plant Foods on Long Island and Block Island Sounds," in Hart, *Current Northeast Paleoethnobotany*, 101–19; Michael J. Heckenberger, James B. Petersen, and Nancy Asch Sidell, "Early Evidence of Maize Agriculture in the Connecticut River Valley of Vermont," *Archaeology of Eastern North America* 20 (1992): 125–49; Tonya B. Largy, Lucianne Lavin, Marina E. Mozzi, and Kathleen Furgerson, "Corncobs and Buttercups: Plant Remains from the Goldkrest Site," in Hart, *Current Northeast Paleoethnobotany*, 69–84; and Nancy Asch Sidell, "Prehistoric Plant Use in Maine: Paleoindian to Contact Period," in Hart, *Current Northeast Paleoethnobotany*, 194–222.
34. For further discussion see Elizabeth S. Chilton and Dianna L. Doucette, "Archaeological Investigations at the Lucy Vincent Beach Site (19-Dk-148): Preliminary Results and Interpretations," in *A Lasting Impression: Coastal, Lithic, and Ceramic Research in New England Archaeology*, ed. Jordan E. Kerber (Westport, Conn.: Praeger, 2002), 41–70; Elizabeth S. Chilton, Tonya Baroody Largy, and Kathryn Curran, "Evidence for Prehistoric Maize Horticulture at the Pine Hill Site, Deerfield, Massachusetts," *Northeast Anthropology* 59 (2000): 23–46; Tonya Baroody Largy, Peter Burns, Elizabeth S. Chilton, and Dianna L. Doucette, "Lucy Vincent Beach: Another Look at the Prehistoric Exploitation of Piscine Resources Off the Coast of Massachusetts, U.S.A.," *Northeast Anthropology* 64 (2002): 67–73.
35. For example, see William F. Keegan and Kristen Noble Keegan, eds., *The Archaeology of Connecticut: The Human Era—11,000 Years Ago to the Present* (Storrs: Bibliopola Press, University of Connecticut Co-operative, 1999).
36. Elizabeth S. Chilton, "The Origin and Spread of Maize (*Zea mays*) in New England," in *Histories of Maize: Multidisciplinary Approaches to the Prehistory, Biogeography, Domestication, and Evolution of Maize*, ed. John Staller, Robert Tykot, and Bruce Benz (Burlington, Mass.: Elsevier, 2006), 539–47.
37. Elizabeth S. Chilton, "Mobile Farmers of Pre-Contact Southern New England: The Archaeological and Ethnohistoric Evidence," in Hart, *Current Northeast Paleoethnobotany*, 157–76, esp. 161–71; see also Elizabeth S. Chilton, " 'Towns They Have None': Diverse Subsistence and Settlement Strategies in Native New England," in *Northeast Subsistence-Settlement Change, A.D. 700–1300*, ed. J. P. Hart and C. B. Reith (Albany: University of the State of New York, State Education Department, 2002) 289–300.
38. Chilton, "Towns They Have None," 293–95.
39. Chilton "Mobile Farmers," 163.
40. Dincauze, "Prehistoric Archaeological Resources," 40.
41. Ibid.
42. Donta, "Hockanum School Project," 16.

43. Mulholland and Savulis, "Survey of Stockbridge Road."
44. Donta and Wendt, "Natural Gas Pipeline," 16; Peter A. Thomas, "Cultural Change on the Southern New England Frontier, 1639–1665," in *Cultures in Contact: The Impact of European Colonization on Native American Cultural Institutions A.D. 1000–1800*, ed. W. W. Fitzhugh (Washington, D.C.: Smithsonian Institution Press, 1985), 131–61.
45. For further discussion see Margaret M. Bruchac, "Native Presence in Nonotuck and Northampton," in *A Place Called Paradise: Culture and Community in Northampton, Massachusetts, 1654–2004*, ed. Kerry W. Buckley (Amherst: University of Massachusetts Press, 2004), 18–38; Sylvester Judd, *History of Hadley, including the Early History of Hatfield, South Hadley, Amherst and Granby, Massachusetts*, 2nd ed. (Springfield, Mass.: H. R. Huntting, 1905), 114; and Peter A. Thomas, "In the Maelstrom of Change: The Indian Trade and Cultural Process in the Middle Connecticut River Valley, 1635–1665" (PhD diss., Department of Anthropology, University of Massachusetts Amherst, 1979), 3.
46. Bruchac, "Earthshapers and Placemakers," 58.
47. Bruchac, "Native Presence in Nonotuck," 18.
48. Eric S. Johnson, "Community and Confederation: A Political Geography of Contact Period Southern New England," in *The Archaeological Northeast*, ed. M. A. Levine, K. A. Sassaman, and M. S. Nassaney (Westport, Conn.: Bergin and Garvey, 1999), 155–68; Eric S. Johnson, "Some by Flatteries and Others by Threatenings: Political Strategies among Native Americans of Seventeenth-Century New England" (PhD diss., Department of Anthropology, University of Massachusetts Amherst, 1993); and Thomas, "Cultural Change," 156.
49. Massachusetts Historical Commission, "MHC Reconnaissance Survey Report, Hadley, Massachusetts" (MHC, 1982).
50. Judd, *History of Hadley*, 118–20; Massachusetts Historical Commission, "Reconnaissance Report."
51. Thomas, "Maelstrom of Change"; see also discussion in Nash, this volume.
52. Bruchac's work on this topic includes "Historical Erasure and Cultural Recovery," "Earthshapers and Placemakers," "Native Presence in Nonotuck," and two working papers for the Five College Repatriation Committee: "Background History: Regional Collections of Native American Indian Skeletal Remains from the Middle Connecticut River Valley" (2004); and "Collecting Indians for the Colleges: Constructing Native Invisibility in the Connecticut River Valley" (2003; both papers are on file at Amherst College).
53. Bruchac, "Native Presence in Nonotuck," 21.
54. Quoted in ibid., 22.
55. Dincauze, "Prehistoric Archaeological Resources," 6, 12.
56. Donta, "Hockanum School Project," 12.
57. F. D. Huntington, "Professor Huntington's Address," in *Bicentennial Celebration of Hadley*, 28–29.
58. Bruchac, "Historical Erasure and Cultural Recovery"; Dincauze, "Prehistoric Archaeological Resources," 9.
59. Judd, *History of Hadley*, 104.
60. Bruchac, "Historical Erasure and Cultural Recovery," 117.
61. Dincauze, "Prehistoric Archaeological Resources," 9–13.
62. Charles Willoughby, *Antiquities of the New England Indians* (Boston: Peabody Museum, 1935); Harry Andrew Wright, *The Story of Western Massachusetts*, vol. 1 (New York: Lewis Historical Publishing, 1949).
63. Donta and Wendt, "Natural Gas Pipeline," 9. The Massachusetts Archaeological Society was founded in 1939 to stimulate the study of archaeology and Native American cultural

history in Massachusetts and build relationships among people interested in archaeology. Howes's works include "Artifacts Found on the Judd Tract in South Hadley, Massachusetts," *Bulletin of the Massachusetts Archaeological Society* 7 (1946): 68–70; "Aboriginal New England Pottery," *Bulletin of the Massachusetts Archaeological Society* 5, no. 1 (1943): 1–5; "An Unusual Pipe from Hadley, Massachusetts," *American Antiquity* 8 (1942): 175–77; and "A Trading Center for Local Products found on the Hoccanum Road in the Town of Hadley, Massachusetts," *Bulletin of the Massachusetts Archaeological Society* 3, no. 4 (1940): 58.

64. Dincauze, "Prehistoric Archaeological Resources," 12. Fowler published a number of articles: "Comparative Study of Hoe and Spade Blades," *Bulletin of the Massachusetts Archaeological Society* 35, nos. 1–2 (1973): 1–8; "The Hoe Complex of the Connecticut Valley," *American Antiquity* 12 (1946): 29–34; "A Chronology and Classification of Connecticut Valley Projectile Points," *Bulletin of the Massachusetts Archaeological Society* 6 (1945): 53–57; "The Norwottuck Complex," *Bulletin of the Massachusetts Archaeological Society* 6 (1945): 58–63. On Rodimon, see Eric Johnson, "Rodimon Collection Report" (MHC, 1985).
65. Bruchac, "Historical Erasure and Cultural Recovery"; Dincauze, "Prehistoric Archaeological Resources," 11.
66. Wilder's publications include "Notes on the Indians of Southern Massachusetts," *American Anthropologist* 25 (1923): 197–218; "The Physiognomy of the Indians of Southern New England," *American Anthropologist* 14, no. 3 (1912): 415–36; "Excavation of Indian Graves in Western Massachusetts," *American Anthropologist* 7, no. 2 (1905): 295–300; and, with Ralph Wheaton Whipple, "The Position of the Body in Aboriginal Interments in Western Massachusetts," *American Anthropologist* 19 (1917): 372–87.
67. For further discussion see Bruchac, "Historical Erasure and Cultural Recovery," 171–90.
68. For a discussion of the legacy of Harris Hawthorne Wilder and other Connecticut River Valley collectors and impacts on repatriation today, see Bruchac, "Historical Erasure and Cultural Recovery," and Alice Nash's essay in this volume.
69. Margaret Barstow, personal communication, 2 January 2008.
70. Thomas Ulrich, "Phase I / Reconstruction—Phase II / Intensive Cultural Resource Survey for Three Pumping Stations, North Hadley, Massachusetts" (report, MHC, 1977); Mulholland and Savulis, "Survey of Stockbridge Road"; M. B. Folsom, "Draft Report of South Hadley Canal Archaeological Monitoring and Survey" (MHC, 1979); D. C. Skivas, "Massachusetts Natural Resources Conservation Service Cultural Resource Activities Report" (MHC, 1994); Donta, "Hockanum School Project."
71. Dincauze, "Prehistoric Archaeological Resources."
72. Rita Reinke and Ed Hood, "Report on the Hadley Palisade Project" (report on file with the Hadley Historical Commission, 1990).
73. Shirley Blancke and John Peters Slow Turtle, "Indigenous Peoples' Control over and Contribution to Archaeology in the United States of America: Some Issues," *Bulletin of the Massachusetts Archaeological Society* 57, no. 2 (1996): 64–68.
74. For examples see Linda Derry and Maureen Malloy, eds., *Archaeologists and Local Communities: Partners in Exploring the Past* (Washington, D.C.: Society for American Archaeology, 2003); Jordan Kerber, ed., *Cross-Cultural Collaboration: Native Peoples and Archaeology in the Northeastern United States* (Lincoln: University of Nebraska Press, 2006); Paul Shackel and Erve Chambers, eds., *Places in Mind: Public Archaeology as Applied Anthropology* (New York: Routledge, 2004).

3

While Quanquan's mortgage and the language within it provide one avenue of insight into the first period of Hadley's history, archaeological evidence of the fortifications that once surrounded the village provide another, and shed light, too, on the nineteenth- and twentieth-century communities that remained fascinated with Hadley's so-called palisade. As late as 1996, the members of the Hadley Historical Commission chose to add a monument to the town common celebrating and interpreting the long-lost structure. The artist's conception of the landscape captured the way many citizens have envisioned the fortifications that once encircled the village, and the monument continues to attract the interest of the many cyclists who cross the common along the Norwottuck Rail Trail.

The commission's formal interest in the fortifications began earlier, when they contacted archaeologists at the University of Massachusetts to see if a study could be made of this long-gone artifact. The findings reported here by Ed Hood and Rita Reinke, the archaeologists who undertook that investigation, enlarge our understanding not only of the structure itself, but also of the nature of relationships between the European and Native communities who came to exist alongside one another in the last half of the seventeenth century (including fears as well as realities) and also how the English families who settled this place conceived the nature of community in ways that encompassed both cooperation and coercion.

The Fortification of Hadley in the Seventeenth Century

J. Edward Hood and Rita Reinke

IN 1996 THE HADLEY Historical Commission created a new monument and plaque to commemorate the fortification constructed in the town during the latter part of the seventeenth century. The plaque, based on nineteenth-century descriptions of the town's "palisade," depicts a substantial, well built, and symmetrical stockaded structure. The image conveys the sense of a community united in its response to an outside threat. The descriptions of Hadley's fortification in local histories, such as Sylvester Judd's 1863 *History of Hadley*, which combine information from original source documents, personal observations, and hearsay, also often suggest something more substantial and effective than what actually existed. In this chapter we review the historical and physical evidence for the Hadley fortification and present an interpretation that is literally grounded in the results of our archaeological investigation.[1] As we will see, the nature of the fortification's actual construction and maintenance says as much about the conflict between individual and community interests within a frontier English colony as it does about the external conflicts that gave rise to it: the struggle for ownership and dominance of the Connecticut River Valley region between continental European powers, local English settlers, and Native American inhabitants.

Fences and Defenses

The construction of fortifications was common in New England during the early and mid-seventeenth century, especially at times of heightened conflict, such as the Pequot War of 1636–37. Fortifications might be built as specific points of defense or retreat, around all or parts of settlements, or even around individual houses. In many cases they were just high fences, intended to keep out sudden attacks and to provide cover from enemies firing into the settlement. They generally did not have battlements from which defenders could fire on attackers, and they were often of a relatively unsubstantial construction. They were never intended to withstand anything as formal as a siege, as William Hubbard notes in his 1677 account of King Philip's War: "The English Plantations about Hadley . . . concluded it the safer way to make a kind of Barricado about their Towns, by setting up Pallizadoes or cleft wood about eight foot long, as it were to break the force of any sudden assault which the Indians might make upon them; which counsel proved very successful; for although it be an inconsiderable defense against a Warlike Enemy, that hath strength enough, and confidence to besiege a place, yet it is sufficient to prevent any sudden assault of such . . . Enemy as these were."[2]

Only a small number of such fortifications have been discovered or examined archaeologically. A Native American settlement in Springfield, Massachusetts, known as Fort Hill, which was set up in 1666 by the English colonists for the protection of the Indian inhabitants (and presumably so the English could keep an eye on them), had such a fortification.[3] Excavations conducted by Harry Andrews Wright in 1895 uncovered evidence for posts set into the ground, believed to be a part of that palisade.[4] At an early English house site

(1630s to 1650s) in Kingston, Massachusetts, archaeologists uncovered a trench that held a palisade of vertical poles, interpreted as part of an unfinished fortification that was intended to surround a single house but was never completed.[5] With the outbreak of King Philip's War (fought between Native American residents of southern New England and the English colonists) in 1675, many of the English settlements in the Connecticut River Valley in Massachusetts, including Hadley and nearby Springfield, Northampton, Hatfield, and Deerfield, built protective fortifications.

Town records indicate that the fortification in Hadley (figure 3.1) stood from 1675 until at least 1693. In order to understand this structure better, it is helpful to consider first a common element of the seventeenth-century landscape being created by English colonists—fences. The construction of fences to bound agricultural land and protect it from damage by livestock was a fundamental element of the land use practices of English colonists in New England.[6] In Connecticut River Valley towns such as Hadley and Deerfield, landowners created large common agricultural fields and meadows. Plots of land within them were privately owned, but fencing to protect the fields from livestock was placed around the entire common field. Although this resulted in a fence scores of miles long, it required less total fencing than the individual bounding of private parcels.[7]

J. Ritchie Garrison has documented the physical remains of a portion of the common field fence, of a type known as "ditch and bank," in Deerfield, just north of Hadley.[8] It consisted of a two- to three-foot ditch, with the excavated earth used to create a ridge or bank on the inner side of the ditch. This type of earthwork, also know as a ha-ha or sunk fence, was capable of restricting the flow of animals, having a total height from the bottom of the ditch to the top of the bank of close to four feet. That Hadley also used ditch and bank fences for its common fields is attested by Frederic Dan Huntington in his address at the town's bicentennial celebration in 1859: "Enclosures were made chiefly at common expense, by fences, embankments and deep ditches, traces of the latter still remaining in some parts of the town."[9]

A fence could be added to the top of the bank, making the total fence, when properly maintained, a very effective livestock barrier. Garrison documents such a construction for Deerfield, and the use of post and rail fences as part of the common field fencing there is amply documented.[10] As we will see, there is a close relationship between the design of common field fences in Hadley, and probably other Connecticut River Valley towns as well, and the type of fortifications these towns constructed during the last quarter of the seventeenth century.

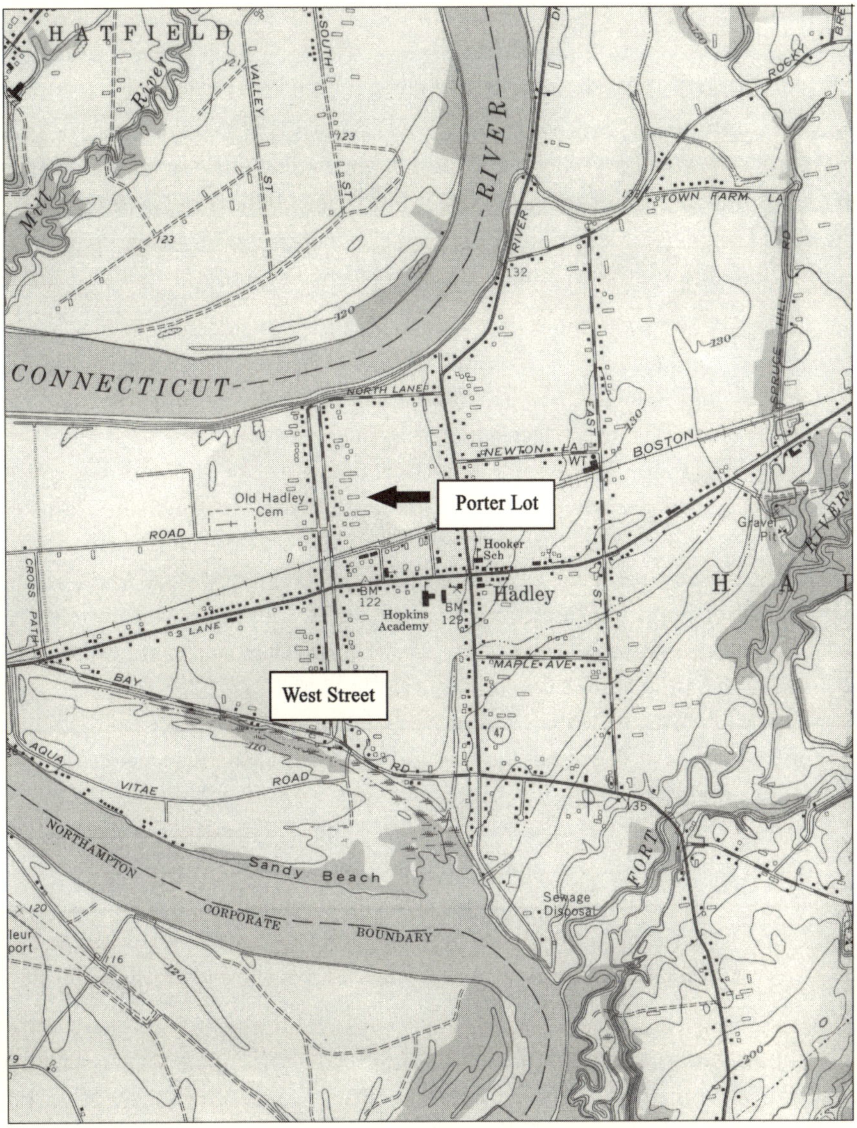

FIGURE 3.1. *Main area of the early colonial settlement of Hadley, along the wide strip of land defined by the two parallel streets shown here as "West Street," known as "the common." The town of Hadley is much larger than the area shown here, but the main part of the earliest settlement was in homelots along the common.*

The Historical Evidence

We have little good documentation of physical evidence for what the fortifications of Connecticut River Valley towns such as Hadley looked like, apart from the discovery of the Fort Hill fortification in Springfield and William Hubbard's 1677 description, quoted above. Sylvester Judd's 1863 *History of Hadley* provides the most complete description of the Hadley fortification, drawing on a number of sources, some identifiable and others of uncertain origin:

> In the latter part of autumn [1675] and in the ensuing winter, the people . . . constructed about their plantations [meaning the English settlements], a palisade or palisado. It consisted of rows of pales, stakes or posts about ten feet in length, having two feet in the ground and eight feet above the ground. These posts were made by splitting sticks of timber into two or more pieces, and hewing off the edges of the cleft-pieces so that no part should be less than two or three inches in thickness. These were set close together in the earth, and were probably fastened to a piece of wood near the top. Many of the rails of fences were used for palisades. These fortifications which would have been a very inadequate defense against an attack by Europeans, were a sufficient barrier against the assaults of the Indians. . . .
>
> The first vote of Hadley . . . relating to the fortifications was on the 11th of February 1676. It was not then completed. It was a palisade fence crossing the homelots, in the rear of the buildings, on both sides of the street and crossing the street some rods from each end. The two sides of the palisade were each almost a mile in length and the two ends near forty rods each. There were strong gates at the ends, and at the highways on the sides. There was little danger of an attack on the western or meadow side of the street, and the fortification on that side was not so strongly made as the other.[11]

In his manuscript notes, Judd, who was doing historical research around the middle of the nineteenth century, records the best direct observation of the remains of the fortification: "In Colonel Porter's homelot there is a portion [of the fortification] that has never been ploughed & here the earth of the old palisade shows itself. There is a gentle ridge, with a depression on each side, lower than the adjoining surface. The east depression was where the palisade stood, the ridge is the earth thrown against it, now settled down: and the west depression is the ditch from which the earth was thrown."[12] (See figure 3.1 for location of the Porter lot.) Judd uses the word "palisade" to describe the fortification, but the town records never specifically use this term; rather, they consistently use the terms "fortification," "breastwork," and "defensive fence." The contemporary observer

William Hubbard does use "pallizadoes" to describe the specific wooden posts used to create this "kind of Barricado." Here, we use the term "palisade" specifically to describe a fence built of vertical posts or pales set into the ground, forming a continuous, solid barrier, perhaps with narrow gaps between each vertical post.

Judd's comments on the date of the original construction match those of Hadley's town records, which suggest that work began during the winter of 1675/76, while armed colonial forces were garrisoned in the town. On October 6, 1675, the Reverend John Russell of Hadley, in a letter to Governor Leverett in Boston, noted that the "empowering of some man or men . . . to direct & order us in our fortifications, might not be unuseful."[13] The first concrete reference to fortifications, in the town records of February 11, 1676, show that they were already either wholly or partially in place by that date: "Voted and ordered by the town that the whole fortification set up for the defense and security of the town on east and west side shall be sufficiently maintained and kept up and that on the west side [of] the street to defend the meadows from spoils and damage, and to be subject to the inspection of the fence viewers."[14]

This town record also shows that the role of supervising the construction and maintenance of the fortification was initially given, at least in part, to the men who normally inspected agricultural fences in the town, the fence viewers (an elected and important town office), and not a military officer. By 1678, however, the records show that official "surveyors of the town fortification" had been appointed, acknowledging the unique duties required of this position, though at an even later date, 1693, the records once again indicate that this responsibility belonged to the fence viewers. From its original construction, then, the Hadley fortification, and probably those of other Connecticut River Valley towns, had direct technological and administrative links to the creation and maintenance of the common field fences used in these towns. Judd's observations on the remains of the Hadley fortification and the archeological evidence discovered during our research, detailed below, indicate that, at least on the east side of the town, it consisted of a ditch and bank, akin to the common field fence documented by Garrison for Deerfield. In an entry in the Hadley town records for May 3, 1693, the fortification is specifically referred to as a "defensive fence."

Location and Size

There is nothing in any of the town records to suggest the dimensions or exact location of the fortification. Judd states that it was approximately one mile long (covering almost the full length of the village street) and about forty rods (640 feet) wide.[15] Wherever Judd may have obtained this information, he did not leave a record of it, and we have not identified a contemporary source for these measurements. Judd may have felt that forty rods was simply the logical width; the town common was twenty rods wide, and an additional twenty rods (ten on each side) would have placed the fortification behind the houses and most or all outbuildings on the village homelots. Judd had observed a surviving trace of the fortification prior to 1860, however, and he may have taken direct measurements from this to establish its dimensions. For this reason we chose to use his information to guide our initial fieldwork. As we will see, our findings do support Judd's assertion of the location of the fortification, at least on the east side of the town.

Figure 3.2 is a 1909 reconstruction of the original homelots, showing the Hadley settlement's location in a bend, or oxbow, of the Connecticut River. The settlement is on a north–south axis, running all the way across the open end of the oxbow, effectively cutting off the west "meadow" land of the town from the mainland east of the river. The town common is a band of public land running the full length of the village along the north–south axis. Today the common includes two streets and adjacent sidewalks running north–south, with the outer edges of the sidewalks defining the outer edge of the common. Originally the streets or travel routes may have been less formal; pedestrians and animal-drawn vehicles may have crossed the common more or less as they desired, though there may have been a few well-worn paths. This public land served as the location of the meetinghouse, as a training ground for the militia, and as a site for grazing animals, as well as other public and private activities.

The 1909 reconstruction of the village shows the nucleated character of the settlement, with Russell Street (today's Route 9), which bisects the settlement going east–west, and other roads noted. Each parcel had its homelot fronting on the common, with a rear lot extending east or west out toward the common agricultural fields. It also shows a heavy line about a fifth of the way back from the common on each side, running north–south. The lines are unidentified, but they are in the approximate location of the fortification as Judd described it. If these lines do represent the fortification, they do not show clear north or south walls for it. Thus we cannot be sure whether the fortification was in fact a long rectangular enclosure or simply two long barriers running north–south that would protect the town from attack or sniping along the greater part of its length.

Another characteristic noted by Judd and supported by the town records is that the east and west sides of the fortification seem to be, at times, of slightly different character or construction, and they are certainly referred to in differing ways over time. Town records consistently refer to the "east" and "west"

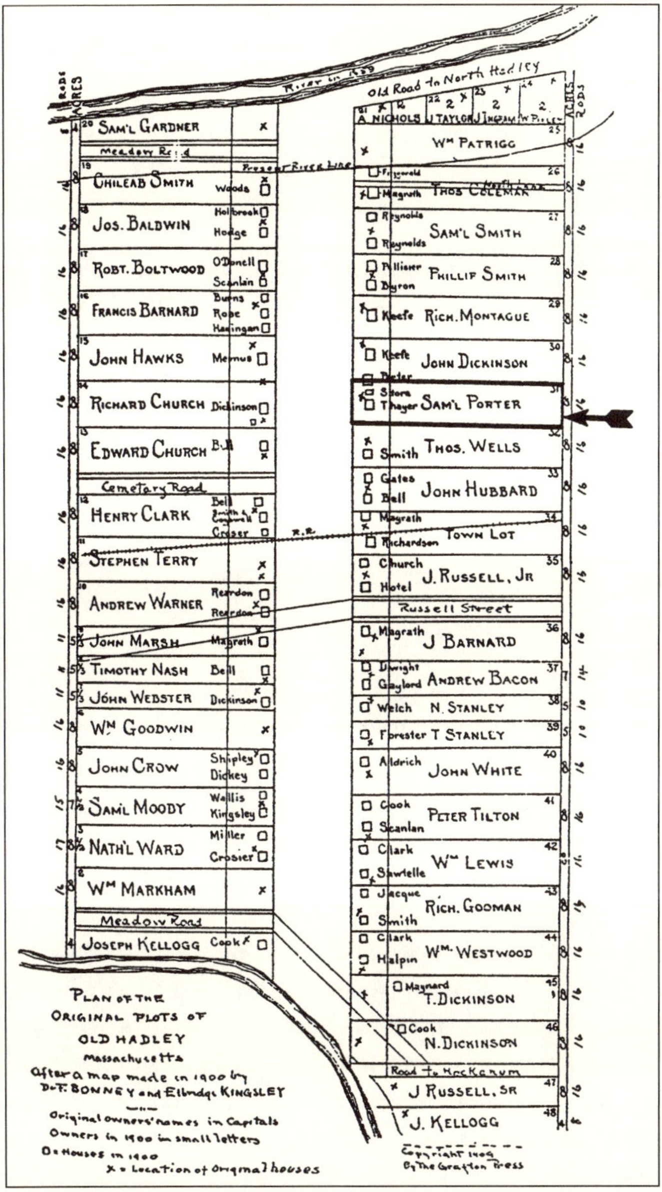

FIGURE 3.2. *A 1909 reconstruction of the original homelots of Hadley. The common is the wide strip of land running north–south between the two columns of homelots. The heavy black lines running parallel to the common, just behind the houses, are in the approximate location of the fortification, at least on the east side. From Franklin Bonney and Elbridge Kingsley, "The Original Settlers of Hadley and the Lots of Land Granted Them,"* Grafton Magazine of History and Genealogy 2, *no. 1 (August 1909), 5.*

sides of the fortification, but never to the north or south sides, or what Judd describes as the "two ends," although their existence is sometimes implied by the mention of gates, which presumably would have been on the north and south ends. Generally each side is discussed separately in the town records, and not necessarily as part of a single fortification. For example, the record from December 10, 1678, notes:

> Voted that all the inhabitants that live on the *west* side of the street shall sufficiently repair and make up the rear *fence* of all their house lots to secure the meadow from damage according to a town order at or before the last of March next.
>
> Voted also that all the inhabitants on the *west* side that have had warning to set up the *fortification* against their lot that they have broken down or is fallen down shall speedily repair and set up the same and then afterward it shall be maintained by a common public charge.
>
> Voted that the *fortification* on the *east* side the town shall be proportioned to every man according to the town list which shall be taken in January next. (Emphasis added.)

Of the entries from fourteen different dates in the town records that refer to the repair, upkeep, or other modification of the fortifications, eight entries specifically mention the east side, but only four mention the west side, and two of those suggest that something rather less than a fortification was being repaired (such as the "rear fence" mentioned in the record from December 1678).

It is difficult to reconstruct the physical reality from occasionally cryptic town record entries, but we can make some inferences. The fortification does appear to have been different, at least part of the time, on the east and west sides of the street. As we have seen, one of the stated purposes of the original west-side construction was to "defend the meadows from spoils and damage," an injunction repeated again in December 1678. These entries suggest an animal barrier rather than a military construction; "spoils and damage" more likely refers to the result of livestock getting into crops than to damage caused by Native American tactics, which during King Philip's War typically did not include the destruction of crops. The difficulty in interpretation lies in the context of these statements. In each case, the same records contain references to "the whole fortification" or "all the town fortification." Were there two structures on the west side of the street? Was there only one, but one that served a different function on the west than it did on the east?

Our investigations were not able to resolve this question. Perhaps a primary, overall intent of the fortification was to cut off the oxbow on which the settlement was built from land attacks from the east, with the west or river-side fortification of secondary importance. The palisade at Salem, Massachusetts, apparently served this function, fencing off the peninsula where the main body of the community was located.[16] If that were the case in Hadley, we would expect that the structure on the east side would be more substantial than that on the west, which indeed is generally what the town records imply. It remains uncertain, however, what form the fortification took beyond the fact that it had two long walls running north–south on either side of the central part of the village. The east and west sides of the fortification were treated differently, and quite possibly were not of the same character and served different purposes. It is also unclear whether the fortification was a closed box with gates, or if its builders left the north and south ends open, relying on the river passing nearby as a protective barrier.

Construction

A series of town records provide some details of the construction of the Hadley fortification, beginning with the entry for February 19, 1677: "Voted by the town that the fortification on the east side [of] the town shall be repaired[,] made strong and defensible in every part of the same against the Enemy, and that every Inhabitant of the town shall do his proportion now of [?] the Breastwork was laid out and in the place where he did then his proportion and shall maintain the said Breastworks according to its first appointment 5 foot and ½ in height with the rails or outworks belonging thereto."

The wording is a little awkward, but the basic import is clear. The fortification, at least on the east side of the town, consisted of a "breastwork," which means some sort of earthwork, most likely a ditch and bank fence of the type documented by Garrison for Deerfield and observed by Judd in Hadley prior to 1860, topped by a palisade. The breastwork was to be five feet six inches in height "with the rails." It is unclear from this wording if the total fortification of breastwork and palisade is supposed to be five and one-half feet, or if just the breastwork was this height, with the palisade providing additional height. If this represents the total height of the fortification, it suggests a barrier far less substantial than most of us imagine for an effective fortification. This could suggest that the total height of the breastwork from bottom of ditch to top of bank was five and one-half feet, which capped by a palisade would be a more formidable height. Whatever the actual height, this 1677 town record fits with Sylvester Judd's nineteenth-century observation that the fortification included a ditch and bank.

Less than two years later, however, this configuration seems to have been considered inadequate by the voters of Hadley, as the town records for December 10, 1678, show:

> Voted that all the fortification on the east side of the town shall be made new.
>
> Voted that the length of the staffs shall be ten foot long[;] . . . rails[,] such as are substantial, and all other staffs 3 fingers thick set two foot into the ground and to be all set up by the last day of May, next ensuing.

This is the most explicit description of the construction methods for the palisade part of the fortification in any of the contemporary documents that we have seen, and it describes very clearly its total height: it was a palisade of posts, approximately two inches thick, set two feet into the ground and extending eight feet above the ground. The record uses the words "staffs" and "rails" to describe the vertical posts of the palisade, terms that indicate their insubstantial nature—they were little more than (and in many cases may have been) fence rails. This was clearly not a sturdy fortification meant to withstand any sort of effort to break it down. Nor was it intended to be a place from which to mount a defense, as no accommodations are made for firing over or through it, with the exception of the "flankers" noted in the town records for January 10, 1678, discussed below.

A palisade consisting of eight-foot-high posts or staffs, placed on top of a ditch and bank breastwork (with a total height of three to five and a half feet), would present an eleven- to thirteen-and-a-half-foot-high obstacle on its exterior side. The purpose of such a barrier would be to prevent a surprise or rush attack on the settlement and also to inhibit sniping into it. It would also serve as a disincentive to hostile intrusion by constraining the escape route out of the settlement for would-be attackers. This is precisely what William Hubbard says happened during an attack in March 1676 on the "Barricado" at Northampton (one of the English settlements near Hadley whose fortifications were described at the beginning of this chapter): "Although [the Indians] did afterwards in the Spring break through those Pallizadoes at Northampton, yet as soon as ever they began to be repulsed, they saw themselves like Wolves in a Pound, that they could not fly away at their pleasure, so as they never adventured to break through afterward upon any of the towns so secured."[17]

On January 10, 1678, the Hadley town records make reference to "flankers" as part of the fortification, and in January 1679 the records call for "watch houses" to be built. These flankers were most likely projections from the long flat face of the fortification; they presumably had interior battlements or other features that would allow defenders to observe and even fire over the top of, or through, the fortification at the enemy's side, or flank. The number of flankers is not given, but any such features would make the otherwise flimsy fortification more effective.

Nothing else is said about the flankers, however, nor is greater detail provided about the other types of fortifications mentioned in passing: "the meetinghouse shall be fortified" (February 19, 1677), "several watch houses" (January 9, 1679), "the garrison houses" (February 10, 1692), and "two more fortified houses" (June 16, 1693). It is clear that the defense of the village was premised on several elements that probably varied in importance over the seventeen years that the palisade stood, but the only defensive structure that is consistently mentioned through this time span is the breastwork-palisade. Town records specifically refer to it as the "fortification"; other defensive elements, such as the flankers and watch houses, are always specified separately.

Some further light is shed on the specifics of the construction of the fortification in the town record entry of March 28, 1679, which notes that the town voted to have all of the east side of the fortification "made new" and that "the fortification abovesaid shall be removed or set a foot and half further out or eastward from the place where now it stands." To move the fortification one and a half feet to the east would seem to be a major undertaking, given that it was about a mile in total length and included an excavated breastwork. What purpose would this relocation accomplish? We suggest that the order reflects the realization that the common field fence design of the fortification could be made more formidable by placing the palisade posts or pales closer to the front of the bank facing the ditch of the breastwork. A foot and a half is roughly the distance from the center to the edge of a bank created with the fill excavated from a three-foot-wide ditch. If the posts were placed in the center of the bank, the result would be a narrow foothold in front of the palisade. By moving the palisade to the front edge of the bank, this foothold would be eliminated and the net height of the palisade made greater in relation to the ditch in front of it. Such a measure would involve far less labor than moving the ditch and bank breastwork itself to the east.

As we have seen, Sylvester Judd, who observed the remains of the fortification still visible in the mid-nineteenth century, described "a gentle ridge, with a depression on each side," and noted that "the east depression was where the palisade stood," which suggests just such a scenario—that the palisade was "in" the east depression, that is, on the inside of the ditch. The westerly depression that he notes suggests an additional effort to bolster the palisade by piling up dirt against its back, to make the bank higher and perhaps prevent attackers from pushing it down.

Community Cooperation

The town records show that there was some difficulty in getting individual residents to build and maintain the fortification, and they suggest an interesting pattern in the dynamics of persuading individuals to subordinate their private property rights and increase their efforts for the good of the community. The town record of February 19, 1677, documents that each landowner was obligated to build his own section of the fortification. Such a method seems an improbable way to effectively build and maintain a common defensive structure—one that presumably was only as strong as its weakest parts. Some landowners might be disinclined or unable to do more than the bare minimum; some might not complete the job at all. Judging from town records, this does appear to have been a problem. For example, in March 1679 it was resolved that "where there are any breaks in the fortification above said in any mans proportion as it was last laid out the said person or persons shall forthwith sufficiently repair and set up the same under the penalty of the former order in case of neglect." On December 10, 1678, it was "voted also that all the inhabitants on the west side that have had warning to set up the fortification against their lot that they have broken down or is fallen down shall speedily repair and set up the same and than afterward it shall be maintained by a common public charge." And on June 16, 1693, "that all defensive fence the owners thereof having had notice by the fence viewers and not done up in one days time, the said viewers shall be and are hereby empowered to make good such defective fence and to have double pay from the owners of such fence."

Thus, it is clear that much time was spent on keeping the structure in good repair and attempting to ensure that each property owner did his fair share of the work. Various town officials were appointed and empowered to enforce compliance. All of this required substantial effort on the part of the town's leadership, and it indicates that the townspeople were not of a single mind about the necessity of the fortification—or at least not uniformly inclined to do the work required to build and maintain it.

Town records also indicate that some landowners were willing to sacrifice safety for convenience. Because of the way the fortification was situated, lots on the common were effectively bisected by a fence running along the street, separating homelot from farm fields. To get to their fields, these owners would have had to travel down the street from their homelot, exit the fortification through one of the official gates, and then travel back to the fields on the outside of the fortification. Perhaps not surprisingly, it seems that some owners preferred to create, or perhaps threatened to create, their own gates to allow them direct access to their fields. On February 11, 1676, it was ruled that "no man in any part of the fortifications abovesaid shall have or make any particular outlet for himself or cattle into meadows or lots under the penalty of five shillings." Certainly if property owners maintained their own private gates (and these quite possibly were just holes), the fortification would have been much less effective.

The Archaeological Evidence

Our review of town records, local town histories, and the manuscript notes of Sylvester Judd laid the groundwork for our search for the physical remains of the Hadley fortification. Judd's observation of the surviving remains of the fortification on the east side of the common on the Porter Lot, recorded at some time prior to his death in 1860, as well as his unsourced observation about the width of the fortification, led us to conduct our first excavations on the site of the historic Porter homelot. Other test excavations were made to explore the east and west sides of the common and the northerly and southerly portions of the town. These additional test locations were chosen based on visual inspection of the landscape and our estimate of the amount of disturbance to the ground caused by construction, agriculture, or other activities.

The funding for our work was limited, so the amount of excavation we conducted was relatively small. Six different sites were examined archaeologically, with hand-dug trenches 50 centimeters (20 inches) wide, of varying lengths. Since the area of possible location was large, and the fortification was presumed to be only several feet wide in cross-section, running north–south, the most expedient way to locate it was by excavating several narrow east–west trenches. Twelve excavation units were dug, with a total linear length of 40 meters (about 130 feet), placed to intersect the most likely location of the fortification based on Judd's observations of its distance from the town common. This was by no means a foolproof method, and the fortification might well have lain ten or twenty feet in either direction.

Excavation was done by hand, primarily by shovel skimming—scooping up shallow, horizontal slices of soil with a sharpened, flat-bladed shovel. Where archaeological remains of any sort were encountered, including any disturbance to the natural soil layers (called "features"), further excavation was made with a mason's trowel and dustpan. Excavated soil was sifted through a ¼-inch mesh screen in order to catch any artifacts not recovered during the digging process. All excavation units and soil strata were recorded, and the excavation units were photographed. All artifacts were washed, identified, and catalogued.

Findings

The majority of the excavation units revealed a fairly typical sequence of soil layers, starting with a homogeneous organic soil, generally around 12 to 20 inches deep, created by repeated plowing and tilling—what archaeologist refer to as a "plow zone." The plow zone usually abruptly gives way to the lower, less organic undisturbed soils, called B-zone soils. The sharp contrast between the two soil layers marks the boundary created by the continued deep passage of the plow. Naturally occurring rocks are unusual in the soil layers of this part of Hadley, so excavation was very easy and soil layers distinctive.[18]

In two of the excavation units, at the site labeled "Porter Lot" shown in figures 3.1 and 3. 2, where Judd claimed to have seen evidence of the fortification in the nineteenth-century landscape, we uncovered remains that can clearly be identified as belonging to the fortification. This property, located on the east side of the Hadley common, north of Route 9, is the site of the Samuel Porter house, dating to the first quarter of the eighteenth century and considered to be the oldest house still standing in western Massachusetts.[19] Judd mentions that the lot had never been plowed, and this preserved the evidence of the fortification in the form of undulations on the ground surface. He suggests that previously (meaning in the mid-nineteenth century or earlier) more evidence of the fortification had been visible elsewhere on the lot, but by the time of his writing some had disappeared; presumably plowing and tilling were done in these spots, leveling the ground surface.

Judd wrote that the fortification was 40 rods, or 640 feet, wide. He obviously would have been able to measure the location of the visible evidence for the east side fortification, though what his assertion that the west side of the fortification would have been equidistant from the common is based on is unknown. Since the common is 20 rods wide, and since the general understanding of the fortification is that it ran the length of the village enclosing the houses along the common, it may be presumed that Judd reasoned, or perhaps knew somehow, that the fortification was *centered* on the common. If so, this would suggest that the physical location of the fortification was 10 rods beyond the outside edges of the common, today defined by the outer edges of the sidewalks that run in front of the houses.

At the time of our research, in 1990, there were no surface remnants of the fortification visible on the Porter property. In fact, its approximate location, based on Judd's observations, was either in a level yard or a well maintained garden or agricultural field (figure 3.3). Neither the property owners nor any other residents had any recollection of physical remains of the fortification; clearly such evidence had long ago been erased. With little other evidence for the location of the fortification to go on, we determined that the best strategy for locating any subsurface remains was to try to bisect it with an excavated trench, at the location where it was last reported seen by Judd on the Samuel Porter lot.

Using Judd's measurements, we began excavations 20 rods from the center of the common onto the Porter Lot, a distance 10 rods (160 feet) from the east

FIGURE 3.3. *Excavation unit 2 at the Porter Lot (view from the west). Clear physical evidence for the fortification was found in this trench and at another unit just to the south.*

edge of the common. Here we then excavated a trench measuring 2 meters by 50 centimeters (approximately 6 feet 8 inches by 20 inches) perpendicular to the north–south course of the fortification (unit 1). As it turned out, we came directly down on buried remains of the fortification, though this was not immediately apparent (or believable—it was "too good to be true," we thought).

At the bottom of the plow zone, 26 centimeters (10 inches) below the ground surface, our excavation discovered undisturbed B-zone soil, cut through by a large feature, roughly 3 feet in width (east to west), running north–south through the middle of the excavation unit. It extended to a depth of 57 centimeters (23 inches) below the ground surface and clearly appeared to be the bottom of a more or less symmetrical pit or ditch. The dark color of this feature was due to the highly organic topsoil that filled it (distinct in color and texture from the adjacent undisturbed B-zone soil). There was also a fair amount of charcoal mixed into the organic fill. The top of the original feature was probably higher, but subsequent plowing or tilling of the soil would have destroyed this evidence, creating the homogeneous upper plow-zone layer. The only identifiable artifact was a nineteenth-century nail, indicating when the feature was filled in.

Based on our understanding that the fortification ran north–south parallel to the common, our next step was to look for this same feature further to the north or south. A new excavation trench (unit 2) was placed 10 meters (about 33 feet) north of unit 1. This time a much longer trench (6 meters, or almost 20 feet) was excavated to help confirm the unique character of the feature and identify any other features in its vicinity (figure 3.3). Here we found very clear physical evidence for the early fortification, including some specific evidence for its construction.

In this site the feature was buried more deeply, most likely by soil deposition or agricultural activity (figure 3.4). There was a modern plow/tilling zone of approximately the same depth as unit 1. But in unit 2 there was an older, deeper plow zone extending to a depth of 50 centimeters (20 inches) below the ground surface. This is very deep for a historic plow zone, and it indicates that soil has built up more rapidly, or perhaps even been added, in this area of the property. At the bottom of the old plow zone, 20 inches below the modern ground surface, the remains of an old ground surface, or A-zone, were discovered (labeled "Buried A-Zone" in figure 3.4), representing the actual location of the ground surface layer at some point in the past, which in this case we know to be 1675 or 1676. The upper part of this layer was churned into the overlying "old" plow zone at a later point in time, but the bottom portion of this early A-zone was still intact. A clearly visible trench had been dug *through* this old ground surface layer and down into the underlying subsoil (labeled "A/B-zone" and "B-zone" in figure 3.4). This trench had subsequently been filled in with organic soils from above the buried ground surface.

The shape of the cross-section of this feature was distinctive, with a deep ditch on the east side of the feature and an irregular shallow trench on the western edge of the ditch. The west side of the feature had the distinct appearance of having been truncated by later plowing or other soil-leveling activity. This suggests that it previously extended higher on its west side but that this part of the remains had been obliterated. Based on this evidence, we concluded that the ditch would originally have been approximately 80 to 100 centimeters (31.5–39 inches) wide and at least 40 centimeters (15.75 inches) deep. The small, irregular trench on the west side of the feature was generally about 10 to 15 centimeters (4 to 6 inches) wide. A few artifacts were found in the fill, including some shards of eighteenth- and nineteenth-century ceramics (thin white salt-glazed stoneware, Rhenish-type stoneware, green shell-edged ware, and lead-glazed redware), as well as one small piece of lead shot. These articles would have fallen into the trench as it was filled back up.

The rest of the excavation unit for approximately 2 meters (about 6 feet) both west and east showed no other features related to this ditch or any evidence of activity other than plowing, and this indicates that the feature was

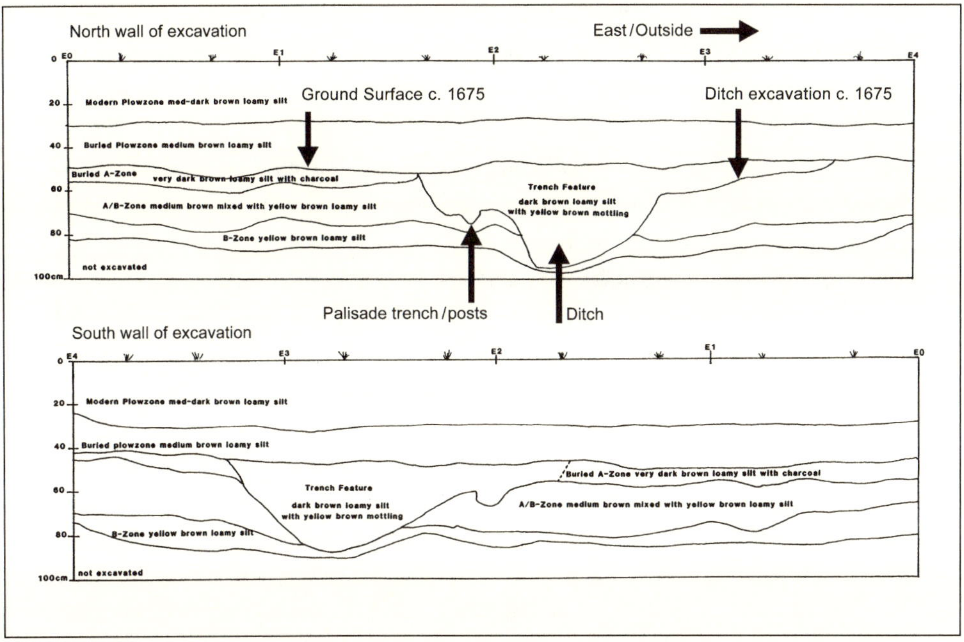

FIGURE 3.4. *Cross-section of the soil strata in excavation unit 2 at the Porter Lot, showing physical remains of the fortification. Top drawing shows the north side of excavation trench, with east or "outside" of the fortification to the right. Bottom drawing shows the south side of the excavation trench, with east side of the fortification to the left.*

isolated and distinct on the landscape when it was originally constructed. In order to see whether the ditch was continuous between units 1 and 2, we used a hand-held soil corer to take samples along the same north–south axis as the ditch feature between the two units. These samplings indicated that the ditch was in fact continuous, and that it extended further to the north of unit 2.

INTERPRETATION

The physical remains of the Hadley fortification we found on the Porter lot closely resemble the description made by Sylvester Judd of what was visible on the ground surface in the mid-nineteenth century on this property. We discovered a substantial ditch on the fortification's east side (what Judd described as the "east depression") with a shallow, narrow trench on its western edge. The western portion of the feature was clearly cut away by later plowing or other activity (figures 3.4 and 3.5). The small, westerly trench is almost certainly the base of the actual palisade wall, which would have contained posts set into either individual holes or a trench, or perhaps a combination of both. These posts were presumably on the front side of an embankment on the "inside" of the ditch, to raise the palisade to a more effective height and to place some additional soil behind the palisade posts for greater strength. As we noted earlier, the town records show that in 1679 residents voted to have all of the east side of the fortification moved a foot and a half to the east, and our hypothesis was that this indicated that the palisade was placed in the western edge of the ditch, on the eastern edge or face of the corresponding bank to the west (or "inside") of the ditch.

The "ridge" that Judd describes was undoubtedly the bank that supported and backed the palisade. The town records of February 19, 1677, describe the fortification as a "breastwork," a term that strongly suggests a ditch and bank structure of the type we found at the Porter lot. The bank part of the fortification has been plowed away, and the lower depression on the west side of the fortification that Judd noted has also been obliterated. But the defensive ditch and the very bottom of the palisade post trench are preserved. It is also arguable that the easterly trench provided adequate fill to create a high enough bank, though Judd's description suggests that the bank would have been made even higher by the addition of soil excavated from the west side of the main bank. This westerly depression, visible in the mid-nineteenth century, has been plowed away, along with the bank, and therefore must be presumed to have been substantially shallower than the main ditch.

After 1693, when there was no longer any perceived need for the fortification, property owners were undoubtedly quick to disassemble it. Pales from the palisade might have been reused for fencing or other purposes, or they might have been burned in household fires or simply allowed to rot. Much of the breastwork was probably plowed away in active farm areas. Over time its traces would have been softened by natural processes of erosion, with the ditch becoming shallower and the bank lower as time passed. As Judd noted, in the mid-nineteenth century the last remaining section of the fortification that had not been plowed down was still visible at the surface, more than 150 years after it had been abandoned. It is this section of the fortification that our archeological investigation discovered—a remarkable artifact that exists today solely as distinctive staining in the soil.

Figure 3.5 shows our interpretation of the sequence of construction, use, and abandonment of the fortification in this location. This portion of the abandoned trench was not used as a trash dump (only a tiny number of small artifacts were found in its fill), and it was not completely filled in until sometime after the mid-nineteenth century, when Judd observed it. A shard of green shell-edged refined earthenware was recovered from the upper section of the ditch, indicating that the fill was deposited sometime after 1800, when such

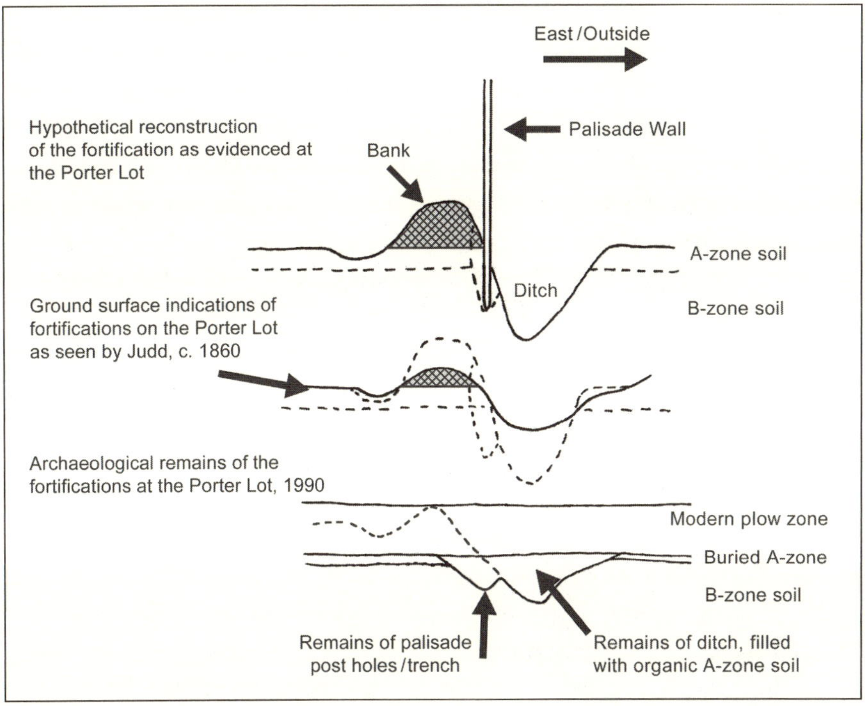

FIGURE 3.5. *Reconstruction of the Hadley fortification: This sequence of drawings shows how the soil layers of unit 2 at the Porter lot were transformed by the construction of the breastwork-palisade fortification, its abandonment, and the refilling and plowing down of the site.*

ceramics came into common use. This evidence supports the conclusion that the date of the filling-in of this feature corresponds to the time when Judd observed remains of the fortification.

Our archaeological excavations at other locations along the common did not locate remains of the east fortification. We presume that these remains were destroyed by subsequent land-use activities. Nor were we able to locate any physical remains of the west fortification.

Landscape and Land Use

What is most remarkable to us, as experienced archaeologists, is that Judd's unsupported statement that the fortification was forty rods wide, and our hypothesis that this measurement was centered on the town common, turned out in fact to be correct, with only a foot or two of error in either direction. That the landmarks we used in the late twentieth century to demarcate the edges of the common, the present sidewalks, matched the edges of the seventeenth-century common attests to the longevity of this feature on the landscape. Clearly the east fortification *was* twenty rods from the center of the common, a distance Judd could have measured from the physical remains he could see. Whether or not the west fortification was the same distance from the center of the common was not verified by our research, though some indirect evidence discussed below does suggest that the west side fortification was also twenty rods from the center of the common and that the fortification may in fact have been forty rods wide, symmetrical placed around the settlement, as Judd suggests.

Our fieldwork at other locations along the Hadley common identified an intriguing pattern that may represent a possible indirect trace of the fortification. Many of the houses along the common today have well defined yards planted with grass, shrubs, and trees. These then give way to plowed fields, often without a fence separating them. In some cases there is a noticeable bank of soil built up at this break between yard and field, the result of plowing: as the plow turns at the near edge of the field, it deposits a strip of soil that is not planted, and this soil continues to accumulate with each new plowing. The location of these plow banks—the break between yard and field—corresponds surprisingly closely to the forty-rod width that Sylvester Judd gives for the fortification. We examined one of these plow banks on the west side of the common, but did not find any physical remains of the fortification there.

As we have seen, landowners did not always cooperate with the town's efforts to keep the fortification in good repair, and they may even have weakened the defensive value of the fence with private gates. Nonetheless, the fence was there, periodically reinforced by town votes, for at least seventeen years, and it may well have imprinted long-term patterns of land use. Even today, when more than two hundred years of plowing and other land use have obliterated almost all direct physical remains of the fortification, a shadow of the long-vanished structure still seems to be visible in the break between yard and field behind the houses lining the Hadley common.

A New Image of the Hadley Fortification

By bringing together fragmentary documentary and physical evidence, we have been able to gain new insights into the specific nature of the Hadley town fortification as it existed from approximately 1675 to 1693. Its design was most likely derived from the ditch and bank agricultural fence, a type found in Hadley and nearby Deerfield. This consisted of a two- to three-foot ditch on the outside of the fence, with the fill from the ditch used to create a ridge or bank on the interior side. Rather than a post and rail fence on top of the bank, however, the Hadley fortification employed a palisade wall of vertical posts or pales set into the outward face of the bank, which increased the total height by several feet and made it more difficult for enemies to climb the structure or push it in.

This was not a substantial fortification in the traditional sense of the word. The structure itself may not have been symmetrical around the settlement, and some sections were probably better built than others. Its intent was to thwart or discourage a rush attack into the settlement, and the apparent differences between the east and west sides suggest that its primary function may have been to isolate the village from the mainland to the east, protecting the houses and fields within the Connecticut River oxbow. Town records indicate that the fortification was occasionally (or perhaps frequently) in a state of disrepair, and that getting the townspeople of Hadley to maintain it required some cajoling on the part of the town government. Indeed, one of the most interesting aspects of our research is the contrast it provides to nineteenth-century descriptions of life in an early New England community.

Notes

We thank the Hadley Historical Commission for their support of the research and archaeological fieldwork discussed in this chapter, as well as the landowners who gave us permission to work on their property. Elise Feeley, reference librarian at Forbes Library, Northampton, was most generous with her time and knowledge of the collections there. More recently, reference librarian Katie Krol rescued us from twenty-year-old memory lapses. Eric Johnson provided valuable consultation on the illustrations. At the University of Massachusetts Amherst, we thank UMass Archaeological Services and the Department of Anthropology, particularly Dr. Robert Paynter and Dr. Mitchell Mulholland, for their assistance and support. The authors also thank Claire Carlson and Marla Miller for their support in bringing this essay to publication.

1. Our full study, "Report on the Hadley Palisade Project," is on file with the Hadley Historical Commission. The research and fieldwork were commissioned in 1990 by the Historical Commission, which wanted to determine the location and integrity of any existing remains of the town's seventeenth-century fortification, as well as whether these remains might be affected by future development.
2. William Hubbard, *Narrative of the Troubles with the Indians in New England* (Boston: John Foster, 1677), 46.
3. Generally, however, Native Americans in southern New England do not appear to have used fortifications prior to contact with Europeans, although by the seventeenth century they were employed in times of need, including defense against English colonists. See Eric S. Johnson, " 'Released from Thraldom by the Stroke of War': Coercion and Warfare in Native Politics of Seventeenth-Century Southern New England," *Northeast Anthropology* 55 (Spring 1998): 1–13.
4. Harry Andrew Wright, "Discovery of Aboriginal Remains near Springfield, Massachusetts," *Scientific American* 76, no. 1 (1897): 170.

5. James A. Deetz, "Plymouth Colony Architecture: Archaeological Evidence from the Seventeenth Century," in *Architecture in Colonial Massachusetts*, ed. Abbott Lowell Cummings (Boston: Colonial Society of Massachusetts, 1979), 50–51.
6. Robert B. St. George, " 'Set thine house in order': The Domestication of the Yeomanry in Seventeenth-Century New England," in *New England Begins: The Seventeenth Century*, vol. 2, *Mentality and Environment*, ed. Jonathan Fairbanks and Robert Trent (Boston: Museum of Fine Arts, 1982), 159–88.
7. John Sheldon, "The Common Field of Deerfield," in *History and Proceedings of the Pocumtuck Valley Memorial Association*, vol. 5 (Greenfield, Mass.: T. Morey & Son, 1912), 238–54.
8. J. Ritchie Garrison, *Landscape and Material Life in Franklin County, Massachusetts, 1770–1860* (Knoxville: University of Tennessee Press, 1991), 118–19.
9. F. D. Huntington, "Prof. Huntington's Address," in *Celebration of the Two Hundredth Anniversary of the Settlement of Hadley, Massachusetts* (Northampton, Mass.: Bridgman and Childs, 1859), 22.
10. Garrison, *Landscape and Material Life*; Sheldon, "The Common Field of Deerfield," 245–50.
11. Sylvester Judd, *History of Hadley, including the Early History of Hatfield, South Hadley, Amherst and Granby, Massachusetts*, 2nd ed. (Springfield, Mass: H. R. Huntting, 1905; repr., Somersworth: New Hampshire Publishing Company, 1976), 151–52.
12. Sylvester Judd, undated Judd manuscripts, vol. 3:43, microfilm, Forbes Library, Northampton, Mass.
13. L. Everts, *History of the Connecticut Valley in Massachusetts*, vol. 1 (Philadelphia: Everts Publishing, 1879), 340.
14. Hadley town records, 1660–1693, microfilm, Forbes Library, Northampton, Mass. We have regularized the spelling in passages from the town records.
15. Judd, *History of Hadley*, 152.
16. Sidney Perley, *History of Salem Massachusetts*, vol. 3, *1671–1716* (Salem, Mass.: S. Perley, 1909), 92–93.
17. Hubbard, *History of the Indian Wars*, 46.
18. In addition to remains of the Hadley fortification, these excavation units revealed a variety of other historic remains, including evidence for three barns now long gone from the landscape, two dating to the nineteenth century and one potentially earlier, as well as distinct evidence of the flood of 1936 that caused extensive damage to the region. All of these findings are discussed in our 1990 report to the Hadley Historical Commission (see note 1).
19. Kevin M. Sweeney, Department of History and American Studies, Amherst College, personal communication.

4

No story is better known in the annals of Hadley history than that of the regicides Edward Whalley and William Goffe, two men who, having participated in the overthrow of Charles I, found refuge in the colonies on the western fringe of England's empire. The two men had sat in judgment over the executed king, and when his son was restored to power, fled for their lives. They eventually found safe harbor in Hadley, a fact that continues to loom large in the town today. As if the documented account of these events wasn't dramatic enough, the town has also long nurtured the legend of the Angel of Hadley, which tells the story of an attack on the town during King Philip's War that was miraculously thwarted when a mysterious bearded gentleman in ancient clothes—the aged Goffe—appeared to warn the startled villagers of the imminent threat; the apparition then disappeared just as quickly, leaving the wondering colonists safe, grateful, and perplexed. Much ink has been spilled as historians have debated the legend's veracity. As Mark Sargent points out in his 1992 essay "Thomas Hutchinson, Ezra Stiles, and the Legend of the Regicides," the destruction of Goffe's papers, including the journal on which Thomas Hutchinson had based his account of the regicides (see Martin Antonetti's essay in this volume), left the field wide open for myth to thrive.

The idea that Hadley sheltered men who rebelled against their king held obvious appeal for the Americans of the early Republic, and during the romantic era of the early nineteenth century authors embraced the regicides' story with zeal. It is not surprising that, as Hadley approached its two hundredth anniversary, the regicides played a significant role in the celebrations. The engraving that today is arguably the most famous in Hadley history was produced in connection with that earlier moment in Hadley pastkeeping; as the town approached its 1859 bicentennial, the Scottish-born engraver and publisher John McRae created a steel-plate engraving (figure 4.1) modeled on an oil painting of the event by Connecticut artist and stained-glass designer Frederic A. Chapman (in an 1882 version by Selmar Hess, the flowing white beard that is the centerpiece of the original is mysteriously excised). Reproductions of that image kept the story alive for generations.

In his introduction to the 1905 edition of Judd's history of Hadley, Deerfield historian George Sheldon refuted the story of the Angel of Hadley. Subsequent writers assumed that the story was basically mythical, and more appropriate for juvenile literature. In 1966, Bianca Bradbury's Sam and the Colonels *appeared; not be outdone, Myra Clarke Crandell's children's book* Molly and the Regicides *followed two years later. Other iterations have been plentiful, too. In his consideration of these events, Douglas Wilson counters Sheldon's skepticism with a new and careful review of the evidence. In this thoughtful essay, which won the 1986 Walter Muir Whitehill Prize in Colonial History from the Colonial Society of Massachusetts, he reminds us not to mistake silence for absence, and to consider more carefully the significant pressures under which the regicides and their supporters acted.*

Web of Secrecy

Goffe, Whalley, and the Legend of Hadley

Douglas C. Wilson

During most of the nineteenth century, one of the most popular tales of early New England was the legendary story of the Angel of Hadley, who dramatically appeared in the Massachusetts frontier village in the 1670s, during King Philip's War. No report of the episode was published until nearly ninety years later, when it was related by Thomas Hutchinson, then lieutenant governor of the Bay Colony, in a footnote to *The History of the Colony and Province of Massachusetts-Bay* (1764). He wrote: "I am loath to omit an anecdote handed down through Governor Leverett's family.... Hadley was alarmed by the Indians in 1675, in the time of public worship, and the people were in the utmost confusion. Suddenly, a grave elderly person appeared in the midst of them. In his mien and dress he differed from the rest of the people. He not only encouraged them to defend themselves; but put himself at their head, rallied, instructed and led them on to encounter the enemy, who by this means were repulsed. As suddenly the deliverer of Hadley disappeared. The people were left in consternation, utterly unable to account for this strange phenomenon."[1] Hutchinson identified the stranger as Colonel William Goffe, one of the Parliamentary officers known as regicides who had condemned England's King Charles to the scaffold in 1649. Goffe and another regicide, his father-in-law, Colonel Edward Whalley, had fled from the vengeance of Charles II and the Restoration in 1660 and sailed to New England, where they eventually found a hiding place in Hadley on the Connecticut River.

It was Ezra Stiles, president of Yale College, who later introduced the angel motif. In his moralizing narrative, *A History of Three of the Judges of Charles I*, printed in 1794, Stiles wrote that the townspeople "could not account for the phenomenon, but by considering that person as an angel sent of God upon that special occasion for their deliverance."[2] The story was popular for the next seventy years, especially in the upsurge of nationalism that followed the War of 1812, when American intellectuals self-consciously looked for native writers and subjects. Many authors turned to scenes of early New England, and one of their favorite topics was the regicide. Ironically, however, it was not an American but a Briton who made the most notable early use of Hadley's angel in fiction. Walter Scott told the anecdote in *Peveril of the Peak*, published in 1823, and it was *Peveril* that spurred American interest in the regicides.[3]

Between 1820 and 1850 a regicide judge appeared in eight—a full third—of the two dozen romances that were written in America about the American Puritans.[4] The most important writers to develop the subject were James Fenimore Cooper in 1829 and Nathaniel Hawthorne in 1835. In Cooper's novel *The Wept of Wish-Ton-Wish*, a regicide appears as a stranger again and again to help a settlement in western New England fight off the Indians during King Philip's War. In Hawthorne's famous story "The Gray Champion," the ghostly figure of a regicide appears in Puritan Boston to turn back English troops led by Governor Edmund Andros.

The regicide possessed three qualities that appealed to romantic taste: antiquity, national spirit, and individualism; and Stiles's embellishment of the story added another romantic element, the supernatural. Writers saw in the regicides what Michael Davitt Bell calls their "symbolic possibilities . . . as . . . types of the American revolutionary spirit."[5] In Hawthorne's story, for instance, it is said that the Gray Champion continues to reappear at times of national danger (at Lexington, for example, and Bunker Hill). "His hour is one of darkness, and adversity, and peril. But should domestic tyranny oppress us, or the invader's step pollute our soil," wrote Hawthorne, "still may the Gray Champion come; for he is the type of New England's hereditary spirit; and his shadowy march, on the eve of danger, must ever be the pledge, that New England's sons will vindicate their ancestry."[6]

By the 1850s the regicides' story was so well known that in *Walden* Henry David Thoreau could use their names as household words. A visitor to his cabin, "an old settler and original proprietor," kept himself "more secret," wrote Thoreau, than "did Goffe or Whalley." English and American tourists stopped at Hadley in the 1850s to see where the regicides had lived, and they took away slivers from a house beam as souvenirs. The artist Frederic Chapman painted a dramatic picture of Goffe rallying the people to fight off the Indians. His work, *Perils of Our Forefathers*, was reproduced in 1859 by a New York engraver (whose advertisement claimed absurdly that the episode helped establish the nation's "civil and religious freedom") (figure 4.1). The regicides' story also became a standard feature in popular New England chronicles written by historians like John Gorham Palfrey and, later, John Fiske.[7]

FIGURE 4.1. *William Goffe as the Angel of Hadley. Engraving by John McRae, 1859, from Frederic Chapman's painting* Perils of Our Forefathers. *Collection of the author.*

After the 1870s, however, writers began to abandon the legend. Eventually Goffe the rescuer faded from public awareness much as Hawthorne's Champion disappeared from Boston's King Street—"melting slowly into the hues of twilight, till, where he stood, there was an empty space."[8] The new glare of realism in literature had something to do with the decline of the story; and an aggressive local historian, George Sheldon of Deerfield, Massachusetts, sped the process along, claiming to disprove the whole episode.[9]

But Sheldon looked too hastily at a legend that is veiled in secrecy and woven in a network of ties that reached back into England. The story of Goffe and Whalley merits closer scrutiny, for it shows how intricate those ties were, how resilient they were under pressure, and how they served perhaps, at one time, to keep history silent.

I

When they arrived at Boston in July 1660, Whalley and Goffe were the most prominent public figures of the mother country ever to land in New England.

The turmoil of the Puritan revolution had raised both men from modest beginnings to military renown, and then to high station in the government of Oliver Cromwell. Whalley was a first cousin of the Lord Protector. His mother, Frances, was Cromwell's aunt, and his father, Richard, was a sheriff of Nottingham and member of a locally prominent family. When the religious and political struggle between Charles I and Parliament erupted into civil war in 1642, Whalley, like other Puritans, sided with Parliament. In the following year he was a captain in the regiment formed by Cromwell at Cambridge—the famous Ironsides. Eventually he would become one of the five officers celebrated by John Milton in his "Second Defence of the People of England."[10]

In Cromwell's shattering victory over the king's army of Cavaliers at Naseby in 1645, Whalley, now a colonel, led the Roundhead cavalry divisions of Parliament that swept across the wide clangorous field of battle and routed the royalist force under Marmaduke Langdale.[11] Naseby was the dramatic turning point of the war. Charles afterward found himself hemmed in at his capital in Oxford, and Whalley, laying siege to the royalist stronghold of Banbury to the north, helped tighten the circle. After Banbury surrendered in May 1646, Whalley went on to force the surrender of the royalist garrison at Worcester.

Meanwhile the king had fled Oxford in disguise and thrown himself upon Parliament's unsteady ally, the Scots in the north. His cause lost in the field, he hoped the Scots would secure better terms for him than he could win at the hands of the English. In a twisting course of events, however, the Scots turned the beleaguered king over to Parliament, and a restless force then seized Charles in the name of the army. The army's commander-in-chief, Thomas Fairfax, ordered Whalley's troop to take charge of Charles, but he escaped in November 1647 after five months in captivity. Whalley told his superiors he could do nothing to prevent the king's flight: his orders, he recalled, were to let the king move freely about his lavish prison, the thousand rooms of his Hampton Court Palace; consequently, the soldiers "could no more keep the king (if he had a mind to go) than a bird in a pound."[12]

Charles fled to the Isle of Wight, only to become prisoner, there, of the island's Parliamentary governor, Colonel Robert Hammond. At the island's Carisbrooke Castle the king courted his enemy, Parliament, while plotting new onslaughts against it. These royalist conspiracies led early in 1648 to the outbreak of the Second Civil War—new hostilities that stirred the Roundheads to the end of their patience.

One of the younger officers under Fairfax and Cromwell at this time was William Goffe, the devout and prayerful son of a strict Puritan minister from Sussex.

Goffe had fought in the first war as an infantry officer in Colonel Thomas Pride's regiment. He now held the rank of major. With Whalley—then or soon to be his father-in-law—he belonged to the army's large council of officers who thought that with God on their side they had finally triumphed over the king and his Romish clergy. In true Puritan fashion, seeing the resurgence of their enemies as a sign of God's anger, the heads of the army gathered in a prayer meeting at Windsor Castle that April to discover the cause of His wrath. Like other enthusiasts in the New Model Army, Goffe was a fervent lay preacher. He now helped determine the army's fateful resolve. One officer at the prayer meeting, William Allen, years later recalled what transpired. On the third and final day of their soul-searching, the army leaders decided that God was angry because their "cursed carnal conferences, our own wisdom, fears, and want of faith, had prompted us the year before to entertain with the King and his party." Whereupon, Allen related, Goffe spoke movingly about the Lord's admonition that begins, in Proverbs 1:23: *Turn you at my reproof. . . . I have called, and ye refused; I have stretched out my hand, and no man regarded; But ye have set at nought all my counsel, and would none of my reproof.* "In this path," remembered Allen, "the Lord led us not only to see our sin, but also our duty"—led the council "to come to a very clear and joint resolution . . . to call Charles Stuart, that man of blood, to an account for the blood he had shed, and the mischief he had done to his utmost, against the Lord's cause and people."[13]

As if in answer to the anguish and prayers there came, swiftly, a second resounding defeat of the Cavaliers capped by Cromwell's victory that summer at Preston. In December the army again took the king into its own hands. Six days later it purged Parliament of members sympathetic to Charles, and—obligingly—the remaining members, or "Rump" Parliament, then brought Charles to the bar.

Goffe—the future "Angel of Hadley"—was as responsible, then, as anyone for the execution of Charles I. He and Whalley were among the Cromwellian colonels who formed the core of the High Court of Justice that in January 1649 arraigned the king for the "high and treasonable" offense of "levying and maintaining a cruel war against the Parliament and kingdom." The king of course was found guilty, and Whalley and Goffe were among the fifty-nine judges who signed his death warrant. The execution that followed was unprecedented, the most shocking political event of its time. The king himself faced it calmly: baring his neck to the headsman, he said "I go from a corruptible to an incorruptible crown, where no disturbance can be, no disturbance in the world."[14]

Whalley and Goffe figured prominently in subsequent military and government affairs. When Cromwell campaigned in Scotland to halt the advances of Charles II, bent on recovering his father's realm, Whalley helped lead the cavalry assault in the decisive battle of Dunbar. Cromwell reported after the victory that Whalley was "cut in the handwrist, and his horse (twice shot) killed under him; but he well recovered another horse, and went on in the chase." In the reserve Goffe commanded Cromwell's own foot regiment and led it to regain the advantage when the first English infantry faltered. Goffe and his men came "seasonably in," related Cromwell, "and, at the push of the pike did repel the stoutest regiment the enemy had."[15] But not until the following year, 1651, was young Charles finally repulsed.

In the Interregnum that followed—the nine years of Commonwealth and Protectorate—Whalley and Goffe were appointed district governors, elected to Parliament, and later named by Cromwell to the House of Lords he established in 1657.[16] When the Protector's health declined the following year, both belonged to an inner circle of nine councilors who directed the nation's affairs. The seventeenth-century historian Anthony Wood wrote that during the Protectorate Goffe "was in so great esteem and favor in Oliver's court, that he was judged the only fit man to have Maj. Gen. John Lambert's place and command, as major general of the army of foot, and by some to have the protectorship settled on him in future."[17]

After Cromwell's death in 1658, however, the country was ripe for the restoration of monarchy. A new Parliament and a military takeover by General George Monck, one of Cromwell's old officers who was receptive to Charles II, led finally to the new king's return in May 1660.

Goffe and Whalley had seen the change coming. From the Netherlands in April the king had issued his Declaration of Breda offering pardon to all his subjects "excepting only such as shall hereafter be excepted by Parliament." Knowing that as regicides their lives were in peril, the two men said farewell to their families and took passage aboard a vessel bound for New England.

On May 14, the Commons ordered the arrests of Whalley, Goffe, and many others. In the case of the old Naseby hero and his son-in-law, the order came too late to apprehend them. Their ship had lifted its anchor the day before.

II

In the 1640s and 1650s a strong relationship of common interests developed between many Old and New Englanders, reinforced by religious and family ties that crossed the Atlantic. Thus, the asylum that Whalley and Goffe found in New England was welcoming and familiar. Both men were solidly in the party of orthodox, moderate Puritans in England, the party with whom New England's establishment shared the greatest affinity. The moderate group in

England was led by men like John Owen, who advocated New England's form of congregationalism, and Thomas Goodwin. Ministers like Owen and Goodwin, along with lay Puritans like Goffe and Whalley, opposed sectarians who thought the civil magistrate should have no control over matters of religion, just as John Cotton and other authorities in Massachusetts had opposed Roger Williams.[18]

Puritan leaders in the New World had applauded the Puritan triumph at home. In 1651 the churches of New England had celebrated news of Cromwell's victory at Dunbar with a day of thanksgiving; and Cotton, the leading clergyman of Massachusetts, also used the occasion in his First Church at Boston to endorse the overthrow of Charles I. "There is," declared Cotton, "a lawful and loyal conspiracy as well as a disloyal and wicked conspiracy"; and he said loyal subjects might conspire "against those that have been set over them by the Lord, when once they depart from God and do such acts, as have been dangerous and destructive to the commonwealth."[19]

If New England was a good refuge for Whalley and Goffe ideologically, other ties made it so personally. Puritans in New England and England were knit closely together by many threads of kinship and acquaintance. This was certainly true of the regicides. First among the two men's connections were Jane and William Hooke, Whalley's sister and his brother-in-law. The husband, a minister, was a founder of Taunton, Massachusetts, who had moved in 1644 to New Haven, where for twelve years he was a teacher in the church of the Reverend John Davenport. Encouraged by the Puritan ascendancy in England—perhaps also by his brother-in-law Whalley's influence at Whitehall—Hooke and his family had returned to the home country in the 1650s. Hooke soon won appointment as one of six chaplains in the court of the Lord Protector.[20]

Then there was Daniel Gookin of Cambridge, Massachusetts—later prominent as a friend of the Indians and author of *An Historical Account of the Doings and Sufferings of the Christian Indians in New England*. As a member of the General Court at Boston he was one of the handful of men who governed the Bay Colony. Gookin had crossed and recrossed the Atlantic on various missions and was returning to Massachusetts in 1660 when he found the fugitives, Goffe and Whalley, aboard the same vessel. Whether or not he had known the two earlier, the long crossing cemented their friendship. The regicides stayed with Gookin at his house in Cambridge for their first seven months in America, and Gookin later was charged with secretly managing their estates.[21]

Also a valuable friend of the two regicides was Richard Saltonstall Jr., an early colonist who spent many years both at Ipswich, Massachusetts, and back in England. Saltonstall had represented the English government in Edinburgh when Whalley and Goffe were there in 1651, and he surely knew both at the time. As a commissioner for confiscated estates in Scotland he surveyed lands that were awarded to Whalley the following year. Working with Hooke, Saltonstall raised charitable funds for Massachusetts in 1660, and years later—when Goffe and Whalley had long been in exile—he sent the regicides a personal present of fifty pounds.[22]

The fugitives almost certainly had known another Massachusetts man as a comrade in arms: John Leverett, a Roundhead officer who returned to New England in 1662 and served his colony as major general and then as governor during King Philip's War. Leverett had fought on Parliament's side throughout the Civil War as a captain in Colonel Thomas Rainsborough's regiment of foot. The regiment fought at Naseby and took part under Whalley's command in the Banbury siege. Later Leverett was an agent for Massachusetts during the Protectorate. He would visit Hadley at least once, in the 1660s, while the regicides were there.[23]

Connecticut's governor, John Winthrop Jr., was an old friend of the Hookes, and Whalley and Goffe may have paid their respects to him when they traveled through Hartford in 1661 on their way to New Haven. Winthrop went to England soon thereafter, to secure the Connecticut charter. Before his return voyage, he arranged to have Whalley's twenty-year-old nephew, Ebenezer Hooke, who was eager to return to New England, serve him for four years; Winthrop in exchange would see that the young man got started in a livelihood.[24]

The regicides' ties ran south from Massachusetts and Connecticut into the New Haven Colony, where the two colonels knew William Jones, an assistant and later deputy governor of the colony. Like Gookin, Jones was a passenger on the ship that brought Goffe and Whalley to Boston. His father was the regicide Colonel John Jones, who was married to Whalley's cousin Catherine Cromwell, Oliver's sister. Colonel Jones had gone into hiding on the eve of the Restoration but was "discovered one evening about twilight in Tinsbury Fields, apprehended, and carried prisoner to the Tower." With nine others who approved the death of Charles I, he was tried and executed. Colonel Jones faced the end courageously in October 1660, saying the sledge that took him to the scaffold was "like Elijah's fiery chariot, only it goes through Fleet Street."[25] Goffe and Whalley were in the vicinity of New Haven when news of the execution—a sharp reminder of their own mortal danger—reached the colonel's son William, their neighbor and friend.

One person who welcomed Whalley and Goffe to New Haven was the colony's leading minister, John Davenport, Hooke's former colleague. After a brief sojourn in Holland, Davenport had fled to New England in 1637 and with other Puritans established New Haven the following year. Many years later, in tribute to Davenport's piety and learning, Cotton Mather wrote that Davenport was such a "close and bent" student that the Indians called him "So Big Study-Man." When the regicides were expected at New Haven, Davenport preached on the text of Hebrews 13:2: *Be not forgetful to entertain strangers: for thereby some have entertained angels unawares*, and on Isaiah 16:3–4: *Hide the outcasts; betray not him that wandereth. Let mine outcasts dwell with thee, Moab; be thou a covert to them from the face of the spoiler.*[26] Davenport's veiled reference to the two colonels was unmistakable.

Another clergyman who assisted the fugitives was Increase Mather of Boston, father of Cotton Mather. Increase Mather became minister of Boston's Second Church in 1664, when he was twenty-five. Seven years earlier he had gone to England, where he was a protégé of the Reverend John Howe, a Puritan serving with Hooke as a chaplain at Whitehall. At the Restoration, Mather was a minister with the English garrison at Guernsey; years later he boasted that "when the King was proclaimed in Guernsey, I did out of conscience openly refuse to drink his health . . . professing that I would pray for the King's health but drink for my own."

Mather soon realized that England under Charles II held no promise for a headstrong young Puritan minister, and he returned to Boston in September 1661. Soon he was forwarding concealed letters back and forth between the regicides and their families in England—a clandestine service he provided for many years.[27] The list of New England leaders who were closely involved with the regicides includes, then, such important names as Gookin, Saltonstall, Leverett, Winthrop, Jones, Davenport, and Mather. Most of these names will reappear later, in the riddle of the legend of Hadley.[28]

III

To that wide network of the regicides' connections, indeed to most of New England's leaders, Goffe's and Whalley's presence among them posed an awkward and difficult challenge in the context of a larger dilemma. There did not seem to be any problem when the pair first arrived at Boston in late July 1660. They were given a warm reception. Massachusetts's governor, John Endecott, "embraced them, bade them welcome, and wished more such men as they would come over." In a rare gesture, the General Court granted them "liberty of the House," so they quickly made the acquaintance of the colony's leaders. They lived openly for several months with Gookin and his family in Cambridge and were regally entertained. A young Bostonian and former Harvard student, John Crowne, reported that they received "universal applause and admiration." He added, almost prophetically, that they "were looked upon as men dropped down from heaven."[29]

With the regicides' arrival came news of the Restoration, but it was not an immediate cause for alarm. Not only had Massachusetts since its founding been the refuge of exiles, but its leaders regarded their domain as a commonwealth that was virtually independent of England. The charter granted by Charles I in 1629 had established "one body corporate and politic" with power to make any laws "not contrary" to those of England.[30]

At the outbreak of the Civil War the Bay government had dropped the ceremonial oath of allegiance to the king. And when a few colonists in 1646 said they would appeal grievances to Parliament, the General Court replied stoutly that Massachusetts people were not bound to the laws of England "any longer than while we live in England, for the laws of the Parliament of England reach no further, nor do the King's writs under the great seal."[31] This remarkable declaration of independence went unchallenged for many years. (The more famous Declaration would not be proclaimed until 130 years later.)

Goffe and Whalley had not been in New England long, however, when their hosts began to learn that the new regime under Charles II was taking a stricter attitude toward the colonies. King and Parliament expected all to comply with London's wishes, and one of their first commands was to arrest regicides who had gone into hiding. On June 6, 1660, the king, reinforcing Parliament's arrest order published three weeks before, issued a proclamation listing the names of Goffe, Whalley, and others who had "out of the sense of their own guilt lately fled and obscured themselves," and he ordered them to surrender "under pain of being excepted from any pardon or indemnity both for their respective lives and estates." The decree also stated that none should "presume to harbor or conceal any [of] the persons aforesaid, under pain of misprision [that is, failure to make a report] of high treason.[32] The penalty for misprision was the same as that for treason itself: the guilty could be hanged, cut down while still alive and disemboweled, then beheaded and quartered.

The two men were excepted from Parliament's Act of Indemnity that August. The king issued a warrant for their arrest and put a £100 price on their heads.[33] The warrant, eventually reaching Boston, brought an early test of the king's new authority. The choice of whether or not to respect the king's orders caused political strain; in New England, of course, the strain was also religious—a test of conscience. For if Whalley and Goffe were political exiles, they also were the Puritans' co-religionists in flight from the Stuart monarchy.

As pressure to surrender the regicides and, more broadly, to accept London's authority intensified during the next six years, New Englanders were bedeviled by a group of choices that overlapped and were roughly parallel: resistance or obedience, commonwealth or colony, God or Caesar.[34] To this manifold dilemma they responded with a natural instinct for self-preservation—responded also with remarkable combinations of hypocrisy, anxiety, and courage. Their agility under the circumstances would astound William Hooke. Whalley's brother-in-law wrote to Davenport in 1661: "I am almost amazed sometimes to see what cross capers some of you do make. I should break my shins should I do the like."[35]

When Captain Thomas Breedon, a royalist in Boston, told Endecott that the two celebrities were traitors and ought to be arrested, the governor responded that as long as there was no commission from England, none should disturb them. The marshal general of the colony, Edward Michelson, taunted Breedon by grinning in his face and chanting, "Speak against Whalley and Goffe if you dare, if you dare, if you dare!"[36] Eventually reports from New England would reach London, however, and some would be hard to explain. Massachusetts leaders saw that sooner or later they needed to address the new king on their own behalf, and in February Charles received a humble petition from Endecott in the name of the General Court. The petitioners asked the king not to believe any objections he heard against them until they had an opportunity to speak in their own defense. This precautionary step was wise: Crown authorities were already hearing complaints about the intolerance of the Massachusetts leaders, and now Breedon, much aggrieved, was en route to England.

Goffe and Whalley were not mentioned in Endecott's letter, but on February 22 he summoned the General Court to discuss the problem of the regicides. No action was taken, but the message was clear: it would be unwise for them to stay in Massachusetts. No doubt Gookin, a magistrate, participated in this discussion and told his house guests about it. Four days later Goffe and Whalley set out with horses and a guide for New Haven. After a stop at Hartford they arrived at the minister Davenport's house on March 7. By then, Endecott must have known they were beyond his jurisdiction. It was time now to spruce up the record, and on March 8 he and his council prepared an order for the regicides' arrest. The warrant was given to the marshal general—none other than Breedon's old tormentor, Edward Michelson.[37]

The king by this time had learned the whereabouts of his quarry. To Endecott he wrote on March 5: "Trusty and well-beloved,—Wee greete you well. We being given to understand that Colonell Whalley and Colonell Goffe, who stand here convicted for the execrable murther of our Royall Father, of glorious memory, are lately arrived at New England, where they hope to shroud themselves from the justice of our lawes;—Our will and pleasure is, and we do hereby expressly require and command you . . . to cause both the said persons to be apprehended, and with the first opportunity sent over hither under a strict care, to receive according to their demerits. We are confident of your readiness and diligence to perform your duty; and so bid you farewell."

When this letter reached Endecott at the end of April 1661, the governor feared he had shown too little diligence. He now took action on the king's side by sending two eager royalists, Thomas Kellond and Thomas Kirke, to hunt down the fugitives. Endecott asked them to deliver the king's disturbing letter to Governor John Winthrop Jr. at Hartford, to New Haven's Deputy Governor William Leete at Guilford, and to the Dutch governor at New Amsterdam, Peter Stuyvesant.[38]

Someone warned Whalley and Goffe in advance. They had been Davenport's guests in New Haven for seven weeks; now they moved secretly to William Jones's house nearby. When Kellond and Kirke arrived in the area on May 11 they moved again—this time to the forest outside New Haven, where they spent most of the next four weeks hiding at a cavelike pile of boulders on the top of West Rock.[39] Kellond and Kirke pressed Leete to take action immediately. The deputy governor stalled for time, consulted several deputies of the colony for hours, and was finally going to issue a warrant when two magistrates, Robert Treat and Matthew Gilbert, won a further delay. The colony's leaders then said they could not proceed "until they had called a general court of the freemen." The two royalists were exasperated and warned Leete "how ill his sacred majesty would resent such horrid and detestable concealments and abettings of such traitors." Impatiently they rode on to New Amsterdam.[40]

New Haven's General Court finally met three days later and, perhaps knowing that Goffe and Whalley were now in the forest, it cleverly issued a warrant authorizing searches only in "buildings" and "vessels in the harbor." The members of the Court also lied shamelessly in their record book, saying they did not know the two fugitives were even *in* the colony. "And whereas there have been rumors of their late being known at New Haven," they reported, "it hath been inquired into, and several persons examined, but could find no truth in those reports."[41] One man, though, still felt unprotected. Kellond and Kirke understood that Davenport had been the regicides' host in New Haven, and they certainly would report the fact to London. Before the end of June, Goffe and Whalley made a public reappearance in New Haven on the pretext of surrendering. Apparently they hoped this would lift the onus from Davenport. Then they again disappeared.

The ruse gave Davenport a weak opportunity to defend himself, which he did in a written "apology" to Massachusetts and English authorities. "You will find mine innocency in reference to the two colonels to be such as might secure me from all fear of danger," he asserted. Davenport also wrote that New Haven officials "wanted neither will nor industry to have served his majesty in apprehending the two colonels, but were prevented and hindered by God's overruling providence."[42]

After their brief reappearance in New Haven, Goffe and Whalley returned to their hideout at West Rock for a short time and then moved to the home of a Micah Tompkins near Milford, where they lived in obscurity for the next few years. Massachusetts consoled Kellond and Kirke with gifts of 250 acres of farmland each, and Endecott sent London an account of their mission "so his majesty might understand," he said, "the sincerity of my efforts to serve him."[43]

As the year of the Restoration drew to a close, Goffe and Whalley had put Massachusetts in an awkward position, but the Bay government took no action until they had left. The leaders of New Haven, too, let the regicides escape, then lied about where they had been. And Davenport almost lied. Hooke was right: they cut some amazing capers!

The dilemma posed by the regicides diminished somewhat after August 1661. Goffe and Whalley went underground, living almost entirely in seclusion from that time onward. But the political problem they had created for New England was the first sign of a larger quandary now facing Massachusetts: the hard question of how to keep peace with London while denying London's authority. In 1661 the General Court reiterated its belief that Bay officials had "full power and authority, both legislative and executive . . . [in] ecclesiastics and in civils, without appeal, excepting law or laws repugnant to the laws of England." On the other hand it agreed that Massachusetts owed Charles II at least token allegiance, and the king was finally "proclaimed" that August. In an acknowledgment sent the following year, Charles showed he, too, was skilled in the mixing of signals. He said he was "well satisfied"; he confirmed the colony's charter and guaranteed "all the privileges and liberties" it granted. At the same time he insisted that the oath of allegiance be reinstated, that freedom of conscience be permitted to all except Quakers, and that Massachusetts allow individuals to use the Book of Common Prayer.[44]

To the Puritan authorities of Massachusetts this was good news and bad. At last the charter appeared to be safe, but the religious purity of the colony now seemed to be threatened. Not able to grant all that the king demanded, they explained later that to allow use of the Book of Common Prayer, for instance, would be to tolerate the same religious practices that had caused them to leave England in the first place. Charles disliked their response and early in 1663 declared he would send commissioners to investigate affairs in New England. He asked the commissioners to learn, among other things, whether any traitors were in the colonies and "by whom they were received and entertained," so that such sympathizers could "be taken more notice of, and may . . . take the more care for their future behavior."

The commissioners received another, more disturbing instruction: to hear complaints against the colonial governments. As the scholar Paul R. Lucas has noted, Massachusetts's leaders were now placed in an awkward position, for if "they refused to allow the commission to hear complaints they would be denying, in effect, the authority of the king in Massachusetts. On the other hand, if they allowed the commission to proceed . . . they would be admitting that the government of Massachusetts was not sovereign on its own soil."[45]

Soon after the commissioners arrived in July 1664, the Massachusetts General Court told them that the colony's guarantees under the charter seemed inconsistent with one of the king's orders—"with your hearing and determining complaints and appeals against us."[46] The investigators carried out their work in Connecticut, New Haven, and Rhode Island before they took on the Bay's obstinate leaders.

Their visit south of Massachusetts alarmed Goffe and Whalley, so in October 1664 the fugitives stole up the Connecticut River Valley to distant Hadley. It may have been Davenport who arranged for their removal from Milford. Church splinter groups led by the Reverend John Russell of Wethersfield, Connecticut, had moved north in 1659 and 1660 to establish Hadley on the Massachusetts frontier. Davenport had sided with Russell's party during controversies that led to the separation; no doubt he felt that Russell was conscientious and trustworthy, and that his remote new village in the wilderness would be for Goffe and Whalley the refuge they needed.

Russell sheltered them safely in Hadley for more than ten years.[47]

Bay leaders resisted most of the demands made by the commissioners and refused to let them sit as a court of appeals. The inquisitors wanted to examine many complaints, including one of their own. Hearing that Daniel Gookin held property for his friends Whalley and Goffe, they had seized cattle he owned in Rhode Island. But Gookin "refused to answer . . . so no more was done." One of the emissaries, George Carr, returned to London in 1665 and that December delivered a report on the colonies detailing Massachusetts's "refractoriness," including Gookin's.

Crown authorities now lost patience with Massachusetts and demanded that three of its leaders—Endecott's successor as governor, Richard Bellingham, Major William Hathorne, and the unruly Gookin—come to England to answer the allegations.[48] The reaction was an anguished debate in the General Court on September 13, 1666, "concerning the duty we owe to his majesty." Some members urged compliance but others objected. Deputy Governor Francis Willoughby, for one, said the Court "must as well consider God's displeasure as the King's, the interest of ourselves and God's things, as his majesty's prerogative: . . . for if the King may send for me now, and another tomorrow, we are a miserable people." Another summed up the colony's dilemma: "To come to a narrow," he exclaimed, "what is our privilege and what is prerogative?"[49]

Privilege carried the day; no men were sent over. Instead the Court brazenly replied to London that "We have in all humility given our reasons, why we could not submit to the commissioners . . . whereof we have not to add; and therefore can't expect that the ablest persons among us could be in a capacity to declare our case more fully."[50]

At this point London officials might have taken sharp measures against the colony. Strangely enough they did not, and the issue was left unresolved. During the next ten years the king's government concentrated on Europe and two wars with the Dutch, while the activities of the Council for Foreign Plantations declined until by 1668 they had ceased altogether. Not until 1675 did a new colonial affairs board, the Lords of Trade, turn again to the question of New England's loyalty. When Charles sent a zealous new agent, Edward Randolph, on a mission to Boston, the board asked him to investigate conditions throughout the colonies. One thing it wanted Randolph to find out was how the inhabitants "stand affected to the Government of England."[51]

Randolph arrived in New England just as King Philip's War, which had raged through the Plymouth, Rhode Island, and Massachusetts colonies for the past year, was finally burning out. On June 12, 1676, two days after Randolph landed at Boston, the Indians made one of their last assaults in the conflict. Their target, as it happened, was Hadley.

IV

Whalley and Goffe had moved to Hadley more than eleven years earlier, and they spent most of their days there living secretly in an upstairs chamber at the house of the minister, John Russell. Thomas Hutchinson says few persons in the colony knew where they were. In the floor of a passage behind their room, a secret opening led to an "under closet" designed for their concealment "in case of search or surprise." For a time—perhaps a few years—Goffe and Whalley were joined by a less famous regicide, John Dixwell, who afterward settled in New Haven, where he lived more openly under the assumed name of James Davids.[52]

Throughout the regicides' exile Goffe corresponded secretly with his wife, Frances, Whalley's daughter, in England. He wrote in a simple code and as a further precaution addressed his wife as his mother and referred to his daughters as his sisters. He signed the letters "Walter Goldsmith" and gave all his residences the same fictitious place name, "Ebenezer."[53] Mather continued to serve as the correspondents' intermediary at Boston.

The letters that survive express the poignancy of the couple's forced separation. In one, Frances Goffe wrote to her husband: "Though we should never meet in this world again, yet I hope, through grace, we shall meet in heaven, and so ever be with the Lord, and it will not be in the power of men to part us." He grieved when she wrote about the death of one of their daughters, and the death of a grandchild soon after; but tenderly he urged her to "rejoice in the Lord alway, and again I say rejoice; and I beseech you to remember that weak eyes are made weaker by too much weeping." They did not give up hope. As late as 1675 Goffe wrote to his wife, "These are dying times, wherein the Lord hath been and is breaking down what he hath built, and plucking up what he hath planted . . . let us account it a great mercy if he gives us our lives . . . and bring us again to see the faces of one another with comfort."[54]

By then, Whalley apparently had suffered a stroke. Goffe told his wife that her father's "understanding, memory and speech doth so much fail him, and [he] seems not to take much notice of anything that is done or said. . . . [He has] not been able, of a long time, to dress or undress himself, nor to feed, or ease nature either way, orderly, without help, and it's a great mercy to him that he hath a friend that takes pleasure in being helpful." The old warrior—the cavalry hero of Naseby and warden of Charles I—died soon thereafter, and was buried in the land of his exile.

Goffe was perhaps sixty-five, and if either regicide appeared suddenly out of hiding to help defend Hadley during King Philip's War, it was certainly Goffe and not Whalley.[55] To investigate the historical validity of the legend of Hadley—the remarkable story from King Philip's War that stirred Scott, Cooper, and Hawthorne—one must reexamine the sources and circumstances and view them in the light of two factors already set forth: the sympathetic network of Goffe's and Whalley's friends in New England, and the strain in the colonies' relations with London.

Hutchinson wrote that the Indian attack against Hadley occurred on "a fast day," September 1, 1675, "while the people were at church, which broke up the service, and obliged them to spend the day in a very different exercise." His source appears to be Increase Mather's *Brief History of the War with the Indians in New*

England, which he paraphrases roughly. He then connects the Leveretts' story of Goffe's dramatic appearance to this date in September. But Hutchinson may have been led astray. Mather wrote only that the residents of Hadley that day "were driven from the holy service they were attending by a most sudden and violent alarm, which routed them the whole day after." Debunking the Angel legend in 1874 and later as "a pure romance," a "baseless episode" and a "fabrication," Deerfield's historian George Sheldon observed that Mather had reported only an alarm on September 1, and he argues correctly that there was in fact no attack that day upon Hadley. Sheldon concluded that, consequently, Hutchinson's tale of the rescue (and the subsequent legend) could not be true.[56]

The fact that Indians did not attack Hadley on September 1, however, does not prove that Goffe never helped save the village. Did it happen another time? No one has found contemporary evidence that Goffe fought the Indians at any time, and the story remains conjectural. Yet in the field of conjecture much remains to be said.

A fresh look at the Angel episode may begin with a tantalizing "contemporary hint" that the historian Franklin B. Dexter, in 1870, discovered in a letter John Russell wrote to Mather on April 18, 1677. It is the only hint known to survive. The Hadley minister commented on Mather's *Brief History of the War*, which had been published the previous fall. "I find nothing considerable mistaken in your history," he told Mather. "That which I most fear in the matter is lest Mr B. or some of Connecticut should clash with ours and contradict each other in the story as to matter of fact. Should that appear in print which I have often heard in words, I verily fear the event would be exceeding sad."[57]

Dexter and Sheldon disagreed about the significance of those mysterious words, but neither did much to decode them. Neither followed the natural path from Russell's text back to Mather's to see what "story" in Mather's book might be open to contradiction. Surely it was not Mather's report of the alarm of September 1, 1675: the book's mention of that was too simple and brief to cause Russell concern. The only passage that could have made him nervous is a detailed narrative later in Mather's book—a description of the attack upon Hadley that occurred nearly ten months later, on June 12, 1676.

Sheldon took little interest in the assault of June 12, declaring that the Angel story could not have happened then for several reasons, the main one being that, on that day, "nearly 500 Connecticut men were in Hadley under Major Talcott." Goffe's intervention, he said, would have been wholly unnecessary.[58] But the only original contemporary report of the attack is Mather's, and evidence shows that on this point Mather's narrative is ambiguous—maybe even deceiving.

Ever since Mather's volume was published, historians have misunderstood what happened that June day in Hadley. First, we should look at the military situation that faced the Connecticut River towns in 1676.

With the approach of spring that year came a renewal of war with the Indians. King Philip's party returned to western Massachusetts from winter quarters near Albany and attacked Northampton, across the river from Hadley, on March 14. Although the assailants were driven off, the commander of Bay forces in the area, Major Thomas Savage, reported to Boston that the outlook was grim. "We perceive as near as we can gather," he said, "that their aim is at these towns on the river to destroy them."[59] By early April, however, there had been no further hostilities in the area. Trouble threatened the eastern part of the colony instead, and Savage and most of his forces were withdrawn to the east.

In May, when warm weather stirred a new confidence in the towns of the Connecticut River Valley, the remaining garrison soldiers grew restless. Hearing that Indians were camped in large numbers above Hadley near Deerfield, the towns' militiamen organized a raiding party that crept into the sleeping Indian village at daybreak on May 19 and launched a deadly assault. The carnage that morning—later known as the Falls Fight massacre—cost the English dearly when neighboring Indians attacked their retreating column and killed thirty-seven men.[60]

The settlers' blood now ran high. Soon after the Falls Fight, when scouts observed new Indian campfires near the scene of the massacre, Russell suggested to authorities at Hartford that they send a large expeditionary force to destroy the foe once and for all. On May 24 Captain Benjamin Newberry, in charge of the small garrison of Connecticut soldiers at Northampton, made a similar appeal to his commanders at Hartford. The main body of Connecticut soldiers was then at Norwich under the command of Major John Talcott, and Newberry suggested that if Talcott "would please to come this way with his forces, he might do a good service."[61]

Similar pleas reached officials in Boston. Seeing an opportunity to strike hard at the enemy, Connecticut and Massachusetts now planned a double offensive: in a pincer movement the Connecticut soldiers would conduct a sweep up the west side of the Connecticut River from Northampton, while Bay forces, commanded by Captain Daniel Henchman, swept up the east side from Hadley.

Talcott's Connecticut force, an imposing array of 250 colonists with 200 Indian allies under Oneko, son of the Mohegan chief, Uncas, marched into Hadley on Thursday, June 8. Later the same day, headquarters were established across the river at Northampton.

Talcott then wrote to his superiors at Hartford. His message, though confusing, suggests strongly that his entire English contingent—either with or without its Indian allies—had crossed to Northampton. Talcott reported that the Bay forces had not yet arrived at Hadley, "and upon advice with those of my council of war, [I] judge that it is not prudence to divide our forces and engage the enemy on both sides of the river being too weak, rationally expecting that they will endeavor to make over to one side and so overpowering it may be to our ruin and your loss, and judge it a bootless undertaking to drive but one side, knowing they will fly (if beaten) over to the other side and scornfully reproach us, and have quartered our soldiers and are waiting for your further orders."[62] The Bay soldiers under Henchman would not arrive in Hadley for another six days.

Since the plan was for Talcott's men to launch their sweep up the river from Northampton, because Talcott and his officers thought it was unwise to divide their forces, and since he wrote on June 8 and thereafter from Northampton, never Hadley, it is logical to assume that most if not all the Connecticut forces were in Northampton rather than Hadley on June 8 and after. That is why Mather's account of the June 12 attack on Hadley is suspect.

Mather began writing his history on the first of May, 1676, and completed it seven weeks later, on August 21. He does not identify the source for his account of the Hadley engagement; whoever it was, Mather wrote about the action within ten weeks of its occurrence.[63] He begins:

> June 12. The enemy assaulted Hadley in the morning, sun an hour high. Three soldiers going out of the town without their arms were dissuaded therefrom by a sergeant who stood at the gate, but they alleging that they intended not to go far, were suffered to pass. Within a while the sergeant apprehended that he heard some men running, and looking over the fortification, he saw twenty Indians pursuing those three men, who were so terrified, that they could not cry out. Two of them were at last killed, and the other so mortally wounded as that he lived not above two or three days. Wherefore the sergeant gave the alarm. God in great mercy to those western plantations had so ordered by his providence, as that Connecticut Army was come thither before this onset from the enemy.[64]

The clear, perhaps deliberate implication of the last sentence is that the Connecticut army defended Hadley, although Mather doesn't actually say that: he reports only that it had come "thither"—that is, to "those western plantations"—and that its arrival was fortunate. Could Talcott's men have dashed back across the wide river that early morning when Hadley was threatened? Would the Indians have allowed them to cross? Russell once wrote to Governor Leverett and his Council, "Experience shows us that a hundred men on the other side of the river can send little relief."[65]

Ever since Mather's book was published, historians have concluded that Talcott's Connecticut forces drove off the Indians. But Talcott's men were based at Northampton.

William Hubbard of Ipswich, Massachusetts, whose *Narratives of Troubles with the Indians in New England* was published in April 1677, six months after Mather's volume appeared, was the first historian to write later that the Connecticut men defended Hadley. Sheldon's tale of the battle is more dubious still. The Deerfield historian knew that Talcott had his headquarters at Northampton, and he placed his entire force in that town thirty hours before the attack. Yet he wrote that when the Indians assaulted Hadley, the Connecticut men were there. The attackers, he said, were surprised to find "the stockades lined with soldiers and Indians, and soon fell back in disorder." In the early 1900s George M. Bodge wrote mistakenly that Talcott and his men actually had been quartered in Hadley, rather than Northampton. And in the 1950s our most rigorous historian of the war, Douglas Edward Leach, repeated the general story: when Hadley was assaulted, he wrote, it "gave the Connecticut men a chance to work off their pent-up energy. They and the townsmen beat off the savages rather readily."[66]

Mather's narrative continues to reinforce the initial impression it has created. "Besides English," says Mather, "there were near upon two hundred Indians in Hadley, who came to fight with and for the English against the common enemy, who was quickly driven off at the south end of town."

So we have it that a force of the Indian allies, at least, had quartered in Hadley. But the "English" are unspecified. Although Henchman's detachment would not arrive until two days later, there were, of course, English in Hadley: not only the settlers themselves, but also the small remnant of Massachusetts soldiers whom Savage had left under Capt. William Turner. Turner had been killed three weeks earlier in the disastrous rout from the Falls Fight. The surviving force was commanded by Capt. Jeremiah Swain.

Mather writes that the attacking enemy "was quickly driven off at the south end of town," and "whilst our men were pursuing of them here, on a sudden a great swarm of Indians issued out of the bushes and made their main assault at the north end of the town. They fired a barn which was without the fortifications, and went into a house, where the inhabitants discharged a great gun upon them, whereupon about fifty Indians were seen running out of the house in great haste, being terribly frighted with the report and slaughter made amongst them by the great gun."

A bewildering tale! Was the house itself outside or inside the fortifications? Was the gun fired by the "inhabitants" of the fortifications, of the house, or of the town? Was it fired at the Indians from inside the house or outside? Whatever happened, Mather implies that this episode turned back the main assault, that it began while Hadley's defenders were pursuing the enemy at the opposite end of town (a mile to the south), and, quite possibly, that this turning point in the struggle involved townspeople rather than soldiers. He concludes by noting that as soon as the Indians fled the house, "ours followed the enemy (whom they judged to be about five hundred, and by Indian report since, it seems they were seven hundred) near upon two miles, and would fain have pursued them further, but they had no order so to do. Some in those parts think that as great an opportunity and advantage as hath been since the war began was lost at this time, the Lord having brought the enemy to them and there being English and Indians enough to pursue them. But others supposing that then they should impede the design of coming upon them at the Falls, nothing was done until it was too late, only the towns in those places were eminently saved, and but few of ours that lost their lives in this skirmish."[67] The odd remark that the combatants "had no order" to continue pursuing the Indians suggests that there was no one present with authority to make that decision—another sign that Talcott was absent. That, in fact, is what Hubbard reported. Led apparently by Mather into writing that the Connecticut troops helped repel the attackers, he grants that their leader was elsewhere. "The commander in chief, it is said, quartered at one of the towns on the west side of the river," wrote Hubbard, "and did not apprehend the advantage till the season was over."[68]

What, then, did Russell mean in April 1677 when he nervously wrote to Mather, "That which I most fear in the matter is lest Mr B. or some of Connecticut should . . . contradict . . . the story" Mather had published? If the Connecticut forces were not in Hadley and did not save the village, a key part of Mather's narrative was suspect. What different version of the attack, which Russell "often heard in words," would have dire results if it were printed? Was Russell afraid that Connecticut men would give public credit to Goffe, instead, as the savior of Hadley?

Mather's ambiguous narrative leaves room for the version of an attack on Hadley that Hutchinson learned from Leverett's family. One can summarize the piecemeal evidence by speculating about what might have happened—about an origin, at last, for the Angel legend:

The Connecticut troops arrived in Hadley four days before the attack, but all or most of them then crossed the river to Northampton, the town from which they were to launch the expedition up the west side of the river. There they waited for Henchman to arrive at Hadley, where the Bay forces would begin a simultaneous march up the opposite shore. Before the Bay troops arrived, however, Hadley was a tempting target—either because its garrison was small, or because it sheltered the Indian mercenaries led by Oneko. With a feinting ambush the enemy lured the defenders, at least the remnant of Massachusetts soldiers whom Savage had left in garrison, to the south end of town, and then they attacked the north, striking terror among the civilians. In the emergency Goffe, ever the professional soldier, quickly came to their rescue. The prompt firing of the "great gun," a cannon, with deadly aim, indicates military skill and presence of mind in battle.[69] This repelled the attack; the Hadley forces then rallied and pursued the Indians for nearly two miles, and the town was "eminently saved." But if the story of Goffe's appearance ever became widely known, he and his hosts would have been mortally endangered; also, New England's leaders would have been politically embarrassed at a time when their relations with the Crown were at risk once again. A cover-up was essential. When Mather published a deceptive and incomplete story, Russell feared it would backfire. It never did; instead, the improbable rescue of Hadley by Connecticut forces became the accepted version, repeated by historians ever after.

The plausibility of a cover-up is supported by other puzzling circumstances that surround the assault. First, in addition to the works by Mather and Hubbard, only two other contemporary histories of the war describe that summer's fighting in western New England. Neither mentions the attack. *A True Account of the Most Considerable Occurrences That Have Happened in the Warre between the English and the Indians in New England* was published in London in the fall of 1676. Arranged chronologically, it consists of reports sent from a well-informed New Englander to a friend in London. It gives news of Talcott's activity and describes events of June 9, 14, and 30 but says nothing of the June 12 attack on Hadley.[70] The writer is unidentified, but the letters' exceptional praise of the Christian Indians makes it likely that he was none other than the regicides' old companion, Daniel Gookin.

The oldest son of Goffe and Whalley's friend Richard Saltonstall also wrote about the war in the west. *A New and Further Narrative of the State of New-England*, by Nathaniel Saltonstall of Haverhill, Massachusetts, was published in London toward the end of 1676. It gives only a brief paragraph to events in June. While Saltonstall reports that Talcott that month "slew and took captive" twenty-four Indians, he says nothing about the attack on the 12th. Elsewhere he mentions "Great spoil made at Hadley, Hatfield and Chelmsford"—but that is all.[71]

One may well ask why Saltonstall and, presumably, Gookin both omitted the Hadley engagement.

It is also odd that no reference to the Hadley fight survives in the military records of Massachusetts or Connecticut. This omission is a curious gap in the voluminous war correspondence. But perhaps it should not be surprising, in light of a third coincidence: the men who were first and second in command of the English forces closest to Hadley on June 12, Connecticut's Talcott and Newberry, were both brothers-in-law of John Russell.[72] The family ties make it likely that they knew and protected Russell's secret about the fugitives, and if Goffe emerged from hiding to help defend the village, it would not have been in the family interest for Talcott or Newberry to record it.

Instead, Russell singled out a mysterious "Mr B." as one who might dispute Mather's story. The best guess as to Mr. B.'s identity is made by Lemuel Welles in his *History of the Regicides in New England*: he suggests it was the Reverend Gershom Bulkeley of Connecticut. Bulkeley, wrote another historian, was a man of "overweening self-importance" and "litigious spirit" who was "almost continually at strife with his parish, his neighbors, or the government" of Connecticut. He had succeeded Russell as minister of the anti-Russell faction that remained at Wethersfield, and on June 12 he was serving with the Connecticut forces in Northampton as a military surgeon and member of Talcott's council of officers.[73] In later years Bulkeley proved to be a king-fearing royalist and an outspoken critic of New England's Puritan leaders; in 1692 he complained of a deep "antimonarchical spirit" in the colonies and said it was "well known . . . in what admiration some had the persons of, and what entertainment was given to, some of [the king's] murderers" who had fled to the region. A tract published by Bulkeley in 1694 warned readers: "He that disobeys the King, as King, or exercising his kingly office, disobeys God."[74]

Bulkeley may have expressed such royalist sentiments as early as 1676. If so, Russell probably knew them and was afraid that Talcott's surgeon could not be trusted with news of a regicide's appearance in Hadley.

Bulkeley's superiors Talcott and Newberry, and even the highest authorities in Connecticut, were more reliable. Connecticut's governor and deputy governor were now respectively William Leete and Robert Treat, the same men who fifteen years earlier had frustrated Kellond's and Kirke's pursuit of Whalley and Goffe in New Haven. Goffe likewise had a friend in Leverett at Boston. If the governor received any report that the regicide had made a public appearance the week of June 12, it could not have come at a worse time. The king's aggressive agent, Edward Randolph, had just arrived on his fact-finding mission, and Leverett would have done his best to suppress the story.

The only account of Goffe's role in the episode that survived, then, was the "anecdote handed down through Governor Leverett's family" and reported by Hutchinson more than eighty years later. Trying to reconcile the story with accounts of the war, perhaps the Leveretts or Hutchinson, or both, confused the date and certain other details.

Three months after the Hadley engagement Goffe wrote to Mather from Hartford. The letter mentions his "remove to this town." Perhaps he had left Hadley after twelve years of residence there because he knew he had been discovered. Goffe's last surviving letter is dated April 2, 1679. His death is unrecorded. The hunted fugitive was never reunited with his family, but the man who helped turn the army fatally against Charles I at Windsor and led Cromwell's regiment to victory over the Scots at Dunbar was stoical at the end: "Not any one ingredient which my tender-hearted and wise Father hath put into my cup could have been spared," he wrote to Mather; "my affliction hath been for my good."[75]

In choosing whether to obey or disobey the king's orders for the capture and arrest of the regicides, Mather and other New Englanders chose between temporal and what they saw to be higher law. It was not always an easy choice, for if it was piety to obey the "higher law," it could be treason as well. Conflicts between temporal and higher law have been posed again and again in our history. The historian Alan Simpson has referred to the potential "subversive" result of the Puritans' religious zeal.[76] That same piety—the root of New England's treason in harboring the regicides—is a root of the political morality that appears throughout the American experience. The Puritans' choices here were forerunners of similar choices claimed by New Englanders later on: In 1750 by Jonathan Mayhew, for instance, in his pre-Revolutionary "Discourse Concerning Unlimited Submission," and by Theodore Parker in his 1854 sermon, "The Law of God and the Statutes," opposing the Fugitive Slave Law. In that sense it is not the regicide alone, but his host even more, who can be seen—to use Hawthorne's expression—as "the type of New England's hereditary spirit."

Goffe's death, and that of Charles II in 1685, did not end the fear of what might happen to the regicides' protectors if they ever became known. Charles's successor was his ruthless younger brother, James II. After the failure of Monmouth's Protestant uprising against James, Russell and his colleagues must have heard about the trial in England in 1685 of Alice Lisle, whose daughter was Bridget Usher of Boston, widow of Harvard's third president, Leonard Hoar. Lisle had sheltered two of the Monmouth rebels overnight at her home in Hampshire. Troops the next day found one of them in the malthouse and the other concealed in a chimney. Under the law against harboring traitors, Lisle herself was condemned and beheaded.[77]

News of Lisle's sentence must have shaken Goffe's New England benefactors, so deepening their silence that, with time, stories about the regicides, unconfirmed and unrecorded, became wisps of memory only—the myth makers' skein.

Notes

1. Thomas Hutchinson, *The History of the Colony and Province of Massachusetts-Bay*, ed. Lawrence Shaw Mayo, 3 vols. (Cambridge, Mass.: Harvard University Press, 1936), 1:187.
2. Ezra Stiles, *A History of Three of the Judges of Charles I* (Hartford, 1794), 109.
3. Sir Walter Scott, *Peveril of the Peak*, Waverly Novels, 25 vols. (Philadelphia, 1887), 15:222–23; G. Harrison Orians, "The Angel of Hadley in Fiction," *American Literature* 4 (November 1932): 262.
4. Michael Davitt Bell, *Hawthorne and the Historical Romance of New England* (Princeton: Princeton University Press, 1971), 28.
5. Ibid., 31. See also Ursula Brumm, "A Regicide Judge as a 'Champion' of American Independence," *Amerikastudien* 21 (1976): 177–86.
6. Nathaniel Hawthorne, "The Gray Champion," in *Twice-Told Tales* (Boston, 1872), 24.
7. Henry David Thoreau, *Walden*, ed. J. Lyndon Shanley (Princeton: Princeton University Press, 1971), 137; *Hampshire Gazette*, 25 September 1855; circular issued for the engraving by John C. McRae of New York City, 1859 (it and Chapman's painting are at the Forbes Library in Northampton, Mass.); John G. Palfrey, *History of New England*, 5 vols. (Boston, 1859–90), 3:164; John Fiske, *The Beginnings of New England* (Boston, 1898), 244–46.
8. Hawthorne, "Gray Champion," 23.
9. George Sheldon, "The Traditionary Story of the Attack upon Hadley and the Appearance of Gen. Goffe, Sept. 1, 1675: Has It Any Foundation in Fact?" *New England Historical and Genealogical Register* 28 (October 1874): 379–91.
10. *The Writings and Speeches of Oliver Cromwell*, ed. Wilbur C. Abbott, 4 vols. (Cambridge, Mass.: Harvard University Press, 1937–47), 1:216; John Milton, "Second Defence of the People of England" [1654], in *The Works of John Milton*, 18 vols. (New York: Columbia University Press, 1931–38), 8:233. Milton wrote that in the "fiercest battles" Whalley could always be found "among the thickest of the enemy."
11. Henry Lockinge, *Historical Gleanings on the Memorable Field of Naseby* (London, 1830), 74.
12. *The Clarke Papers*, ed. C. H. Firth, 4 vols. (London, 1891–1901), 1:130; "Colonel Edward Whalley to John Lenthall, Esq., touching the manner of the King's departure from Hampton-Court," in Francis Peck, *Desiderata Curiosa* (London, 1779), 374–77.
13. Sir Charles Firth, *The Regimental History of Cromwell's Army*, 2 vols. (Oxford: Clarendon Press, 1940), 1:359; William Allen, "A faithful Memorial of that remarkable Meeting of many Officers of the Army in England, at Windsor Castle, in the Year 1648," in *Somers Tracts*, ed. Sir Walter Scott, 13 vols. (London, 1811), 6:501.
14. J. G. Muddiman, *Trial of King Charles the First* (Edinburgh: W. Hodge., 1928), 193; C. V. Wedgwood, *A Coffin for King Charles: The Trial and Execution of Charles I* (New York: Macmillan, 1964), 22.

15. *Original memoirs written during the Great Civil War; being the life of Sir H. Slingsby, and memoirs of Capt. Hodgson . . . with notes*, ed. Sir Walter Scott (Edinburgh, 1806), 298; Cromwell, *Writings and Speeches*, 2:324.
16. Whalley was governor, or major general, for his home county of Nottinghamshire and four others: Lincolnshire, Derbyshire, Warwickshire, and Leicestershire. Goffe was in charge of his home county of Sussex and two others, Berkshire and Hampshire. Cromwell, *Writings and Speeches*, 3:844, 4:839; *The Harleian Miscellany: A Collection of Scarce, Curious, and Entertaining Pamphlets and Tracts . . .* , ed. Thomas Park, 10 vols. (London, 1808–13), 3:483.
17. Anthony Wood, *Athenae Oxonienses. . . . To which are added, The FASTI, or Annals, of the said University to the Year 1690* (London, 1721), 2:79.
18. Austin Woolrych, *Commonwealth to Protectorate* (Oxford: Oxford University Press, 1982), 32, 38, 58, 121n, 333.
19. Francis J. Bremer, "In Defense of Regicide: John Cotton and the Execution of Charles I," *William and Mary Quarterly*, 3rd ser., 37 (1980): 105, 118.
20. Ray Charles Palmer, *Rev. William Hooke, 1608–1678* (New Haven: Old Colony Historical Society, 1912), 9, 12. Goffe's wife, Frances, and their children lived for a time with the Hookes, her aunt and uncle, after Goffe and her father, Whalley, escaped from England. "Mather Papers," *Massachusetts Historical Society Collections*, 4th ser., 8 (1868): 133.
21. Lemuel Welles, *The History of the Regicides in New England* (New York: Grafton Press, 1927), 24, 26, 28, 31. Welles's rare volume is the best book-length history of Whalley's and Goffe's New England exile.
22. Massachusetts Archives 57:42, Massachusetts State Archives, Boston, Mass.; *The Manuscripts of the Duke of Portland Preserved at Welbeck Abbey*, 10 vols. (London: Historical Manuscripts Commission, 1891–1931), 1:658; Abbott, *Writings and Speeches*, 2:379n, 422; "Mather Papers," 135.
23. Abbott, *Writings and Speeches*, 4:338; *Calendar of State Papers, Domestic Series, Charles I, 1645–47* (London, 1891), 339; Hutchinson, *Massachusetts-Bay*, 1:187.
24. "Winthrop Papers," *Massachusetts Historical Society Collections*, 4th ser., 7 (1865): 590, 594. To this writer's knowledge, there is no record of Ebenezer Hooke's subsequent life in New England.
25. Ibid., 501; James Caulfield, *The High Court of Justice: Comprising Memoirs of the Principal Persons who sat in Judgment on King Charles the First, and Signed his Death-Warrant* (London, 1820), 49.
26. Cotton Mather, *Johannes in eremo: Memoirs. . . .* (Boston, 1695), 25; Welles, *Regicides in New England*, 28–29.
27. "The Autobiography of Increase Mather," ed. Michael G. Hall, *American Antiquarian Society Proceedings* 71, part 2 (1961): 271–360; "Mather Papers," 162.
28. No roster of prominent seventeenth-century New Englanders is complete without the name of John Pynchon, the most important man in western Massachusetts. Pynchon served with Gookin, Leverett, and others in the General Court. Although the evidence is inconclusive, he also may have kept the secret of Goffe and Whalley while pretending to plot for their apprehension. See *Massachusetts Historical Society Collections*, 3rd ser., 8 (1843): 326; "Mather Papers," 171.
29. *Calendar of State Papers, Colonial, America and West Indies, 1661–1668* (London, 1880), no. 161, 54 (herafter cited as *CSP Colonial*); *The General Court of Massachusetts, 1630–1930*, Tercentenary Exercises held at the State House, 1930 (Boston: Wright & Potter, 1931), 61.
30. *Records of the Governor and Company of the Massachusetts Bay in New England*, ed. Nathaniel B. Shurtleff, 5 vols. (Boston, 1853–54), 1:10, 12.

31. Richard S. Dunn, *Puritans and Yankees: The Winthrop Dynasty in New England* (Princeton: Princeton University Press, 1962), 40; Herbert L. Osgood, *The American Colonies in the Seventeenth Century*, 3 vols. (New York: Macmillan, 1904–7), 1:262.
32. *By the King, A Proclamation to summon the Persons therein named who sate, gave Judgment, and assisted in that horrid and detestable Murder of His Majesties Royal Father of blessed memory, to appear and render themselves within Fourteen days, under pain of being excepted from Pardon* (Whitehall, 6 June 1660).
33. *By the King: A Proclamation for the apprehension of Edward Whalley and William Goffe. . . .* (Whitehall, 20 September 1660).
34. Paul R. Lucas skillfully examines the political uncertainty of this period in his article "Colony or Commonwealth: Massachusetts Bay, 1661–1666," *William and Mary Quarterly*, 3rd ser., 24 (1967): 88–107.
35. "Mather Papers," 178–79.
36. Welles, *Regicides in New England*, 27; *CSP Colonial*, no. 45, 15; *The Humble Petition and Address of the General Court Sitting at Boston in New-England, unto the High and Mighty Prince Charles the Second and presented to his Most Gracious Majesty Feb. 11, 1660* (Worcester, Mass.: American Antiquarian Society, n.d.), 4.
37. Hutchinson, *Massachusetts-Bay*, 1:184; *CSP Colonial*, no. 81, 27.
38. *Massachusetts Historical Society Collections*, 3rd ser., 7 (1838): 123; *CSP Colonial*, no. 81, 27–28.
39. Hutchinson, *Massachusetts-Bay*, 1:185n. The "Judges' Cave" can be seen today at West Rock State Park outside New Haven.
40. *CSP Colonial*, no. 96, 34.
41. Stiles, *Three Judges*, 50.
42. Hutchinson, *Massachusetts-Bay*, 1:185n; *Massachusetts Historical Society Collections*, 3rd ser., 8 (1843): 328.
43. Hutchinson, *Massachusetts-Bay*, 1:185n; "Mather Papers," 181; *Massachusetts Historical Society Collections*, 3rd ser., 7 (1838): 126; and 3rd ser., 1 (1825): 52.
44. Shurtleff, *Records*, vol. 4, part 2, 25, 165; *Massachusetts Historical Society Collections*, 3rd ser., 1 (1825): 53.
45. Shurtleff, *Records*, vol. 4, part 2, 165, 200, 161, 193; Lucas, "Colony or Commonwealth," 105.
46. Shurtleff, *Records*, vol. 4, part 2, 199.
47. Hutchinson, *Massachusetts-Bay*, 1:186; *Connecticut Historical Society Collections* 2 (1870): 38.
48. *CSP Colonial*, no. 1103, 344–46; Lucas, "Colony or Commonwealth," 106.
49. "Danforth Papers," *Massachusetts Historical Society Collections*, 2nd ser., 8 (1826): 99–100.
50. Ibid., 109.
51. Osgood, *Seventeenth Century*, 3:152; "Randolph Papers," *Prince Society Publications*, 7 vols. (Boston, 1898–1909), 2:198.
52. Stiles, *Three Judges*, 200; Hutchinson, *Massachusetts-Bay*, 1:186n.
53. Hutchinson, *Massachusetts-Bay*, 1:123n. In the Old Testament, Ebenezer is the name that Samuel gave the stone he set up to mark the place where the Lord protected the Israelites from the Philistines.
54. Ibid., 1:442; "Hutchinson Papers," *Prince Society Publications*, 2 vols. (Albany, 1865), 2:186, 193. Several of the Goffes' letters are preserved at the Boston Public Library. Some were published in these volumes and others in the "Mather Papers."
55. "Hutchinson Papers," 188–89; Welles, *Regicides in New England*, 88; *Alumni Oxonienses: The Members of the University of Oxford, 1500–1714*, ed. Joseph Foster, 4 vols. (Oxford, 1891), 2:578.
56. Hutchinson, *Massachusetts-Bay*, 249; Increase Mather, *A Brief History of the War with the*

Indians in New England (Boston, 1676), 7–8; George Sheldon, "Introduction to the New Edition," in Sylvester Judd, *History of Hadley, including the Early History of Hatfield, South Hadley, Amherst and Granby, Massachusetts*, 2nd ed. (Springfield, Mass.: H. R. Huntting, 1905), vii, ix, xviii; Sheldon, "Traditionary Story," 389, 391.

57. Franklin B. Dexter, "Memoranda Respecting Edward Whalley and William Goffe," *New Haven Colony Historical Society Papers* 2 (1877): 139; "Mather Papers," 81.
58. Sheldon, "Traditionary Story," 391.
59. Mass. Archives 241:279.
60. Judd, *History of Hadley*, 162–66.
61. Conn. Archives, War Records, 1:74, 76; Benjamin Newberry to John Allyn, Northampton, 26 May 1676, H. H. Edes Papers, Massachusetts Historical Society, Boston, Mass. Quoted by permission.
62. *Massachusetts Historical Society Proceedings*, 2nd ser., 8 (1894): 66; Conn. Archives, War, 1:83, 88a.
63. Thomas James Holmes, *Increase Mather: A Bibliography of His Works*, 2 vols. (Cleveland: Harvard University Press for William Gwinn Mather, 1931), 1:74. Perhaps Mather's source was his nephew, Rev. Samuel Mather, who may have been at Hatfield, across the river from Hadley; it also could have been Rev. Solomon Stoddard at Northampton, or even John Russell.
64. Mather, *Brief History*, 33. (Here and in the following excerpts from Mather, punctuation has been modernized for clarity of analysis.)
65. Mass. Archives 67:288.
66. William Hubbard, *The Present State of New England, Being a Narrative of the Troubles with the Indians in New-England* (1677), ed. Samuel G. Drake, 2 vols. (Roxbury, Mass., 1865), 1:245; George Sheldon, *A History of Deerfield, Massachusetts*, 2 vols. (Deerfield, 1895–96), 1:173; Sheldon, "Traditionary Story," 391; George M. Bodge, *Soldiers in King Philip's War* (Boston: privately printed, 1906), 38; Douglas Edward Leach, *Flintlock and Tomahawk: New England in King Philip's War* (New York: Macmillan, 1958), 206.
67. Mather, *Brief History*, 33.
68. Hubbard, *Narrative*, 1:246.
69. Artillery pieces were scarce and rarely used in King Philip's War; also, firing a seventeenth-century cannon was complicated and laborious: a knowledgeable person had to load a careful measure of powder into the muzzle, ram the projectile in after it, place more powder at the touchhole, light and put the taper to the primer, and move smartly out of harm's way.
70. *A True Account of the Most Considerable Occurrences That Have Happened in the Warre between the English and the Indians in New England* (London, 1676), 4.
71. N.S. [Nathaniel Saltonstall], *A New and Further Narrative of the State of New-England* (London, 1676), 4.
72. Russell's first wife had been Talcott's sister Mary, who died before 1660; his second wife was Newberry's sister Rebecca, who lived until 1688. Sherman W. Adams and Henry R. Stiles, *The History of Ancient Wethersfield, Connecticut*, 2 vols. (New York: Grafton Press, 1904), 2:594.
73. Welles, *Regicides in New England*, 95; *The Public Records of the Colony of Connecticut, May, 1678–June, 1689*, ed. J. Hammond Trumbull (Hartford, 1859), 389; Conn. Archives, War, 1:90.
74. Gershom Bulkeley, "Will and Doom, or The Miseries of Connecticut by and under a Usurped and Arbitrary Power" [1692], in *Connecticut Historical Society Collections* 3 (1895): 92; Gershom Bulkeley, *Some Seasonable Considerations for the Good People of Connecticut* (New York, 1694), 14.

75. "Mather Papers," 158, 163.
76. Alan Simpson, *Puritanism in Old and New England* (Chicago: University of Chicago Press, 1955), 16.
77. Thomas Babington Macaulay, *The History of England from the Accession of James the Second*, 6 vols. (London: Macmillan, 1913–15), 2:630, 634.

5

If for decades the legend of the Angel of Hadley seemed to many in the community dramatic and appealing, but utterly intangible, the story was unexpectedly brought to life during an inventory of the Hadley Historical Society's manuscript collections funded by the Bay State Historical League. Among the most exciting discoveries was a sixteenth-century bible in the possession of the society, stowed away so securely that the present membership was largely unaware of its presence in their collections. A small note tucked inside its pages suggested that the book had once been the property of William Goffe, one of the two men who, having signed the 1660 death warrant for King Charles I, fled to New England after the Restoration, eventually finding secure hiding in Hadley. The discovery of such an important artifact associated with some of the most significant events in the early modern Atlantic world sparked the interest of a number of local scholars. Martin Antonetti, curator of rare books at Smith College, kindly agreed to examine the book and attempt to determine whether it could indeed have been associated with the regicides. The bible, because it seemed to all but demand a showcase, provided an opportunity to bring together other scholars who had recently undertaken work on Hadley during its first period of English settlement: the lively 2003 conference on Hadley in the Renaissance at the University of Massachusetts Center for Renaissance Studies.

Antonetti's research enriches the human dimension of the events recounted by Douglas Wilson elsewhere in this volume, and he also helps us understand better how the legend of the regicides unfolded in the nineteenth- and twentieth-century community. Most tantalizing are the presences and absences Antonetti notices about the regicides and the bible at the time of the 1909 celebration, when a float in the local parade (designed by none other than poet Clarence Hawkes) honored Whalley and Goffe, and the bible garnered a place of honor in local exhibitions, but the story and the artifacts were apparently unconnected at that time. Antonetti's research raises puzzling and fascinating questions about the bible's whereabouts and meanings in the early twentieth century. That we are left us with yet more mystery reminds us that there are always new questions to ask, even about very old stories.

The "Goffe Bible"

Succor for the Regicides?

Martin Antonetti

In the summer of 1933 an eighty-eight-year-old woman boarded a train in Champaign-Urbana, Illinois, where she had been living with her daughter for the previous four years, and traveled north to spend a few weeks with her son and his family in Manitowoc, Wisconsin. This had become an annual journey in recent years; it was cooler there on the shores of Lake Michigan, and she loved spending time with her grandchildren, who were then entering adolescence. As it happened, this would be the last time she saw them, since she died, peacefully in her sleep, just before Christmas that year.

On this particular visit she brought a special gift for her twelve-year-old grandson, Robert. Perhaps she sensed that her time on earth was limited. Perhaps, too, she considered him to be mature enough now to understand its value. As they were sitting in together in the parlor of the house, "her black eyes as alive and sparkling as ever," she asked him, "So you are interested in collecting books, Robert?" When he eagerly responded that he was, she said, "Well, I have some books upstairs that you will want to see. I might even make you a present of them." She then made her way, quite laboriously, up the stairs to her room. There she unpacked her trunk, found what she was looking for, and, with the help of Robert's younger sister, made her precarious way back down, all the while leaning heavily on her cane. The epic ascent and descent together consumed no fewer than forty-five minutes.

Once safely back in her chair she opened her treasure, which was "wrapped in brown paper and secured with twine." There were three old books. "The third and largest book was a bible. It was very old. . . . When I finally got down to examining the bible grandma said: 'Now Robert, that bible is very valuable. It was found in a secret room of the John Russell house in Hadley. It is the bible of William Goffe who hid in the Russell home for many years.' "

This small but touching incident was described fifty years later in a letter from that grandson, Robert Bayne of Carmel, Indiana, to Dorothy Russell of Hadley.[1] Robert's grandmother was Julia Taft Bayne (1845–1933), a noted poet and essayist with a significant Hadley association.[2] Julia had just bequeathed to her grandson an artifact that she believed was owned and read by William Goffe, the "Angel of Hadley," the regicide who, along with his father-in-law,

Edward Whalley, sought shelter from the avenging hand of Charles II in the frontier outpost of Hadley for over fifteen years, from 1664 until around 1680.[3] Robert, a midwesterner with no connection to Hadley himself, had kept the bible in his care from 1933 until 1983. Then, seeking a permanent home for the "old relic" (as he called it), where it might be restored and studied, he wrote to Dorothy Russell for help. Her reply does not survive, but its message can be inferred by the presence in the Hadley Historical Society of a dog-eared and disbound copy of a bible which has, since 1983, been know as the "Goffe Bible" or the "Hadley Bible" (figure 5.1).

In the spring of 2003 Marla Miller, the editor of this volume, asked me to examine the "old relic" in order to ascertain whether the association with Goffe might be verified. I made a careful study of the book and its previous owners—at least those I was able to discover—and, along with James Freeman, a colleague from the University of Massachusetts, reported my findings at a conference on early Hadley held at the Renaissance Center at the university in May of that year.[4] Jim and I were able to trace the trajectory of this bible's history from the present day all the way back to Hadley in the late seventeenth century; in the end we got very close to Goffe himself. In fact, it is possible to say with some certainty that the bible was present in at least one, and perhaps two, of the houses in which Goffe hid during his long internment in Hadley. Just two small but crucial pieces of the puzzle remain unsolved. Even so, we nonetheless have a fairly clear picture of this bible's place in town history.

Julia Taft Bayne was the wife of John Bayne, the minister of the First Congregational Church of Hadley from 1869 to 1893. The spirited daughter of a federal official, she was raised in Washington, D.C., during the Buchanan and Lincoln presidencies and, owing to her social position and the fortunate circumstance of living directly across the street, was a frequent houseguest at the White House and playmate of the Lincoln children, Willie and Tad.[5] In her later years she wrote a popular memoir of life in wartime Washington and her personal experiences of the Lincoln family.[6] After the Civil War, having attended Elmira Female College for a year, she took a teaching position at Hopkins Academy in Hadley. The young instructor of French soon fell in love with the new minister of the First Church, John Bayne, and the couple married in 1869. Gregarious and popular, Julia actively assisted her husband in his pastoral duties and played a central role in the social life of the town. She clearly enjoyed her years in Hadley; she later celebrated the town and its traditions in poems like "The Hadley Weathercock" and "The Hadley Elms," published in magazines such as *The New England Magazine*, *Youth's Companion*, and *St. Nicholas*.[7]

THE NEW TESTAment of our Lord IESVS CHRIST, Translated out of Greeke by Theod. Beza: With briefe Summaries and expositions vpon the hard places by the said Authour, Ioac Camer. and P. Loseler. Villerius. Englished by L. TOMSON. Together with the Annotations of Fr. Iunius vpon the Reuelation of S. IOHN.

IMPRINTED AT LONDON by the Deputies of Christopher Barker, Printer to the Queenes most Excellent Maiestie. 1599.

FIGURE 5.1. *Title page of the Goffe Bible. Courtesy of the Hadley Historical Society.*

Bayne departed her beloved Hadley in 1893, when she and her husband were sent to LaSalle, Illinois, where he assumed the leadership of a new congregation. Later, they moved to other congregations in Illinois and Nebraska before Rev. Bayne's death in 1915.[8] All the while she continued to write—more poems and a memoir—and to lecture on her days with the Lincoln family. When she gave the historic bible to her grandson shortly before her death, she passed along as well her belief that it had once belonged to the famed regicide.

The History of the Tradition

Had this bible belonged to, or been used by, William Goffe? Perhaps a better question might be, *could* it have belonged to Goffe? How had Julia Taft Bayne come to possess it and what was the basis for her claim that it was associated with Goffe? Had there been a long-standing local tradition linking the bible and the regicides?[9] Did someone give this important artifact to Julia in 1893, when she and her husband immigrated to Illinois, as a parting gift, as a keepsake or remembrance of happy decades in Hadley?

Evidence suggests that Julia had not assumed ownership of the bible during her stay in Hadley and that she acquired it much later. In fact, it is likely that the book was in the possession of the Samuel Dudley Smith family of Hadley in 1909—fully sixteen years after her departure—when it was put on public view during the Old Hadley Quarter Millennial Celebration, which took place over a period of four days in early August of that year. On Monday morning of that week the Central School Building was thrown open and visitors were invited to view "the historical and arts exhibitions" assembled by a committee chaired by Mrs. F. H. Smith. These items, culled from family collections and "as replete in historical value as are the annals of the town," were displayed in glass cases throughout the schoolhouse, and they were later recorded by Clifton Johnson in some detail in the descriptive program of the entire event that he later compiled.[10] Among the other heirlooms we find one case "entirely filled with the many beautiful articles belonging to the family of S. D. Smith," such as "exquisite embroidery over 100 years old," including thirty samplers. Among the books, Johnson records, is "a Bible bearing the date 1599."

Johnson gives no further description of that bible, so we cannot know for sure that this is the same one that eventually made its way to Manitowoc and back, but it seems likely that it is. Yet Johnson's program does not give any indication of the bible's provenance or ascribe previous ownership to Goffe or Whalley. This is a highly significant omission, for in 1909 the townspeople of Hadley were well aware of this chapter in the town's history, and were quite proud of it. Indeed, the Old Hadley Quarter Millennial Celebration made much of the legend of Goffe and Whalley. Many of the fulsome speeches given during the festivities referred to the regicides and the assistance they received from Rev. John Russell,

Peter Tilton, and Lt. Samuel Smith. Wednesday's parade featured an "Angel of Hadley" float,[11] and there were regicide-related artifacts on display in other places, including "a chair in which the regicide judges sat while inmates of the home of Pastor Russell."[12]

If that "Bible bearing the date 1599" had been even remotely associated with Goffe, if there had been a regicide tradition attached to it in 1909, no doubt it would have been exhibited as such at the celebration. But Johnson's exhaustive program does not record that it was. Given the bible's age and the Smith family's role in the early history of the colony, family members may have speculated that the bible was one that had come over on the *Mayflower* or soon after, and that its value derived from its association with the early Pilgrims rather than with the regicides.[13] All of this taken together suggests, first, that the bible that was later owned by Julia Taft Bayne was still in Hadley in 1909, in the possession of the S. D. Smith family; and second, that it was not associated with the regicides at that time, but was displayed simply as a family heirloom.

The question of how the bible was passed from the S. D. Smith family to Julia Taft Bayne at some point between 1909 and 1933 is perhaps impossible to answer now. It is clear that she was well known and well loved in Hadley, both during her years of residence and after her departure. Her obituary in the *Daily Hampshire Gazette* of Northampton even calls her "one of Hadley's immortals," recalling that "during her years here she won the admiration of all who came to know her."[14] Given what is known of her personality and her fondness for the town, it is probable that she maintained a correspondence with friends from Hadley after she left in 1893. From them she may have learned about the great celebration of August 1909 and was perhaps even invited or encouraged to attend. Indeed, we learn from Clifton Johnson's program that her poem "A Song of Hadley" (music by Johnson himself), written specially for the occasion, was publicly sung as part of the festivities.

> In the story of the ages, told by poets and by sages,
> Where the world's great cities shine on imperishable pages,
> Stands no name more loved than thine, Dear Old Hadley!
> And we sing thy praises gladly, elm-bow'red tranquil Hadley,
> Let no lip salute thee sadly, Dear Old Hadley, Dear Old Hadley!

Could it have been sung by Julia herself, who had returned to "elm-bow'red tranquil Hadley" for the great event? It is certainly possible that she was present at the commemoration. If so, might the bible have been given to her as a gift or keepsake by a member of the Smith family at that time?

The Early History of the Hadley Bible

Fortunately, by examining evidence left on the bible by earlier owners it is possible to trace its history before 1909. The book now safely ensconced in the Hadley Historical Society is an incomplete (randomly lacking some pages in various sections) small-format bible, a quarto, containing both the Old and New Testaments, printed with hand-set lead type on handmade rag paper, purportedly in London in 1599.[15] It is important to note here that the Hadley volume contains the Geneva version of the biblical text, a sixteenth-century translation made by the English Protestant scholars who sought refuge from persecution in Calvinist Geneva during the reign of Catholic Queen Mary. These expatriate scholars were lead by John Knox, a radical reformer and "apostle to the Scots" who rejected Thomas Cranmer's High Church Anglicanism. They railed against the *Book of Common Prayer* as being contaminated with "popery and superstition on every page" and undertook to compile a new prayer book more closely linked to the teachings of John Calvin.

Also central to their program of reform was the creation of a new translation of the Bible based on the Greek and Hebrew originals, rather than on St. Jerome's Latin Vulgate text. The Geneva Bible, as it came to be called, was the most scholarly and most thoroughly annotated version up to that time, and it quickly replaced the Great Bible of 1539 in popularity: in the 85 years between 1560, the date of its first appearance, and 1644 it was reprinted in 140 separate editions.[16] From 1580 until 1615, all of the quarto editions of the Geneva Bible contained the Calvinistic Catechism inserted between the Old and New Testaments.[17] This, and the very strong Calvinist bias in the marginal notes that frame every page, made the Geneva Bible a powerful instrument of Puritan reform in the English church. Thus, given the strictly reformist, even radical, tendencies of the churches of the Plymouth and Massachusetts Bay colonies, it is easy to understand why the Geneva version was particularly attractive to Puritan colonists.[18] It is certainly indicative of its spiritual relevance to the American colonists that Increase Mather himself owned a copy of the London 1599 edition.[19] Its small size made it considerably cheaper than the folio—or "great"—bibles used in churches.[20] Thus it became, in the late sixteenth and early seventeenth centuries, the favored household bible of English-speaking Protestants, wherever they lived.

It is also significant that the 1599 edition was probably not printed in London, as it states on the title page, but actually in Amsterdam for the use of English Puritans living in self-imposed exile in the Low Countries—and it may not have been printed in 1599 at all.[21] So large was this community of religious expatriates that it could easily support a local industry in bible production, rather than having

London-produced copies imported, at some expense, from across the channel. Indeed, so great was this market that the typical press-run for an edition of the quarto bible printed in Holland for resident Englishmen was 3,000 copies.[22] But Dutch printers were prevented by law from freely publishing biblical texts, and so resorted to various subterfuges to meet the considerable demand; as one scholar notes, the nominal date of 1599 is "probably untrue in almost every case; they were apparently published at different times in Amsterdam and Dort and adopted by Barker [whose name appears on the imprint]."[23] Or these printers may have co-opted Barker's name, as he and his heirs were granted by the Crown the sole franchise for the printing of bibles of this sort in this period. That is, it was illegal for any other printer to issue that text without permission; still they did, merely substituting Barker's name for their own in the imprint. Because ships with English Puritan settlers bound for New England routinely stopped in Amsterdam to pick up fellow pilgrims before heading west across the ocean, it is quite possible that this copy came aboard in Amsterdam, crossed the Atlantic in the hands of an early pilgrim to Plymouth or Boston, and eventually made its way to Hadley.

The Hadley bible was originally bound in panel-stamped calfskin over boards. That first binding has now largely deteriorated; only fragments of the old leather remain. The original spine is missing (and an unprofessional repair was made in the eighteenth or nineteenth century with thick cloth) and the front and back covers have become detached. Inside, the pages are very worn, but the wear is not consistent throughout the volume: the New Testament is largely intact, but the Old Testament, especially the book of Psalms, is quite well-thumbed. Indeed, some parts of Psalms are completely detached and simply laid in.[24] Numerous ink spots and wax blobs throughout the volume suggest that someone may have been reading it and taking notes in the dark, by candlelight. Unusually for a bible of this age, there are almost no handwritten inscriptions on the book or its covers, except for a few marginal lineations and indecipherable scribblings in the Song of Solomon, chapter 7, at the verses "thy thighs are like jewels, thy navel is like a round goblet, which wanteth not liquor, thy belly is like a heap of wheat set about with lilies, thy two breasts are like twin roebucks."[25] It would be very gratifying indeed to be able to identify Goffe's hand in some of these scribblings, but there is no evidence to be found: no signature, no notes, nothing stuck between the pages, no positively identifiable trace whatsoever of the seventeenth-century regicide.

There are, however, several personal names penned in later (childish) hands seemingly at random in the text: "Lois Smiths Book" (verso of title page) and "Lois Smith Born in the year 0770 [meaning 1770]," "Justin" (first page of gospel of John), and "Submit" (inside back cover),[26] among others. There were many Lois

Smiths in Hadley throughout the years, but only one born in 1770,[27] and she had a brother named Justin, who was born in 1775. Their father was Warham Smith; his father was Noah Smith; his father was "Orphan John" Smith; his father was John Smith; and *his* father was Lt. Samuel Smith, one of the founders of Hadley. This lineage is remarkable inasmuch as Lt. Samuel Smith—along with Peter Tilton and Rev. John Russell—was traditionally associated with the conspiracy to shelter Whalley and Goffe. Russell's home was in the center of town, both geographically and administratively, and because of his high standing and public duties it would have been a very busy place, full of people coming and going. Ezra Stiles, writing in 1794, surmised that Smith and Tilton would have been asked to house the regicides if activities at the Russell house became so intense as to require their removal to another hiding place, as during the period of military activity in 1675.[28]

At some point after the death of Justin in 1806 the bible passed to his cousin Dudley Smith, who died in 1858. It was then inherited by his son, Samuel Dudley (b. 1843), the "S. D. Smith" of the Old Hadley Quarter Millennial Celebration, in whose family's exhibition case the "Bible bearing the date 1599" is first noticed. Thus we can locate the bible in Hadley at the exact period of the regicides' sojourn there and conclude that it stayed in Hadley, in the possession of the Lt. Samuel Smith family, from that time until at least 1909.

An Unnoticed Inscription

Another inscription, one that can barely be seen by the naked eye, provides a tantalizing clue. Very faintly written on the inner front cover is "Dorothy Russell her book." This is, of course, not the latter-day Dorothy Russell to whom Robert Bayne's 1983 letter was addressed, but rather the seventeenth-century Dorothy Russell, the second wife of John Russell of Wethersfield, who was the father of the Reverend John Russell, one of the founders of Hadley and its principal leader in the early decades of the settlement. Before her marriage to John Russell, she had been Dorothy Smith, the widow of the Reverend Henry Smith of Wethersfield. At some point she and her husband followed their son, Rev. John Russell, to Hadley.[29] This was the Rev. Russell who offered Goffe and Whalley asylum in Hadley in 1664 and in whose house they spent many years.

When Dorothy Russell died in 1694, a complete inventory of her possessions was taken for estate purposes.[30] Being rare and thus noteworthy in a frontier outpost, her books were listed along with their estimated values: "great book 10s, 1 great bible 10s, Doctor Preston's book 6s, one book 5s, 1 book Preston's 5s, psalm book 2s, small book 1s." The "great bible" noted here would have been a folio volume, distinctive for its large size. There is no mention of a small quarto bible. Clearly, the 1599 Geneva bible was not in the Russell home when this inventory of Dorothy's goods was made. The barely legible inscription proves that she once owned the bible, but its absence from the probate inventory indicates that she must have given it away before she died. It is possible that at some point between 1664 and 1680 she made a present of the bible to Goffe, who devoutly read it by candlelight for spiritual sustenance during his long hours of confinement in her stepson's house. If he had such a bible in his custody he may well have carried it with him to his other hideaways in Hadley: the nearby houses of Peter Tilton and Lt. Samuel Smith.

After Goffe died, probably in Hadley around 1680,[31] his "papers," including his journal and letters, were collected by Rev. Russell and forwarded to Increase Mather in Boston. These papers remained in the Mather family library until Thomas Hutchinson acquired them at some point in the middle of the eighteenth century. As Douglas Wilson's essay elsewhere in this volume explains, Hutchinson used these papers to reconstruct the story of the regicides, which was published in his *History of the Colony of Massachusetts-Bay* in 1764; this was the first public exposition of the tale.[32] The following year Hutchinson's house was pillaged by a violent mob angry at his support of the Stamp Act, and his library of printed books and manuscripts was despoiled, most of the Goffe papers perishing ignominiously in the muddy street in front of the house. In his *History*, however, Hutchinson never mentions a bible or any other books among the Goffe papers that survived into the eighteenth century.[33]

The bible, then, must have stayed in Hadley. Keeping in mind that Lois Smith and her brother Justin—the ones who penned their names in it around 1790—were direct descendants of Lt. Samuel Smith, it is possible to conjecture that Goffe, the recipient of a gift from Dorothy Russell, the mother of his first benefactor in Hadley, later left the bible at the home of Lt. Samuel Smith, another benefactor, where it remained. It might then have been passed down in Smith's family from Samuel to John, "Orphan John," Noah, Warham, Lois and Justin, all the way to S. D. Smith, who exhibited it during the anniversary celebrations in 1909. Perhaps at that point the bible was presented by the Smith family to Julia Taft Bayne, "one of Hadley's immortals," when she returned to sing her "Song for Hadley" on that illustrious occasion, then handed down to her grandson Robert in Manitowoc, Wisconsin, in 1933, where it spent the next fifty years before being wrapped up and sent back home to another, much later, Dorothy Russell in 1983.

In the end, much of this tale is only conjecture. The best that can be said is that there is no physical evidence in the bible itself, or no other tradition, to contradict it. The colonial Dorothy Russell may never have spoken to either of the regicides, or had anything whatever to do with them, for all we know. Nor do we know how (or when) the bible came into the possession of the Smith family or how (or when) it was transferred to Julia Taft Bayne. Indeed, it is probable that we will never uncover those crucial bits of the history and so never ultimately be certain of the veracity of the tale. Thus, like any number of "*Mayflower* Bibles" or "Washington's Bibles," the "Goffe Bible" of Hadley may be fated to remain in the realm of historical tradition and hopeful supposition, rather than of archaeological certainty. But does this diminish its value or meaning for us? Perhaps we should consider the Goffe Bible as something else, a powerful talisman that serves to reconnect us with a defining episode in Hadley's history. As such, it also vividly brings into focus for us the world-altering events of the English Civil War and Restoration, and the not inconsequential role that little Hadley played in the drama. The Goffe Bible also stands for the roiling crucible of religious faith and its action as a catalyst on men and women everywhere and in every age. It teaches us that history is nothing more, or less, than the individual striving and struggle of countless men and women, most of whom will always remain nameless and forgotten, against inexorable circumstance. And it reminds us of the hardships present on all frontiers, whether they are cultural, geographical, or psychological. These are some of the valuable insights that this numinous artifact offers up, and for these alone the Goffe Bible should be treasured by this and future generations, as it was by those many generations of Russells and Smiths and Baynes. Knowing whether William Goffe ever thumbed the pages of this particular book may after all be of less importance than its value as a brilliant, and tangible, symbol of Hadley's role in American history.

Notes

1. Robert Bayne to Dorothy Russell, 9 August 1983, Dorothy Russell Papers, Hadley Historical Society, Hadley, Mass.
2. Robert's father was Reed Taft Bayne (1885–1954), the managing editor of the *Manitowoc Evening Times*.
3. See George Sheldon, "Introduction to the New Edition," in Sylvester Judd, *History of Hadley, including the Early History of Hatfield, South Hadley, Amherst and Granby, Massachusetts*, 2nd ed. (Springfield, Mass.: H. R. Huntting, 1905), xi–xiv. The most complete account of the history and legend of the regicides is found in Douglas C. Wilson's article elsewhere in this volume.
4. "General William Goffe: King Killer, Bible Reader, Angel of Hadley," at the conference "Hadley in the Renaissance," Center for Renaissance Studies, University of Massachusetts Amherst, May 2003.
5. Mary A. DeCredico, "Introduction," in Julia Taft Bayne, *Tad Lincoln's Father* (Lincoln: University of Nebraska Press, 2001), xii. Her father was the chief inspector of the U.S. Patent Office, appointed by James Buchanan.

6. The first edition was published in Boston by Little, Brown in 1931; Bayne had already published an excerpt in the *Atlantic Monthly* (133 [May 1924], 660–65).
7. These were later collected and published as *Hadley Ballads* (Chicago: Open Court Publishing Company, 1903). According to an anonymous notice of *Hadley Ballads* published in *Open Court: A Quarterly Magazine Devoted to the Science of Religion* (October 1903), Open Court Publishing Company was founded in 1887 by E. C. Hegeler in LaSalle, Illinois, for the purpose of "establishing ethics and religion on a scientific basis" (569). Bayne may have met the free-thinking Hegeler in LaSalle.
8. These churches were in Mendota, Elwood, and Lockwood, Illinois, and Holdridge and Kearney, Nebraska. Biographical information on Bayne is scarce and derived primarily from obituaries, in particular those found in the *Champaign News-Gazette* (14 December 1933) and the *Daily Hampshire Gazette* of Northampton, Mass. (28 December 1933). Other information can be gleaned from the alumnae publications of Elmira College, which Bayne attended in 1860/61, and which awarded her an honorary AB degree in 1931.
9. I can find no trace of a tradition of a "Goffe Bible" before Robert Bayne's letter to Dorothy Russell. The locus classicus of the tradition of the regicides in Hadley, Ezra Stiles's *History of Three of the Judges of King Charles I* (Hartford, Conn.: Elisha Babcock, 1794), makes no mention of a bible, nor do Lemuel Wells's *History of the Regicides in New England* (New York: Grafton Press, 1927) or Judd's *History of Hadley*.
10. Clifton Johnson, *Old Hadley Quarter Millennial Celebration* (Springfield, Mass.: F. A. Bassette Company, 1909), 26–27. There is no mention of the display of a "Goffe Bible" in the description of an earlier anniversary: *Celebration of the Two Hundredth Anniversary of the Settlement of Hadley, Massachusetts, at Hadley, June 8, 1859* (Northampton, Mass.: Bridgman & Childs, 1859); in fact, it is clear from this publication that the legend of the regicides and the Angel of Hadley did not yet loom large in the imaginations of the residents of the town.
11. Johnson, *Hadley Quarter Millennial*, 57: "Model of the church, with arms of the worshippers stacked on either side of the door and sunflowers growing near the steps; Indians partly concealed in a thicket, and arrows and tomahawks sticking in the door; the regicide, Goffe, known in Colonial history as the angel of Hadley, pushing open the door and pointing toward the Indians with his sword." There is a photograph of the float in the plate following p. 30.
12. Johnson, *Hadley Quarter Millennial*, 29. The chair belonged to the Reverend A. N. Somers of Montague, who had learned of its whereabouts when he overheard two people in "York State" (i.e., upper New York State) quarreling about an old chair in which "somebody sat who killed a king" (ibid.).
13. Historical bibles with important colonial associations were often exhibited at fairs and expositions in the late nineteenth and early twentieth centuries. Interestingly, "John Alden's Bible," or at least one of the three purporting to be his, was also the Geneva edition of 1599. For more on the curious tradition of "the Bible that came over on the *Mayflower*" see Edwin A. R. Rumball-Petre, *America's First Bibles* (Portland, Maine: Southworth Anthoensen Press, 1940), 121–29 and passim; several of those cited there with *Mayflower* provenance are the 1599 edition.
14. *Daily Hampshire Gazette*, Northampton, Mass., 28 December 1933. The fact that she was eulogized so far from her home, by a newspaper in a place she had quit forty years previously, attests the enduring strength of her connection to Hadley.
15. *The Bible, that is, the Holy Scriptures conteined in the Old and New Testament: Translated according to the Ebrew and Greeke, and conferred with the best Translations in divers Languages; With most profitable Annotations upon all hard places, and other things of great*

importance (London: by the Deputies of Christopher Barker, Printer to the Queenes most Excellent Maiestie, 1599).

16. Benson Bobrick, *Wide as the Waters: The Story of the English Bible and the Revolution It Inspired* (New York: Simon and Schuster, 2001), 174–76. The annotations in the New Testament alone contained two thousand alternate readings and more than seven hundred literal renderings from the ancient languages.
17. Nicholas Pocock, "Some Notices of the Genevan Bible, Part II," *The Bibliographer* 2 (September 1882): 97.
18. In this context it is also important to remember that the Cromwellian republic that emerged in England after the beheading of Charles I in 1649 strongly favored the Puritans. Goffe, a political reformer and regicide, was certainly in sympathy with the party of religious reform as well. No doubt he was most comfortable with the readings found in the Geneva version even before he reached Hadley in 1664.
19. This copy, which bears Mather's signature and the family record in his own hand, survives in the collection of the Massachusetts Historical Society; see John Wright, *Historic Bibles in America* (New York: Thomas Whittaker, 1905), 108–9.
20. See Christopher Hill, *Society and Puritanism in Pre-Revolutionary England* (New York: Schocken Books, 1964), 49.
21. A. S. Herbert, *Historical Catalogue of Printed Editions of the English Bible, 1525–1961* (London: British and Foreign Bible Society; New York: American Bible Society, 1968), 115. For more on the complex problem of the bibliography of the English bible in this period see Lea Wilson, *Bibles, Testaments, Psalms and Other Books of the Holy Scriptures in English* (London, 1845), 90–92, and Nicholas Pocock, "Some Notices of the Genevan Bible, Part IV," *The Bibliographer* 3 (January 1883): 28–31.
22. This number is significant, especially when multiplied by the number of editions of the quarto bible published each year. See Herbert, *Historical Catalogue*, 184, citing Michael Sparke's *Scintilla* of 1641, a scarce pamphlet that sheds light on English book trade practices of the period. Historical bibles, like historical children's books, have notoriously low survival rates: they were simply read to pieces, like the Hadley bible. WorldCat, the giant bibliographic database, which contains holdings information for most American and many foreign libraries, lists fewer than fifty copies of all eight of the 1599 editions (on these see Herbert, *Historical Catalogue*, 115–16, nos. 248–55).
23. Herbert, *Historical Catalogue*, 115.
24. The heavy wear to the book of Psalms is not surprising; Puritans, including those who settled the Plymouth and Massachusetts Bay colonies, made extensive use of the Psalms in public and private worship. The importance of the Psalter in colonial tradition is most clearly attested by the fact that the first book printed in North America was *The Whole Booke of Psalmes Faithfully Translated into English Metre* (Cambridge, 1640). Most of the translations were the work of a number of ministers in the Massachusetts Bay colony (hence its sobriquet, *Bay Psalm Book*), chief among them Richard Mather of Dorchester, and Thomas Welde and John Eliot of Roxbury. See John T. Winterich, *Early American Books and Printing* (Boston: Houghton Mifflin, 1935), 28–29. For more on the reading habits of early New Englanders see Jill Lepore, "Literacy and Reading in Puritan New England," in *Perspectives on American Book History: Artifacts and Commentary*, ed. Scott E. Casper, Joanne D. Chaison, and Jeffrey D. Groves (Amherst: University of Massachusetts Press, 2002), 17–46.
25. It may be poignant to note here that Goffe was married and was in periodic—if secret and pseudonymous—epistolary contact with his faithful and long-suffering wife in England, who was attempting to keep their family together, against nearly impossible odds,

pending his return. The letters, "as between a mother and son," were passed through a series of intermediaries thanks to the good offices of Increase Mather. One, from her to him, dated 1662 and suffused with concern and solicitousness, was transcribed as Appendix XIV in Thomas Hutchinson's *The History of the Colony of Massachusetts-Bay* (Boston: Thomas and John Fleet, 1764), 532–34.

26. We could not positively identify Submit: there is no record of anyone bearing this name in the line of Lt. Samuel Smith. The Submit Smith who married Jonathan Dickinson of Amherst in 1807 could be a younger, but unrecorded, sibling of Lois and Justin.
27. Genealogical information about the Smith family is derived from Lucius Boltwood's appendix, "Genealogies of Hadley Families," in Judd's *History of Hadley*.
28. This element of the story is first found in a letter from Samuel Hopkins to Ezra Stiles of 26 March 1793 quoted in Judd, *History of Hadley*, 210–11. See also Stiles, *History of Three of the Judges*, 198–200.
29. See Boltwood, "Genealogies of Hadley Families," 117–18. The histories of the Smith and Russell families are difficult to elucidate, in large part because so many of them shared the same names.
30. Probate Record Office, Hampshire Division, Northampton, Mass., box 125, no. 41. The inventory is dated 22 December 1694. In her last will and testament, which is appended to the inventory, she bequeaths to Samuel Smith (not, however, *Lt.* Samuel Smith), her son by Henry Smith, all of her immovable property; to daughter Dorothy and daughter-in-law Mary Smith she bequeaths all of her movable property "to be equally shared and divided between them."
31. For more on the circumstances of Goffe's death see Douglas C. Wilson's article in this volume.
32. Hutchinson, *History of the Colony of Massachusetts-Bay*, 213–19: "Goffe kept a journal or diary, from the day he left Westminster [England, in flight from the agents of Charles II], until the year 1667; which, together with several other papers belonging to him, I have in my possession." Judd's *History of Hadley* includes some of the relevant passages from Hutchinson (207–11).
33. By great good fortune a few letters to and by Goffe and some of his other papers, mostly manuscript transcriptions of newsletters from England, have survived, having been separated from the main collection in Hutchinson's house at some point previous to the pillage. These were collected and bound by Thomas Price and deposited in the Boston Public Library. They were later transcribed and published with the Mather Papers in the *Collections of the Massachusetts Historical Society* (Boston: For the Society, 1868), 4th ser., vol. 8, 122–25. Among Goffe's correspondents, apart from his wife, were Increase Mather, William Hooke, and Edward Collins. These letters are replete with chapter-and-verse quotations from Scripture—"too much religion in their letters for the taste of the present day," as Hutchinson wrote—but none makes reference to a bible he has in his possession. A fragment of Goffe's diary for the year 1660 was published in the Winthrop Papers in *Proceedings of the Massachusetts Historical Society* (Boston: For the Society, 1864), vol. 7, 281–83. It documents the period of his arrival and first months in Boston, but is much more a record of spiritual matters than of temporal ones. After two weeks in Boston he records that "the L^{d} was graciously pleased to refresh my Soul wth his pressence, in reading ye word, & in prayer, in my private morning Exercise." This is the only reference to the act of reading the bible I have found in any of Goffe's extant writings.

6

If it is clear that the seventeenth-century villagers feared attacks from the Native nations around them, they perceived other, less corporeal threats as well. Satan stalked the English settlements, and any neighbor, no matter how familiar, could be among his allies. The historian Mary Beth Norton, in her book In the Devil's Snare: The Salem Witchcraft Crisis of 1692, *posits a direct relationship between those threats, arguing that the 1692 Salem witchcraft hysteria was at least in part a product of anxiety over the threat of Indian wars. In 1683, almost a decade earlier, Hadley residents contemplated the possibility that evil spirits dwelled among them. It had been only seven years since the assault on the village during King Philip's War, when William Goffe, as Douglas Wilson suggests, may well have risen to the aid of his local benefactors. The fortifications Edward Hood and Rita Reinke describe were in place, providing some sense of security, but earth-fast timbers were no match for the Devil inside.*

"There shall be a wonder in Hadley!"

Mary Webster's "Hideous Witchcraft"

Bridget M. Marshall and Brian W. Ogilvie

During the Salem witch hysteria of 1692, more than a hundred and fifty men and women were accused and jailed, nineteen men and women were hanged, one man was pressed to death, and another four adults and one unnamed infant died in their dungeon cells awaiting trial. The story of Salem's "witches" is well-worn territory, both in scholarly research and in popular imagination.[1] But while Salem was an extreme case, it is far from unique. Accusations of witchcraft (and trials following them) occurred routinely in seventeenth-century New England. Every town seems to have had at least one official accusation, and no doubt many more had local legends and suspicions. Nearly every New England town dating back to the seventeenth century has a record somewhere of a supposed witch.[2] But few of those accused and tried were executed; court records frequently show that they were acquitted or that a higher court overturned a guilty verdict. Such was the case in Hampshire County: although several infamous cases of witchcraft came to trial, county magistrates never executed any witches.

Witchcraft in Hampshire County, at least officially, began long before the events at Salem. County records show that the first witchcraft trial occurred in 1651, when a Mary Parsons of Springfield (at that time part of Hampshire County) was imprisoned for witchcraft and the murder of her infant. The court cleared her of the charge of witchcraft, but found her guilty of infanticide and sentenced her to death; however, no records indicate that the sentence was carried out. Mary's husband, Hugh, was also accused of witchcraft a year later; the jury found him guilty, but reversed the verdict a short time later. In 1674, another Mary Parsons, wife of Joseph Parsons and unrelated to Hugh Parsons or his wife, was accused of witchcraft in Northampton.[3] She too was found not guilty.

Of course, acquittal did not mean that the accused witches were welcomed home. Although the courts refused to inflict punishments, it seems that communities were far less forgiving. Shunned by their town, Hugh and Mary Parsons lived in poverty. Although Mary Parsons of Northampton was comparatively well off because of her husband's social and economic standing, she moved to Springfield after her acquittal. Nowhere is the difference clearer than in the fourth case of witchcraft in Hampshire County, that of Mary Webster of Hadley.[4] In 1683, Webster was accused of and tried for witchcraft, but was found not guilty by the court. One year after her acquittal, her neighbors tried to hang her anyway. In the most remarkable twist, she survived the hanging. And if there was anything that might make people think you were a witch or that you had a deal with the Devil, it was probably escaping death, particularly in such a public way. Mary Webster's case illustrates the challenges of finding facts about cases in the face of limited and perhaps exaggerated evidence; it also provides fascinating insights into some of Hadley's first citizens and New England beliefs about witchcraft.

Witchcraft trials underscore the connections between the New England colonies and the mother country. It is sometimes believed that New England witchcraft trials were a late aberration, coming to bloom in the hothouse atmosphere of colonial Puritanism only after the witch hunt in England itself had withered and died. But the cases of Mary Webster, the two Mary Parsonses, and others, along with the dramatic events of 1692, show that this was not so. When Northampton held its trials and Salem was possessed, belief in witchcraft was still widespread in the English countryside and widely defended in learned circles. By the 1680s, the skeptics were more numerous, and more deeply skeptical, than they had been a century earlier at the height of the European persecution of witches. But there had been skeptics before, and there continued to be fervent believers at all levels of society. Witchcraft belief was still normal in England, and women and men identified as witches continued to pay the price. *Wonders of the Invisible World*, a defense of belief in spirits and witches by the Boston clergyman Cotton Mather, had an eager audience in England, as Mather's London publisher well knew.

Many people associate witch trials with the Middle Ages, but witchcraft belief was not a medieval phenomenon. Anxiety over witchcraft was at its height from the Renaissance through the Restoration, during the century and a quarter from the 1560s through the 1680s. English courts took an active hand in prosecuting it, executing between five hundred and a thousand women and men as witches. The majority of English witches were convicted and executed in the fifty years between 1570 and 1620; thus it is fair to point out, as John Demos has, that New England witchcraft persecution peaked as English witchcraft trials were in decline—so long as we remember that the trials did continue, along with the popular beliefs that led witnesses to testify about the harm done to them by witches. Many of these trials took place in the county of Essex, a hotbed of anxiety about witchcraft.[5] Essex contributed a disproportionate number of colonists to New England, which may go a long way toward explaining the willingness of New Englanders to take suspected witches to court.[6]

English courts did not blindly condemn accused witches; juries convicted fewer than half of those accused, and judges set aside a significant fraction of those convictions. Though from 1563 to 1736 witchcraft was continuously forbidden by statute in England, 94 percent of the Home Circuit indictments accused witches of crimes that would have been crimes anyway: harming or killing humans or livestock, or damaging property. The legislation that governed witchcraft prosecution in the secular courts during the period that concerns us defined witchcraft above all as specific instances of *maleficium*: the use of supernatural power to cause harm to individual human beings or their property.[7] The interesting historical questions are why common people believed that witches caused them harm and why legal authorities were willing to take them seriously. Only by answering these questions can we understand why Mary Webster's neighbors feared her and why she was brought to trial.

A close study of the English trials—or, more precisely, the pamphlet literature that is our best guide to what happened in those trials—reveals that looming behind the specific charges of *maleficium* was a strong sense of supernatural, indeed diabolical, power. In a very real way, the felt experience of this power is what led victims to attribute specific acts of *maleficium* to a witch. The Devil was a frighteningly real figure to the English—and to their compatriots in New England.

Victims' testimony bears this out. In a 1664 trial, the mother of a girl allegedly murdered by witchcraft testified that she had had an argument with the witch, who parted with angry words: "*You need not be so angry, for your Child will not live long*: and this was on a *Saturday*, and the Child dyed on the *Monday* following."[8] This exchange was only the last in a long series of disputes between the women. The pattern was described well enough by Reginald Scot, a skeptic, in 1584. Suspected witches, he wrote, "go from house to house, and from doore to doore for a pot full of milke, yest, drinke, pottage, or some such releefe; without the which they could hardlie live. . . . It falleth out many times, that neither their necessities, nor their expectation is answered or served, in those places where they beg or borrowe; but rather their lewdnesse is by their neighbors reprooved. And further, in tract of time the witch waxeth odious and tedious to her neighbors; and they againe are despised and despited of hir: so as sometimes she cursseth one, and sometimes another. . . . Thus in processe of time they have all displeased hir, and she hath wished evill lucke unto them all."[9] No wonder, Scot continued, that any evil that *did* befall someone would be connected with these curses. In an age when disasters were common and people were unwilling to attribute their misfortunes to chance, the witch was a convenient scapegoat.

In folk tradition, witches were old women, often widowed, often ugly. They were sharp-tongued and difficult to get along with, though some hid their malice behind a fair appearance. And they possessed familiar spirits who took the form of animals and did their bidding. Descriptions of these spirits leave no doubt that they were viewed as demons in disguise. In a 1566 trial, the witch's cat was even named Satan.[10] The accused woman's daughter was visited by a "black Dog" who offered to harm the daughter's enemy but demanded "her body and soul, and so upon request and fear together she gave him her body and soul."[11] Legally, courts required evidence of *maleficium* to convict, so statute law gave little weight to diabolical pacts. But interactions with demons, and the diabolical pact, were part of the English stereotype of the witch.

Tales of witches transmitted belief from one generation to the next, and they explain why witches who confessed told similar stories, even without torture, which was illegal in English witchcraft trials. Pressed to confess their crimes and sins, perhaps urged on by assurances that the court would be lenient, or perhaps convinced themselves of their own guilt, accused witches who confessed retold the stories they had learned. Their rambling, often contradictory stories suggest as much. They also suggest the small horizons of the accused. One witch claimed her cat Satan had given her eighteen sheep—apparently the greatest wealth she could imagine.[12] Another sold her soul so that the Devil might strike fear into the heart of a twelve-year-old girl who had been unkind to her. Perhaps that should not surprise us: the village *was* the world for most accused witches. And we should also keep in mind that the Devil of folklore was a less imposing figure than the mighty Satan of medieval and early modern theology: the Devil could always be tricked by a clever man. Old women might be less fortunate, but that, they knew, was the way of the world.

Why, then, did ministers and judges take these stories seriously? Because they, too, were afraid of Satan. Indeed, the Devil was most fearsome to learned clerics and philosophers. The literature and art of the Renaissance and Baroque featured witches engaged in a diabolical conspiracy, like the witches in Ben Jonson's *Masque of Queens* or the Weird Sisters in *Macbeth*. The Renaissance revival of classical literature contributed Circe and other enchantresses, who were cited by fifteenth- and sixteenth-century demonologists as proof of the Devil's wiles.[13] Demonology was part of a system of thought in which spirits exist, possess natural wisdom, and are capable of feats of natural magic but not miracles. Thomas Aquinas assigned those feats to the realm of the preternatural, because demons followed natural laws but produced effects that were out of the ordinary course of nature. Demonologists attempted to specify the limits of natural effects in their discourse, much like natural philosophers—the scientists of the day—with whom they shared many interests.[14]

Like villagers, who thought of witches as antisocial outcasts, demonologists and witch-hunting lawyers saw them as the opposite of good society. But there was a significant difference. The demonologists' Satan was far more powerful and majestic than the Devil of folklore. And the learned man's witch was more threatening, in a cosmic sense, than the village witch. Not only had she made an individual pact with the Devil, but she was also, in fact, part of a diabolical conspiracy against all Christendom. This kind of thinking lay behind the willingness of legislators, judges, and lawyers to accept that witchcraft was real. Here too, the cultural stereotype, reinforced by pagan poets and Christian theologians, both transmitted belief in witches and legitimated individual accusations.

Demonologists had yet another reason to be interested in witches. To men who feared a lapse into materialism, witchcraft seemed to offer the most striking proof of the reality of demons. Demons, in turn, demonstrated the reality of the entire spirit world. The Dominican inquisitor Heinrich Kramer, author of the late fifteenth-century witch-hunting manual *Malleus Maleficarum* (*The Hammer of Witches*), held that belief in witches was an essential tenet of the Catholic faith. Some Catholics disagreed, and some Protestants would mock the papists' credulity. But the majority of thinkers in both camps accepted that demons existed and that witches were in league with them. One of them, Cotton Mather, would play a tragic role in the story of Mary Webster.

Our sources on Webster's case are notoriously difficult to pin down, but they do make entertaining reading. *The Records of the Court of Assistants* provides the most reliable information, but it is sorely lacking in details. Several accounts, including those found in Cotton Mather's *Memorable Providences Relating to Witchcraft and Possessions* (1689) and *Magnalia Christi Americana* (1702), Thomas Hutchinson's *History of the Colony and Province of Massachusetts-Bay* (1767), Sylvester Judd's *History of Hadley* (1863), and Samuel Drake's *Annals of Witchcraft in New England* (1869) provide considerable embellishment, but are less reliable, since none of these authors was present at either the events in Hadley or the trial.[15] These authors, especially Judd and Drake, drew primarily on local lore. Judd mentions that the stories about Webster "were told with gravity by old persons, seventy years ago, and were believed by some and laughed at by others."[16] These tales may very well reflect prejudice, and perhaps they were exaggerated over time. For instance, Drake wrote that Webster "could ride through the Air on Broomsticks or without them"; however, he does not give his source, and her broomstick-riding appears in no other record.[17] Such fanciful details make it very difficult to know what really happened leading up to the trial and the later attempt to hang her.

Mary Webster's unfortunate story is deeply entwined with the very founding of Hadley, in 1659. The man who would become her husband, William Webster, was the son of John Webster, a deputy governor and governor of Connecticut, who was one of the founders of the Hadley settlement. The majority of Hadley's original settlers were a small group of religious dissidents from Hartford and Wethersfield, Connecticut, but the town soon grew to include immigrants from other towns in the Connecticut River Valley. A map of Hadley homelots in 1663 shows lots belonging to forty-six men,[18] and Kevin M. Sweeney has estimated that seventy-two male heads of family or single males over the age of twenty-one settled in the town between 1654 and 1675.[19] Sylvester Judd's history provides some useful dates for establishing the growth of Hadley's town infrastructure. In 1665, the town voted to fund a schoolmaster, but the first schoolhouse would not be built until 1696. The first ordinary license (to serve intoxicating beverages) was granted in 1667. A church meeting-house in the center of the village was complete by 1670. There were notable setbacks in progress that resulted from King Philip's War, particularly an attack on the town in 1675, but in general Hadley experienced continued growth throughout the later seventeenth century.[20]

These broad strokes paint a picture of early Hadley, but many of the details specific to Mary Webster's situation have been obscured over time. The 1663 map of Hadley homelots shows that John Webster (the father of Mary's husband) held a homelot; we also know that in 1660 he was appointed magistrate for the town. His tenure in Hadley did not last long; he died in 1661, leaving a wife and seven children. According to his will, Webster left his lot in Hadley to be shared equally between his sons Thomas and William Webster,[21] but by 1681 a John Taylor is listed as the owner of the lot. What happened to Thomas and William Webster after the death of their father is unclear from the documents we have. Although they were the sons of a founder of Hadley, both appear in the town records as recipients of assistance; as Judd explains, Thomas lived in a small house erected by the town in the middle highway, and William and his wife were aided by the town.[22] But the records do not reveal how they sank into indigence. William Webster's apparent fall from grace goes unmentioned and unexplained by Judd, who either did not know the reason for the fall or perhaps chose to maintain a discreet silence rooted in a nineteenth-century sense of propriety.

Mary Webster was born Mary Reeve; she married William Webster "in 1670, when he was 53 years old, and she probably some years younger."[23] When or how Mary Reeve came to be in Hadley is not clear, and we have very little information about the couple.[24] Judd claims that the Websters' problems with their neighbors stemmed from the fact that they were poor and required financial assistance from the town, and that "Mary Webster's temper, which was not the most placid, was not improved by poverty and neglect, and she used harsh words when offended." Judd further supposes that "despised and sometimes ill-treated, she was soured with the world, and rendered spiteful toward some of her neighbors,"[25] but we have no testimony from Webster herself about her feelings toward her community or her situation.

It does seem clear, however, that Mary and William Webster, despite their connection to the town founder, were on the bottom rung of the social ladder. This is a common characteristic of suspected witches in both England and New England, as Reginald Scot claimed and many historians have confirmed.[26] All accounts concur that Mary was an unpleasant character, widely disliked in the community. Drake somewhat sympathetically remarks, "Poverty is discouraging, and it is intimated that it did not improve the Temper of Mary Webster; and it is also intimated she became spiteful, and . . . looked upon all those about her as Enemies, and acted accordingly."[27] The fact that Webster saw her neighbors as enemies seems reasonable considering how they treated her. Most accounts indicate that the supposed victims of her witchcraft took immediate action against her. Drake (repeating Judd's examples) reports: "Cattle refused to draw as they approached her House, and Horses balked, and could not be driven past her Door. In such Cases Drivers would enter the House and beat her, or threaten to do so, and then she generally let them pass."[28] Whether Mary was the cause of these problems near her home or not, it is notable that the men were not afraid to threaten or physically harm her, despite her supposed powers. Drake further relates that "on one occasion she overturned a Load of Hay as it was about to pass, and the Man in Charge of it entered the House to whip her, but in the mean Time his Load of Hay was placed right Side up by an invisible Hand."[29] One wonders whether some were so certain that Mary would interfere with anyone who passed by her house that they would harm or threaten her in advance to prevent her from casting spells.

Some of the more colorful anecdotes are less easily explained, as with one tale recorded by Drake: "At another Time, by looking at a Child in a Cradle at a Neighbour's House, she caused it to ascend to the Chamber Floor three successive Times when no visible Hands touched it."[30] The Websters themselves had no children, and this may have added to local suspicions. But the majority of stories of bewitching seem to involve what might be called coincidence; for example, "Once a Hen came down Somebody's Chimney and was somewhat scalded in a pot which happened to be over the Fire. It was found that Mary Webster was suffering from a Scald, about that Time."[31] While a modern reader might not see a connection between the scalded hen and Mary, it is probably an example of the commonly held belief in witches' familiars, which were thought to spy on others. This familiar nursed (typically, drinking blood) from the witch; the presence of a familiar (and thus proof of witchcraft) could be inferred from the presence of a "witch's teat" on the suspected woman. The witch's teat could be anywhere on the body, and might be any sort of odd mark, mole, or protuberance of skin. Presumably, the import of this story is that Mary sent out her familiar, the hen, and when it was scalded, she too felt its effects. Similar explanations of injuries associated with familiars appear in witchcraft testimonies across New England.

Hadley residents were collecting (or perhaps creating) strange stories about Mary Webster for many years before she was finally called to court to account for her behavior. According to the court records for Hampshire County, Mary Webster appeared before the court at Northampton on March 27, 1683. The record lists John Pynchon of Springfield and Peter Tilton of Hadley as the "honored Assistants of this jurisdiction," and three men—Philip Smith (of Hadley), William Clarke, and Aaron Cooke—as "Associates of the court."[32] Joseph Kellogg and John Hubbard, two of the thirteen jurors, were Hadley residents themselves; Hubbard's homelot was directly across from the Websters' house on the middle highway to the meadows, so he may have had particular knowledge of what went on there. Among the jurors, one name in particular stands out: Joseph Parsons Senior, husband of Mary Parsons, who not long before had had her own brush with this same court. The record provides limited detail, indicating only that Mary Webster was "under strong suspicion of having familiarity with the devil, or using witchcraft," that she was examined by "the worshipfull Mr. Tilton," and that "many testimonies [were] brought in against her."[33] Unfortunately, the specific testimonies are not included in the record. It is not clear whether they were recorded at the time; presumably, the testimonies consisted of the various tales of overturned loads and scalded hens. Deeming, as they did in the case against Mary Parsons, that the crime of witchcraft was beyond the scope of their court, they agreed to send the case to Court of Assistants in Boston, and that Mary should be "by the first convenient opportunity sent to Boston Jail and committed thence as a prisoner to be further examined."[34]

Mary Webster and all the evidence in the case were sent to Boston in April 1683. On May 22, she appeared before Governor Bradstreet, Deputy Governor Danforth, and nine Assistants at the court, where she was indicted. As it appears in the court records, the accusation was that "not having the feare of God before her eyes & being instigated by the divill, [she] hath entred into Covenant & had familliarity with him in the shape of a warraneage [wild black cat][35] & had hir Imps sucking hir & teats or marks found in hir secret parts as in & by severall testimonyes may Appear Contrary to the peace of our Soveraigne Lord the king his Crowne and dignity the lawes of God & of this Jurisdiction."[36] Almost four months later, on September 4, she was tried in Boston, but the records provide few details of what went on during the session. We learn that she responded "making no exception against any of the Jury leaving hirself to be tryed by God & the Country," and that "After ye Indictment & evidences in the Case were read Comitted to the Jury . . . the Jury brought in hir virdict they found hir not guilty."[37] What the evidence, arguments, or opinions were, we do not know; but the acquittal must have been a huge relief to Mary and her husband. Judd supplements the court records with notations from the colony's Treasurer's books, which list the costs of Mary Webster's court case, including "Bringing down Mary Webster from Hadley to prison" (£5), "Witnesses about Goodwife Webster" (£12 15s. 2 d.), "Robert Earl for keeping Mary Webster in Boston" (£4), and "Cash for carrying Mary Webster to Hadley" (£2), for a total of £23 15s. 2d. expended on the trial.[38] And with that, the official record of Mary Webster ends. We know that she returned to Hadley, but no other official information appears regarding her. It is at this point, *after* her official acquittal for witchcraft, that her remarkable legend begins.

In an early example of the discontent in western Massachusetts with decisions made in Boston, the residents of Hadley disagreed with the Boston court's "not guilty" verdict. The following year, in the winter of 1684/85, Lieutenant Philip Smith of Hadley became gravely ill. A copy of his will appearing in the Hampshire County Record books shows that he had the will made on January 5, 1685, "through God's dispossessing hand being weak and all of body and know[ing] not how soon this life may terminate and yet through Grace of God."[39] He died five days later. Smith was a prominent member of the Hadley community, and in fact had served on the Hampshire County court that had previously sent Mary Webster's case to Boston. Apparently Mary was suspected of causing his illness, and some residents attempted to hang her for it.

At this point, sources disagree on what happened and why. The key source for the details of Mary's witchery is Cotton Mather's *Memorable Providences*, published in 1689; later historians seem to have relied on his account almost exclusively. Drake gives much credence to Mather's version of the story, remarking in his own history that Mather, "being contemporaneous with the Events, ought to have been well informed with all the Particulars"; however, Mather was not present for the events, and, more important, he had a very strong reason to represent the witchcraft in its most frightening possible way. While Mary Webster's neighbors recounted specific incidents in which she had caused harm—that is, *maleficium* in the legal sense—Mather put the emphasis on the supernatural elements of the story, evidence that Webster had consorted with the Devil. As Drake later admits, "it should be remembered that all, or nearly all [Mather's] Accounts came to him, at least, second handed; and often, perhaps, through a third or fourth idle Head, all Lovers of the Marvellous; ready at all Times, especially in the Night, to believe the Air full of ill shapen Monsters, bearing Commissions from the Devil, to enlist Followers, of whom he might make Witches and send them forth to vex and torment Mankind."[40] Despite such misgivings about Mather's motivations, Drake and others report his findings without much critique, often inserting several pages of his text verbatim into their own.

Mather told Mary Webster's story again, with only a few small variations, in a chapter of his *Magnalia Christi Americana* (1702).[41] From the opening, he clearly establishes where he stands on the events in Hadley: "Mr. Philip Smith, aged about Fifty years, a Son of eminently vertuous Parents, a Deacon of a Church at Hadley, a Member of our General Court, an Associate in their County Court, a Select-man for the affairs of the Town, a Lieutenant in the Troop, and, which crowns all, a man for Devotion and Gravity, and all that was Honest, exceeding exemplary; Such a man in the Winter of the Year 1684, was murdered with an hideous Witchcraft, which filled all those parts with a just astonishment."[42] Mather is clearly using the case of Philip Smith in his ongoing fight against the dark powers that, as he saw it, manifestly threatened New England. Furthermore, he stresses Phillip Smith's high moral and social standing. Mather paints Webster as vicious and ungrateful to her generous benefactor: "[Smith] was concerned about Relieving the Indigencies of a wretched woman in the Town; who being dissatisfied at some of his just cares about her, expressed her self unto him in such a manner, that he declared himself apprehensive of receiving mischief at her hands."[43] Mather's account stresses the difference between the two figures' status; in his mind, Smith's particularly high standing and Webster's particularly low one aggravated the situation. Mather's disdain for Mary Webster, to whom he never even gives a name other than "wretched woman," is apparent throughout his narrative; his focus is on Smith's story, not Webster's.

Mather describes Smith's illness at great length, emphasizing Smith's own suspicions about the causes of his pains. From Mather's telling, it is easy to imagine how distraught and suspicious Smith's family and friends would have been:

> About the beginning of January he began to be very Valetudinarious. . . . Such Weanedness from, and Weariness of the World, he shew'd, that he knew not (he said) whether he might pray for his continuance here. Such Assurance had he of the Divine Love unto him, that in Raptures he would cry out, "Lord, stay thy hand, it is enough, it is more than thy frail servant can bear!" But in the midst of these things, he uttered still an hard suspicion, That the ill Woman who had threatened him, had made impressions on him. While he remained yet of a sound mind, he very sedately, but very solemnly charged his Brother to look well after him. . . . "[B]e sure" (said he) "to have a care of me for you shall see strange things. There shall be a wonder in Hadley! I shall not be dead when it is thought I am!" This Charge he pressed over and over; and afterwards became Delirious.[44]

From the description, it is obvious that Smith suffered in the extreme, and his very visible struggle with his illness no doubt appeared to his audience to be a fight with the Devil.

Whatever the cause, his fits and delirium were frightening not only to him but also to his nurses and watchers. Several of his symptoms echo those that appear in other witchcraft cases. Mather claims that "he had a Speech Incessant and Voluble beyond all imagination, and this in divers Tones and sundry voices, and (as was thought) in various languages." He "cryed out not only of sore pain, but also of sharp Pins, pricking of him: sometimes in his Toe, sometimes in his Arm, as if there had been hundreds of them. But the people upon search never found any more than One." The pins in particular (and the search for them) seem similar to those described in several transcripts in the Salem cases. Also like the Salem accusers, Smith claimed to see an apparition of his tormentor when no one else in the room could: "In his Distresses he exclaimed very much upon the Woman afore-mentioned, naming her, and some others, and saying, 'Do you not see them; There, There, There they stand.' "[45] Who the mysterious "others" were remains unexplained. According to Mather, the strangeness was not limited to Smith's person. There were continuous weird occurrences in the sickroom: "pots of medicines, provided for the sick man, were unaccountably empty'd," "audible scratchings were made about the bed, when his hands and feet lay wholly still," and, most spectacularly, "they beheld fire sometimes on the bed; and when the beholders began to discourse of it, it vanish'd away." A familiar seemed to skulk around him: "Divers people actually felt something often stir in the bed, at a considerable distance from the man; it seem'd as big as a cat, but they could never grasp it."[46] As Mary was previously accused at trial of having "imps" and a "familiar," specifically a "warraneage" or wild black cat, it is not surprising that she would continue to be associated with such diabolical presences.

As further proof that Smith was bewitched, Mather mentions curious details about his corpse: "a Swelling on one Breast, which rendered it like a Womans. His Privities were wounded or burned. On his back, besides Bruises, there were several pricks, or holes, as if done with Awls or Pins." Moreover, the body didn't seem quite dead: "After the Opinion of all had pronounc'd him dead, his Countenance continued as Lively as if he had been Alive; his Eyes closed as in a slumber; and his nether Jaw not falling down."[47] Adding to this concern about the "liveliness" of the body was the fact that a whole day after his death, "those that took him out of the Bed, found him still Warm, though the Season was as Cold as had almost been known in an Age."[48] Whether in fact Smith was actually alive and in some kind of coma we cannot know at this point; in any case, his distraught friends and family did not see his death as a normal one. After his body was moved, there seemed to be a swift degeneration: "On Monday Morning, they found the Face extremely tumified and discolored; 'twas black and blue, and fresh blood seem'd to run down his Cheek in the Hairs."[49] But less explicable than the bodily changes were the apparently supernatural happenings: "Divers noises were also heard in the room where the corpse lay; as the clattering of chairs and stools, whereof no account could be given."[50]

Any of these occurrences would be disturbing to anyone, of course, but especially to people in the seventeenth century. Doctors were often called in to examine suspected victims of witchcraft. While contemporaries knew that some diseases were natural, others—especially those with such visible, painful symptoms—came from either God or the Devil. If bad things were happening to good people, then witchcraft was afoot.[51] The last sentence of Mather's account shows that he had no doubt about what killed William Smith: "Upon the whole, it appeared unquestionable that Witchcraft had brought a period unto the life of so good a man."[52]

Hadley residents seem to have agreed that Mary Webster was responsible. According to Mather, witnesses to Smith's agonies sought to alleviate them at their suspected source: "Some of the young men in the town being out of their wits at the strange calamities thus upon one of their most belov'd neighbors, went three or four times to give disturbance unto the woman thus complain'd of: and all the while they were disturbing of her, he was at ease, and slept as a weary man: yea, these were the only times that they perceiv'd him to take any sleep in all his illness."[53] Mather does not elaborate on what exactly the men did to "disturb" Webster, but the practice of beating or restraining a suspected witch to prevent her from further mischief was a common occurrence; similar activities are referred to in the Salem witch trials. Thomas Hutchinson, in his history of the Massachusetts Bay colony, describes the incident: "While [Philip Smith] lay ill, a number of brisk lads tried an experiment upon the old woman. Having dragged her out of the house, they hung her up until she was near dead, let her down, rolled her sometime in the snow, and at last buried her in it, and there left her."[54] Mather never specifically mentions the hanging, and Hutchinson seems to be the first to describe it. Judd and Drake's versions follow Hutchinson, but the source of the story remains unconfirmed. Mary Webster did indeed survive whatever "disturbance" the men put her through. She lived for another eleven years, and was probably seventy or so when she died in peace in 1696. Thus it is likely that she would have heard about the far more calamitous effects of witchcraft accusation in Salem in 1692. Whether she feared being accused again, we cannot know. After she had escaped the noose once, Hadley residents might well have wondered whether she could be killed at all.

Later tellers of the story show less sympathy toward Smith and his comrades than Mather did. For instance, Hutchinson describes Smith as "an hypocondriack person" who "fancied himself under an evil hand, and suspected a woman, one of his neighbours, and languished and pined away, and was generally supposed to be bewitched to death." Hutchinson reports the outcome with apparent glee: "It happened that she survived and the melancholy man died."[55] Drake also casts aspersions on the behavior of the witch-hunters, and often points out what he perceives to be their foolishness: "The Tormentors must have been Infidels of the worst Type, else they would never have dared to molest one whom they believed to be a Witch, and hence able to afflict them as sorely as Mr. Smith was afflicted. And yet they doubtless believed that a Witch 'could take off her Shoes and go through a Keyhole' to torment whoever she pleased. Such are the Inconsistencies of Believers in Witchcraft."[56] Whether the community really believed Mary was a witch, or simply disliked her and were looking for an excuse to get rid of her, is a question that we can't answer. But Mary Webster ultimately triumphed over them, and one has to imagine that she remained a feared figure in the community after her escape from death.

While surely Mary Webster's troubles are not amusing, it is enjoyable to imagine the community's displeasure at finding they have a quite powerful, death-defying witch among them. Two poems from different periods exemplify two very different kinds of reactions posterity has had to the singular case of Mary Webster. In September of 1893, Julia Taft Bayne published a poem in *New England Magazine* called "Molly Webster" that imagines Mary Webster as a fearsome woman who still had a hold over Hadley almost two hundred years after her death.[57] It is a forty-line poem of rhyming couplets, written in a faux-antique form with archaic spelling and diction. The speaker is a Hadleyite, who opens by asking: "Heard ye e'er of Molly Webster, Molly Webster ye Hadley witch? / Heavie her Curse hath layn vpon Hadley, feered on by Poore & Riche." The speaker insists that Webster was a powerful witch, and that she is still much feared in the town. In one particularly notable line, the speaker proposes an explanation for her acquittal by Boston courts: "Pray God it was not for her bright black eyes & her long curling hair" (line 20). Webster's appearance is never mentioned in the court records, and this detail seems to spring from the poet's imagination. The poem asks for the audience's intervention: "Pray Christian people who here ys Tayl, whoever ye may bee, / Pray for ye Peece of Hadley, for sorely try'd are wee!" (lines 33–34). The final couplet entreats, "God keep vs alle from Salvages, God keep vs alle from Worse;— / Ye Idyl Sport of wicked FRIENDS & Molly Webster's curse!" According to Baynes's own footnotes to the poem, the story comes from Mather's *Magnalia Christi Americana*, and it seems that her speaker has fully imbibed the spirit of fearfulness that Mather enjoined.

On the other end of the spectrum are those who admire Mary Webster's strength and endurance in the face of colonial intolerance. One of her descendants is the well-known Canadian novelist and poet Margaret Atwood.[58] In an address she gave in 1980 when she received the Radcliffe Alumnae Medal, Atwood said of Mary Webster, "She is my favourite ancestor, . . . and if there's one thing I hope I've inherited from her, it's her neck."[59] Atwood dedicated her novel *The Handmaid's Tale* (1985) to Mary Webster, and she made her the subject of her poem "Half-Hanged Mary" (1995).[60] Each of the poem's sections chronicles an hour of Mary's hanging from the tree, from seven at night until eight the next morning. The section in which Mary tells the story of being cut down after hanging is particularly effective at conveying a tone of defiance and almost glee:

> When they came to harvest my corpse
> (open your mouth, close your eyes)
> cut my body from the rope,
> surprise, surprise:
> I was still alive.
>
> Tough luck, folks,
> I know the law:
> you can't execute me twice
> for the same thing. How nice.
>
> I fell to the clover, breathed it in,
> and bared my teeth at them
> in a filthy grin.
> You can imagine how that went over.
>
> Now I only need to look
> out at them through my sky-blue eyes.
> They see their own ill will
> staring them in the forehead
> and turn tail.
>
> Before, I was not a witch.
> But now I am one.[61]

Atwood's final lines sum up the story of Mary Webster best: her Hadley neighbors made a witch out of her in their minds, and their actions only made her more powerful. In a community struggling to maintain order, safety, and sustenance, they easily fell victim to the worst superstitions, and in fact their story was used by Mather and others to foment still more fears and anxieties about the Devil in Massachusetts, eventually culminating in the Salem witch hysteria.

Of course, witches with supernatural powers did not really exist. At the center of witchcraft belief, accusation, and prosecution was a gaping void—a void filled by early modern Englanders and New Englanders by an inverted image, a reflection not of themselves but of their own ideal self-image. Reginald Scot discovered this when he tried to join witch covens himself, sending old women as his agents lest reputed witches be suspicious of the learned Kentish gentleman.[62] Needless to say, he failed, for there were no covens to infiltrate.[63] In New England, the strands of law, popular belief, and demonology were even more closely intertwined than in the old country. In this sense, New England did provide something of a hothouse atmosphere.

For Cotton Mather, what was most important about witchcraft was the evidence it offered for the Devil's activity. If the London edition of *Wonders of the Invisible World* emphasized trials, the original Boston edition leaves no doubt that Mather's main concern was *devils.* Several convicted witches testified that they had signed a pledge in the Devil's book to engage in the "Hellish Design of *Bewitching,* and *Ruining* our Land." Mather's emphasis on the sufferings of Philip Smith served the same purpose. No stronger evidence of "the Invisible World" could be imagined.

Even clear evidence that the accused were innocent did not suffice to shake belief in this invisible world. When the Salem jurors recanted, they blamed "the mysterious delusions of the powers of darkness, and prince of the air" for their errors.[64] In New England, as in Europe, witchcraft trials ended not because judges and juries grew skeptical of the existence of witches but because they came to doubt the evidence linking real individuals to specific acts of witchcraft. The decline in witchcraft belief is a much more complex story than we have been able to tell here. But an important part of it is the absence, in the eighteenth century, of judicial legitimation for the belief. After 1700, witchcraft entered the courts only in slander trials. That is one important reason why we no longer live amid the wonders of the invisible world.

Notes

1. Important and recent readings in the field include Paul Boyer and Stephen Nissenbaum, *Salem Possessed: The Social Origins of Witchcraft* (Cambridge, Mass.: Harvard University Press, 1974); Frances Hill, *A Delusion of Satan: The Full Story of the Salem Witch Trials* (Cambridge, Mass.: Da Capo Press, 1997); Bernard Rosenthal, *Salem Story: Reading the*

Witch Trials of 1692 (New York: Cambridge University Press, 1995); Carol Karlsen, *The Devil in the Shape of a Woman* (New York: W. W. Norton, 1987); and Mary Beth Norton, *In the Devil's Snare: The Salem Witchcraft Crisis of 1692* (New York: Knopf, 2002).

2. For a thorough listing of cases before Salem, see John Demos, *Entertaining Satan: Witchcraft and the Culture of Early New England* (New York: Oxford University Press, 1982), 401–9. Richard Godbeer's *Escaping Salem: The Other Witch Hunt of 1692* (New York: Oxford, 2005) is an excellent source for information on witch trials in Stamford and Fairfield, Connecticut.
3. For more information on the case of Mary Parsons, see Demos's chapter "Hard Thoughts and Jealousies," in *Entertaining Satan*, 246–74.
4. Samuel G. Drake, *Annals of Witchcraft in New England, and Elsewhere in the United States, from Their First Settlement* (Boston: W. Elliot Woodward, 1869), reported that Webster's case "is said to be the most notable of any that ever occurred in the County of Hampshire" (168), echoing Sylvester Judd, *History of Hadley, including the Early History of Hatfield, South Hadley, Amherst and Granby* (Northampton, Mass.: Metcalf & Company, 1863), who called Mary Webster "the most notable witch in Hampshire county" (228).
5. Demos, *Entertaining Satan*, 12–13.
6. James Sharpe, *Instruments of Darkness: Witchcraft in Early Modern England* (Philadelphia: University of Pennsylvania Press, 1997), provides a reliable overview of English witchcraft beliefs, trials, and panics.
7. Keith Thomas, *Religion and the Decline of Magic* (New York: Charles Scribner's Sons, 1971), 436–68.
8. *A Tryal of Witches, at the Assizes Held at Bury St. Edmonds . . . on the Tenth Day of March, 1664* (London, 1682), reprinted in Gilbert Geis and Ivan Bunn, *A Trial of Witches: A Seventeenth-Century Witchcraft Prosecution* (London: Routledge, 1997), 215.
9. Reginald Scot, *The Discoverie of Witchcraft* (New York: Dover Publications, 1972), 4–5 (book 1, chap. 3).
10. *The Examination and Confession of Certain Wytches at Chelmsford . . .* (London, 1566), quoted, in modernized form, in Alan Charles Kors and Edward Peters, eds., *Witchcraft in Europe, 400–1700: A Documentary History* (Philadelphia: University of Pennsylvania Press, 2001), 304–5.
11. Ibid., 306.
12. Sharpe, *Instruments of Darkness*, 71.
13. On demonology, see Stuart Clark, *Thinking with Demons: The Idea of Witchcraft in Early Modern Europe* (Oxford: Oxford University Press, 1997).
14. Lorraine Daston and Katharine Park, *Wonders and the Order of Nature, 1150–1750* (New York: Zone Books, 1998), 121–22, 128.
15. Many of these primary texts are collected and excerpted in *Witch-Hunting in Seventeenth-Century New England: A Documentary History, 1638–1692*, ed. David D. Hall (Boston: Northeastern University Press, 1991), chap. 16, "The Strange Death of Philip Smith (1683–1684)," 260–64.
16. Judd, *History of Hadley*, 237.
17. Drake, *Annals of Witchcraft*, 168.
18. Judd, *History of Hadley*, 31.
19. Kevin M. Sweeney, "From Wilderness to Arcadian Vale: Material Life in the Connecticut River Valley, 1635–1760," in *The Great River: Art and Society of the Connecticut Valley, 1635–1820*, ed. Gerald W. R. Ward and William N. Hosley Jr. (Hartford, Conn.: Wadsworth Atheneum, 1985), 20, table 2. The table indicates the number of male heads of family or single males over age twenty-one arriving from various towns: Windsor (5), Wethersfield

(15), Hartford (25), "Other Connecticut Towns" (4), "Other Hampshire County Towns" (2), "Eastern Massachusetts Towns" (9), and "Unknown" (12), for a total of 72. Hadley was second only to Northampton (with 99) in Hampshire County.

20. Such destructive attacks, and the ongoing threat of further violence, fits a pattern proposed by Norton in *In the Devil's Snare*, which posits a connection between witchcraft accusations and the threat of violence from Native communities. Hadley was certainly vulnerable to such attacks, as other essays in this volume show in greater detail.
21. John Webster's will, dated 25 June 1659, appears in the Hampshire County (Mass.) Probate Court Records (Hampshire County Probate Court and Registry of Deeds, Northampton, Mass.), vol. 1, 20–21. Webster appointed another son, Robert, as his executor. The financial lot of the children (and grandchildren) varied widely. One son, Matthew, received only a sum of £10; William received £70 and Thomas £50, in addition to the split of the Hadley homelot.
22. Judd, *History of Hadley*, 242.
23. Ibid., 228. One of the few notices regarding them appears in the Hampshire County court records for 1668: "Wm Webster of Hadley took the Oath of Fidelity to this Common Wealth."
24. *Records of the Court of Hampshire County*, vol. 1, 1660–1690 (Hampshire County Registry of Probate), 93r.
25. Judd, *History of Hadley*, 236.
26. Robin Briggs, *Witches and Neighbors: The Social and Cultural Context of European Witchcraft* (New York: Viking, 1996); Sharpe, *Instruments of Darkness*, 62–63; Boyer and Nissenbaum, *Salem Possessed*, 31–33; Karlsen, *Devil in the Shape of a Woman*, 46–76.
27. Drake, *Annals of Witchcraft*, 168.
28. Ibid., 168–69. Drake's account is quite similar to that of Judd: "Teams passing to and from the meadow went by her door, and she so bewitched some cattle and horses that they stopped and ran back, and could not be driven by her house. In such cases, the teamsters used to go into the house and whip or threaten to whip her, and she would then let the teams pass" (*History of Hadley*, 237).
29. Drake, *Annals of Witchcraft*, 169. In Judd's version: "She once turned over a load of hay near her house, and the driver went in and was about to chastise her, when she turned the load back again" (*History of Hadley*, 237).
30. Drake, *Annals of Witchcraft*, 169. Again, Drake echoes Judd: "She entered a house, and had such influence upon an infant on the bed or in the cradle, that it was raised to the chamber floor and fell back again, three times, and no visible hand touched it" (*History of Hadley*, 237).
31. Drake, *Annals of Witchcraft*, 169. Judd reports: "There is a story that at another house, a hen came down chimney and got scalded in a pot, and it was soon found that Mary Webster was suffering from a scald" (*History of Hadley*, 237).
32. *Records of the Court of Hampshire County*, fol. 225v.
33. Ibid.
34. Ibid., fol. 226r.
35. Judd includes a transcript of this record in his text and adds in a footnote that "warraneage" is "in some Indian dialects . . . the same as the Nipmuck wallaneag or woollaneag. It was the name of the fisher, or pecan, or wild black cat of the woods. All the testimony on which the indictment was founded, came from persons in Hadley. She had undoubtedly been searched for witch marks by some of the women of Hadley" (238).
36. *Records of the Court of Assistants of the Massachusetts Bay, 1630–1692*, vol. 1 (Boston: The County of Suffolk, 1901), 229–30.

37. Ibid., 233.
38. Judd, *History of Hadley*, 238.
39. *Records of the Court of Hampshire County*, fol. 243v.
40. Drake, *Annals of Witchcraft*, 175, 178–79.
41. Cotton Mather, *Memorable Providences, Relating to Witchcrafts and Possessions* (1689), in *Narratives of the Witchcraft Cases, 1648–1706*, ed. George Lincoln Burr (New York: Charles Scribner's Sons, 1914), 131–34; Cotton Mather, *Magnalia Christi Americana; or, The Ecclesiastical History of New England, from its First Planting, in the Year 1620, unto the Year of Our Lord 1698* ([1698] Hartford, 1852; repr., New York: Russell & Russell, 1967), 454–55.
42. Mather, *Memorable Providences*, 131–32.
43. Ibid., 132.
44. Ibid.
45. Ibid., 132–33.
46. Mather, *Magnalia Christi Americana*, 455.
47. Mather, *Memorable Providences*, 134.
48. Mather, *Magnalia Christi Americana*, 454.
49. Mather, *Memorable Providences*, 134.
50. Mather, *Magnalia Christi Americana*, 454.
51. Briggs, *Witches and Neighbors*, 208–16.
52. Mather, *Memorable Providences*, 134.
53. Mather, *Magnalia Christi Americana*, 455.
54. Thomas Hutchinson, *The History of the Colony and Province of Massachusetts-Bay, from the Charter of King William and Queen Mary, in 1691, until the year 1750*, ed. Lawrence Shaw Mayo, 3 vols. (Cambridge, Mass.: Harvard University Press, 1936; repr., New York: Kraus Reprinting, 1970), 2:14.
55. Ibid.
56. Drake, *Annals of Witchcraft*, 179–80.
57. Julia Taft Bayne, "Molly Webster," *New England Magazine* 15, no. 1 (September 1893): 23. cdl.library.cornell.edu/cgi-bin/moa/moa-cgi?notisid=AFJ3026-0015-4 (accessed 30 June 2008).
58. In her biography, *The Red Shoes: Margaret Atwood Starting Out* (Toronto: HarperFlamingo Canada, 1998), Rosemary Sullivan describes Atwood's connection to Mary Webster as "a kitchen story" (334 n. 13). The authors have not been able to document the nature of Atwood's relationship to Webster.
59. Margaret Atwood, "Witches," in *Second Words: Selected Critical Prose* (Boston: Beacon Press, 1984), 331. This speech has been reproduced in several other publications.
60. Margaret Atwood, "Half-Hanged Mary," in *Morning in the Burned House* (Toronto: McClelland & Stewart, 1995), 58–69.
61. Ibid., 66–67. Quoted by permission.
62. Scot, *Discoverie of Witchcraft*, 27 (book 3, chap. 6).
63. The anthropologist and archaeologist Margaret Murray, in a series of works beginning in the 1920s, claimed that covens were real survivals of an ancient, pre-Christian religion, a belief that has been taken up by some practitioners of the modern religion of witchcraft. Murray has been decisively refuted; see, for instance, Norman Cohn, *Europe's Inner Demons: An Enquiry Inspired by the Great Witch-hunt* (New York: Basic Books, 1975).
64. Kors and Peters, *Witchcraft in Europe*, 437.

7

Hannah Barnard was born in the summer of 1684—in the narrow space of time between Mary Webster's acquittal and the illness of Philip Smith that would throw suspicion Mary's way once more. Hannah was an infant when Hadley boys strung up the newly accused witch. Mary and Hannah shared Hadley's lanes until 1696, when Mary died and young Hannah turned twelve.

Both women are well remembered in Hadley today, but while Mary's memory engages the supernatural, Hannah's legacy is much more tangible. The collections of Michigan's Henry Ford Museum include a spectacular painted cupboard once owned by Hadley's Hannah Barnard, her name boldly inscribed in large letters across the front. Hannah's cupboard is related to a genre of early American furniture of some renown. People familiar with the world of early American antiques know Hadley because of the famous "Hadley chests," ornately carved joined chests, richly embellished with tulip and leaf motifs, sunflowers, hearts, pinwheels, curling tendrils, and undulating vines, that are distinctive to the region. These objects—the "Mercedes of American chests," as curator William Hosley has said—were popular in Hadley and throughout the Connecticut Valley (primarily the upper Connecticut River Valley from Springfield to Deerfield) in the seventeenth century. Decades of scholarship have explored many aspects of their design, construction, and use, but until Ulrich's landmark article, no one had taken full notice of the fact that the initials so prominently displayed on these assertive artifacts belonged not to their maker or buyer, but to the women who acquired and bequeathed them. Her study rewrote not only the history of these important artifacts of seventeenth- and eighteenth-century New England domestic life, but also the history of women, gender, and families in colonial Massachusetts.

Hannah Barnard's Cupboard

Female Property and Identity in Eighteenth-Century New England

Laurel Thatcher Ulrich

> Ah, when she moved, she moved more ways than one:
> The shapes a bright container can contain!
>
> *Theodore Roethke, "I Knew a Woman" (1961)*

Hannah Barnard's cupboard was the most engaging, if not the most elegant, object in an exhibit of Hadley chests mounted at Israel Sack in New York, at the Wadsworth Atheneum in Hartford, and at Memorial Hall Museum in Deerfield, Massachusetts, in the spring of 1993 (figure 7.1). In describing the installation at Israel Sack, curator Suzanne Flynt told a reporter for the *Hartford Courant*: "No doubt about it. It was the dominant object of the show. I set up the other chests like so many little pews leading up to the cupboard, which sat there like a kind of throne or altar at the end of the line." "Altar" seems like the right word to describe this exuberant cupboard with its electric blue columns flanking a symbolic garden. But who or what did it celebrate? Could it have been Hannah Barnard herself? The Hartford reporter thought so. Expressing amazement that a woman could emblazon her own name on an article of furniture in "this rigidly patriarchal period," he pronounced it "a remarkable cupboard with a proto-feminist message." A Hartford collector, on the other hand, reverted to a more traditional interpretation of family life in time past. Surely the cupboard must have been an extravagant gift from Barnard's future husband. It was "a Valentine in furniture."[1]

The authors of the exhibit catalog were more circumspect. Although acknowledging that the woman's name "made a strong statement" about her role "as keeper of the household and a major portion of its assets: valued textiles and silver," they concentrated on stylistic analysis ("The Barnard cupboard was a stage for new Baroque concepts conveyed through traditional Hampshire County ornament") and on details that could be empirically affirmed (under polarized light microscopy the paint on the columns turned out to be a mixture of white lead and Prussian Blue, an artificial pigment first synthesized in Berlin in 1704). Their choice was understandable. In an effort to avoid the romantic excesses of early

FIGURE 7.1. *Hannah Barnard cupboard. Henry Ford Museum and Greenfield Village. Photo courtesy of Pocumtuck Valley Memorial Association, Memorial Hall Museum, Deerfield, Mass.*

twentieth-century collectors, decorative arts scholars are often cautious about exploring the social implications of their materials.[2] Unfortunately, social historians have been even more indifferent to the decorative arts. Most turn to objects, if at all, in the last stages of their projects, looking for illustrations to enliven arguments developed from written sources.[3]

My own interpretation of the Barnard cupboard, therefore, has both a methodological and a content objective. I want to make a particular argument about female identity in early America, and I want to demonstrate the value of object-centered research in social history. These two objectives came together quite by accident. Asked in the same season to write an essay on female identity and to keynote a symposium held in conjunction with the Hadley chest exhibit, I decided to see what would happen if I brought the two projects together. Although I had begun working with museum textile collections in an effort to expand available sources in women's history, I had never considered furniture. I thought of wood and things made of wood as belonging to the male domain. Hannah Barnard's cupboard took me by surprise.

Here was a seemingly expressive, highly personal object marked with a woman's name, but what did it mean? Were the words on the cupboard idiosyncratic or representative of some larger pattern in early American culture? Combined with vines and flowers, were they symbols of fertility, assertions of self, markers of one woman's command of her household goods, or emblems of everywoman's subordination to domestic duty? Or were they merely design conventions or expressions of style? At the most basic level, I wanted to know what the cupboard could tell me about property. In a world where most forms of wealth were controlled by male heads of household, were certain objects in fact owned by women? The cupboard led me backward and forward between objects and documents, suggesting new ways of looking at gender and material life in early America. Hannah's cupboard is neither a protofeminist statement nor a valentine in furniture. It is an index to the shifting sources of female identity in early America. Surviving through three centuries, it exposes the contradictions in our inherited notions of family and the potent mix of violence and refinement in our history.

Hadley, Massachusetts, is a town rich in both history and antiquarian lore. Founded in 1658 by disaffected Puritans from Wethersfield, Windsor, and Hartford, Connecticut, it became one of the founding towns of Hampshire County, Massachusetts, in 1662. Battered during King Philip's War, the town still had only 50 families in 1682, but by the end of what the town history labels the "Fourth Indian War, 1722–1726," there were 117 households. Hadley entered the annals of furniture history in the next century, when in 1883 a Hartford banker began to speak of an antique chest he had found on a summer excursion as his "Hadley chest." By then, similar chests had already found their way into the exhibition space of the Pocumtuck Valley Memorial Association in Deerfield, one of the nation's landmark regional museums. Founded to commemorate the deaths of Deerfield settlers in the French and Indian attack of 1704, the PVMA soon became the guardian of antiques of every description—from a massive door bearing the marks of Indian hatchets to delicate silk embroideries.[4]

The conjunction of war and refinement is not an invention of the nineteenth century. Those who thrived in the "rough, rude, violent, and unpredictable world" of frontier Massachusetts were determined to conquer their French and Indian antagonists and to perpetuate an English culture expressed not only in sermons but in things. Men like Deerfield's famous minister John Williams returned from captivity in Canada to commission carved chests and silver tankards as well as to write of God's providence.[5] Hannah Barnard's cupboard reflects this combination of frontier exigency and English aspiration. Decorated with conventional emblems of fecundity and equally stylized symbols of British sovereignty, it celebrates the wealth and ambition of Hannah's family. The cupboard relates to two important and well-documented furniture traditions—the Connecticut Valley joined-oak cupboard and its close cousin, the equally famous and exhaustively researched "Hadley" chest.

In seventeenth-century New England, a cupboard was an ostentatious and expensive form owned primarily by ministers, merchants, and government officials. When the Reverend Mr. Solomon Stoddard of Northampton, Massachusetts, died in 1729, he left silver, "needle wrought cushions," and fine linens as well as a "cupboard in the Parler." Mary Rowlandson, the author of the famous captivity narrative, inherited a cupboard when her first husband, the Reverend Mr. Joseph Rowlandson, died in Wethersfield, Connecticut, in 1678. The Rowlandson cupboard is typical of the so-called sunflower furniture made in Wethersfield (figure 7.2). The maker of the Wethersfield cupboards used black paint to imitate the ebony turnings on English cupboards, which were often ornamented with exotic woods or mother-of-pearl. Such cupboards were designed both to store and to display wealth. Turned columns supported an overhanging top shelf that was draped with a rich textile called a "cupboard cloth." Often the cupboard, though valuable, was worth much less than the textiles stacked in its dark and almost inaccessible lower section. The textiles in the Rowlandson inventory, for example, were valued at almost fifty pounds. The cupboard, appraised at two pounds, was roughly equivalent to twenty-eight towels and napkins, worth less than ten pillowbeers (pillow cases).[6]

If few families in this period had cupboards, fine linen, or silver, most had at least one chest. An ordinary chest was merely a large box with a hinged lid. The cheapest ones were made of plain boards, nailed together, but the sturdiest and most valuable were constructed like a cupboard (or a house), with panels fitted into a heavy frame with mortise-and-tenon joints. Some of these "joined" chests had one or two drawers beneath. In probate inventories, they are often described

FIGURE 7.2. *Mary Rowlandson cupboard. Lancaster Public Library, Lancaster, Mass.*

as "chests *with* drawers." Joiners also made "chests *of* drawers," a furniture innovation that abandoned the hinged top of the conventional chest, allowing easier access to stored linens or clothing by devoting all of the space to drawers. Hannah Barnard's cupboard is a compromise between a traditional cupboard, like the one inherited by Mary Rowlandson, and a chest of drawers. The upper half has doors, like a cupboard; the lower half drawers, like a chest. In fact, a chest of drawers with dark blue (almost black) paint at Historic Deerfield is almost identical to the lower half of Hannah's cupboard and was perhaps made by the same joiner.[7] (In the eighteenth century, the "joiners" who made the Rowlandson and Barnard cupboards and hundreds of chests, chests of drawers, and chests with drawers in rural towns like Hadley were succeeded by "cabinetmakers" who made lighter, more modern pieces using dovetailed boards and fine veneer. These were sometimes called "cases" rather than "chests" of drawers.)

Furniture scholars have identified at least sixteen variants of the so-called Hadley chest, made in Hadley and nearby Hampshire County towns from the 1680s to about 1730.[8] Some have drawers, some do not. Since most are marked with initials or a name, genealogists have been able to link many to young women born in nearby towns. In contrast, plain nailed chests made during the same period often have men's initials. Although early collectors wrote of the Hadley chest as a "folk" form, furniture scholars today emphasize its dynamic origins in a cluster of seventeenth-century shop traditions, ranging from Wethersfield, Connecticut, to the north-country joiners employed by John Pynchon at Springfield, Massachusetts. The name derives from an early piece, found in Hadley, carved with a distinctive, two-petaled tulip. The exuberant and varied decoration led early collectors to label them "dower" or "marriage chests."[9]

Although what furniture scholars consider true Hadley chests include tulips in some form, the variety of styles is really quite remarkable. Two initialed chests made about the same time as Hannah's cupboard suggest the range. The "MS" chest, with its undulating vines and explicit sexual imagery in the central panel, places the owner's initials in tight lozenges to the right and left. The "SH" chest, in contrast, splashes tulips over the entire ground, the shallow carving highlighted in red paint over a stippled background. The initials on the SH chest command the central panel, standing out all the more boldly because, with the exception of a small area just above, they occupy the only plain field on the chest (figures 7.3 and 7.4).

Almost all Hadley chests are marked in some way. Like the linens they were designed to protect, most have two initials, though a handful have three.[10] Only 8 of the more than 120 marked chests have complete names. With one exception, all of those with full names seem to have been made for women from the towns of Northampton and Hadley. Esther Lyman, Sarah Strong, Esther Cook, and Mary Burt all came from Northampton, and Elisabeth Warner and Thankful Taylor from Hadley, though they married men from Enfield and Suffield (now in Connecticut). Mary Pease, who was born in Enfield, was related to Warner by marriage (figure 7.5).[11] The four Northampton chests employ a distinctive fleur-de-lis pattern as well as a variant of the Hadley tulip, though there are differences in the way the names are handled. Esther Lyman's uses the curling tendrils typical of the SH and many other Hadley chests; on the other chests, the names are carved in unadorned letters. The placement of the names also varies. On five chests, including three from Northampton, the name marches boldly across the upper rail (figure 7.6). Mary Pease's appears on the lower rail,

Figure 7.3. *"MS" chest with drawers. Hatfield, Mass., area, c. 1715. Wadsworth Atheneum, Hartford. Wallace Nutting Collection. Gift of J. Pierpont Morgan, by exchange, and the Evelyn Bonar Storrs Trust Fund.*

just above the drawers; Esther Cook's, which seems to have been altered or replaced in the twentieth century, sits somewhat awkwardly in the central panel.[12]

All of that suggests consumer choice. At any given point, several joiners were capable of creating carved chests, varying the final product, including the placement of names and initials. Ironically, as Philip Zea has observed, "regional acceptance of these hybridized expressions of American joinery was accelerated by the devastation of King Philip's War, particularly in Hampshire County where wholesale rebuilding and refurnishing was required."[13] The Hannah Barnard cupboard, probably made just after the end of Queen Anne's War

FIGURE 7.4. *"SH" chest with drawers. Hadley or Hatfield, Mass., c. 1710. Pocumtuck Valley Memorial Association, Memorial Hall Museum, Deerfield, Mass. Gift of George Sheldon, before 1886.*

(1713), explodes with new adaptations of old ideas. It builds on the Hadley chest tradition, but it is not carved. Although many Hadley chests were painted before assembly, not so with the Barnard cupboard. In fact, it belongs to a small cluster of Hampshire furniture related by surface decoration alone. The "SW" chest at Memorial Hall in Deerfield is a chest *with* drawers (figure 7.7). A chest *of* drawers at Winterthur was made in a different manner by a different joiner, yet both seem to have been decorated by the person who painted Hannah's cupboard. This unknown painter could have been the joiner who made Hannah's

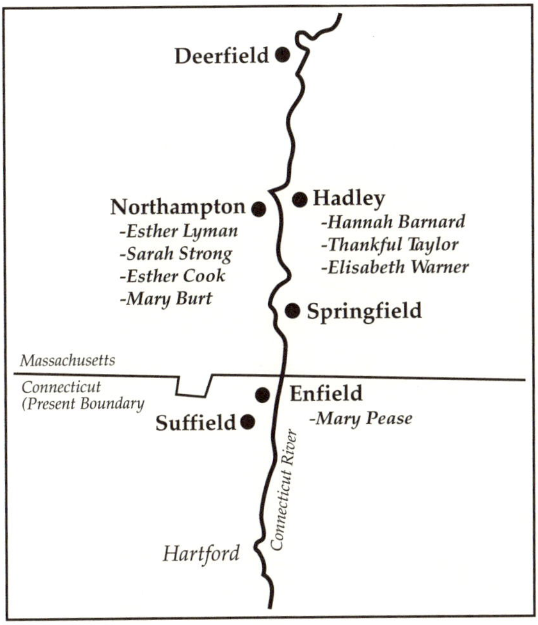

FIGURE 7.5. *Sites associated with chests. Melinda Chiou, Colophon Type and Design.*

cupboard, one of the men who made the other chests, or a different person entirely. The character of the painting suggests someone used to working with wood, however. The designs were laid out with a straightedge and compass, the outlines incised into the wood, then filled in with pigment.[14]

The Barnard cupboard draws from most of the Hadley variations, interpreting each motif in paint rather than carving. It has undulating vines like the MS chest, curling letters like the Esther Lyman chest, inverted hearts like those on the SH chest, leaf and diamond constructions like those on the "EE" and "LB" chests, and a row of half-circles like those on the bottom rail of an uninscribed example. But it doesn't stop there. The painted drawer "moldings" are shaped like the actual moldings on early cupboards or chests. Glorying in paint, the creator of Hannah's cupboard bent tradition in yet another way. The turned posts of cupboards were meant to be black. The flamboyant blue on Hannah's cupboard shows off a vibrant new tint unavailable before. An awareness of European imports is also evident in the segmented roses that march across the drawers. Although they might have been laid out with a straightedge and compass, they look very much like the roses on a tin-glazed plate owned by Esther Williams of Deerfield, who married in the same year as Hannah Barnard (figure 7.8). In English delftware, flat "roses" were sometimes combined with checkered "thistles." The upright blossom in the central panel of Hannah's cupboard

FIGURE 7.6. *Sarah Strong chest with drawer. Northampton, Mass., early eighteenth century. Historic Northampton.*

is in fact a thistle. The plump fruits on either side of the central panel are pomegranates, another widely used motif in English decorative arts.[15]

The designer brought all of these elements together in a unified and powerful composition. Hannah's name is integral to the design, yet its placement sets it apart from the Hadley and Northampton chests, perhaps because the cupboard form demanded a different treatment. A chest, with its lidded top, left several unbroken surfaces for decoration. A cupboard required a vertical opening. Unless the designer wanted to string the name across a drawer, he (or she) had to fit it into one of the panels on the top, easy to do with an initial, hard to accomplish with a full name. The solution was brilliant. The name "Hannah" is a palindrome, a word that reads the same backward or forward. The composition takes advantage of this repetition allowing the three letters *H*, *A*, and *N* to form two strong columns. "Barnard," despite its tantalizing internal rhyme, was more difficult, since seven letters required four rows rather than three. Again the painter allowed *A* and *N* to dominate, keeping the curved letters, *B*, *R*, and *D*

FIGURE 7.7. *"SW" chest with drawers. Hadley, Mass., area, c. 1718. Pocumtuck Valley Memorial Association, Memorial Hall Museum, Deerfield, Mass. Gift of George Sheldon, 1892.*

somewhat narrower, filling in the extra space with a square.[16] (The handling of the curved letters seems to be typical of Hadley chests, however, as the narrowness of the *S* on the SH chest shows.)

Inside the columns formed by Hannah's name are two bold towers formed of seemingly unrelated things—paired leaves, pomegranates, hearts, and diamonds. Nothing on the cupboard seems more "folklike," yet the composition is probably an abstracted version of the borders often used in late-Renaissance tapestries and engravings. A cushion cover owned by Edward Taylor, the pastor of nearby Westfield, Massachusetts, shows a central vase of flowers bordered by pillared constructions of fruit, flowers, leaves, urns, and masks, the massing

FIGURE 7.8. *Plate. Tin-glazed earthenware, England, early eighteenth century. Pocumtuck Valley Memorial Association, Memorial Hall Museum, Deerfield, Mass. Gift of Mrs. Bessie Gamons, 1954.*

strikingly similar to the borders on the Barnard cupboard (figure 7.9). The busy turnings on seventeenth-century cupboards are, of course, a three-dimensional version of the same thing.

Thus, Hannah's cupboard is both idiosyncratic and representative of larger patterns in the decorative arts. Looking backward to the sober seventeenth-century households that sent the first settlers up the river toward Hadley, it embraced the expanding world of eighteenth-century commerce. Made by an unknown local joiner who knew how to construct both chests of drawers and cupboards, it was likely decorated by a second person who added a flamboyant new pigment to a repertoire of designs familiar from local carved furniture and English ceramics to create a highly personal rendition of a traditional "woman's chest." The cupboard itself can tell us that much.

One of the staples of social history—probate records—can tell us a bit more. In Hampshire County, Massachusetts, as elsewhere in the English-speaking

FIGURE 7.9. *Tapestry cushion cover. England, c. 1610–1615. Pocumtuck Valley Memorial Association, Memorial Hall Museum, Deerfield, Mass. Gift of the Reverend John Taylor to Deerfield Academy Museum, before 1806. Brought by the Reverend Edward Taylor from England in 1662.*

world, cupboards and chests, like the textiles, ceramics, and silver they were designed to store, belonged to that category of property known as "movables." According to English law, movables, or "personalty," formed the core inheritance of women. Unless other circumstances required a different arrangement, sons received buildings and land, daughters a combination of household goods, animals, and occasionally servants or slaves. There was a principal of equality in seventeenth-century New England, but it assumed differential treatment of males and females. When John Billings of Hatfield died unmarried, the court divided his worldly possessions among his siblings "in Equall and proportion, the said Brothers to have all the Lands Equallie divided to them and the said Sarah to have her share in the Moveable goods." The court used similar language when it ordered that Joseph Barnard's sons were "to injoy all the lands in Equall proportions . . . and the daughters to be payd out of the moveable Estate so farr as they will Extend." When another man willed his lands to his sons and brother but neglected to provide for his daughters, the court added "that the daughters of the said deceased shall have their portions Out of the Movables."[17]

Anthropologist Annette Weiner suggests that the Western concepts of "real property" and "movables" are one manifestation of "the world's most ancient and profound economic classification"—the distinction between alienable and inalienable possessions. "What makes a possession inalienable," Weiner explains, "is its exclusive and cumulative identity with a particular series of owners through time." In English property law, that series of owners was the patriline. Movables might pass freely, but real property was protected from indiscriminate inheritance. Typically, widows inherited the use of land rather than the land itself. At death or remarriage, real estate reverted to male heirs. For the possessors, Weiner argues, inalienable possessions resolved the paradox of "keeping-while-giving": "Some things, like most commodities, are easy to give. But there are other possessions that are imbued with the intrinsic and ineffable identities of their owners which are not easy to give away. Ideally, these inalienable possessions are kept by their owners from one generation to the next within the closed context of family, descent group, or dynasty."[18] The association of males with land and females with movables was not, therefore, a neutral division of resources. The possession of "real" property secured male identity. A man who passed his name and land to a son transcended his own mortality as he validated his own authority. He kept while giving.

In the classic "thirds" offered to a widow, land reverted to the male line at the woman's death. In the Connecticut River Valley, as Toby Ditz has shown, daughters received land only when personalty was lacking; the value of that land was always significantly less than that inherited by their brothers. By custom and law, fathers "could simply exclude all daughters and members of daughters' families from heritable rights in land and confine their share of property to personalty."[19] In such a system, women themselves became "movables," changing their names and presumably their identities as they moved from one male-headed household to another. But what if some portion of these goods retained the daughter's maiden name even as she lost it? That is the puzzle presented by Hannah Barnard's cupboard.

Hannah Barnard married John Marsh in 1715. She died in 1717, leaving an infant daughter Abigail. That daughter married Waitstill Hastings in 1736, and in

1742 Abigail and Waitstill had a daughter. They named her, not just Hannah, but Hannah *Barnard* Hastings (figure 7.10). The use of middle names is extraordinarily rare in Hadley (or anywhere else in New England) in this period. Hannah Barnard Hastings may be the only child in eighteenth-century New England named for a cupboard. Not surprisingly, she inherited it.[20] The cupboard preserved her grandmother's name, but the name also transformed the cupboard. Marked in this way, it became less portable, less exchangeable. It had become an inalienable possession.

Hannah's cupboard points toward invisible and little understood notions of inheritance lying just beneath the surface of early probate records. Hannah Barnard had been John Marsh's second wife; he had married the first time in 1704. After Hannah's death, he married a third time. He was only in his forties when he died in 1725, but he was already a wealthy man, in part, one suspects, because of the goods brought to marriage by three wives, all daughters of substantial families.[21] He owned parcels of "meadow," "woodland," "upland," and "outland" in addition to his homestead with its buildings and orchard. He owned horses as well as two yoke of "fat oxen" and tools for farming and lumbering. He also owned an "Indian [perhaps West Indian] Boy

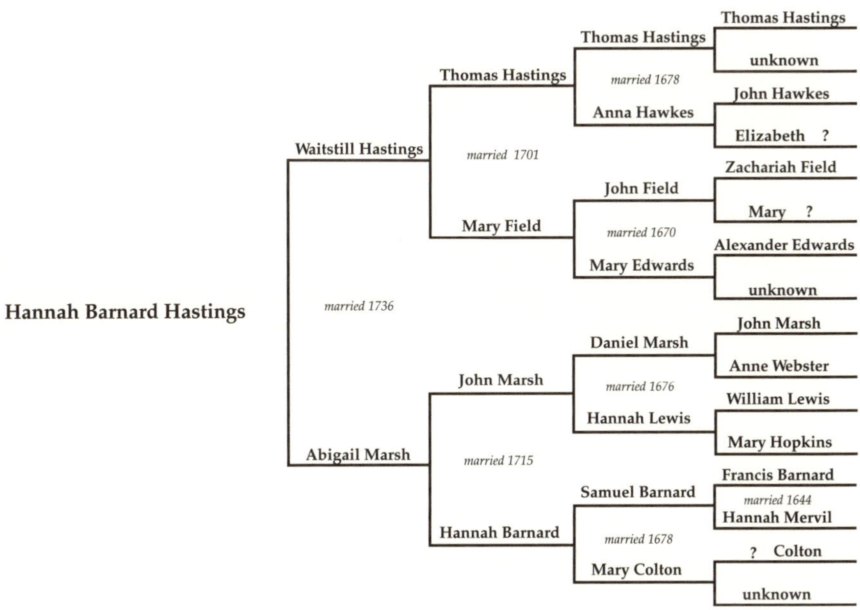

FIGURE 7.10. *Hannah Barnard Hastings pedigree. Melinda Chiou, Colophon Type and Design.*

Sippey about 14 Years Old," and at the time of his death he had five minor children, including Hannah's daughter Abigail.

His will and inventory make clear what the cupboard only suggests, that within the clutter of household goods defined as "movables," certain objects were marked, literally or figuratively, with female lineages. The inventory lists household goods in three separate places, in the general list following land and cattle and under the subtitles: "3d Wives Goods" and "2d Wives Goods." Marsh's only son, then two years old, was promised all of his father's real estate, but Abigail was to receive £120 "to be paid in what was her own Mothers," plus "her Mothers Wearing Cloaths . . . to be given her free." The younger girls were to receive portions worth £100. The inventory suggests that these goods, too, were to come from property their mother brought to marriage.[22]

The three lists are strikingly parallel in both organization and value. Each includes brass, iron, and pewter, earthenware and glass, "wooden ware," including furniture, and a range of valuable textiles divided into "Woolen," "Linnen," and "Bedding." The household goods on the general list amount to seventy-two pounds, Hannah Barnard's goods total eighty-five pounds, the third wife's goods eighty-seven pounds. The goods on the first list, some of which might have originated with Marsh's first wife, include "A Carved Work Chest" valued at thirty shillings. One can easily imagine a Hadley chest here, perhaps one marked with initials or a name. The furniture listed with the "2d Wives Goods," our Hannah Barnard, includes "a floward Chest" valued at thirty-two shillings and another "ditto" at ten. There is no mention of a "cupboard," though there must have been one at some point because the list of linens includes "2 Cupboard Cloths." The furniture listed with the "3d Wives Goods" includes a more modern (and expensive) item: "A case of drawers," valued at four pounds. The third wife, like Hannah, had a store of sheets, towels, tablecloths, and napkins, but she had no cupboard cloth.[23]

Perhaps the more expensive "floward chest" on Hannah's list was the "cupboard" that survives today, though it is strange that the inventory takers, who carefully distinguished between the "carved" and "floward" chests and who knew the difference between a "chest" and a "*case* of drawers," would call a cupboard a chest. Perhaps the cupboard was too visible a reminder of the dead wife to remain in the household after Marsh married again. Hannah's section of the inventory includes nine pounds, "money due for sundries in Ensign Moses Cooks hands." Moses Cook was Hannah Barnard's brother-in-law. Could Mary Cook have taken the cupboard (and perhaps little Abigail) at the time of her sister's death? We cannot know. There is no question, however, about the intent of

Marsh's will. The goods Hannah Barnard brought to marriage formed the core of her own daughter's inheritance.

Marsh's inventory has been known to furniture researchers since the 1930s, yet none has noted the importance of the separate listing of each wife's goods. When Hannah's cupboard surfaced in the antiques market in 1936, the Reverend Clair Franklin Luther, the first systematic cataloger of Hadley chests, was certain Marsh's inventory contained the clue to the identity of the similar SW chest. Marsh's third wife was named Sarah Williams. Surely the first flowered chest in the inventory was Hannah's cupboard and the second belonged to Sarah. It was an attractive notion, yet it ignored the structure of the document. Unless one assumes that Hannah Barnard conveniently anticipated the initials of her successor, the least likely place to find a chest marked "SW" was with her goods![24] Surprisingly, the 1992 catalog of the Hadley exhibit repeated the error. The problem was not so much faulty scholarship as an inability to break free of patriarchal paradigms.

In scholarly as well as common usage we speak of the "Marsh family," the "Barnard family," or the "Hastings family." Biologically, of course, there is no such thing. One can speak of a particular family through time only by ignoring the fundamental basis of reproduction, that every child requires both a mother and father. Barring sibling incest, in each generation half of the genes must come from outside the original group. But law, culture, and convenience conspire to make us forget that. The pedigree of Hannah Barnard Hastings illustrates the fragility—and complexity—of female lineage (figure 7.10). Notice how easy it is to trace the "Hastings" line, reading along the top of the chart from Hannah to her father Waitstill Hastings, then to Waitstill's father, grandfather, and great-grandfather, all named Thomas Hastings, the repetition of names illustrating Weiner's concept of "keeping while giving." Everywhere on the chart, going from child to father to grandfather is simple—from Abigail Marsh to John Marsh to Daniel Marsh to John Marsh, for example, or from Hannah Barnard to her father and grandfather. But to trace daughter-mother lineages is more difficult. The names of all eight of Hannah's great-great-grandfathers survive; only three of her great-great-grandmothers have complete names. Two are simply "unknown."

Even though biologically the notion of descent from mother to daughter makes every bit as much sense as from father to son, it is extraordinarily hard to define such a "line" within Western genealogical conventions. To enfold a female lineage in the patrilineal line of descent, a girl would have to carry a chain of surnames that grew heavier with each generation. Abigail and Waitstill Hastings acknowledged just one link in that chain when they named their daughter for her maternal grandmother. Yet the name persisted for two more generations. Hannah Barnard Hastings had a daughter named Hannah Barnard Kellogg (born 1769) and a granddaughter named Hannah Barnard Hastings Kellogg (born 1817).[25] The cupboard perpetuated one woman's identity for more than a century after her death.

In the Marsh family, demographic accidents—the early deaths of two wives, the husband's own premature demise—exposed female lineages. More commonly, the formulaic dispersal of movables, as in "one-third of my household goods," concealed the female labor that created and maintained those goods and the social customs if not the female voices that directed their disposal. Because daughters customarily received their portions at marriage rather than at the death of their father, wills and inventories actually mask much of what moved from one generation to another. Land can be traced in deeds, but movables, by definition, flowed outside the constraints of law. That is why object-centered research is so useful. Probate records can tell us what sorts of objects people possessed at any one time and what kinds of things fathers (and occasionally mothers) willed to their children at the end of life, but well-documented histories of surviving objects can tell us how certain movables were actually transmitted—or lost—over time.

Almost inadvertently, decorative arts historians produce a great deal of social history simply by pursuing their most basic enterprise—establishing provenance. Challenging the attribution of a Hadley chest first documented in 1935, Marius Peladeau demonstrated lineal descent from mother to daughter. Making a slight detour to include a posthumous stepdaughter, the line stretched from 1700 to the early twentieth century. Museum curators can no doubt point to many other examples of this sort, on unmarked as well as marked objects.[26] One need not assume awareness of a "female line." All that is required is a belief in each generation that certain objects ought to pass from mother to daughter. Establishing provenance is seldom that easy, however, nor is direct transmission from mother to daughter the only alternative to patrilineal descent.

The mystery of the SW chest suggests the complexity of the enterprise. The first accession records for Memorial Hall listed the chest as an "Ancient oak cabinet—not carved but painted—bought of Jonathan A. Saxton about 1870 Long in the Saxton [—] / Geo. Sheldon." The blank is in the original, perhaps reflecting Sheldon's uncertainty. By 1908, he had in fact changed his story, writing that the "Oak chest, marked SW . . . came down in the White family." A printed catalog published at the same time attributes it to Susanna White of the Mayflower.[27] The 1992 exhibit catalog understandably debunked the Mayflower connection, noting the propensity of nineteenth-century antiquarians to assign English origins to every piece of old furniture, yet they too offered a somewhat fanciful explanation of the origins of the chest. Since George Sheldon purchased it from Jonathan Saxton about 1870 and since the only payment to Saxton recorded in Sheldon's daybook relates to the estate of Charles Williams, "The 'SW' Chest was probably a Williams family heirloom." Their reasoning was straightforward. Since Charles Williams was a "collateral descendant" of John Marsh's third wife, Sarah Williams, the Barnard cupboard and the SW chest were probably "successively brought into the Marsh household in 1715 and 1718."[28] Notice once again how patrilineal constructions ("Williams family heirloom," "Marsh household") simplified the story. The catalog does not explain why an object ostensibly belonging to the third wife was listed with the second wife's goods, nor does it attempt to show how a piece of furniture belonging to a woman married successively to a Marsh and a Grey ended up, six generations later, in the "Williams family."

Working with the same set of documents but with a different set of assumptions about family history produces alternative routes to Jonathan Saxton. One of these even connects to a Sarah Williams who died in Deerfield in 1720. This Sarah was a second cousin of John Marsh's Sarah and a first cousin of the Esther Williams who owned the tin-glazed plate with the rose that looks so much like the ones on the Barnard cupboard and the SW chest. Born in Roxbury, this Sarah Williams married Samuel Barnard, Hannah's cousin, in 1718. Like Hannah, she died giving birth to an only child. Sarah's infant, however, did not survive. Samuel Barnard left Deerfield after his wife's death and though he married again had no children. When he died in 1762, he left land and property to the sons of his brother Ebenezer Barnard. Although there is no way of proving this, at any time between 1720 and 1762 he could also have given movables to his brother's daughters. One of those daughters became the grandmother of Jonathan Saxton, whose sister Tirza was the wife of the Charles Williams mentioned in George Sheldon's daybook.[29] Thus, the SW chest, if it belonged to Sarah Williams Barnard, could easily have been both a Saxton and a Williams "family heirloom."

It could also have come down "in the White family" either as an heirloom or as a piece of junk left behind in one of the many family migrations. Jonathan Saxton's mother-in-law, Mercy White, was the daughter of Salmon White, a *male* with the initials "SW." Although Salmon was too young to have been the original owner of the chest, his aunt Susannah Wells, who became Susannah White at marriage, might have been the "Susannah White" who inspired the Mayflower legend. She moved to Hardwick, Massachusetts, and later to Vermont.

But this trail, too, leads back to Hannah Barnard's cousin Samuel and his wife Sarah Williams. Samuel's sister Sarah Wells was Susannah White's adoptive mother. One can imagine the initials directing the chest from Sarah Williams to Sarah Wells to Susannah White and then by some forgotten path, perhaps through Salmon White, to Jonathan Saxton. By then the chest might have been less a treasure than a burden. The first Hadley chests were often discovered on back porches, in barns, or in slaughterhouses. One even traveled to the Midwest as a shipping crate.[30]

Barring the discovery of a forgotten will, inventory, account book, or letter with an explicit reference to the SW chest, there is no way of knowing how it reached Jonathan Saxton, nor can we know for certain whether the *S* stands for Sarah, Susannah, or Salmon, or the *W* for White, Wells, Williams, Wright, Wait, or any other of the ubiquitous *W*'s in Hadley or Deerfield. The first families of Deerfield and Hadley are so intertwined that it is almost impossible to trace one line of descent without encountering another. The very difficulty of establishing provenance reinforces the central insight of this essay, however. Families are social constructions, made and remade over time. Family identities, like personal identities, are built from selective fragments of the past—names, stories, and material objects.

Fortunately, enough well-documented objects survive to help us see how gender intersects with property in the continuing struggle to define the meaning of family. Historian Barbara Ward became interested in the subject of female inheritance when she was researching provenance for the silver entries in *The Great River*, a catalog produced for a major exhibit of Connecticut Valley objects. Probate records revealed, for example, that the silver caudle cups John Davenport bequeathed to his minor daughters in 1731 were to be engraved "D / IE" to represent the girls' parents. But a surviving cup, belonging to an older daughter and not mentioned in the will, is engraved "AD." Since the daughter's name was Abigail, the initials were appropriate, but the form of the cup marked it as much older. Ward believes it was made for the paternal grandmother, a woman whose name also happened to be Abigail Davenport. The "AD" cup might well have been a prototype for later gifts from the father and mother to their younger daughters. The same process was at work in the case of Prudence Stoddard, who owned two pieces of Stoddard silver, a teapot with the family coat of arms given her at marriage in 1750, and a standing salt made half a century earlier and inscribed with the initials of her paternal grandparents, the Reverend Solomon Stoddard and his wife, Esther Mather. Prudence, in turn, passed these objects on to her daughters.[31] Ward's catalog entries demonstrate the power of combining object analysis with genealogical research.

Women did not always pass on their gifts to female descendants, however, as a silver tankard from the collections of Historic Deerfield shows. Fortunately, the tankard, dating from 1700–1710, bears its genealogy on its handle (figure 7.11). The first set of initials belonged to Mary Williams Cook of Newton, Massachusetts, who bequeathed it to her nephew, Dr. Thomas Williams of Deerfield. It then descended to several generations of Williamses, each heir adding his or her initials in turn. In this case, a lineage obscured in marriage returned to the paternal line in a gift from a woman to her brother's son. The inscription on another Deerfield piece, also associated with the Williams family, shows a different line of descent. The inscription reads: "This Cann Is Presented to Mrs: Anna Williams / By her Uncle and Aunt Hindsdale / 1754." Aunt Hinsdale, born Abigail Williams, was Anna Williams's paternal aunt. Although Anna might already have married Jacob Cushing, the "Mrs" before her name denotes social rather than marital status. The cann (a type of mug), which symbolized a familial relationship between two women whose maiden names were "Williams," bore the Hinsdale coat of arms and descended in the Cushing family. Meanwhile, "Aunt Hinsdale" was widowed twice, becoming first Madame Hall and then Madame Silliman. When she died in 1783, she left more silver with the Hinsdale arms to the church at Deerfield and to her niece Sarah Williams. She also manumitted her slaves, honoring gendered notions of property by giving her male

FIGURE 7.11. *Silver tankard, c. 1700–1710. Jeremiah Dummer, Boston, 1645–1718. Historic Deerfield, Inc., Acc. #59–88. Photo by Helga Studio.*

servant, Jockton, one hundred acres of New Hampshire land, and her female servant, Chloe, "a Bible, a cow, a feather bed, a brass kettle, a pot, 2 tramels, chests, hand irons, chairs and pewter things." In addition, she gave clothing, jewelry, and other valuables to seven female relatives, including nieces Abigail Norton and Abigail Woodword and stepgranddaughters Frances Silliman and Abigail Williams Hall.[32] Such bequests assert an expansive, almost fluid, notion of family that undercuts simple notions of patrilineal *or* matrilineal descent. It also suggests how a woman, particularly a much-married woman, might accumulate multiple lineages. Identity for such a person derived less from membership in a group than in the ability to move between and among groups.

In a legal system that required the subordination of women, one might imagine a female identity that was inherently fragile and derivative, shaped through attachment to others rather than assertion of self. Yet, ironically, the force of patriarchy might have encouraged certain women to develop a more complex and in some ways autonomous sense of self than their brothers or sons. Never able to step into a ready-made identity, they learned to mediate between a family of origin and one or more families of marriage. Surely, for men as well as women, "family" meant brothers and sisters, aunts, uncles, and cousins as well as husbands, wives, parents and children, but for women lived relationships almost always cut across patrilineal markers. In Annette Weiner's words, "To draw on other social identities, to enhance one's history, and to secure the appropriate transmission of inalienable possessions for the next generation involve voluminous exchanges, elaborate strategies, and productive efforts." The bequests of Mary Cook and Abigail Hinsdale point to one of the central themes in Weiner's work—exchanges between brothers and sisters and their offspring, "the kinship counterpart of keeping-while-giving."[33]

Such exchanges did not require marked objects, of course, only a continuing effort to cultivate and maintain associations across generations. Still, the marking of objects, like the naming of children, tightened connections. Since brothers and sisters commonly named children for each other, relationships between a woman and her namesakes might take on heightened significance. At her death in 1720, Joanna Dyer of Exeter, New Hampshire, divided her pewter among her sisters' daughters, Joanna Perryman, Joanna Leavitt, and Joanna Thing, though her ring marked "JG" went to a brother's daughter who like herself had been born Joanna Gilman.[34] A sister might honor a sibling with a given name, but only exchanges between a sister and her brother's daughter fully returned the gift to the giver.

With that insight, we return once again to Hannah Barnard, moving back a generation to consider the life of her paternal aunt and namesake, Hannah

Barnard Westcarr Beaman, a childless and twice-married woman who left a fragmentary but colorful history. Born in Hartford, Connecticut, about 1646, she was already the wife of John Westcarr (or Wescar) when she was charged at the county court in Springfield, Massachusetts, in March 1673 for wearing silk "contrary to law" (see Lynne Z. Bassett's chapter in this volume). She was presented again in 1675 and in January 1677 was admonished "for wearing silk in a flaunting garb, to the great offence of several sober persons in Hadley." Hannah was not alone in her rebellion. In 1673, her brother Joseph Barnard and his wife Sarah were presented, as well as Sarah's two unmarried sisters, daughters of Elder John Strong of Northampton. In 1675, "38 wives and maids and 30 young men" were charged, "some for wearing silk and that in a flaunting manner, and others for long hair and other extravagancies." At a 1677 court, Abigail, the wife of Mark Warner, and Hannah Lyman, the sixteen-year-old daughter of Richard Lyman of Northampton, were among the defendants. Hannah Lyman was fined ten shillings for "wearing silk in a flaunting manner in an offensive way and garb, not only before, but when she stood presented, not only in ordinary but in extraordinary times."[35]

If the names Warner, Strong, and Lyman sound familiar, they are. Like Hannah Barnard Westcarr, several of these silk-wearing offenders of late seventeenth-century Hampshire County were paternal aunts of young women who many years later put their full names, in an assertive if not a flaunting manner, on chests and cupboards (figure 7.12). The fathers of the silk wearers were not the river gods of the upper Connecticut, the Stoddards, Williamses, Dwights, Ashleys, Porters, Partridges, and Pynchons who dominated religion and politics in Hampshire County for generations, but a group of ambitious families a step down on the social scale. Their children's insistence on the right to wear clothing reserved only for elites suggests as much. Hannah's father, Frances Barnard, was one of the "perpetual pioneers" of early New England. Born in England, he was first in Hartford, then Hadley, then by the 1670s in Deerfield. In a frontier environment, his children moved from rebellion to respectability. The oldest son, Thomas, graduated from Harvard College in 1679 and was ordained pastor of the First Church of Andover, Massachusetts, in 1682. The middle son, Joseph, was convicted in 1681 of selling liquor to Indians but by 1687 was clerk of the Deerfield town meeting, serving until he died from wounds received in an ambush of "Enymy Indians" in August 1695. Joseph's widow soon married Captain Jonathan Wells, a man who had also overcome his youthful transgressions to become a military and political leader.[36]

Hannah Westcarr Beaman's own trajectory was similar. A year after her presentation in court for outraging "several sober persons" with her flaunting apparel,

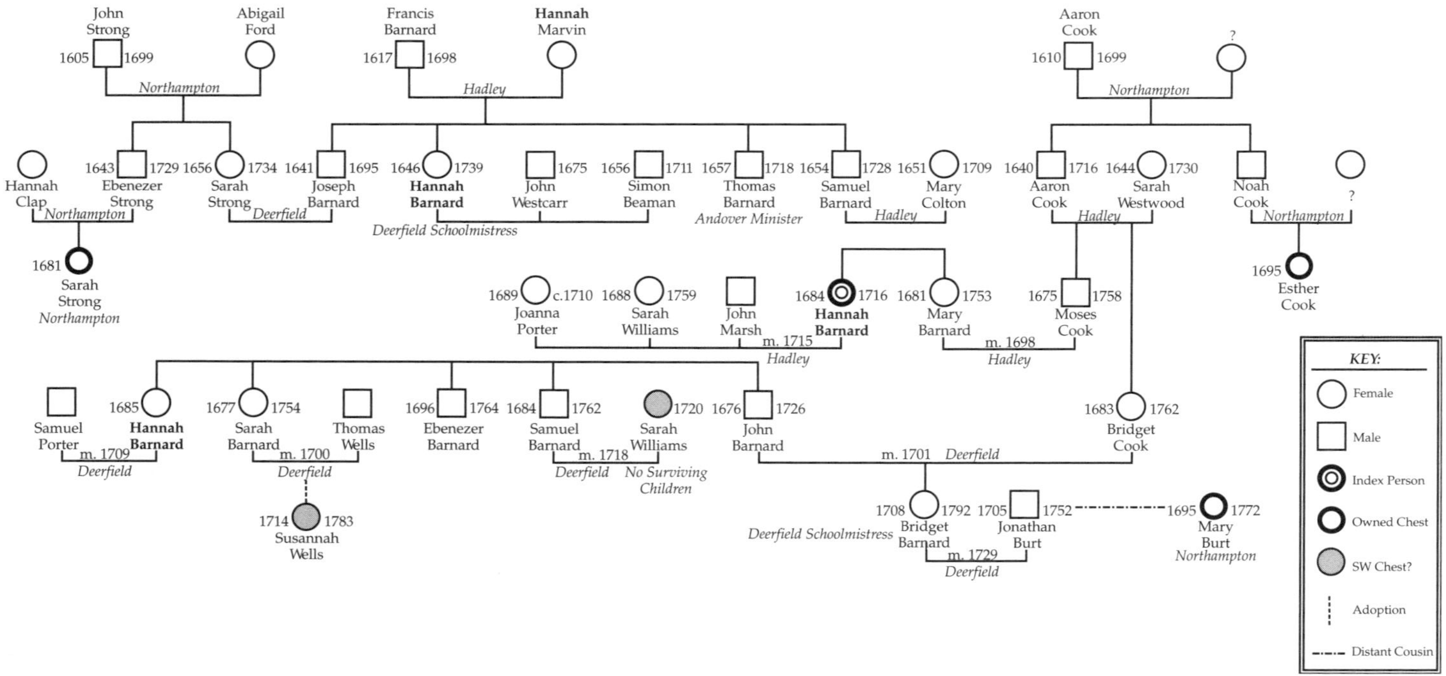

FIGURE 7.12. *Hannah Barnard relatives. Melinda Chiou, Colophon Type and Design.*

Hannah Wescar had acquired at least one serious book. By 1694, she had become Deerfield's schoolmistress, though we know of her work only because she hustled the town's children to the fort during an attack. The book, Richard Baxter's *Reformed Pastor*, bears her name, the inscription somewhat obscured by the effort of a later hand to copy it (figure 7.13):

Hanah Wescar
Ejus Liber
1678
[Hannah Wescar, Her Book.][37]

The use of Latin in the inscription led Deerfield's nineteenth-century historian, George Sheldon, to conclude that the gentle school dame could never have written it herself.[38] Yet there is no reason why an educated woman of her generation could not have used a common Latin phrase like "Eius Liber." Minus the flourishes, the inscription is quite compatible with her later signature. Regardless of who wrote it, the flourishes in the handwriting are characteristic of the time and strikingly similar to the curling tendrils on many Hadley chests (figure 7.14). A flowing inscription in a book—or on a chest—set a person apart. Even the letters on Hannah Barnard's cupboard, which appear at a distance to be straight Roman letters, have tiny curls at the tips.

Hannah Westcarr was a widow in 1678. Because she had no children and her husband no competing male heirs, she had inherited everything. At the estate settlement, witnesses, including her own sister Sarah, testified that "Mr John Wascarr sayd upon his Death Bed that he would Leave all his Estate to his Wife and that it was not his minde to take away One Penny of it from her." An inventory taken by Hannah's father, Francis Barnard, documents Westcarr's work as a frontier trader, listing "mooseskin" as well as fifty-nine pounds worth of "English goods," the latter still at Hartford. Other goods in the inventory, a chest of drawers, cupboard, carpets, and cushions, might have been part of Hannah's portion.[39] The Baxter book might have been among the unnamed volumes valued in the inventory at more than seven pounds. Whether Hannah inherited it from her first husband or acquired it later, she eventually gave it to her brother, Thomas Barnard, pastor of the church at Andover, Massachusetts. On the title page of the book is *Thomas*'s name and a tiny inscription in Latin, "Ex dono charissima Sorosis, H.B." (A gift from my dear sister, H.B.). The "H.B." stands for "Hannah Beaman." Hannah had married for the second time in 1680. She and her second husband, Simon Beaman, were among the Deerfield captives taken to Canada in 1704. There is no other record of her life in Deerfield until 1718, when, widowed again, she is listed

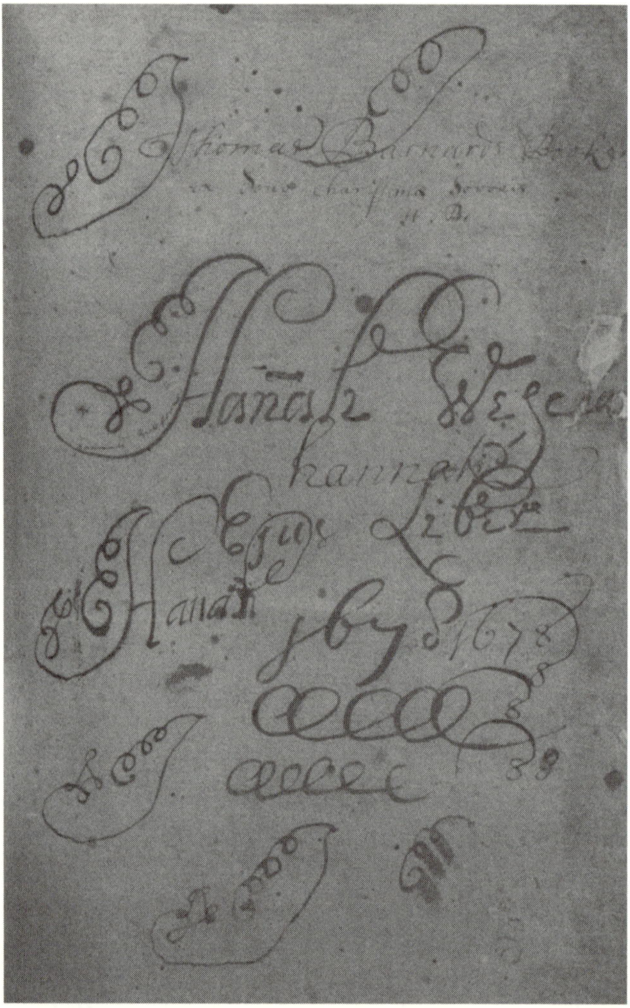

FIGURE 7.13. *Handwritten inscription, Hanah Wescar Ejus Liber. In Richard Baxter,* Gildas Salvianus: The Reformed Pastor. . . . *(London, 1656). Pocumtuck Valley Memorial Association Library, Deerfield, Mass. Photo by Amanda Merullo.*

among household heads. When she died in 1739, she left ten shillings to each of her brothers' children and the rest of her estate to the town of Deerfield for the support of schools.[40]

Perhaps Hannah Beaman bequeathed her brothers' daughters and granddaughters more than shillings. It is not farfetched to think that she was her niece's first teacher. The invisible work of some schoolmistress surely lies be-

FIGURE 7.14. *"RA" chest with drawers (detail). Hadley or Hatfield, Mass., c. 1700. Pocumtuck Valley Memorial Association, Memorial Hall Museum, Deerfield, Mass. Gift of Chester Graves Crafts, 1887.*

hind the bold assertion of literacy on Hannah's cupboard and on other Hampshire County chests. Perhaps some of the owners of these chests were themselves schoolmistresses. Hannah Barnard was almost thirty when she wed John Marsh. Could she, like her aunt, have been a teacher? There is no way to know, since proprietors of "dame schools" were paid by parents, leaving no record in town accounts. In 1728, however, Deerfield did pay a female teacher. Significantly, she was Bridget Barnard, Hannah Beaman's grandniece.[41] A comparison between Hannah Barnard's cupboard and an illustration from a Renaissance writing manual broadens the point (figure 7.15). On the cupboard as in the engraving, a row of half-circles underlays the central panel. In the engraving, a woman, a writing master, and a neatly printed text stand at the center of a windowlike opening, flowering stalks at the side. On the cupboard, the symbolic woman, through the letters of her name, frames the flower. Although the cupboard and the engraving have no direct connection, both partake of design conventions common in the early modern era. Hannah's cupboard may be less a valentine in

ALLA ILLVSTRA: ET ECCELL. S.
Marcheſa Del Guaſto. Giouanbattiſta Verini Fio
rentino ſuo dedicatiſſimo ſaruitore, che
inſegna Abbacho, & de ogni
ſorte littre Scriuere al
mal Cantone al ſe
gno del Ballone
ĩ Milano.

CON GRATIA, ET PRIVILEGIO

FIGURE 7.15. *Giovanni Bapttista Verini,* Alla Illustra . . . , *title page. John M. Wing Foundation, Newberry Library, Chicago, Ill.*

furniture than a protosampler, a deft combination of letters and flowers marking femininity, gentility, and literacy.

Early American historians have had a great deal to say about "consumer revolutions," but the social implications of the expansion of material goods have remained elusive. Material culture studies, like much scholarship in the decorative arts, have concentrated on defining differences among regions and on tracing the spread of "amenities" from one status group to another. Even so powerful a work as Richard Bushman's *Refinement of America* is fundamentally a "diffusion" study. Somewhere between the broad contours of "refinement" and the microscopic examination of paint pigments, there must be room for a social history of objects that focuses on the small politics of everyday life. As Amanda Vickery has written, "Social emulation and conspicuous consumption are useful concepts . . . but as portmanteau descriptions of eighteenth-century consumer behavior and material culture they are dangerously misleading." Material goods not only served as markers of status but as "crucial props in unobserved, intimate rituals." A woman might use them not only to assert status and define relationships but "to create a world of meanings and ultimately to transmit her history."[42]

Although few families in rural Massachusetts owned press cupboards, silver, fine textiles, or embroideries, many owned chests, sheets, blankets, and cheap imported ceramics. As Gloria Main has demonstrated, the stock of movables in the Connecticut Valley, as elsewhere in New England, was growing in the second quarter of the eighteenth century. Thus, the opportunity for people to attach names, genealogies, and stories to material objects, to create inalienable possessions, was expanding. At the same time, more and more women were learning to write their own names not only on documents but on personal possessions—bed rugs, sheets, towels, weaving drafts, books, letters, and diaries.[43]

The meanings of those names were highly variable, never fixed. Some women claimed ownership: "Martha Ballard, Her Diary"; "Polly Lewis, Her Verses"; "Mary Comstock, Her Rugg." Others made claims on posterity:

> When I am dead and in my grave,
> And all my bones are rotten.
> When this you see remember me,
> That I won't be forgotten.

Similar verses appear in the meditations of the seventeenth-century poet Anne Bradstreet, in the autobiography of an eighteenth-century Connecticut farm woman, Hannah Heaton, on schoolgirl embroidery from the seventeenth through the eighteenth century, on nineteenth-century patchwork quilts, and even in graffiti on Virginia furniture.[44]

Cary Carson has argued that the growth of marked objects in England and America in the seventeenth century was part of a social revolution that predated and helped to stimulate the so-called commercial revolution of the eighteenth century. He contrasts the inscribed drinking vessels of rural England, the "pot laureates" of a forgotten world, with the labeled chests, textiles, silver, and ceramics that became increasingly common in the eighteenth century. In an earlier world, a pot might speak for itself, advising all who saw it to take their "mery fill." In the more individualized world of an emerging middle class, "inscriptions on ordinary utilitarian objects bespeak not comradeship, but ownership." As we have seen, however, ownership took different forms for men and women. Marked objects appear everywhere in early America, but the forms they take vary widely. Among German-speaking settlers, for example, cupboards frequently bear the names of married couples rather than individuals. Does that suggest differences in the meaning of property or simply contrasting methods of outfitting young women for marriage? There are also significant differences in the same region over time. In Hampshire County (as elsewhere), heavy joined chests bearing women's initials or names gave way in the early eighteenth century to sleek cabinetry with no marks at all. Did refinement mean greater anonymity for women as well as greater freedom to purchase and display movable goods? Finally, the relationship between the construction and the ownership of objects bears more study. What did it mean when women became producers as well as purchasers of household goods? Did other women share the exuberant materialism of the Vermont woman who in the early nineteenth century wove into the center of her decorative all-white coverlet: "The Property of Susan Bailey"?[45]

Hannah Barnard's cupboard forces us to consider the so-called marriage chest, not as a romantic relic of a bygone day, but as one element in a complex gender system. About the time the first Hadley chests were being carved, the Hampshire County minister Edward Taylor wrote a poem titled "Upon Wedlock and Death of Children." Taylor's poem, like Hannah's cupboard, uses flower imagery to celebrate marriage and the establishment of a new household. The poem puns on the word "knot," which in seventeenth-century usage could connote a decorative flower bed, a bud on a plant, a calligraphic flourish, sexual intercourse, marriage, a believer's relationship with God:

> A Curious Knot God made in Paradise,
> And drew it out inamled neatly Fresh.
> It was the True-Love Knot, more sweet than spice,
> And set with all the flowres of Graces dress.
> . . . .
> When in this Knot I planted was, my Stock
> Soon knotted, and a manly flower out brake.
> And after it my branch again did knot:
> Brought out another Flowre; its sweet breath'd mate.

In the poem, Taylor's sweet flowers are both children and the words used to remember them. When his children die, he writes, "I piecemeale pass to Glory bright in them."[46] His description of reproduction is lush, yet curiously asexual, almost parthenogenetic. There is no female presence, unless it is the earth itself. Taylor's poem may unconsciously reflect the ancient notion of the womb as a passive receptacle for male seed.

A cupboard, too, is a container. Yet framed with a woman's name, Hannah Barnard's cupboard lays claim both to the garden and the branching flower. Whether or not she willed it, her name asserts her identity as an educated person, an heir to the material wealth of an ambitious family, and the future mistress of a household. The hearts, vines, pinwheels, thistles, and roses that embellish it are both traditional and imitative, relics of English tradition and emblems of a new possessive individualism as it developed among aspiring gentry in the Connecticut River Valley. Hannah's cupboard tells us that, in a world where most forms of wealth were controlled by male heads of household, certain objects were in some sense owned by women. Ownership of precious household goods offered the power not only to shape a material environment but to build lineages and alliances over time. Yet Hannah's cupboard is also a sign of the fragility of life and the transience of female identity in a world circumscribed by the cycles of marriage, childbearing, and death. When Hannah Marsh gave birth to a daughter, then died, her cupboard became both a monument and a knotted puzzle for future generations.

Notes

This essay owes a special debt to William Hosley of the Wadsworth Atheneum, who invited me to keynote a furniture conference even though I knew nothing about furniture. He and Karen Blanchfield introduced me to the topic and, in the initial stages of my research, provided photocopies of key sources as well as advice and direction. Later, Suzanne Flynt of Memorial Hall and David Proper and Philip Zea of Historic Deerfield gave generously of their time and knowledge, correcting many errors in earlier drafts of this essay.

1. Owen McNally, " 'Furniture from New England Towns': Window to the Past," *Hartford Courant*, 6 February 1993.
2. Philip Zea and Suzanne L. Flynt, *Hadley Chests* (Deerfield, Mass.: Pocumtuck Valley Memorial Association, 1992), 20, 28. An exception to the cautious approach of decorative arts scholars is Richard Lawrence Greene, "Fertility Symbols on the Hadley Chests," *Antiques* 112 (1977): 250–57. One of the first scholars to urge a cultural approach to the study of early American furniture (and later to decorative arts scholarship in general) was Robert Blair St. George (*The Wrought Covenant: Source Material for the Study of Craftsmen and Community in Southeastern New England 1620–1700* [Brockton, Mass. Brockton Art Center–Fuller Memorial, 1979], 13–17). For a vigorous statement of the problems of what he calls "scientific antiquarianism" in the decorative arts, see Michael J. Ettema, "History, Nostalgia, and American Furniture," *Winterthur Portfolio* 17 (1982): 135–44.

3. Even Richard L. Bushman, whose work has done so much to bridge the gap between the two disciplines, explains that he did not attempt to learn "the methods of curatorial scholarship with its emphasis on vast quantities of highly specific and exact knowledge"; see *The Refinement of America: Persons, Houses, Cities* (New York: Knopf 1992), xiii.
4. Sylvester Judd, *History of Hadley, including the Early History of Hatfield, South Hadley, Amherst and Granby, Massachusetts*, 2nd ed. (Springfield, Mass.: H. R. Huntting, 1905), 10–14, 85, 283, 284; Zea and Flynt, *Hadley Chests*, 5–6; Suzanne L. Flynt, Susan McGowan, and Amelia F. Miller, *Gathered and Preserved* (Deerfield, Mass.: Memorial Hall, 1991), 5–15.
5. Richard I. Melvoin, *New England Outpost: War and Society in Colonial Deerfield* (New York: W. W. Norton, 1989), 287; Douglas Edward Leach, *The Northern Colonial Frontier, 1607–1763* (New York: Holt, Rinehart and Winston, 1966), 208. Also see Kevin M. Sweeney, "From Wilderness to Arcadian Vale: Material Life in the Connecticut River Valley, 1635–1760," in *The Great River: Art and Society of the Connecticut Valley, 1635–1820*, ed. Gerald W. R. Ward and William Hosley Jr. (Hartford, Conn.: Wadsworth Atheneum, 1985), 17–21.
6. Gerald W. R. Ward, "Some Thoughts on Connecticut Cupboards and Other Case Furniture," *Old-Time New England* 72 (1987): 66–69 (Ward attributes the phrase to Charles Montgomery); Hampshire County Probate Records, 5 (1719–1738), 15, Hampshire County Courthouse, Northampton, Mass. The so-called Rowlandson cupboard now stands in the public library in Lancaster, Massachusetts, the town the Rowlandsons fled after their house and possessions were destroyed in the war that took Mary into captivity. Since Rowlandson apparently had a prenuptial contract reserving her inheritance at the time of her second marriage, the "great cupboard" listed in the estate of her second husband, Samuel Talcott, was probably a different piece of furniture (Estate Records, Hartford District Probate Court, nos. 4658, 5380, Connecticut State Library). On Mary Rowlandson's second marriage, see David L. Greene, "New Light On Mary Rowlandson," *Early American Literature* 20 (1985): 24–38. On the cupboard, see Ward, "Some Thoughts," 67–69; Walter A. Dyer, "The Tulip-and-Sunflower Press Cupboard," *Antiques* 27 (1935): 140–43. On the textiles, see Rowlandson Inventory, Estate Records, Hartford District Probate Court, no. 4658. On the inaccessibility of storage space in early cupboards, see Ward, "Some Thoughts," 70.
7. Patricia E. Kane, "New Haven Colony Furniture: The Seventeenth-Century Style," *Antiques* 103 (1973): 950–62; William N. Hosley Jr., "The Wallace Nutting Collection at the Wadsworth Atheneum, Hartford, Connecticut," *Antiques* 126 (1984): 860–74; Ward, "Some Thoughts," 74–77; Dean A. Fales Jr., *American Painted Furniture, 1660–1880* (New York: Dutton 1972), 16, 17; Zea and Flynt, *Hadley Chests,* 22, fig. 14. On the distinction between chests *with* drawers and chests *of* drawers, see Brock Jobe and Myrna Kaye, *New England Furniture: The Colonial Era* (Boston: Houghton Mifflin, 1984), 130–11.
8. Although some Hadley chests, like the Barnard cupboard, did indeed originate in Hadley, Massachusetts, related examples are found throughout the Connecticut River Valley. See Zea and Flynt, *Hadley Chests*, 5, 16; Clair Franklin Luther, *The Hadley Chest* (Hartford, Conn.: Case, Lockwood, and Brainard, 1935), xix–xxvi; Patricia E. Kane, "The Seventeenth-Century Furniture of the Connecticut Valley: The Hadley Chest Reappraised," in *Arts of the Anglo-American Community in the Seventeenth Century*, ed. Ian M. G. Quimby, Winterthur Conference Report, 1974 (Charlottesville: University Press of Virginia, 1975), 79–122; Philip Zea, "The Fruits of Oligarchy: Patronage and the Hadley Chest Tradition in Western Massachusetts," *Old-Time New England* 72 (1987): 1–65.
9. William N. Hosley Jr. and Philip Zea, "Decorated Board Chests of the Connecticut River Valley," *Antiques* 119 (1981): 1146–51.

10. Kane, "Seventeenth-Century Furniture," in Quimby, *Arts of the Anglo-American Community*, identifies 126 chests, 102 with two initials, 6 with three, 11 with none, and 7 will full names. Philip Zea believes the NDM/1700 chest might have been made for Nathaniel and Margaret (Pynchon) Downing; see Zea, "The Fruits of Oligarchy," 9, fig. 12.
11. Further research may refine the connections between Mary Pease and Elisabeth Warner, who married a Pease. The information in figure 7.6 is based on my own research in the International Genealogical Index, on genealogies in Judd, *History of Hadley*, and George Sheldon, *A History of Deerfield, Massachusetts*, 2 vols. (1895–96; repr., Deerfield, Mass.: Pocumtuck Valley Memorial Association, 1983), vol. 2; Luther, *The Hadley Chest*, 98, 121, 144; C. F. Luther, "The Hadley Chest," *Antiques* 14 (1928): 338–40; Preston R. Bassett, "Collectors' Notes: An Unrecorded Hadley Chest," *Antiques* 75 (1959): 460–61; *Catalogue of the Bertram K. Little and Nina Fletcher Little Collection* (New York: Sotheby's, 1994), 71; "Researches among Funeral Sermons," *New England Historical and Genealogical Register* 8 (1854): 180–83; and telephone conversations with Lynne Bassett, curator, Historic Northampton, and Olive Blair Graffam, curator of collections, Daughters of the American Revolution Musuem, Washington, D.C.
12. See illustration in Edith Gaines, "Collectors' Notes," *Antiques* 82 (1962): 172. Philip Zea doubts the authenticity of the name panel in the Cook chest.
13. Simpler versions of the same design elements appear on a nailed chest owned by a Northampton woman; see Zea, "Furniture," in Ward and Hosley, *The Great River*, 187.
14. Fales, *American Painted Furniture*, 20–23; Zea and Flynt, *Hadley Chests*, 19–23. For early images and the provenance of the three pieces, see "The Editor's Attic: The Frontispiece," *Antiques* 10 (1926): 188–90; "Connecticut Valley Polychromed Press Cupboard," *Antiques* 25 (1934): 129; "The Editor's Attic: Which Hannah Barnard?" *Antiques* 26 (1934): 168; "The Editor's Attic: The Vindication of Hannah," *Antiques* 29 (1936): 139–40. The SW chest has been heavily repainted, but enough of the original work remains to demonstrate the technique. Although the Winterthur chest was stripped of a later coat of paint, the original paint, when exposed, was in excellent condition. The design, pigments, and methods of application are strikingly similar to the Hannah Barnard cupboard. I would like to thank Suzanne Flynt for looking at the Barnard cupboard and the SW chest with me and Brock Jobe for showing me related physical evidence in the Winterthur chest.
15. Fales, *American Painted Furniture*, 19, fig. 16; Kane, "Seventeenth Century Furniture," 94, 101, 102, figs. 9, 10, 17, 19; Zea, "Furniture," 202, 206, figs. 81, 84. The rose-and-thistle motif connects Hannah's cupboard to a large group of unrelated chests, chests with drawers, chests of drawers, and standing high chests made in Guilford and Saybrook, Connecticut, between 1700 and 1725. The Connecticut chests are painted in a flowing and lyrical style, yet they too employ some version of the stylized rose and thistle that was so much a part of English decorative arts from the early seventeenth century onward. The Guilford-Saybrook chests are closely related to printers' ornaments that combined the rose and thistle with the fleur-de-lis, symbolically linking the crowns of England, France, and Scotland. I do not know whether there was any political significance to the appearance of these ornaments in eighteenth-century New England. Using a different painting style, a Connecticut chest of drawers from the same period alternates roses and thistles on the four drawers. Among the Hadley chests, the carved Northampton chests seem to be the only ones with fleur-de-lis. See Fales, *American Painted Furniture*, 24–29, 36–38, 39, 42–43; Charles F. Montgomery, "Country Furniture: A Symposium," *Antiques* 93 (1968): 357–58, figs. 3, 3a; and John T. Kirk, "The Tradition of English Painted Furniture, Part 1: The Experience in Colonial New England," *Antiques* 117 (1980): 1082–83, figs. 8, 8a, b; Elizabeth Carroll Reilly, *A Dictionary of Colonial*

American Printers' Ornaments and Illustrations (Worcester, Mass.: American Antiquarian Society, 1975), 187. See, for an example of the pomegranate motif, the slip-decorated plate made by John Burslem in Staffordshire in exactly this period, in Leslie B. Grigsby, *English Slip-Decorated Earthenware at Williamsburg* (Williamsburg, Va.: Colonial Williamsburg Foundation, 1993), 10, 41, figs. 2, 46.

16. The visual rhymes formed by the repeated *A*'s might have been accidental. When the cupboard was restored in 1994, the conservator discovered faint marks of an *E* below the first *A*, suggesting that the painter had been uncertain about the spelling of Hannah's name (conversation with Susan Buck, Society for the Preservation of New England Antiquities Conservation Center; Zea and Flynt, *Hadley Chests*, 28 n. 56). Variant spellings of names were common in this period. A piece of silver owned by one of Hannah's relatives was marked "Bernard"; see Silver Beaker, "The Gift of Samuel Bernard to the Church in Deerfield 1723," c. 1723, L-20-85, Historic Deerfield.
17. John Billing Distribution, 8 September 1698, Joseph Barnard Distribution, n.d., Charles Fierre Will and Distribution, 29 July 1699, Hampshire County Probate Records, Book 1690–1700.
18. Annette B. Weiner, *Inalienable Possessions: The Paradox of Keeping-while-Giving* (Berkeley: University of California Press, 1992), 6 (quotation), 32, 33, 37, 42–43, 154.
19. Toby L. Ditz, *Property and Kinship: Inheritance in Early Connecticut, 1750–1820* (Princeton: Princeton University Press, 1986), 65. In the case of daughters, Ditz argues, bequests of land were substitutes for personal property. She notes, however, that wills undervalue bequests to daughters, since most probably received all or part of their portions of moveable goods at marriage (69–70).
20. Court Cupboard, 36.178.1, Henry Ford Museum and Greenfield Village Files; "Connecticut Valley Polychromed Press Cupboard," *Antiques* 25 (1934): 129; "The Editor's Attic: Which Hannah Barnard?" 168; "The Editor's Attic: The Vindication of Hannah," 139–40. I can find only three girls in colonial Hadley given a surname for a middle name, none before Hannah Barnard Hastings; see Lucius M. Boltwood, "Family Genealogies," in Judd, *History of Hadley*, 8, 64, 91–92.
21. Sheldon, *History of Deerfield*, 2:298. Of the 117 names in the Hadley valuation list of 1720, Marsh's father-in-law, Samuel Porter, ranked first, his father, Daniel Marsh, was fourth, and his father-in-law, Samuel Barnard, was seventh. On the valuation list of 1731, "Heirs of John Marsh, and Widow Sarah Marsh" rank fifteenth out of 87 (Judd, *History of Hadley*, 278, 283). Marsh's third wife, Sarah Williams, was the daughter of Isaac Williams of Newton and a first cousin of Deerfield's minister, John Williams; see Sheldon, *History of Deerfield*, 2:376–77.
22. John Marsh Will, 5 June 1725, Hampshire County Probate Records, 4:134, Microfilm, Latter-day Saints Family History Library, film number 0879184. As it turned out, little John never did come of age. He died 3 July 1726, age three; see Boltwood, "Family Genealogies," in Judd, *History of Hadley*, 92.
23. John Marsh Inventory, Hampshire County Probate Records, 4:138–40. I thank Suzanne Flynt for the suggestion that the cupboard might have left the household. The identity of Moses Cook reinforces the possibility.
24. "The Editor's Attic: Which Hannah Barnard?" 168; Zea and Flynt, *Hadley Chests*, 22.
25. [Lydia Nelson Hastings, ed.], *The Hastings Memorial: A Genealogical Account of the Descendents of Thomas Hastings of Watertown, Mass., from 1634 to 1864* (Boston: Samuel Drake, 1866), 7, 8, 11; Thomas Hopkins, *The Kelloggs in the Old World and the New*, vol. 1 (San Francisco: Sunset, 1903), 172, 369. The last of the Hannah Barnards died childless in San Jose, California, in 1889.

26. Marius B. Peladeau, "A Hadley Chest Reconsidered," *Antiques* 117 (1980): 1084–86. But such lineages are difficult to trace. Some scholars seem to assume descent from male, some through female lines. See, for example, entries concerning different objects inherited by the same woman, discussed by Philip Zea, "Furniture," and Jane Nylander, "Textiles, Clothing, and Needlework," in Ward and Hosley, *The Great River*, 223, fig. 103, 374–75, 380, figs. 245, 249.
27. Suzanne Flynt to Laurel Ulrich, 10 March 1995, citing Pocumtuck Valley Memorial Association Accession Book, I, 181, and *1908 Catalogue of Relics in Memorial Hall*, 94, MH 702, PVMA Library, Deerfield; Zea and Flynt, *Hadley Chests*, 22, 29 n. 67.
28. Zea and Flynt, *Hadley Chests*, 20–23.
29. Stephen W. Williams, *The Genealogy and History of the Family of Williams . . .* (Greenfield, Mass.: Merriman and Mirick, 1847), 21, 33, 34; *Vital Records of Deerfield, Massachusetts*, vol. 1 (Boston: New England Historic Genealogical Society, 1920), 2, 264; *Vital Records of Roxbury, Massachusetts*, 2 vols. (Salem, Mass.: The Essex Institute, 1925–26), 1:383, 2:437; Sheldon, *History of Deerfield*, 2:66, 67, 279–80. Sheldon incorrectly states on page 377 that Sarah, daughter of Samuel Williams Jr., married John Polly.
30. Sheldon, "Genealogies," *History of Deerfield*, 2:66, 67, 281, 358, 393. Sarah and Thomas Wells both left property to nieces and nephews; see Thomas Wells Estate, Hampshire County Probate Records, 7:272–73; Sarah Wells Estate, Hampshire County Probate Files, box 9, 25; Zea and Flynt, *Hadley Chests*, 3–4.
31. Barbara McLean Ward, "Women's Property and Family Continuity in Eighteenth-Century Connecticut," in *Early American Probate Inventories* (Dublin Seminar for New England Folklife Annual Proceedings, 1987), ed. Peter Benes (Boston: Boston University, 1989), 74–85; catalog entries in Ward and Hosley, *The Great River*, 279, 281–82, 288–89.
32. Registration Records, Historic Deerfield. In 1777, Madame Silliman occupied pew number one, next to the pulpit, in Deerfield Church. See Sheldon, *History of Deerfield*, 1:479; 2:744, 904; "Genealogies," 2:204–5, 378, 380, 382.
33. Weiner, *Inalienable Possessions*, 67.
34. Albert S. Batchellor, ed., *Probate Records of the Province of New Hampshire*, vol. 2 (Concord, N.H.: Rumford Printing Co., 1907), 128–30.
35. Judd, *History of Hadley*, 91–92.
36. Zea, "The Fruits of Oligarchy," 23–24; Melvoin, *New England Outpost*, 85, 138, 145, 150, 163, 167, 171, 184, 199; Sheldon, "Genealogies," *History of Deerfield*, 2:65. When Francis Barnard died in 1698, he left his son "Mr Thomas Barnard Minister of the Gospel in Andover the full and just sum of fiftie pounds money . . . which I give him to be improved towards the bringing up one of his Sons to Learneing"; see Francis Barnard, Will, Hampshire County Probate Records, 3:46.
37. I am grateful to Deerfield librarian David Proper for finding and photocopying this inscription. George Sheldon, "The Hannah Beaman Book and the Regicides," *History and Proceedings of the Pocumtuck Valley Memorial Association, 1912–1920* (Deerfield, Mass., 1921), 25–33, argues that Wescar got the book from English Civil War general Edward Whalley, who got it from Baxter himself.
38. Ibid., 30. Sheldon was unable to connect the signature with that of any other educated contemporary but thought it looked a bit like three autographs of General William Goffe, the second of his "Regicides." It came to Sheldon's museum from a descendant of Samuel Williams, an associate and teacher of the third Thomas Barnard.
39. Hampshire County Court Records, Book I, 177, and on Westcarr's dealings with Indians, I, 89, 99, 121, 133.

40. Hampshire County Probate Records, 5:66, 6:22, 58, 59, 77; Sheldon, *History of Deerfield*, 1:244, 272, 303, 308, 624, and 2:840; Richard E. Birks, "Hannah Beaman, Deerfield's First School Mistress: Her Times and Her Experiences," in *History and Proceedings*, 496–513.
41. Judd, *History of Hadley*, 56–58, 418; Sheldon, *History of Deerfield*, 2:840. The town also enjoined farmers "to procure School Dames to teach their children."
42. Amanda Vickery, "Women and the World of Goods: A Lancashire Consumer and Her Possessions, 1751–81," in *Consumption and the World of Goods*, ed. John Brewer and Roy Porter (London: Routledge, 1993), 294.
43. See Gloria L. Main, "The Distribution of Consumer Goods in Colonial New England: A Subregional Approach," in Benes, *Early American Probate Inventories*, 153–68. In an effort to measure the distribution of consumer goods in early America, Main has created an "Index of Amenities" that includes some of the things we have been discussing here, particularly linens, earthenware, and silver. "In the Valley," she writes, "the only subregion for which we have a useful sample in the period 1725–1729, the index rose to an extraordinarily high level for householders in the lower and middling class." Although the distribution of amenities varied over time and by region, nearly everyone was accumulating a broader range of consumer goods over the course of the century. See also Gloria L. Main, "An Inquiry into When and Why Women Learned to Write in Colonial New England," *Journal of Social History* 24 (1990–91): 579–89; William J. Gilmore, *Reading Becomes a Necessity of Life: Material and Cultural Life in Rural New England, 1780–1835* (Knoxville: University of Tennessee Press, 1989).
44. Betty Ring, *American Needlework Treasures* (New York: Dutton, 1987), for example, fig. 5, Margret Palfrey Sampler, 32, fig. 51, Cordelia Bennet Sampler, 4, and computations based on Ethel Stanwood Bolton and Eva Johnston Coe, *American Samplers* (Boston: Massachusetts Society of the Colonial Dames of America, 1921). Heaton wrote, "i leaue you her a little book for you to look upon / that you may see your mothers face when she is dead and gone"; Barbara E. Lacey, "The World of Hannah Heaton: The Autobiography of an Eighteenth-Century Connecticut Farm Woman," *William and Mary Quarterly*, 3d ser., 45 (1988): 280–304 (quotation on 282). Jonathan Prown pointed out to me a white pine and poplar desk, Norfolk, Virginia, ca. 1790–1820, Colonial Williamsburg, G1988-427, with a succession of female names inside the lid and the penciled phrase, "If you see remember me."
45. Cary Carson, "The Consumer Revolution in Colonial British America: Why Demand?" in *Of Consuming Interests: The Style of Life in the Eighteenth Century*, ed. Cary Carson, Ronald Hoffman, and Peter J. Albert. (Charlottesville: University Press of Virginia, 1994), 533–41, 555; Tufted Counterpane, 1985–0639.01, National Museum of American History, Washington, D.C.
46. Edward Taylor, "Upon Wedlock and Death of Children," in *The Poetical Works of Edward Taylor*, ed. Thomas H. Johnson (New York: Rockland Editions, 1939), 117, 118.

8

Myths about early American families and their clothing are both familiar and tenacious. Images of Pilgrims clad head to toe in severe ensembles of black and white jostle alongside competing notions of homespun simplicity to create an incongruous picture of communities simultaneously intolerant of fashion and unable to achieve it. Popular historical imagination would lead us to envision the men and women who populate the foregoing chapters dressed in those stereotypical costumes—in fact, part of the legend of the Angel of Hadley involves the bewildered residents noticing the figure's odd, out-of-date finery, but not knowing how to interpret his strange apparel. We may think of Hadley's earliest residents as costumed uniformly in homespun ensembles, but nothing could be further from the truth, as Lynne Bassett shows in the essay that follows. The men and women of seventeenth-century New England were eager to comply with London fashion; the degree to which they did or did not do so reflects, Bassett persuasively argues, values beyond the strictly theological, or mere matters of means.

The Sober People of Hadley

Sumptuary Legislation and Clothing in Hadley Men's Probate Inventories, 1663–1731

Lynne Z. Bassett

Along with their axes, plows, and cattle, the English settlers of the Connecticut River Valley brought their traditions and social values. Of great importance to the new residents was their traditional social hierarchy, for which clothing served as an important symbol. Both Massachusetts and Connecticut enacted sumptuary legislation, which had been a part of English law since Roman times, dictating what was proper and improper apparel for specific social classes. In this essay I examine clothing found in the probate inventories of men who died in Hadley, Massachusetts, during the late seventeenth and early eighteenth centuries, and then discuss sumptuary prosecution of Hadley men and women in the 1670s with the aim of determining whether they complied with the General Court's laws on personal appearance.[1]

If asked to picture what one of our colonial forefathers looked like, most people would probably describe a dour man in dark, drab clothes and a broad-brimmed hat with a buckled band, carrying his Bible under his arm for easy access. In fact, portraits of prominent seventeenth-century colonists (especially those of the merchant class), along with period documents such as probate inventories, letters, diaries, and court records, reveal that many colonists spent large sums of money on their wardrobes, dressing in a colorful variety of rich silks and fine wools, decorated with elegant linen laces, gold braid, and buttons of precious metals. In the last quarter of the seventeenth century, colonists of the Anglican faith increased in numbers, particularly in the Boston area, and they especially felt free to model their "carriage," manners, and fashion closely after the English gentry.[2] But even Puritans often dressed with some flamboyance, for being wealthy was a sign of God's favor.[3] Living in a frontier town did not necessarily limit one's wardrobe to homespun in dull vegetable-dyed colors, either; interaction and trade between coastal cities and inland communities offered (particularly to the wealthy) access to fashion news and imported fabrics, along with elegant trims and accessories such as jewelry, wigs, silk shoes, gloves, and lace collars and cuffs.[4]

The basic wardrobe of an English man in the second half of the seventeenth century and throughout the eighteenth century consisted of a coat, waistcoat, breeches, shirt, stockings, shoes, and hat. More expensive types of garments included greatcoats and boots; a suit with matching coat, waistcoat, and breeches was of greater value than a non-matching outfit. All of these items could be made of materials in a wide range of qualities, and could be embellished with expensive items such as a lace jabot (a ruffle falling from the throat), gold buttons and jeweled shoe buckles, and bunches of ribbon. A sword or cane, finger ring, an elegant powdered wig of curled human hair, and jeweled tassels on the ties of the collar (called a "band" in this period) could add greatly to the value of an outfit.

The drawing in figure 8.1, representing merchant and mariner Captain George Corwin (1610–1685) of Salem, Massachusetts, illustrates an elegant outfit for a man of high status in the last quarter of the seventeenth century. He wears a full-skirted coat over breeches, which are tied at the knee. The coat has pocket flaps and sleeve cuffs ornamented with silver lace or embroidery, representing the "1 Cloth Coat wth. Silver lace" listed in his probate inventory.[5] A lace jabot falls from the neck of his shirt, partially covering a heavily embroidered baldric (an ornamental belt worn over one shoulder). Corwin's silver-headed cane,

FIGURE 8.1 (*above left*). *Conjectural drawing of Captain George Corwin (1610–1685), based on his portrait of c. 1675 and his probate inventory; the portrait is attributed to Thomas Smith, and is in the collection of The Peabody Essex Museum, Salem. Drawing by David Rickman.*

FIGURE 8.2 (*above right*). *Portrait of a man, Boston, ca. 1675–1690. Attributed to Thomas Smith. Oil on canvas, 43½ by 35 7/16 inches. Harvard University Art Museum, Fogg Art Museum, gift of Mr. Robert Winthrop, class of 1926, to Harvard College, 1946.H527. Photo: Imaging Department © President and Fellows, Harvard College.*

FIGURE 8.3 (*below left*). *A lower-class man's costume of the late seventeenth century. Drawing by David Rickman.*

along with his portrait, survives in the collection of the Peabody Essex Museum in Salem.

The unknown Boston gentleman, possibly Elisha Hutchinson, portrayed around 1675–1690 and seen in figure 8.2, particularly belies the idea that Puritans were drab dressers. His full-bottomed wig was the latest in London fashion. He wears the baldric of the Ancient and Honorable Artillery Company, with the elegant silver hilt of his sword visible below his left hand.[6] The needlelace jabot and sleeve ruffles are important indicators that this man did not live by the sweat of his brow. Scores of silver buttons and bunches of silk and silver ribbon at his shoulder and the waist of his breeches add even more glory to his outfit.

In contrast, the clothing of the laboring classes had little embellishment, and consisted of coarse grades of wool and linen. The man depicted in figure 8.3 wears no ruffles or lace at the neck or wrists of his shirt. His coat lies against his shirt, as he has no waistcoat. He wears his own hair, not a wig, and his buttons would have been made of iron or some other lower-quality material. The secondhand market provided much of the clothing for the lower classes; every item in the outfit depicted here could have been purchased from a street peddler with a cart full of old clothes.

The English settlers of Massachusetts Bay Colony valued the visual distinction between the privileged and laboring classes. Such visual cues enabled one to judge a person's worth in an economy dependent on personal credit, and allowed the wearer to show piety. The ministers of Massachusetts Bay frequently pointed to an excess of fashion and pursuit of material goods as a sign of the colony's religious decline.[7] Two sermons by the Reverend Increase Mather, published in 1674 under the title *The Day of Trouble Is Near*, took on the issue of dressing in a "proud" manner: "As to *matters of Religion*, things are not as should be. There is a great decay as to the power of godliness amongst us. . . . We can now see little difference between Church-members and other men, as to their discourses, or their spirits, or their walking, or their garb, but Professors of Religion *fashion themselves according to the world*. And what *Pride* is there? Spiritual Pride, in Parts and common Gifts of the Spirit, and in Spiritual Priviledges; yea carnal, shameful foolish Pride, in Apparel, Fashions, and the like."[8]

The elements of fashion that so appalled Increase Mather also offended the Massachusetts General Court. The first sumptuary law was passed in Massachusetts in 1634; it was soon followed by another in 1639. These two efforts were apparently ineffective, for in 1651 the General Court of Massachusetts Bay Colony wrote with some exasperation:

> Although several Declarations and Orders have been made by this Court, against excess in Apparel, both of Men and Women, which have not taken that effect as were to be desired, but on the contrary; we cannot but to our grief take notice, that intollerable excess and bravery hath crept in upon us, and especially amongst people of mean condition, to the dishonour of God, the scandall of our profession, the consumption of Estates, and altogether unsuitable to our poverty . . . [we] declare our utter detestation and dislike, that men and women of mean condition, should take upon them the garb of Gentlemen, by wearing Gold or Silver lace, or Buttons, or Points at their knees, or to walk in great Boots; or Women of the same rank to wear Silk or Tiffany hoods, or Scarfes, which though allowable to persons of greater Estates, or more liberal education, yet we cannot but judge it intollerable in persons of such like condition.[9]

A major difference between the 1651 law and those of 1634 and 1639 is the distinct line that it drew between those who were able to wear expensive adornments and those who were not allowed that privilege because of their "mean condition." The demarcation was drawn at a £200 estate (about $34,000 in 2007 dollars):[10] "It is therefore Ordered by this Court and the Authority thereof; that no person within this Jurisdiction, nor any of their relations depending upon them, whose visible estates real and personal, [do] not exceed the true and indifferent value of *two hundred pounds*; shall wear any Gold or Silver lace, or Gold and Silver buttons, or any bone lace above two shillings *per yard*, or silk hoods, or scarfs, upon the penalty of *ten shillings* for every such offence."[11] There were, however, exceptions to the £200 rule, revealing the importance of social status as well as wealth: "This Law shall not extend to the restraint of any Magistrate or publick officer of this Jurisdiction, their Wives and Children . . . or any setled Military Officer, or Souldier in the time of Military service, or any other whose education and imployment have been above the ordinary degree, or whose estate have been considerable, though now decayed."[12]

Analyzing the eligibility of a Hadley resident's right to wear the elegant clothing listed in the sumptuary laws requires us to establish each probated male's economic and social status. The 1663 land distribution list, along with Hadley tax lists of 1682 and 1687, provide information on a probated individual's economic status while living, while probate inventories reveal the value of the estate at the time of death.[13] The analysis of social status is based on occupation, dividing occupational prestige into four levels (table 8.1).[14] Occupations are known or surmised for all of the probated men.[15] The period examined begins in 1663 with Hadley's Hockanum Meadow land distribution, and continues through the lifetimes of the probated individuals who appear on that list, to 1731.

TABLE 8.1. *Occupations according to social prestige*

I. Educated Professional	*II. Proprietor, Professional*	*III. Skilled Laborer*	*IV. Unskilled Laborer*
Gentleman	Farmer	Blacksmith	Laborer
Minister	Merchant/Trader	Baker	Gravedigger
Physician	Military Leader	Weaver	
Deacon	Innkeeper/Ordinary Keeper	Carpenter	
		Tailor	
		Maltster	
		Cordwainer	
		Glazier	

Information on the garments found in the inventories, therefore, is categorized two ways. First, according to the sumptuary laws' economic standard, the garments are divided into those found in estates worth over £200 and those worth less than £200. (All monetary values are converted to pounds sterling to remain consistent.) Second, the garments are organized according to their owners' social status as determined by occupational prestige.

Analysis of Data by Economic Standard

The differences in the wardrobes of decedents worth more than £200 and those worth less than £200 are not striking (table 8.2). Shirts—being made of fine, smooth linen or rough tow, with pleats that were difficult to clean and press or made plain, without ruffles—had the greatest potential to express the status of wearers in the seventeenth and eighteenth centuries. In the Hadley inventories, there were approximately three shirts in each of the inventories valued under £200, and approximately four shirts in each of those valued at over £200. At 3s. 5d. (three shillings, four pence), the mean value of the shirts in the wealthier estates was about 1s. 6d. higher than the others. The quality of the fabric used in the shirts from the over-£200 estates does not appear to be a major factor in their slightly higher value. For instance, six dowlas shirts appeared in the over-£200 estates, but none in the poorer estates. According to the 1696 book *The Plain Dealing Linnen Draper*, dowlas was a linen fabric used to make "ordinary shifts and shirts for tradespeople"—thus, this most common fabric used by the wealthier men was actually quite coarse.[16] Holland, however, was a fine quality linen and popular for undergarments. Holland was used in 13 percent of the wealthier decedents' shirts and in 8 percent of the poorer. "Fine," a term used

TABLE 8.2. *Average number and value of wearing linen in +£200 and –£200 estates*

+£200	–£200
4 shirts, 3s. 5d. ea.	3 shirts, 1s. 11d. ea.
5 neckcloths, 1s. 5d. ea.	3 neckcloths, 1s. 1d. ea.
or	or
7 bands, 2s. 7d. ea.	5 bands, 9d. ea.
2 drawers, 3s. 7d. ea.	0 drawers

for high quality linen, described another 10 percent of the shirts in the over-£200 estates, and 8 percent in the under-£200 estates.

Especially fine fabric, then, does not explain the difference in mean value between the two categories. Could these shirts have been more elegantly constructed? In the period under study, the fashionably unbuttoned waistcoat revealed the shirt underneath; ruffles at the shirt's neck opening signaled the wearer's social position, "being inconvenient, uncomfortable and readily soiled."[17] Similarly, the narrow wristbands that gathered the voluminous sleeves of the shirt may have sported ruffles. It becomes obvious, however, that the shirts of Hadley men were not often constructed with ruffles when their value is compared with the shirts found in a similar study of clothing in Boston. In that colonial metropolis, the shirt of a "simple wardrobe" was valued at an average of 3 shillings—only five pence less than the average shirt worn by the very wealthiest men in Hadley![18]

The wealthier men of Hadley in the late seventeenth and early eighteenth centuries generally owned more, but only slightly better quality, undergarments than their less prosperous neighbors. Any visual distinction offered by the undergarments (called "wearing linen" in the probate inventories) was subtle—and probably not even noticeable by visitors from the more flamboyant Boston area.

Several categories of outerwear likewise suggest that the sartorial gap between Hadley's haves and have-nots was not large (table 8.3). Coats were found in similar numbers in both categories of estates, but the mean value was a bit higher in the over-£200 estates (10s. 10d. as opposed to 8s. 3d.). The coat fabrics listed in the inventories of the two different economic classes did not differ strikingly, however. Wealthier men often enjoyed coats made of better-quality wools, but no elegant silks were found. Kersey, a cheap wool cloth, was by far the most common coat fabric in the under-£200 estates. Superior construction or quality

Table 8.3. *Average number and value of outerwear and accessories in +£200 and –£200 estates*

+£200	–£200
3 breeches, 7s. 7d. ea.	2 breeches, 3s. ea.
3 coats, 10s. 10d. ea.	3 coats, 8s. ea.
2 waistcoats, 5s. 3d. ea.	2 waistcoats, 3s. 11d. ea.
2 jackets, 6s. 6d. ea.	1 jacket, 4s. ea.
3 caps, 1s. ea.	3 caps, 3d. ea.
1–2 hats, 3s. 8d. ea.	1–2 hats, 3s. 2d. ea.
1–2 pr. shoes, 3s. 8d. ea.	1–2 pr. shoes, 2s. ea.
1 pr. boots, 4s. 8d.	1 pr. boots, 2s. 3d
3 pr. stockings, 1s. 5d. ea.	3–4 pr. stockings, 1s. 2d. ea.
1 or 2 pr. gloves, 1s. 2d. ea.	1 pr. gloves, 1s. 3d
4 handkerchiefs, 10d. ea.	2 handkerchiefs, 11d. ea.

of buttons may account for the difference in the mean value of coats in the two categories.

Individuals of the lower economic class owned an average of two or three pairs of breeches each. About three pairs of breeches on average were found in the wardrobes of men worth over £200. Again, these breeches were valued higher than those in the under-£200 estates: 4s. 8d., as opposed to 3s. Individuals of modest means tended to own many more linen breeches than their wealthier neighbors. They may have been homespun, as the Hadley inventories frequently list textile equipment such as hetchels (boards spiked with long, iron teeth for combing flax fibers) and spinning wheels. Leather breeches also appeared in quantity among the inventories worth less than £200. Leather breeches, were, in fact, associated with the lower classes and manual labor until the first quarter of the eighteenth century, when they gradually became fashionable with the upper classes—enough so that by the 1730s those who valued social distinctions were complaining that gentlemen resembled their servants.[19] In Hadley, where six pairs of leather breeches were found among 20 percent of the over-£200 inventories and twelve pairs among 42 percent of the under-£200 inventories dated from 1705 to 1731, leather may simply have been the material of choice because of its durability. Leather breeches appeared only in the inventories of farmers and laborers until 1722, when a pair was included in the inventory of Mr. Samuel Porter, gentleman and merchant.

Approximately the same number of pairs of shoes were owned by individuals in both categories (between one and two), but shoes in the over-£200 estates were worth on average 1s. 3d. more. Boots, luxury items listed in the sumptuary laws, were not uncommon in the Hadley estates, but they appeared more often in the over-£200 than the under-£200 estates. Boots in the inventories of Hadley's economic elite were also worth more than twice the mean value of boots in the lesser estates.

Suits (outer garments made of the same fabric and worn together) slightly disrupt the pattern of more and better garments in wealthier estates. They appeared in several combinations in the Hadley inventories: coat and vest; coat, waistcoat, and breeches; jacket and breeches; and jacket and waistcoat. It appears that men of the lower economic class were as likely to own a suit as were wealthier men, as they show up in the two categories of inventories with virtually the same frequency, 27 percent and 25 percent.

Greatcoats were expensive items, made large to wear over the coat, waistcoat, and breeches. Unlike other coats, greatcoats were not lined and were "slit up the back for riding."[20] This garment was listed in 14 percent of the inventories. While Hadley's wealthier men were slightly more likely than their less privileged neighbors to own a greatcoat, the quality of their greatcoats was no better, being valued on average a negligible four pence higher. Capes and cloaks, often made of high-quality wool broadcloth, also provided warmth during cold New England winters.[21] While Hadley residents worth over £200, again, owned cloaks slightly more often than their neighbors worth under £200, the value of those cloaks, at 7s. 6d. higher than the other cloaks, constitute perhaps the clearest signal in Hadley wardrobes of a person's economic status.

Garments and accessories that could be described as "luxurious" were found infrequently in the Hadley inventories: ribbon and galloon (narrow ribbon often woven of gold or silver threads), lace, spurs, gold rings, and gold and silver buttons. Also notably absent were silk fabrics of any sort for outer garments.

In sum, the data indicate that wealthier Hadley men did not dress in a manner that would significantly differentiate them from their less well-off neighbors, even though they could—a considerably different situation than that found in similar studies of eastern Massachusetts.[22] Wealthy Hadley men also did not devote as much of their overall estate to clothing as did the men from eastern Massachusetts.[23] Nineteen of the thirty Hadley men in the over-£200 category had what can be viewed as a "complete" wardrobe listed in their inventories: at least one shirt, neckcloth, coat and breeches, hat or cap, and at least one pair of stockings and shoes or boots. Of these nineteen inventories from Hadley's economic upper crust, the average portion of free estate devoted to clothing was a mere 1.6 percent. (The range was .5 to 4.5 percent.) In eastern Massachusetts in the seventeenth century, "on the whole, both gentlemen and servants had an average of 7 percent of their wealth invested in apparel."[24] (By comparison, the average American today spends 4.2 percent of his or her yearly income on clothing.)[25]

Analysis of Data by Social Status

A comparison of garments owned by Hadley men in each of the levels of social prestige makes it apparent again that there was not much visual distinction between classes (table 8.4). Gentlemen rarely owned a garment significantly more valuable than those of their less distinguished neighbors. In fact, it seems that frequently the most valuable outer garments belonged to men in the second tier of Hadley society. What seems to distinguish men at the highest levels of local prestige is that they owned more rather than better garments than men of other social ranks.

The thirty-nine Hadley inventories that list complete wardrobes reveal that the gentlemen at the pinnacle of Hadley's social order spent an average of 1.8 percent of their estate on clothing. In comparison, the farmers and other proprietors just beneath them in power and influence devoted 2.9 percent of their estate to clothing. Skilled laborers and unskilled workers devoted 2.8 percent and 36.6 percent of their estates to clothing, respectively. From these percentages, one might assume, erroneously, that the unskilled laborers were the best dressed men in town. But their estates were so small, with no land and very little personal property, that their clothing became their most valuable possessions.

In monetary terms, the gentlemen in Level I spent an average of about £5.2.11 on their wardrobes. The farmers and other proprietors spent approximately £5.16.2, while artisans in Level III devoted about £2.14.3 to their wardrobes. Though extremely poor, the unskilled laborers in Level IV appear to have dressed better than the skilled laborers of Level III, as they spent on average £4.15.0 for their clothes. Amazingly, men at the top of Hadley's social ladder, though they often owned estates literally a hundred times more valuable than those of the unskilled laborers in Level IV, spent very little more on their wardrobes than did their less privileged neighbors! The top seven gentlemen in Donna Bartsch's study of eastern Massachusetts owned between £24 and £65 worth of clothing—between five and almost twelve times what Hadley gentlemen owned.[26]

No distinctive garment emerged from any one of the four levels of social status. The most highly respected men in the community were the most likely to own a cloak, greatcoat, and boots, but men of the other social levels owned these

TABLE 8.4. *Average number and value of garments owned by Hadley men in each level of occupational prestige*

I. Educated Professional	*II. Proprietor/ Professional*	*III. Skilled Laborer*	*IV. Unskilled Laborer*
10 bands, 4s. 4d. ea.	4 bands, 1s. 4d. ea.	7 bands, 9d. ea.	0 bands
or	or	or	or
6 neckcloths, 1s. 4d. ea.	4–5 neckcloths, 1s. 6d. ea.	3 neckcloths, 7d. ea.	5 neckcloths, 9d. ea.
8–9 shirts, 4s. ea.	3 shirts, 3s. 7d. ea.	2 shirts, 2s. 10d. ea.	3 shirts, 2s. 3d. ea.
2–3 drawers, 3s. ea.	2 drawers, 3s. 9d. ea.	0 pr. drawers	0 pr. drawers
4 breeches, 7s. 7d. ea.	2–3 breeches, 4s. 5d. ea.	1 pr. breeches, 3s. 5d	3 breeches, 2s. 5d. ea.
1 cloak, £1.5.3	possibly 1 cloak, £1.1.0		
4 coats, 10s. 9d. ea.	2–3 coats, 10s. 5d. ea.	2 coats, 5s. 5d. ea.	3–4 coats, 7s. 11d. ea.
1 greatcoat, 10s. 7d	0 greatcoats	0 greatcoats	0 greatcoats
4 jackets, 3s. 4d. ea.	1–2 jackets, 8s. 1d. ea.	1 jacket, ?	1 jacket, 5s. 5d
1 suit, £1.7.2	1 suit, £1.18.2	0 suits	0 suits
1 waistcoat, ?	1–2 waistcoats, 4s. 7d. ea.	1–2 waistcoats, ?	3 waistcoats, 4s. 11d. ea.
3 caps, 14s. ea.	3 caps, 8s. ea.	2–3 caps, ?	0 caps
1–2 hats, 5s. 4d. ea.	1 hat, 3s. 5d.	1–2 hats, 1s. 10d. ea.	2 hats, 4s. 10d. ea.
1 pr. boots, 3s. 4d	possibly 1 pr. boots, 3s. 10d	0 pr. boots	possibly 1 pr. boots, 2s. 8d.
2 pr. shoes, 2s. 7d. ea.	1–2 pr. shoes, 3s. 1d. ea.	2–3 pr. shoes, 1s. 3d	2–3 pr. shoes, 2s. 8d. ea.
5 pr. stockings, 1s. 3d. ea.	3 pr. stockings, 1s. 4d. ea.	3 pr. stockings, ?	4 pr. stockings, 7d. ea.
2 pr. gloves, 1s. 2d. ea.	1 pr. gloves 1s. 5d. ea.	1 pr. gloves, 1s.	1–2 pr. gloves, 7d. ea.
0 mittens	0 mittens	0 mittens	1–2 pr. mittens, 1s. 6d. ea.
5 or 6 handkerchiefs, 10d. ea.	4 handkerchiefs, 12d. ea.	0 handkerchiefs	0 handkerchiefs

garments as well. Perhaps the most significant garment in terms of ownership was a suit, which appeared only in Levels I and II. Still, this does not indicate that men in any one level of social status dressed in a particular garb. Overall, the data indicate that Hadley men chose to dress very modestly, particularly those who would have been allowed by sumptuary legislation to dress more elegantly. In other aspects of their lives, these men were not afraid to spend money, and they enjoyed beautiful things. The Wadsworth Atheneum's 1985 exhibition *The Great River* uncovered a trove of lovely and valuable items that some early valley residents owned, including elegant silver made in Boston, clocks and caned chairs from England, linen damask and stoneware bottles from Germany, and books printed in London.[27] It is remarkable that this love of elegant things did not extend to their wardrobes.

The Sumptuary Law Prosecutions

Despite this apparent lack of ostentation, a number of Hadley men and women, along with others from Hampshire County, were brought to court by their neighbors for unacceptably fashionable and elegant dress, suggesting that interpretation of the sumptuary laws was not literal and involved more than the precise accounting of wealth or status. An examination of the probated individuals who were prosecuted and the stresses of the period may help to explain the litigation.

The Hampshire County Court records from March 1674 to March 1677 document a particularly large number of sumptuary prosecutions. In that three-year span, no fewer than thirty-two Hadley residents were brought before the county court to be admonished for the "wearing of silk in a flanting manner & Exess in Apparrell to ye offence of Sober people."[28] Apparently the sober people of Hadley, who unfortunately were never named in the court records, were easily offended; even the silk hood belonging to Mrs. Gramis, though the court admitted it was old and worn, was deemed too good for the poor woman to wear. She was fined heavily for the offense.[29] (See figures 8.4 and 8.5 for examples of the typical female dress of this period.)

Several of the accused were themselves, or were related to, men included in this study. In March 1673, when Dr. John Westcarr was twenty-eight years old, he was brought before the court along with his wife, Hannah. As a doctor, Westcarr was in good standing with the community. The same month that he was prosecuted for sumptuary law violations, the court allowed Westcarr to continue his practice of "Physick & Chirurgery" as he had had "good success

FIGURE 8.4 (*left*). *Drawing of Elizabeth Paddy Wensley of Boston, based on her portrait of c. 1675 in the collection of The Pilgrim Society, Plymouth. Drawing by David Rickman. Women's fashionable clothing in the seventeenth century was as elegant as men's. Mrs. Wensley wears the latest fashion for the last quarter of the seventeenth century: a gown with open skirt revealing a brocaded silk petticoat. The bodice, which is stiffly boned to create a conical torso, is embroidered down the front and embellished around the neckline with a lace pinner. The short sleeves are turned back to reveal a colored silk lining. The elbow-length sleeves of her smock extend below the gown sleeves and are decorated with a wide silk bow. Accessories include a fan, pearl necklace, earrings, and a silk hood. Her shoes are of silk, either brocade-woven or embroidered.*

FIGURE 8.5 (*right*). *A working class-woman of the 1670s. Drawing by David Rickman. The costume of a laboring-class woman of this period generally consisted of a hat, coif (or cap), neckerchief, waistcoat, petticoat, apron, smock, stockings, and shoes. The tight sleeves shown here were out of fashion, yet this woman would not have dreamed of obtaining a newer style of waistcoat until this one was worn out. To make the clothes last as long as possible, washable undergarments protected the more valuable outer garments. The inside of the hat was kept clean by the linen coif worn over the hair, and the linen shift and neckerchief kept body oils and perspiration from accumulating in the wool waistcoat and petticoat. The apron protected the front of the waistcoat and petticoat.*

through the hand of God upon his indeavors."[30] When he died in 1675, Westcarr had an estate worth more than twice the minimum set by the sumptuary laws; this fact, coupled with his status as a physician, should have protected him and his wife from prosecution if the sumptuary laws were interpreted literally. The Westcarrs' social and economic status at least protected them from being convicted, even if it could not protect them from prosecution; they were both acquitted. Perhaps conviction was never the goal, only the humiliation of the action. "Severall Sober Persons in hadly" accused Hannah again in 1676 for wearing silk in a "flanting garbe."[31] By this time, Hannah was a widow. Without the protection of her husband's economic and social status, she was "Convicted of her Offence [for which] the Corte did admonish her to be Carefull to reform such things wch are matters of offence."[32]

William Rooker was charged in March 1676 for wearing "Long Hairs & other Extravegences, Contrary to honest & Sober order & Demeanor not Becoming a Wilderness State at least ye Proffession of Christianity & Religion."[33] Rooker was a teenager at the time. He died in 1705, leaving an estate worth about £121. Though he was a farmer and not financially successful, his inventory includes some garments that reveal that his appreciation for fashion had not diminished: two hats, two waistcoats, four coats, a cape, a pair of plush breeches (among others), a blue scarf, and a "bunch" of ribbon, which was rare in the Hadley inventories. Though none of these items of clothing was specifically restricted under the sumptuary laws, the ensembles created from them are easily recognized as being rather gay for modest Hadley.

Standing with William Rooker before the judge that day in March 1676 was Nehemiah Dickinson, also charged with unseemly long hair and flaunting garb. At age thirty-two, Dickinson was older and more prominent in town than Rooker. The year before he had served as selectman, a position he would hold again twelve times. The taxes Dickinson paid in 1681 placed him in the economic top 20 percent of Hadley residents. Dickinson died in 1723 at the age of seventy-nine, leaving an estate worth £348. His inventory lists only modest garments—apparently, he had reformed (or perhaps given away his more valuable clothing). A pair of boots and a "Troopers" scarf were the only items of note. (Dickinson was a lieutenant in the militia, which accounts for the trooper's scarf.) Judging by his economic status as well as his social status, it would seem that Dickinson should have been exempt from prosecution for sumptuary law violations.

Yet another accused individual who should have been exempt was Andrew Warner's daughter, Ruth. Ruth was brought to court in January 1677 along with widow Westcarr. Because Ruth was unmarried, the social and economic status of her father would have determined whether she was eligible to wear silk hoods and the like. Andrew Warner was several times a selectman, and his estate was worth over £356 when he died in 1684; the value of his estate in 1681 was probably not much different from the value at the time of his death only three years later. Ruth Warner, like the Westcarrs and Nehemiah Dickinson, should have been exempt from prosecution for sumptuary law violations. But, as nineteenth-century local historian Sylvester Judd put it, "estates seem not to have been much regarded."[34]

Sitting in judgment of his neighbors was Mr. Peter Tilton, Esq., associate judge of the Hampshire County Court, selectman, deacon, and representative to the General Court. Tilton was perhaps the most respected man in Hadley in the seventeenth century, but he was far from the wealthiest. He was rated at £100 in the 1663 Hockanum Meadow land distribution and taxed 17s. 5d. in 1681, which placed him fifteenth of seventy-two taxed residents (or at the 21st percentile). He left an estate worth £234 on his death in 1696.

The clothing in Tilton's inventory reveals that he dressed more according to his social rank than his economic status. Tilton spent 4.5 percent of his estate on his wardrobe; although this is considerably more than the average of those neighbors who shared his social status, the difference is even greater when compared to those in the same economic category. Garments that revealed Tilton's importance included two suits (one of linsey woolsey worth 15s. 7d., the other of kersey, valued at £2.6.10—both very common and rather coarse fabrics), a new cloth (meaning wool) coat valued at over £2, a serge greatcoat, a new hat valued at 6s. 3d., three pairs of good gloves, five pairs of expensive stockings, and two good pairs of shoes. Surprisingly, his shirts were valued well below the average in both the appropriate economic and social categories. Tilton did, however, own three neckcloths (among others) that were trimmed with lace, valued at slightly over the average. He appears to have owned—at least at the time of his death—no silk, no ribbons, no boots, no gold or silver buttons, not even a cloak. The inventory reveals nothing for which Tilton could have been accused of hypocrisy as he passed judgment on the dozens of people brought before him for immodest dressing.

The terror and upheaval caused in 1675 and 1676 by King Philip's War, "the most destructive war in American history," appears to have played an important role in many of these sumptuary prosecutions.[35] This war, sparked by the execution of three Wampanoags in Plymouth in January 1675, grew into a conflagration that had swept across New England to the Connecticut River Valley by late summer that year. An attack on Brookfield (which lay within the boundaries of Hampshire County at that time) in August caused that settlement to be abandoned. In Hadley on August 22, Major John Pynchon reported that the soldiers "expect nothing but ye enemy to insult & fall upon ye remote Townes . . . they are in great feares."[36] They were right to be concerned. Northfield fell to an Indian attack on September 1. On September 18, in an effort to save the corn crop of Deerfield and prevent starvation of the valley's white residents over the coming winter, a force of sixty-five men were sent out; they were attacked by the Indians and nearly all killed in what has come to be known as the Bloody Brook Massacre. Deerfield subsequently joined the list of abandoned towns. Hadley sheltered the towns' survivors and worried about its own fate.

The wording in the court records in this period makes clear the judges' opinions that misbehavior of all kinds was grievously inappropriate at such a tense time, if not actually the cause of their "afflictions." In September 1676, the Hampshire County Court admonished John Lee of Westfield, saying his behavior was "not becomeing ye gospel Especially at Such a time of sore Affliction & Callamity by Reason of ye warr with ye Indians."[37] The following January Hannah Lyman of Northampton was severely chastised by the court for wearing silk "when ye people of god were falling before ye Lord in publique Humeliation in Respect of ye heavy Judgements & Callamities yt were threateing to Come upon us."[38] Over and over in the court records it is evident that the war made sumptuary prosecutions more urgent: "Considering of How unseemlie a nature such things are in this day of Calamietie, Wast & Destolation."[39] The terror of this period led the deeply religious people of Hadley and their representatives sitting on the county court to shame their "flaunting" neighbors into wearing more humble garb, in the hope of deserving God's mercy.

The Hampshire County sumptuary prosecutions and the clothing found in the inventories reveal Hadley to be a particularly conservative town in which fashionable dressing was seen as excessive and offensive. "Sober" townspeople tried to humble their "prideful" neighbors by accusing them of wearing "flaunting" garb, forcing them to appear in court to justify their appearance.

The men of Hadley continued to reflect their politics and religion in their conservative dress well into the eighteenth century. The luxury items that did appear in the wardrobes listed in Hadley inventories tended to be found at the end of the study period. They also often belonged to two men: Samuel Porter, Esq. (1722) and Dr. William Squire (1731). These were the only men in this study known to have owned a gold ring. They were two of only three men who owned spurs (Squire's were silver). Porter owned an untold number of gold and plate buttons and Squire had silver shoe buckles. Squire owned the only two wigs in town, along with the only banyan (a man's robe, generally of elegant silk or painted cotton, and worn by the educated classes). He also owned a gold watch worth over £11 and a silver-hilted sword worth about £2.

Though Porter and Squire owned among the most expensive clothing and accessories found in the Hadley inventories, their wardrobes were not the most extensive. Lieutenant Samuel Smith Sr. and his son Lieutenant Philip Smith hold that honor. Both men kept ordinaries, but Philip Smith was also a deacon, which made his social status Level I, while his father rated a Level II as a proprietor/professional. Samuel's estate on his death in 1680 was valued at over £606. Philip, who died of "witchcraft" in 1685 (see the essay by Bridget Marshall and Brian Ogilvie in this volume), owned an estate worth £998. Samuel invested 2.4 percent of his estate in clothing; his son devoted 2 percent—both significantly less than elite men in eastern Massachusetts.

Samuel owned two cloaks and five coats, while his son owned one cloak and nine coats. They both owned three hats and one suit. Samuel owned five shirts (including the two most expensive shirts found in this study); Philip had six. Philip also owned six pairs of drawers, eleven handkerchiefs, and fourteen bands. Samuel owned three pairs of shoes and more than fourteen bands. The most valuable garment in Samuel's inventory was a cloth coat worth £1.16.0. In Philip's wardrobe, a cloak valued at over £2 was the most expensive item listed. In general, this father and son represent the Hadley pattern: quantity was preferred over elegance. In Hadley, the ability to have more changes of their plain wool and linen clothing marked men of the upper class, not elegant silk brocade coats trimmed with gold lace, as was the case in Boston.

When higher quality clothing did appear in the Hadley inventories, it often was found in the estates of the proprietor/professionals, rather than the gentlemen. This pattern of material display is seen in at least one other aspect of Connecticut Valley material culture. In his study of eighteenth-century architecture, Kevin Sweeney found that the distinctive Connecticut River Valley doorways on the houses of "men of means . . . but of humble lineage" differed from those of the "River Gods" (the long-standing political, military, and religious leaders of the valley) in that they were "more elaborate and probably more expensive."[40] Perhaps in a similar way, Hadley's innkeepers, farmers, and merchants were attempting to display their success through their wardrobes in the early eighteenth century. Sweeney points out that the strictly Congregationalist River God families displayed a "disdain for certain effete aspects of genteel lifestyles. While the River Gods enjoyed displaying their worldly goods, they did not lead lives filled with dances and fetes."[41] Nor did the male members of the River God families dress in silks and lace like their dapper fellow colonials on the coast. For generations after the founding of Hadley, the example of the region's leading families' conservative ideology led to a tradition of modest dress across economic and social levels.

Notes

1. Probate inventories are lists of a decedent's personal and real estate, made in order to facilitate the distribution of their belongings; probate inventories were particularly important in the case of those who died without a will. This essay is based on Lynne Zacek Bassett, "The Sober People of Hadley: A Study of Clothing in the Probate Inventories of Hadley, Massachusetts, 1663–1731" (MA thesis, University of Connecticut, 1991). For other discussions of clothing in seventeenth- and early eighteenth-century Massachusetts, not otherwise cited in this essay, see Patricia Trautman, "When Gentlemen Wore Lace: Sumptuary Legislation and Dress in 17th-Century New England," *Journal of Regional Culture* 3, no. 2 (Fall/Winter 1983): 9–23; Wendy Kenerson, "A Suit of Clothes: Men's Clothing in the Deerfield Probate Inventories Taken from 1674–1820" (unpublished seminar paper, Historic Deerfield, Inc., 1987); Lynne Zacek Bassett, "Cloathes of his own Wareing: A Study of Clothing Listed in the Probate Inventories of Deerfield, Massachusetts, 1650–1750" (unpublished seminar paper, University of Connecticut, 1986); Alexandra Deutsch, "In Search of the Connecticut River Goddess: Clothing and Status in Eighteenth-Century Hampshire County" (unpublished seminar paper, Historic Deerfield, Inc., 1992). This essay does not include a comparable study of women's clothing, because so few Hadley women's estates were inventoried (as was typical for the period).
2. Bernard Bailyn, *The New England Merchants in the Seventeenth Century* (Cambridge, Mass.: Harvard University Press, 1979), 138–39.
3. Wayne Craven, *Colonial American Portraiture: The Economic, Religious, Social, Cultural, Philosophic, Scientific, and Aesthetic Foundations* (New York: Cambridge University Press, 1986), 14–15.
4. Jane C. Nylander, "Textiles, Clothing, and Needlework," in *The Great River: Art and Society of the Connecticut Valley, 1635–1820*, ed. Gerald W. R. Ward and William N. Hosley Jr. (Hartford, Conn.: Wadsworth Atheneum, 1985), 371–73; see also Gloria L. Main, "The Distribution of Consumer Goods in Colonial New England: A Subregional Approach," in *Early American Probate Inventories* (Dublin Seminar for New England Folklife Annual Proceedings, 1987), ed. Peter Benes (Boston: Boston University, 1989), 157; and Kevin Sweeney, "From Wilderness to Arcadian Vale: Material Life in the Connecticut River Valley, 1635–1760," in Ward and Hosley, *The Great River*, 20.
5. Patricia Trautman, "Dress in Seventeenth-Century Cambridge, Massachusetts: An Inventory-Based Reconstruction," in Benes, *Early American Probate Inventories*, 64–65.
6. The Ancient and Honorable Artillery Company was established in 1638 to train officers for the Massachusetts militia. For more information, see www.ahacsite.org/index.htm. The list of members of this organization includes Elisha Hutchinson, but not George Corwin. It is not known what significance, other than wealth and social position, Corwin's baldric might convey. I thank Paula Richter of the Peabody Essex Museum for checking the members list of the Ancient and Honorable Artillery Company.
7. Bailyn, *New England Merchants*, 139–42.
8. Increase Mather, *The Day of Trouble is Near: Two Sermons Wherein is shewed, What are the Signs of a Day of Trouble being near* (Cambridge: Marmaduke Johnson, 1674), 22.
9. "Excess in Apparel Prohibited" (1651), *The General Laws of the Massachusetts Colony, Revised and Published by Order of the General Court* (Boston, c. 1672).

10. See John J. McCusker, *How Much Is That in Real Money? A Historical Commodity Price Index for Use as a Deflator of Money Values in the Economy of the United States* (Worcester, Mass.: American Antiquarian Society, 2001). One should keep in mind that people did not earn nearly as much in generations past as they do now, so while $34,000 may not seem like that much today, it was a very large estate indeed to a skilled laborer who earned two shillings, or the equivalent of about twenty-seven cents, a day.
11. "Excess in Apparel Prohibited."
12. Ibid.
13. Sylvester Judd provides a transcript of the land distribution and tax lists; the original records are now lost. See Sylvester Judd, *History of Hadley, including the Early History of Hatfield, South Hadley, Amherst and Granby, Massachusetts*, 2nd ed. (Springfield, Mass.: H. R. Huntting, 1905; repr., Somersworth: New Hampshire Publishing, 1976), 26–28, 203–4. Gloria Main points out that among the pitfalls of probate research is the fact that "most probated decedents were males who tended to be older and richer than their neighbors still living." For this reason, tax lists are used to correct the data and gain a better perspective on the community. See Gloria Main, "The Correction of Biases in Colonial American Probate Records," *Historical Methods Newsletter* 8, no. 1 (December 1974): 10–28; Gloria Main, "Probate Records as a Source for Early American History," *William and Mary Quarterly*, 3rd ser., 32, no. 1 (January 1975): 89–100; Kevin Sweeney, "Using Tax Lists to Detect Biases in Probate Inventories," in Benes, *Early American Probate Inventories*, 32–40.
14. This social stratification system is based on Michael B. Katz, "Occupational Classification in History," *Journal of Interdisciplinary History* 3 (1972): 63–88. Though Katz's research was based on nineteenth-century resources, his scale, with a few modifications, is appropriate for this study. The changes were made primarily in Levels I and II: whereas Katz places innkeepers, merchants, and farmers in Level I, seventeenth-century sumptuary laws indicate that Level I should be occupied by men of gentle birth and those with a college degree.
15. Judd, in his *History of Hadley*, along with original court records, give the occupations of a number of Hadley men; information on others was gathered form the probate inventories.
16. Quoted in Margaret Spufford, *The Great Reclothing of Rural England* (London: Hambledon Press, 1984), 121.
17. C. Willett and Phillis Cunnington, *The History of Underclothes*, rev. ed. (Boston: Faber and Faber, 1981), 52.
18. Donna Bartsch, "Social and Economic Mobility of Servants and Gentlemen in Massachusetts Bay as Visible in Costume" (MA thesis, University of Connecticut, 1988), 33.
19. C. H. Spiers, "Deer Skin Leathers and Their Use for Costume," *Costume* 7 (1973): 18.
20. Norah Waugh, *The Cut of Men's Clothes, 1600–1900* (New York: Theatre Books, 1964), 38.
21. Bartsch points to the cloak as a particular status symbol in her study of clothing in eastern Massachusetts ("Social and Economic Mobility," 58–59).
22. Trautman, "Dress in Seventeenth-Century Cambridge," 51–73.
23. See Bartsch, "Social and Economic Mobility."
24. Ibid., 62.
25. U.S. Department of Labor and U.S. Bureau of Labor Statistics, *One Hundred Years of Consumer Spending: Data for the Nation, New York City and Boston*, Bureau of Labor Statistics Report 991 (May 2006), 61. www.bls.gov/opub/uscs/report991.pdf (accessed 19 July 2008).
26. Bartsch, "Social and Economic Mobility," 61.
27. See Ward and Hosley, *The Great River*.

28. Hampshire County Court Records, vol. 1, 186 (26 September 1676). Hampshire County Hall of Records, Northampton, Mass.
29. Mrs. Gramis was fined 10s. 8d. Ibid., 153.
30. Ibid., 144. A "chirurgeon" was a bonesetter. These individuals, Judd writes, were "highly valued," and "some towns in Hampshire County voted pecuniary rewards to induce one to settle among or near them." Judd, *History of Hadley*, 442. Westcarr, however, did not have an entirely clean record. A few years before he got into trouble for wearing elegant clothes, he was prosecuted for selling liquor to the Indians. Judd, *History of Hadley*, 64.
31. Hampshire County Court Records, vol. 1, 185; see also Laurel Thatcher Ulrich's essay in this volume.
32. Ibid.
33. Ibid., 177. Rooker, too, had a run-in with the law on more than this occasion. In February of 1676, he was fined £5 for his part in a "riotous assembly" in Hadley. Judd, *History of Hadley*, 90.
34. Judd, *History of Hadley*, 92.
35. Ibid., 96.
36. Quoted in Richard I. Melvoin, *New England Outpost: War and Society in Colonial Deerfield* (New York: W. W. Norton, 1989), 99.
37. Hampshire County Court Records, vol. 1, 179–80.
38. Ibid., 185.
39. Ibid., 195.
40. Kevin M. Sweeney, "Mansion People: Kinship, Class, and Architecture in Western Massachusetts in the Mid Eighteenth Century," *Winterthur Portfolio* 19, no. 4 (Winter 1984): 249.
41. Ibid., 247.

9

As Laurel Ulrich's and Lynne Bassett's essays demonstrate, women thought carefully about the material objects that surrounded them, and made decisions about their appearance that were deeply grounded in community values. Karen Parsons affirms the conscious way women acquired and made use of goods in a study of gentlewoman Elizabeth Porter Phelps's early nineteenth-century gift of silver to Hadley's First Congregational Church. Eschewing easy analyses that see such gifts merely as gestures to display wealth and privilege, Parsons explores the ways in which donated objects could communicate genuine commitments to spiritual concerns and communities. She, like Ulrich, also reminds us how women used objects to reach beyond the confines of their own lives; whether bequeathed to loved ones or given to congregations, objects allowed women to extend their influence over generations.

"We owe something more than prayers"

Elizabeth Porter Phelps's Gift of Church Silver and Her Quest for Christian Fellowship

Karen Parsons

> May we ever remember that we owe something more than prayers even on offering to the Lord that they who preach the Gospel shall be supported.
>
> *Elizabeth Porter Phelps to Elizabeth Phelps Huntington, August 21, 1811*

Sometime in the years between 1811 and 1813, Elizabeth Porter Phelps, a wealthy Hadley townswoman, donated two communion vessels to the congregation at the Church of Christ (figure 9.1). Such gifts of silver, especially when inscribed with the donor's name, expressed something about the giver to the community. One convention of material culture criticism ascribes the

FIGURE 9.1. *Thomas C. Fletcher (1787–1866) and Sidney Gardiner (1791–1869), two-handled communion cups, Boston, 1808–1813. Courtesy of the First Congregational Church of Hadley.*

gesture primarily to the desire to demonstrate status. Since Phelps belonged to a prominent, moneyed Massachusetts family, it would be easy to see these cups as nothing other than a display of class identity. A careful examination of the context in which Phelps made the gift, however, reveals the complexity of the role that church silver played in early nineteenth-century New England life. In this broader view, it becomes evident that the gift brought together the social networks in which Phelps traveled as a wealthy woman with her intense dedication to her religious principles and community. The meaning of the communion vessels in particular is revealed in this context, since the Hadley congregation advocated a very open and inclusive communion ritual. Furthermore, the time at which Phelps gave the cups coincided with a membership crisis in the church in the years following the death of their beloved pastor, the Reverend Samuel Hopkins.

Taken at face value, Phelps's gift can be read as an expression of status simply by virtue of her family wealth and the high profile she maintained in her church. The family's wealth was certainly no secret to those who worshipped at the Church of Christ. Elizabeth's husband, Charles, owned six hundred acres, making him the largest landowner in town; in 1799 he paid almost twice as much land tax as the next largest property owner.[1] The Phelpses employed church members and local residents as farm workers, domestic servants, and skilled craftspeople at Forty Acres (figure 9.2).[2] The couple's activities within their church also demonstrated, intentionally or not, their financial well-being. Charles, who served as a deacon and played an important role in the 1807–8 construction of the third meetinghouse, sold pews in this new meetinghouse to church members.[3] He also owned three pews: numbers 26 and 28, each valued at $200, and number 70—which he probably rented out—valued at $24 in 1817.[4]

Befitting their financial position, the Phelpses communicated a taste for decor that was fashionable, genteel, and urban: while the surrounding area supplied their household labor, by 1800 the Phelpses looked often to Boston, not to Hadley, to furnish their home.[5] Not insignificantly, the cups themselves were of Boston manufacture, making it all the more likely that Elizabeth's fellow churchgoers would have associated the cups with her social station. Each of the two five-inch-tall cups bears a footed base and two strap handles projecting more than an inch and a half from its body, and an inscription that reads, "Presented / by Elizabeth Phelps to the / Church of Christ in Hadley. / Feby. 1813." On the underside of one cup's base appears the stamp "F.&G." in a rectangular surround—the mark of the silversmithing firm Fletcher and Gardiner. Thomas Fletcher and his partner Sidney Gardiner ran a shop and retail store in Boston between 1808 and 1811. They sold goods produced by other metalworkers but found their greatest profit in merchandising wares made in their own silversmithing shop.[6] Leaving aside the conflict in evidence—maker's mark versus inscribed date—Phelps apparently made the gift between 1811 and 1813.[7]

FIGURE 9.2. *Forty Acres, Hadley, Massachusetts. Courtesy of the Porter-Phelps-Huntington House Museum.*

Considerable evidence and analysis about the social value of material culture appears in a pivotal exhibition catalog titled *The Great River: Art and Society of the Connecticut River Valley*. In her discussion of how silver objects functioned to display the affluence of the area's elite, Barbara McLean Ward notes that gifts of expensive communion silver "made [the donors'] power and position manifest to all . . . their neighbors."[8] In his contribution to the book, Robert Blair St. George asserted that the wealthy elite "preserved the image of corporate communalism to their own advantage" by making generous donations of church plate. Churches had no choice but to be subservient to these donors, who, according to St. George, made "calculated acts of largesse" and thus maintained a level of control over their congregations.[9] The Hadley church certainly did obtain its silver through a particular social network that included Phelps and a number of her friends, including Lucretia Colt Walker. John Hopkins, another close friend of Phelps and the son of Rev. Hopkins, gave an enormous gift of silver fused-plate communion vessels in 1824.[10] The set comprised eight cups, four plates, two flagons, and one baptismal basin. Church records note that "two tankards and some cups were given by Major Erastus Smith" (figure 9.3) on the same day that Hopkins presented his gift. "On July 4, 1824 . . . the church voted 'thanks to Major E. Smith and Captain John Hopkins for furniture for the communion table.' "[11] Phelps also counted Smith among her convivial group of friends.

FIGURE 9.3. *Unknown maker, two-handled communion cup, probably England, 1824. Courtesy of the First Congregational Church of Hadley.*

While many churchgoers certainly recognized Phelps's wealth and her social position as they drank from the cups she had given, that perception does not necessarily encompass the meaning that the objects would have carried for Phelps herself. Phelps's diary and letters reveal that her primary motivation for the gift was not to make a public statement about her wealth nor to gain power within the church community. The tenor of her spiritual life as she recorded it in these documents, as well as the many acts of Christian fellowship she performed, suggest that Phelps prioritized building and maintaining Christian fellowship above all or most other goals. Probably inspired by her friendship with Rev. Hopkins, the gift may have been intended to embody his beliefs about communion participation—a belief manifested in the very design of the cups and the way they functioned during the communion service.

Phelps's day-to-day life was very much a product of her fellowship in Hopkins's congregation. She lived her piety, integrating rigorous spiritual self-examination and dedicated discipleship into almost everything she did. Her forty-nine years of highly introspective diary entries and numerous letters recount her noble deeds, moments of self-doubt, and concern for others' personal salvation. Phelps ardently pursued fellowship through daily acts of generosity—aiding the poor, the parentless, and the distressed. She actively looked to create spiritual fellowship with her husband, her household, townspeople, women in the community, and with Christians around the globe.

A testament to how closely Phelps wished to integrate religion into her daily life appears in her thoughts about her husband, who did not share her focus on spiritual matters. Charles apparently had little tolerance for religion that swayed from traditional Calvinism. In an 1807 letter to her daughter Elizabeth Phelps Huntington, Phelps reported that "we had Mr. Montague all day, a baptist preacher—your father stood it pretty well."[12] Worse yet, Charles often failed to engage in spiritual introspection, and possibly her greatest disappointment resulted from their inability to share thoughts about religion. On the thirty-seventh anniversary of their wedding, Elizabeth reflected, "my feelings on this day have been tender & solemn—when I remember, what my expectations were before I married, respecting a life of religious conversation, & mutual enjoyment of the things of God—I am almost ready to sink in discouragement—my husband has treated me with that reserve & distance which I little expected . . . he finds not that inducement to converse upon experimental religion perhaps, which is requisite to a free Union & endearing interchanging of tho'ts & affections.—O how ought my heart to be humbled, low in the dust before God, that the privilege which I so ardently desired, & confidently expected, has been almost wholly denied me."[13] Elizabeth's relationship with Hopkins may have satisfied her desires to "converse upon experimental religion" and acquired special significance as a result.

Phelps created other opportunities to foster Christian fellowship in her household, especially in the work spaces at Forty Acres, where she interacted with her domestic servants and their children. Approximately thirty women worked and lived at Forty Acres over two decades.[14] Like the church community, this household staff was diverse, including white, African American, and Native American women. Most were young, at least two arrived at Forty Acres unwed and with an infant in their arms, and still others became pregnant while in Phelps's service.[15] Phelps extended concern to these young mothers and in particular to their children. She and Charles sponsored two-and-a-half-year-old Submit West, the daughter of former servant Susanna Whipple, for baptism in the Hadley church in 1794.[16] Later, Phelps kept Submit, or Mitte as she was called, off the town's pauper roles by repeatedly securing her employment; bad behavior cost the teenaged Mitte four jobs in eighteen months.[17]

Phelps showed special concern for two elderly German paupers, George and Mary Andries. While the town paid Charles Phelps a small sum to provide basic necessities and medical services for George and Mary, in the tradition of the local poor relief system, Elizabeth took pains to watch over and nurture a relationship with these two elderly neighbors.[18] Elizabeth cared for Mary in December 1783 when Andries believed she had been poisoned.[19] In 1785, 1788, and 1793 Charles and Elizabeth Phelps visited the Andrieses in "their humble cottage at the edge of the woods opposite Forty Acres" to "eat Christmas supper;" a German tradition not shared in the eighteenth century by most New England Congregationalists.[20] After George's death in 1809, Phelps visited the eighty-five-year-old invalid Mary and "told her she must come live with me but that she must leave all her dirt & rags" behind.[21] Speaking little English and with a heavy German accent, in poor health, and unable to dress herself, Mary brought new challenges to the household. But to Phelps's delight, this poor widow sought God's help while resting at Forty Acres. "She appears to be in prayer a great part of her time, uplifted eyes, with folded hands . . . how should I feel was I such a poor helpless creature in a strange land without any person to depend on? [N]o where else but on clear, pure providence, indeed I can't but hope her eyes are fixed & trusting on God. . . . She says, 'all is good, all is good.' "[22] Evidence of such religious devotion apparently fulfilled Phelps's goals for her charitable work. All of her deeds tended toward bringing Christians together in a greater awareness of God's presence in their daily lives.

These deeds rarely passed without Phelps's self-evaluation of intentions and results. Often she emerged from this introspection humbled and more committed to her goals of spiritual fellowship. Phelps looked to God and through prayer for solace in these dark moments of self-doubt. While Phelps asked for God's guidance in these trying matters, the birth of Submit West's mulatto child in January 1810, just after her nineteenth birthday, drew Phelps into a month-long flurry of reflection. She wrote, "Lord it is a sore grief to me, may my sin be set before me—my neglects be forgiven."[23] Four weeks later she recorded, "we have been taught by experience so often that when we were endeavouring to do our best it has eventually been productive of the most unhappiness. . . . Oh Lord we desire to look to thee for direction . . . if thou seest best that we should be more tried, & grieved by her misconduct may we say in truth, they will be done. Lord there is one favour for [Mitte], which I may beg for . . . may the riches of sovereign Grace be exalted, in the salvation of her & her poor destitute child—we have dedicated her to the Lord in baptism & . . . where is so ever we have done wrong, may we all be forgiven & have true repentance."[24]

Outside of her home, Phelps propagated Christian fellowship no less ardently. She worked closely within her church's congregation in a number of capacities and pursued a discipleship well beyond it. Her efforts within her church ranged from finite tasks to ongoing and much more active organizing. When the congregation built its third meetinghouse, Elizabeth participated in the effort to furnish the new building with textiles. In July of 1809 she "rode into town of arrands. Carried a tablecloth to deacon Smiths for the communion table."[25] On a broader scale, she vigorously organized Hadley women for church patronage and prayer meetings. During 1808, Phelps asked women to join a subscription for dressing the pulpit in the new meetinghouse. She traveled to "the Mills" and the town's Back Street—areas that held some dissension among the residents about where the new building should be located—and she asked the female inhabitants to put aside their differences and unite with women across town.[26] In the spring of 1810 Phelps joined "the good women [who] had agreed to keep as a day of fasting & prayer for a blessing upon their families & others."[27]

While Phelps physically assembled with women for patronage and prayer, she also organized female believers to pray simultaneously, but in the isolation of their own homes. To celebrate the dedication of the new meetinghouse and, more importantly, the resolutions of the divisions that had threatened the community, Elizabeth and other women "agreed to Join in a certain hour (altho' at our respective homes) & offer up our . . . thanks, to the great God who we think has answer'd our prayers."[28] Phelps later invited women from different towns in the river valley, including a neighboring "pious widow" and a family member living in Middletown, Connecticut, to join in prayer at ten o'clock on Saturday evenings. She hoped these women, separated by geography but united in faith, would offer prayers for "our near relations."[29] Phelps's enthusiasm for this dispersed prayer meeting indicates that she enjoyed fellowship on a spiritual level: she envisioned a Christian community that maintained its fellowship even when it could not gather together.[30]

As evidenced in her diary, Phelps also pursued her religious ideals with a missionary zeal, working and praying always for the winning of new souls to God. In 1805, for example, Phelps and other Hadley women took special interest in the "deranged" soul of local resident Samuel Porter: after a prayer session on the Old Street, as Phelps wrote, "a number of women retir'd into a room [and] pray'd—this meeting called upon Lawyer Porters account who continues to be in distress for his soul."[31] During a prayer meeting the following year, Elizabeth was overwhelmed by "a sudden & earnest desire . . . that a dear friend . . . might be fitted for, & brought to the Lords table, & faith immediately followed it—that it would soon be so."[32] By 1807 Porter "appeared a very bright Christian" and in 1809 he joined the church.[33] Phelps remarked that this was the "fulfillment of the faith which was so strongly impressed on my mind . . . in 1806."[34]

During the winter of 1810 Phelps witnessed the "signs of an . . . outpouring of the spirit" in Hadley that excited her hopes: "some are under convictions, may they . . . endure to the end & be saved."[35] Two months later, she enthusiastically reported that two teenage girls "are very much altered, they are together several hours a day with their bibles alone.—have no conversation with anybody, tell none of their feelings unless to each other . . . the Lord is surely carrying on his own work & we will rejoice in it."[36] At the same time that she hoped for increased faith in Hadley, she held great optimism for an apparent "outpouring of the spirit" across New England and even around the globe. She longed to hear reports about religion's impact. She asked her daughter, Elizabeth Huntington, who lived in Middletown, Connecticut, to "tell in your next, how the small awakening process, in those few families by the river, & how religion is with you, as a town—O may there be many sons & daughters born into the *real* family of Christ.[37] The Phelpses hosted regional Missionary Committee meetings at their home and attended numerous ordinations and lectures by missionaries who worked around the globe.[38] In December 1811 a jubilant Elizabeth reported: "O what good tidings are constantly saluting our ears, from many parts of the world. . . . [O]ur hearts leap for Joy when we hear how many instruments God is raising up."[39] In many ways, her desires for the advancement of the gospel seemed to be fulfilled, in Hadley and beyond.

The inspiration for Phelps's hard work and ardent discipleship took shape in the Church of Christ congregation and specifically under the teachings of Rev.

Hopkins, who was called to the pulpit in Hadley just a few months after Elizabeth turned seven years old.[40] He remained her pastor well into her adult life and became an important friend as well. In her diary, Phelps recorded numerous visits to Hopkins's home and wrote enthusiastically about these visits and his preaching. The ideal he inculcated in his congregation all those years was primarily one of religious fellowship. Some years later his successor, the Reverend John Woodbridge, would recall Hopkins as a "distinguished . . . cultivator of peace among his people."[41]

The religious community Hopkins fostered practiced diversity in a variety of ways—not only by including the unconverted along with the converted, but also without discrimination as to race or denominational leanings. Hopkins welcomed African Americans to full membership in this overwhelmingly white congregation. At least five African Americans, four of whom were slaves, were admitted to full church membership between 1765 and 1776.[42] Hopkins performed at least five marriages for African American couples during the years from 1766 to 1808.[43] Evidence suggests that the black congregants were segregated from whites in the meetinghouse: from the mid-eighteenth century, they sat in the gallery's back seats or in the "high pews in the corners over the stairs, which were very conspicuous."[44] No evidence survives revealing where they sat in the third meetinghouse, dedicated in 1808. Despite being physically marginalized from the rest of the congregation, and despite their small numbers, some African Americans were fully integrated into the spiritual fellowship of Hopkins's church. During a June 1768 worship service, "Ralf Way [a free African American] desired prayers for his child sick of the canker which is called the Throat Distemper . . . and has swept away a great many children."[45] Between 1799 and 1809 at least four funerals of African Americans and one of a mulatto girl took place in Hadley. Elizabeth Porter Phelps attended these or burials and prayer meetings for the deceased.[46]

Hopkins also kept his church open to Christians with denominational leanings different from Congregationalism and thus deterred splinter churches from forming. A nineteenth-century Hadley native noted that "in Hopkins's day, it was a great point of interest to keep out other sects. And no small part of the minister's duty was to watch against interlopers."[47] The most significant threat to church unity during his tenure came from Baptists. In 1805 Hopkins encouraged churchgoers to "mark them who cause divisions and offences, contrary to the doctrine which ye have learned," and, more specifically, "those who [are] commonly called Baptists among us." These persons sought to separate themselves from the congregation over differing ideas on the appropriateness of infant and adult baptism. Hopkins adamantly opposed the potential divisions.

He argued that "those . . . Baptists have no pretence of any sufficient ground for separation from our churches, save such of them as behold we are not churches of Christ, because baptized in infancy, and that therefore they can not partake with us at the table of the Lord." Hopkins urged his people to broaden the place of the baptism ritual in the Hadley meetinghouse and to give the so-called Baptists no sufficient grounds for leaving the congregation. He stated that "we are ready to baptize [these people], at the age, and in the mode, they think proper; and when baptized, to receive them to our communion."[48] Hopkins made it a priority to preserve the congregation's unity by identifying and promoting the common beliefs among groups. He thus managed not only to build fellowship within his congregation but also to keep other churches from forming in town.

The communion ritual that Hopkins unfailingly kept open to a broad range of individuals played a vital role in his quest for religious unity.[49] He consistently welcomed "all persons of a sober moral life" to the communion table, "whether they did or did not profess to have been subjected to renewed grace."[50] The diverse group invited to this ritual, one of Christianity's most sacred, included the town's social elite, paupers, African Americans, churchgoers with Baptist leanings, conservative Congregationalists, and most importantly, individuals for whom the communion service offered an opportunity to experience conversion, not affirm an already publicly professed faith. Hopkins and his two predecessors, Isaac Chauncey and Chester Williams, all viewed this sacrament as a converting ordinance, not a reward for those who had publicly disclosed their conversion experience. These ministers, who maintained the church between 1695 and 1809, welcomed the converted and unconverted to full participation in the Lord's Supper.[51]

After Phelps's donation, the church owned six two-handled vessels and used this form exclusively until 1824. Although no evidence reveals who selected Phelps's Fletcher and Gardiner cups for the Church of Christ, whoever made the choice—Phelps or the church deacons—clearly had in mind the communion silver already used in the meetinghouse. The church owned four two-handled cups by 1800.[52] In her essay " 'In a Feasting Posture': Communion Vessels and Community Values in Seventeenth- and Eighteenth-Century New England," Barbara McLean Ward suggested that a preference for a single form of communion vessel can indicate a congregation's desire to blur social distinctions among church patrons and members of the congregation.[53] Since this reading could easily apply to the Hadley church, given its efforts to erase spiritual distinctions among participants during the communion ritual, it helps to explain the church's apparent preference for two-handled vessels in the absence of any other documentation. Its earliest ritual vessels were probably pewter and part of a set acquired after the town's settlement in 1659. Unfortunately, these no longer survive in the church collection.[54] Beginning with the items extant from the eighteenth century, however, a relationship seems to appear between the church's emerging doctrine of an open communion and its preference for the two-handled communion vessels. In 1723 Peter Montague donated a two-handled silver cup made by Boston silversmith John Dixwell. Roughly half a century later the church received another silver cup, made by Zachariah Brigden in Boston, bearing these oversized handles. Between 1781 and 1784 Lucretia Colt gave two silver fused-plate cups to the church in memory of her husband, Benjamin Colt (figure 9.4).[55] Silver and silver fused-plate vessels remained in use at the Hadley church until 1906, when small individual glass cups were introduced.[56]

Among the unusually diverse population in Hopkins's meetinghouse, the passing of the communion vessel from one congregant to the next would have constituted in itself an act of spiritual fellowship. The communion ritual began with the minister's blessing of the wine, after which he poured it from a large vessel into the smaller cups. The blessed wine then stood for the blood Christ shed to forgive the sins of mankind and secure the promise of everlasting life. Thus bearing, in metaphor, the blood of Christ, the two-handled cups traveled through the congregation—"worthy deacons and communicants . . . passed them from hand to hand and from lip to lip as they took the cup and gave thanks."[57]

FIGURE 9.4. *Unknown maker, two-handled communion cup, probably England, 1781–1784. Courtesy of the First Congregational Church of Hadley.*

Drinking from the vessel, each communicant embraced this promise simultaneously with an entire congregation. Each time a participant transferred the cup to the next believer, a moment occurred when two members held the cup together, each grasping one of the handles. In the same way that the promise of an eternal spiritual life held meaning for the group as well as the individual, these two-handled cups facilitated a single participant's communion experience and linked it to that of others in the meetinghouse. Clearly, the two-handled cups favored by the Hadley congregation helped to promote Hopkins's vision of congregational unity.

This inclusive invitation to church rituals had not always been in effect in Hadley. The town's first minister, the Reverend John Russell, who served from 1659 to 1692, subscribed to more conservative ideas about who was eligible for the church's sacraments. The town's founding in 1659 resulted from disagreement in the church in Hartford, Connecticut, partly over who could present their children for baptism. A minority in the Hartford congregation held fast to the conservative teachings of their recently deceased pastor, Thomas Hooker, and believed that only full church members were entitled to baptize their children. These traditional Congregationalists rejected the less rigid view of their current minister, Samuel Stone. As Stone promoted the Half-way Covenant—this loosening of the rules governing baptism—the minority withdrew from the church, aligned with Rev. Russell of Wethersfield, and removed to Massachusetts. In Hadley, Russell enforced "strict Congregationalism" by allowing only members of the church in full communion to present their children for baptism and by administering communion only to "those who gave some evidence of faith and repentance."[58]

A less exclusive perspective about the church community came to the Hadley congregation after Russell's death in 1692 and with the calling of Isaac Chauncey three years later. Chauncey and his two successors, Chester Williams and Samuel Hopkins, subscribed to the theology advocated by Solomon Stoddard, minister in the neighboring town of Northampton from 1669 to 1712. Stoddard, who in his youth had experienced a conversion during a communion service, promoted "open communion" for all worshippers as a means by which they might feel that " 'mighty change' in the heart."[59] He did not require a public affirmation of faith for membership in the Northampton church; one needed only "evidence of good behavior[,] . . . a simple profession of faith," and Stoddard's approval in order to gain access to the communion ritual. Stoddard believed that individuals could experience conversion after "extensive preparation through baptism, education, prayer, communion and much consideration of God's word."[60]

During his lifetime, Stoddard gained limited support in the Connecticut River Valley for redefining the role of the communion service and the part that ministers could play—because they administered that ritual—in conversion. Staunch support came from some nearby churches and their ministers, especially Isaac Chauncey of Hadley and William Williams of Hatfield.[61] After Stoddard's death, however, his views were challenged by his successor and grandson, Jonathan Edwards. Under Edwards's leadership, the Northampton church returned to strict Congregationalist views requiring "those received into the church [to] make a credible profession of piety."[62] This reversal contributed to great controversy in the church and resulted in Edwards's dismissal in 1750. Chester Williams, Hadley's minister at the time, sat on a county-wide ministerial council that heard Edwards's case. Williams voted for the preacher's dismissal, honoring Hadley's longtime allegiance to an open communion.[63] In 1755, when Hopkins took his place at the Hadley pulpit, he joined with a congregation already well versed in the welcoming theology he espoused.

Despite the legacy of decades that gave foundation to Hopkins's principles, the Hadley congregation went into crisis when they lost his leadership. In 1809 Hopkins suffered a number of strokes; about one, Phelps noted in her diary that he "had another shock, one side nearly dead."[64] Paralysis forced him to retire from active ministry, although he remained the senior pastor at the church in name.[65] Elizabeth visited him regularly over the next two years while immobility confined him to his bed. During the week before his death in March 1811, Phelps sat with him for at least two days.[66] Less than a day after his death she was "at the meetinghouse to see about putting the pulpit in black."[67] She later wrote: "Tuesday we attended the funeral of Dr. Hopkins—a dear good friend to us & to all mankind. May all follow him as he followed Christ."[68] Phelps's first opportunity to take communion after Hopkins's death prompted an especially painful moment of self-examination. She wrote in her diary: "One more opportunity at the Lords table, can it be that there is one spark of true grace? Lord awake this dead, hard, stupid heart[.] [W]hat can, what shall I do, but endeavour & really take my place, at the foot of the Cross—Lord, if I perish, surely it will be just—the Sovereign God has a sovereign right to choose who he pleases—to make one vessel to honour & another to dishonour."[69] The loss was certainly a profound and personal one for Phelps, but she took no less personally the threat to the congregation that he had ministered so carefully. After a lifetime of trying to live and support Hopkins's ideals, Phelps would do all she could to bolster the community's commitment after his death. In this context, it became clear that the communion vessels she gave sometime between 1811 and 1813 evoked Hopkins's vision of a unified church dedicated to an inclusive communion ritual.

The gift must also have inspired helpful memories for the congregation as it found itself in a membership crisis.

Phelps's concern about threats to the congregation had already become evident a few years earlier, when the construction of the new meetinghouse stirred disagreement in Hadley. At that time, a number of Back Street residents refused to buy pews in the new building, and six months into the project less than half of the seating had been purchased.[70] With great relief, Elizabeth reported that by the 1808 dedication of the meetinghouse, "those people who have been greatly displeased, & said many hard & bitter things against . . . those who have built the house, are now so far reconciled, that almost the whole of them, are coming into the new meeting-house, & either buying or hireing pews."[71] It was clear to Elizabeth why this change of heart occurred. "This is the Lord's doing. It is marvelous in our eyes . . . we have long been sending up [our prayers] to the throne of grace for this very change of sentiment & conduct."[72]

Just as the church appeared unified after the meetinghouse dedication, and the Lord's good works were apparent in town, Hopkins's illness and death precipitated a dramatic membership crisis. Once Hopkins became bedridden in 1809, the junior pastor, Rev. Woodbridge, took over the pulpit; he did not earn popularity in town quickly. Phelps described him as "very much an orritor[;] has many gestures."[73] By 1811, the year of Hopkins's death, a frustrated Woodbridge noted in his records, "the church diminishes with rapidity." He added an ominous warning: "Consider ye that slight the Lord. Presume his wrath anon."[74] That year the congregation lost twenty-three members to death.[75] Despite an extraordinary increase in new members—a fourfold increase over the previous year in new adult memberships, with thirteen new believers—in 1811 the number of church members who died was almost twice the number of new communicants.[76] The following year brought only one new member to the church, and in 1813 only three adults joined.

Phelps focused her energies on the individuals who did join. She recorded their admissions in her diary and distinguished those who joined by adult baptism, and she took particular interest in the young women, who accounted for eleven—or 85 percent—of these new members.[77] In May 1811 she wrote: "We had had a number join'd to the Church short of a year & there are four new propounded. Polly Shipman is one, & I suppose by what I see & have heard, she rejoices greatly in the Lord. O may there be many sons & daughters, born into the *real* family of Christ."[78] Four months later, Phelps visited Betsey Smith shortly after her baptism and reflected, "I rode out east, the middle way to a cloathers—stopt a few moments at Sereno Smiths—[His wife] was taken into the church last Lords day—was baptized herself & three children, Lord Jesus was not my heart drawn forth in Love to thee, & thy members."[79] The sentiment she expressed here, the dedicated effort to further the growth of the church, provides us with the context so easily overlooked in the standard analysis of church donations. Perhaps Phelps hoped her donation of communion vessels would buoy the spirits of a flagging congregation, drawing churchgoers' hearts closer to Jesus and to their fellow members, as she had felt during her visit with Smith.

The cups physically increased access to Hadley's communion ritual and built fellowship among the congregation. At the same time, they pledged support for the enlargement of a spiritual fellowship around the globe. While Phelps struggled in her life and writings to balance worldly concerns with the promise of eternal life, she clearly stated her belief in salvation through Christian fellowship with her gift of communion silver. In offering "something more than prayers" to Hadley's Church of Christ, Elizabeth Porter Phelps brought together her material and spiritual realms in these cups, and furthered her lifelong pursuit of Christian fellowship.

Notes

I am grateful to the many individuals who offered support of many kinds to this research. They include Dorothy Russell of the Hadley Historical Society; the Reverend Lorain Giles, Ted McQuestion, and the Board of Deacons of the First Congregational Church, U.C.C., Hadley; Susan Lisk of the Porter-Phelps-Huntington House Museum; Bruce Laverty of the Philadelphia Athenaeum; and the staff of the Special Collections at the Amherst College Library. Hilary Anderson Stelling, Jill Meyers, and Jeff Hardwick gave comments on early drafts. Donald Fennimore, curator emeritus at the Winterthur Museum and Country Estate, encouraged this work with his rich understanding of American silver and his unfailing kindness.

1. Christopher Clark, *The Roots of Rural Capitalism: Western Massachusetts, 1780–1860* (Ithaca: Cornell University Press, 1990), 41; Sylvester Judd, *Selected Papers from the Sylvester Judd Manuscripts*, comp. Gregory H. Nobles and Herbert L. Zarov (Northampton, Mass.: Forbes Library, 1976), 523.
2. Marla Miller, "Crossing the Threshold: Interpreting Women and Community in the Phelps Household, 1770–1816," paper given at "Through Women's Eyes: A Colloquium Presenting New Research on Women at 'Forty Acres,' 1750–1850: The Reinterpretation Initiative Phase II," Porter-Phelps-Huntington House Museum, Hadley, Mass., 24 September 1994; Margaret Mary Fitzpatrick, "Forty Acres: A New England Homestead and Its Owners, 1752–1814" (MA thesis, University of Delaware, 1977), 62, 66, 75; Clark, *Roots of Rural Capitalism*, 111.
3. James Lincoln Huntington, *Forty Acres: The Story of the Bishop Huntington House* (New York: Hastings House, 1949), 21; Elizabeth Porter Phelps, Diary, 18 January 1807, Porter-Phelps-Huntington Family Papers, box 7, folder 3 (hereafter cited as Phelps Diary), owned by the Porter-Phelps-Huntington Foundation, on deposit at Amherst College Archives

and Special Collections, Amherst College Library, Amherst, Mass. (hereafter cited as PPH Family Papers).

4. Charles Phelps Estate Division, PPH Family Papers, box 4, folder 33.
5. Tara L. Gleason, "The Porter-Phelps-Huntington Family: The Social Position and Material Wealth of an Elite Family in Eighteenth-Century Hadley, Massachusetts (thesis, Amherst College, 1994, Amherst College Archives and Special Collections), 141.
6. Thomas Fletcher to his father, 4 February 1811, Fletcher Papers, Philadelphia Athenaeum; Ian M. G. Quimby, *American Silver at Winterthur* (Winterthur, Del.: Henry Francis du Pont Winterthur Museum, 1995), 357; Elizabeth Ingram Wood, "Thomas Fletcher: A Philadelphia Entrepreneur of Presentation Silver," *Winterthur Portfolio* 3 (1967): 137.
7. Physical evidence, namely the engraved presentation date of 1813 and the silversmiths' mark used by Fletcher and Gardiner only between 1808 and 1811, presents a vexing mystery about when Phelps donated these cups to the Church of Christ. Documentary evidence is no more clear. In a letter written to her daughter in August 1811, five months after Hopkins's death, Phelps offered a clue, although vague, of her intention to donate the silver cups: "How did my heart burn within me the day before yesterday while I was at Mr. Perkins's, hearing him & Dr. Parsons, conversing upon the opening prospects of the Glory, of the redeemers Kingdom—how animated does it make even stupid me . . . may we ever remember that we owe something more than prayers even on offering to the Lord that they who preach the Gospel shall be supported." She continued, "the publick thanks was returned last Sabbath" (Elizabeth Porter Phelps to Elizabeth Phelps Huntington, 21 August 1811, PPH Family Papers, box 5, folder 10). We know from church records that church members voted thanks to other donors of communion silver. Perhaps this vote of thanks was directed to Phelps. During Fletcher and Gardiner's Boston career, Phelps made five shopping trips to this city, and although no evidence confirms this, it is possible that she purchased these cups during one of her urban excursions. A local merchant or the church deacons may have secured them from Fletcher and Gardiner at this time as well. The 1813 engraved date may have been added later by one of the six Hadley and Northampton area silversmithing firms working at that time. These craftsmen include Joel Brown, Nathaniel Fowle Jr., John Hodge, Nathan Storrs, Huntington & Packard, and Crooks & Phelps. The misspelling of the word presented—"presnted"—on one of the cups suggests that this embellishment was done by an engraver who worked hurriedly or sloppily, or by one who was prone to errors in his work.

   Very few business records survive from Fletcher and Gardiner's business from the years 1808 to 1811, and only three other objects are known to have survived from these early years. They are two-handled cups virtually identical to the Elizabeth Phelps cups: a pair of communion vessels given to the Second Baptist Church in Boston by I. Shedd in 1811, and a cup given to the First Church in Plymouth, Massachusetts, about 1810. The remarkable similarity of these objects suggests that Fletcher and Gardiner recognized and met consumer demand for this form of church silver.

   No Hadley or Hadley area silversmiths' account books survive from the early nineteenth century. For information on silversmiths working in the Connecticut River Valley at this time, see Henry N. Flynt and Martha Gandy Fales, *The Heritage Foundation Collection of Silver with Biographical Sketches of New England Silversmiths, 1625–1825* (Deerfield, Mass.: Heritage Foundation, 1968), and Patricia E. Kane, ed., *Colonial Massachusetts Silversmiths and Jewelers: A Biographical Dictionary* (New Haven: Yale University Art Gallery, 1998).
8. Barbara McLean Ward, "Metalwares," in *The Great River: Art and Society of the Connecticut River Valley, 1635–1820*, ed. Gerald W. R. Ward and William Hosley Jr. (Hartford, Conn.: Wadsworth Atheneum, 1985), 274.

9. Robert Blair St. George, "Artifacts of Regional Consciousness in the Connecticut River Valley, 1700–1780," in Ward and Hosley, *The Great River*, 35. St. George has also suggested that Connecticut River Valley church donors hoped their gifts would preserve social power for their heirs. If Elizabeth Porter Phelps expected this from her donation, she would have been sorely disappointed. Between 1821 and 1828 her daughter, Elizabeth Huntington, faced severe judgment and eventual excommunication by the Hadley church and its leader, Rev. John Woodbridge, for admitting Unitarian leanings. Although Huntington embraced her mother's and Rev. Hopkins's vision of an inclusive, harmonious church, she rejected the doctrine of the Trinity, "narrow[ing] the distance between God and believer by endowing Him with benevolent human attributes." To conservative Congregationalists such as Woodbridge, this denial of the Trinity and allowance of "the human mind to reflect rationally on religious . . . problems" threatened the spirituality of the communion sacrament. While Hopkins actively discouraged splinter groups from forming in Hadley by welcoming diverse theological ideas into his church, Woodbridge, his successor, zealously expelled church members for violating conservative Congregationalist principles or behavior. Also excommunicated were members who were believed to have committed adultery or danced at balls, and those who were thought to be habitual drunks. Because of her views, Huntington was denied attendance at the Hadley communion table and prohibited from drinking from the very cups her mother had donated. This indicates that a donation of church silver was not enough to secure a family's long-term position in the Hadley congregation. Prevailing theological ideas—not an ancestor's status evoked by communion silver—determined who was welcomed to the church's sacraments.

In 1821, four years after Phelps's death, Woodbridge appointed a committee to inquire into each church member's "feelings with regard to religion." Huntington told the committee that she did not believe in the doctrine of the Trinity, and soon after she "was exposed on communion seasons to observations which were extremely trying to her feelings." She concluded that "her presence at the Lord's Table was not desired" and asked to be dismissed from the church. "Only by excommunication," Woodbridge asserted, would Huntington be free of the church. He considered the excommunication case for six years, during which Huntington did not take communion at the meetinghouse, assuming that she was not welcome there. Ironically, in 1827 Deacon Jacob Smith informed Huntington that she was to be disciplined for "withdrawing from the communion" ritual.

Facing a humiliating excommunication, Huntington offered the deacons a statement echoing the message of unity so central to the life and work of her mother and Rev. Hopkins. Church records preserve this statement. "[Mrs. Huntington] rejoices to believe that many who judge their brethren . . . will be admitted to those mansions . . . in her heavenly Father's House—she indulges a very comforting hope, that a place will also be found there for some whose names have been cast out as evil, and who have been esteemed as . . . the disgrace of the church. Anticipating the universal diffusion of light and love through the world, she is happy in the prospect that mankind will one day love together as brethren." On 26 August 1828 the church approved Huntington's excommunication and voted its desire to "express their disassociation of such dangerous sentiments as hers." St. George, "Artifacts of Regional Consciousness," 35; Mary Kupiec Cayton, "Who Were the Evangelicals? Conservative and Liberal Identity in the Unitarian Controversy in Boston, 1804–1833," *Journal of Social History* 31, no. 1 (Fall 1997): 2, 3. All information about Huntington's excommunication is taken from an account written between 1825 and 1827 by Deacons Jacob Smith and Timothy Hopkins. This untitled document is held in the archives of the First Church, Hadley, Mass.

10. In a letter to her daughter, dated 13 November 1810, Phelps noted that John and Lydia Hopkins "really do treat us like parents & their friendship appears in many instances." PPH Family Papers, box 5, folder 10; Boltwood, "Family Genealogies," 71.
11. Book of Remembrance, archives of the First Church, Hadley, Mass.
12. Phelps to Elizabeth Phelps Huntington, 10 March 1807, PPH Family Papers, box 5, folder 9.
13. Phelps Diary, 14 June 1807.
14. Miller, "Crossing the Threshold," 8.
15. Thomas Eliot Andrews, ed., "The Diary of Elizabeth (Porter) Phelps" [part 3], *New England Historical and Genealogical Register* 120 (July 1966): 129; [part 4], *New England Historical and Genealogical Register* 121 (April 1967): 95, 99; Phelps Diary, 11 August 1805; 6 December 1807; 16 July 1809. See also Phelps to Elizabeth Phelps Huntington, 12 November 1807, PPH Family Papers, box 5, folder 9, for her interest in pregnant unwed girls of the lowest class being admitted to the Northampton church.
16. Church records note on 28 September 1794 that "Submit West in the right of Charles Phelps and his wife" was baptized. Hopkins, "Baptisms since ye Burning of my House," archives of the First Church, Hadley, Mass.; Andrews, "Diary of Elizabeth (Porter) Phelps" [part 3], 213.
17. Phelps Diary, 29 November, 7 December 1806; 20 June 1808; Phelps to Elizabeth Phelps Huntington, 14 July, 26 November 1808, PPH Family Papers, box 5, folder 9.
18. Samuel Porter to Charles Phelps, 28 March 1804; Selectmen of Hadley to Charles Phelps, January 1810, Town Records, Hadley Historical Society, Hadley, Mass.
19. Andrews, "Diary of Elizabeth (Porter) Phelps" [part 2], *New England Historical and Genealogical Register* 119 (April 1965): 140.
20. Huntington, *Forty Acres*, 4; Arria S. Huntington, *Under a Colonial Roof-Tree: Fireside Chronicles of Early New England* (Boston: Houghton Mifflin, 1891), 55; Andrews, "Diary of Elizabeth (Porter) Phelps" [part 2], 295, 301; [part 3], 209.
21. Phelps to Elizabeth Phelps Huntington, 15 December 1809, PPH Family Papers, box 5, folder 9. Evidence suggests that Phelps's home county, Hampshire County, may have been an attractive place of residence for paupers and transients because well-established networks of charitable support appear to have been in place. See Douglas Lamar Jones, "The Strolling Poor: Transiency in Eighteenth-Century Massachusetts," *Journal of Social History* 8, no. 3 (Spring 1975): 28–54.
22. Phelps to Elizabeth Phelps Huntington, 15 December 1809, PPH Family Papers, box 5, folder 9.
23. Phelps Diary, 28 January 1810.
24. Ibid., 25 February 1810.
25. Ibid., 23 July 1809.
26. Ibid., 15 May 1808; 20 August 1808. See also Phelps to Elizabeth Phelps Huntington, 21 January 1809, PPH Family Papers, box 5, folder 9.
27. Phelps Diary, 1 April 1810.
28. Ibid., 30 October 1808.
29. Phelps to Elizabeth Phelps Huntington, 21 August 1811, PPH Family Papers, box 5, folder 9.
30. Phelps further integrated herself into the local community with social rituals connected to death, illness, or hardship. In 1785 she drank tea with Major Williams; she later described him in her diary as "not well—has had all his Furniture and most of the family Cloaths taken for Debt and sold at Vendue." (Andrews, "Diary of Elizabeth [Porter] Phelps" [part 2], 213.) Sometimes Phelps was called into private homes to pray for a

church member when death seemed imminent, and she attended the burials and funerals of Hadley's citizens, from those of her own peers among the social elite to those of local African Americans and paupers. (Phelps Diary, 20 December 1807; 3 December 1809; 21 October 1810; Andrews, "Diary of Elizabeth (Porter) Phelps" [part 4], 99; Phelps Diary, 14 October 1804; 19 January 1806; 9 July, 19 November 1809; Phelps to Elizabeth Phelps Huntington, 15 December 1809, PPH Family Papers, box 5, folder 9.)

31. Phelps Diary, 20 October 1805.
32. Ibid., 30 March 1806.
33. Ibid., 12 April 1807; 1 October 1809; Rev. John Woodbridge, "Church Records," archives of the First Church, Hadley, Mass.
34. Phelps Diary, 1 October 1809.
35. Ibid., 25 February 1810.
36. Phelps to Elizabeth Phelps Huntington, 4 April 1810, PPH Family Papers, box 5, folder 10.
37. Phelps to Elizabeth Phelps Huntington, 29 May 1811, PPH Family Papers, box 5, folder 10.
38. "Extracts and Abstracts from Reverend Enoch Hale's Diary," Judd Manuscript, vol. 10, Special Collections, Forbes Library, Northampton, Mass., 52.
39. Phelps to Elizabeth Phelps Huntington, 14 December 1811, PPH Family Papers, box 5, folder 10.
40. Sylvester Judd, *History of Hadley, including the Early History of Hatfield, South Hadley, Amherst and Granby*, 2nd ed. (Springfield, Mass.: H. R. Huntting, 1905; repr., Camden, Maine.: Picton Press, 1993), 324–27.
41. John Woodbridge, *Two Discourses Preached in the First Church in Hadley, Lord's Day, June 24, 1860* (Northampton, Mass.: Bridgman & Childs, 1861), 24.
42. Hopkins, "Baptisms since ye Burning of my House," archives of the First Church, Hadley, Mass.
43. Ibid.
44. Judd, *History of Hadley*, 313.
45. Andrews, "Diary of Elizabeth (Porter) Phelps" [part 1], *New England Historical and Genealogical Register* 118 (January 1964): 19.
46. Andrews, "Diary of Elizabeth (Porter) Phelps," [part 4], 99; Phelps Diary, 14 October 1804; 19 January 1806; 9 July, 19 November 1809.
47. Judd, *History of Hadley*, 327.
48. Samuel Hopkins, *Christ King in Zion: A Half Century Discourse Delivered in Hadley, March 3, 1803* (Northampton, Mass.: Thos. M. Pomeroy, n.d.), 29–30.
49. Sylvester Judd notes that he was remembered for his "rare sagacity in this matter." *History of Hadley*, 327.
50. Woodbridge, *Two Discourses*, 24.
51. Ibid.; Judd, *History of Hadley*, 327; "The Communion Service of Hadley," *Hampshire Gazette and Northampton Courier*, 9 June 1888, 3. They broadened the religious community further by inviting virtually all parents, even those not baptized themselves, to present their children for baptism in the Hadley church.
52. The Hadley church was not atypical in using two-handled cups for communion during the eighteenth and nineteenth centuries. See Anthony N. B. Garvan, "American Church Silver: A Statistical Study," in *Spanish, French and English Traditions in the Colonial Silver of North America* (Winterthur: Henry Francis du Pont Winterthur Museum, 1968), 73–104, for a detailed study of the preference for certain forms of communion silver, including two-handled cups. See also Barbara McLean Ward and Gerald W. R. Ward, eds., *Silver in American Life: Selections from the Mabel Brady Garvan and Other Collections at Yale University* (New York: American Federation of Arts, 1979), 91; E. Alfred Jones, *The Old Silver*

of American Churches (Letchworth, Eng.: Arden Press for the National Society of the Colonial Dames of America, 1913).

53. Barbara McLean Ward, " 'In a Feasting Posture': Communion Vessels and Community Values in Seventeenth- and Eighteenth-Century New England," *Winterthur Portfolio* 23, no. 1 (Spring 1988): 14.
54. A church history notes that these were given to "some feeble Western church" at its formation. See "The Communion Service of Hadley," 3. For information on the tradition of giving communion vessels to fledgling churches see Peter Benes and Philip D. Zimmerman, *New England Meeting House and Church, 1630–1850* (Boston: Boston University and the Currier Gallery of Art for the Dublin Seminar for New England Folklife, 1979), 87.
55. The cup's inscription reads "Presented / by Lucretia / Widow / Lt. Benj. Colt / to the / - Christ Church in / Hadley." Colt died in 1781 and Lucretia married John Walker in 1784. See Lucius Boltwood, "Family Genealogies," in Judd, *History of Hadley*, 23.
56. Book of Remembrances, archives of the First Church, Hadley, Mass.
57. "The Communion Service of Hadley," 3.
58. Judd, *History of Hadley*, 4.
59. Paul R. Lucas, "Solomon Stoddard and the Origin of the Great Awakening in New England," *The Historian* 59, no. 4 (Summer 1997): 2.
60. Ibid., 1.
61. Paul R. Lucas, *Valley of Discord: Church and Society along the Connecticut River, 1636–1725* (Hanover, N.H.: University Press of New England, 1976), 193, 257.
62. Judd, *History of Hadley*, 323.
63. Ibid., 322–23.
64. Phelps Diary, 23 April 1809.
65. William B. Sprague, *Annals of the American Pulpit: Or Commemorative Notices of Distinguished American Clergymen of Various Denominations* (New York: Robert Carter & Brothers, 1857), 1: 521.
66. Phelps noted early in the week that Hopkins was "more unwell" and later "Thursday . . . in the eve . . . we went to see Dr. Hop: . . . he appears very low pulse hardly discernable—fryday we visit at John Hibbards . . . there we heard Dr. Hop: died about 3 that afternoon." Phelps Diary, 3 March 1811.
67. Ibid.
68. Ibid., 10 March 1811.
69. Ibid., 7 April 1811.
70. Phelps to Elizabeth Phelps Huntington, 21 January 1808, PPH Family Papers, box 5, folder 9.
71. Phelps Diary, 30 October 1808.
72. Ibid.
73. Phelps to Elizabeth Phelps Huntington, 3 January 1810, PPH Family Papers, box 5, folder 10.
74. "Ministers of the First Congregational Church of Hadley," archives of the First Church, Hadley, Mass.
75. Rev. John Woodbridge, "Church Records," archives of the First Church, Hadley, Mass.
76. Ibid.; *First Church in Hadley Confession of Faith and Catalogue of Members, April 1, 1832* (Northampton, Mass.: T. W. Shepard, 1832).
77. Woodbridge, "Church Records"; *First Church in Hadley Confession of Faith*. This increased membership appears not to have been the result of one of the religious revivals that periodically swept the Connecticut River Valley in the early nineteenth century. In 1804, thirty-three adults joined the Hadley church during what Phelps called "an

outpouring of the spirit." Rev. Woodbridge, in his 1860 sermon "Two Discourses Preached in the First Church in Hadley," noted that a young male schoolteacher who came to Hadley in 1804 greatly fueled this revival. For evidence of other revivals in the Connecticut River Valley, see Ruth Patten, *Interesting Family Letters of the Late Mrs. Ruth Patten, of Hartford, Conn.* (Hartford: printed by D. B. Moseley, 1845), 162.

78. Phelps to Elizabeth Phelps Huntington, 29 May 1811, PPH Family Papers, box 5, folder 10.
79. Phelps Diary, 29 September 1811.

10

When first published in 1984, Greg Nobles's essay on Hadley's broomcorn craze joined a larger conversation about the market revolution in nineteenth-century New England, and matters no less important than the nature and evolution of capitalism in the early American republic. Nobles's study not only advanced historical understanding of the evolving rural economy, but also illuminated more cultural matters, such as the emergence of new standards of cleanliness that created a market for so many brooms. Since the year this important essay appeared, scholars of the evolution of "capitalism in the countryside" have cultivated a rich picture of the ways in which rural families adapted to economic change, tracking the slow retreat of a world dominated by face-to-face exchanges among neighbors and relatives and the rise of a new world in which transactions became increasingly impersonal and anonymous. Such changes cannot be seen as either an overall gain or an overall loss; rather they were part of ongoing cycles of change that benefited some families at the expense of others.

Commerce and Community

A Case Study of the Rural Broommaking Business in Antebellum Massachusetts

Gregory H. Nobles

In 1797 Levi Dickinson, a farmer in Hadley, Massachusetts, planted a few hills of a strange-looking variety of corn that was virtually useless as food and produced little more than long tassels of brush. Dickinson harvested the brush, dried it, tied it around sticks, and thus made twenty or thirty brooms, most of which he peddled to neighbors in the town. The following year he planted about half an acre of this broom corn, and the year after that a whole acre. By 1800 he and his sons were making several hundred brooms and selling them not just in Hadley but as far west as Pittsfield, Massachusetts, and as far south as New London, Connecticut. Many of Dickinson's neighbors ridiculed him, however, sneering that broommaking was Indian work, too low for white men; as his son would later recall, "We were sometimes mortified with taunts." But Levi Dickinson turned aside the insults and kept on making brooms, even insisting that the local broom business would someday be one of the greatest in the county. He turned out to be right. By 1850 Massachusetts was second only to New York in broommaking, producing well over a million brooms that would be sold throughout the United States and as far away as South America. More important in light of Levi Dickinson's earlier prediction, the bulk of that production came from Dickinson's own Hampshire County and from his own town of Hadley.[1]

On one level this brief sketch of Levi Dickinson suggests a classic portrait of the Yankee farmer as entrepreneur—the independent innovator who tried something new in order to make a little extra money, gradually expanded his operation, and eventually did well enough not only to silence the skeptics but even to lead some of them to follow his example. More to the point, that small portrait of the individual farmer fits into a much broader landscape depicting the economic transformation of rural New England up through the first half of the nineteenth century. Almost from the beginning of white settlement in the seventeenth century, many New England farmers had been involved in a network of trade that reached as far as England and the West Indies, but it was especially the government-sponsored drive for internal improvements in the wake of the American Revolution that accelerated the integration of rural people into a national—indeed global—system of commercial capitalism. Linked to northern cities by an expanding transportation network of turnpikes and canals, inland farm villages became an increasingly important source of supply to match a growing national demand, and even more farm families began to engage regularly in market exchange, producing not only surplus crops but a variety of homemade goods—cloth, shoes, palm leaf hats, and the like—to be traded for cash or credit with rural merchants or urban commission agents.[2]

In some cases, in fact, the increasing emphasis on production for market exchange seemed to bring about a gradual but nonetheless radical change both in the nature of the community and in the lives of the people themselves. Alan Dawley's study of Lynn, Massachusetts, and Jonathan Prude's work on Oxford and Dudley, Massachusetts, both show very strikingly how in the early part of the nineteenth century the inhabitants' increased involvement in nonagricultural enterprises and growing reliance on the marketplace eventually helped prepare the way for the transformation of these communities from farm villages to factory towns.[3] In other cases, of course, the transformation of rural communities was not quite so extreme: market production continued to be carried on within a predominantly agrarian context, and rather than become industrial operatives, most farmers remained independent operators. Indeed, some historians have suggested that the expansion of the market system in rural New England led farmers to become petty capitalists, adopting a more individualistic and profit-oriented outlook, essentially an altogether different system of values from those commonly associated with the more family-centered, self-sufficient style of farming of the eighteenth century. As Percy Bidwell and John Falconer noted in their classic history of northern agriculture, "The introduction of the cash nexus . . . forced the farmers to confront a new set of problems, calling for the exercising of a new set of faculties. Shrewdness in buying and selling must now be added to the simpler qualities of hard work and saving. Farming became a more speculative business." Or, as a contemporary observer urged his fellow New Englanders, "The farmer who is wide awake to his business should watch, as well as follow, the markets. . . . Let our farmers study their true interests. . . . Let them be up and doing something to supply the wants of the towns and cities in their vicinity. . . . Let them raise flowers even, if it will pay a profit. Why not?"[4]

More recently, however, a number of historians—most notably Michael Merrill, James Henretta, and Christopher Clark—have raised important and intriguing questions about the attitudes and aspirations of farmers as they became increasingly involved in the capitalist economy of the antebellum era. While not denying either the existence or the extent of market production, these historians have sought to explain the changing economic activities of rural people in terms that also emphasize the continuities and traditions of rural society. Rather than depict the early nineteenth-century northern farmer as either self-sufficient yeoman or market-oriented entrepreneur, they have explored what Jonathan Prude has described as the "tension that would arise between ensuing economic changes and entrenched community mores." In doing so they have provided a more complex picture of people involved in the process of social change, trying to hold onto part of the past even as they look to the future. Christopher Clark, for instance, has written of the "bifurcation . . . within rural society between those who began to draw back from the system growing up in their midsts because they feared its consequences." If farmers did engage in market production, he argues, they did so "for reasons of family economy, rather than competitive profit-seeking." In general these scholars make a persuasive argument that many farm families approached new commercial opportunities with some degree of ambivalence, hoping at least to accommodate the economic value of market exchange to the cultural values that upheld the enduring importance of both family and community.[5]

In this light the case of Levi Dickinson and his fellow broommakers should contribute to our understanding of the significance of market production within the context of the rural community. Even as the broommaking business grew and became enmeshed in a vast market network, it remained rooted in Hadley and a handful of other farm towns. Moreover, even as the number of brooms produced in these towns began to reach well into the hundreds of thousands, the process of broommaking did not become centralized in a factory or large shop but remained rooted in the traditional process of household production. To be sure, broommaking represented only a small part of the vast system of household manufacture in antebellum Massachusetts. Palm leaf hatmakers, for instance, numbered well into the tens of thousands by the 1830s; by comparison, the number of broommakers probably never exceed five or six hundred.[6] We must be careful, then, about making any overly broad generalizations about household manufacture based on the broommaking business alone. Still, the particular history of broommaking in Massachusetts—especially the expansion of distribution to a national, even international, scale despite the concentration of production within a very limited geographical area—offers us a useful case study not only of the connections between urban markets and rural manufacture, but also of the emerging relationship between commerce and community.

Though not as common or extensive as some other forms of rural manufacture, broommaking seemed to epitomize some of the most desirable aspects of household production. For one thing, brooms could be produced almost wholly from materials grown on the farm, and even a farmer with little land or capital could easily get involved in the broommaking trade. An early nineteenth-century observer estimated that one man working four months could cultivate and harvest about six acres of broom corn, each acre yielding about six hundred pounds of brush; allowing one pound of brush per broom, the farmer could produce enough material for well over three thousand brooms. One additional benefit a farmer gained from growing broom corn was use of the seed as feed for livestock, especially pigs. Indeed, in some cases the value of the seed alone was thought to be enough to cover the cost of cultivating a crop of broom corn. In several respects, then, broommaking was an ideal sideline for northern farmers: it could be accommodated to the normal patterns of outdoor and indoor work in the changing seasons, and it provided both a marketable product and a usable byproduct. In short, it seemed to fit almost perfectly into the rhythm and economy of the family farm.[7]

The actual process of making brooms, moreover, did not require the employment of a skilled labor force or an investment in sophisticated technology. Many rural broommakers made their brooms without any specialized equipment at all: after drying and bleaching the brush from the corn, the broommaker simply secured a piece of twine (or often wire) to a wall, stepped back a few feet, tied the other end of the twine to a hemlock broom handle, gathered a bunch of brush around the handle, and started walking toward the wall, rolling the twine tightly around the brush as he went.[8] Other broommakers used a roller for the twine in order to do part of their work sitting at a bench, and some used even more elaborate devices for holding and tying the brush and handle. Unfortunately, there is very little evidence available on the development, distribution, and cost of this early broommaking apparatus. No broommaking machine was patented until 1849, but several students of New England crafts have suggested that early forms of the device date back perhaps as far as the first two decades of the century. They were not produced or marketed by manufacturing firms but fashioned by broommakers themselves or by local craftsmen according to their own designs. The equipment—basically a set of large wooden vises and clamps—was simple and relatively inexpensive to build, and it has been estimated that a broommaker could build or buy a broommaking machine for around four or five dollars, roughly a week's wage for a laborer. Whatever the case, it seems clear that broom production did not depend on a high degree of mechanization or capitalization but remained a reasonably accessible form of enterprise that relied primarily on human power and human handiwork.[9]

The main obstacle to broommaking, at least until the late 1820s, was not so much in the manufacturing as in the marketing. Like the aforementioned Levi Dickinson, rural broommakers usually peddled their goods themselves, taking them from town to town in the immediate region but seldom going far away from their families or their farms. Homemade brooms represented only one of many commodities exchanged in the intricate but extensive system of local barter that was so commonplace in rural communities. William Warren, one of the first broommakers in Conway, Massachusetts—his section of the town later came to be known as "Broomshire"—traded brooms on a regular basis in neighboring Deerfield for a pound and a half of pork. "He did it," said a local historian, "because he was hungry, being out of meat several years by winter." In addition to this direct form of personal exchange with neighbors, some farmers included brooms among the products they traded for goods or credit with local merchants. But even with this additional outlet for brooms, broommaking remained an essentially small-scale enterprise that grew only gradually within a fairly limited region for the first few years. By 1810, for instance, Hampshire County was the only Massachusetts county that recorded corn brooms among its agricultural products, and the total number of brooms produced was only seventy thousand. Ten years later, in the federal government's Census of Manufactures, Massachusetts broommaking did not receive any mention at all.[10]

The situation changed, however, both rapidly and dramatically. In Hampshire County most local historians date the first major burst of expansion in the broommaking business from the mid-1820s, and by the 1830s broommaking had become a well established economic activity in a handful of the older farming communities in the rich, fertile lowlands of the Connecticut River Valley. In 1831 a government report on manufactures in the United States showed Massachusetts broommaking and broom-related production in only seven towns—all of them in western Massachusetts—but what was striking was the level of production: the number of brooms produced had increased more than tenfold since 1810, approaching well over a million brooms a year. The farmers of Hadley, for instance, had been growing an average of 125 tons of broom corn a year throughout the 1820s, and the 1831 figures for the town showed a half-million brooms valued at $50,000. The expansion of broom production in western Massachusetts even gave rise to a kind of specialized network of broommaking materials within the region. Inhabitants of some of the hilltowns above the Connecticut Valley—where the soil was too rocky and thin for growing broom corn as a cash crop—turned to their woodlots and to the surrounding forests to gather branches and saplings for broom handles. The town of Ashfield alone accounted for seven hundred thousand broom handles in 1831, and Wendell, Plainfield, and Williamsburg provided around a hundred thousand handles each for the broommakers in Hadley, Hatfield, Deerfield, and other valley towns.[11] Throughout the second quarter of the nineteenth century the Connecticut Valley continued to be the main broommaking region of Massachusetts; almost ninety percent of the state's broommakers worked in Hampshire and Franklin counties, and they were responsible for well over ninety percent of the state's broom production. But during this period broommaking also spread to other parts of the state. Figures for 1845 show substantial broom and broom handle production in twenty-five Massachusetts towns in eight of the state's fourteen counties from Plymouth County in the east to Berkshire County in the far west.[12]

It should be clear that this increase in both the number of broommaking towns and the number of brooms produced was a function of a vastly expanded market network. Massachusetts households alone could hardly absorb an annual production of over a million brooms. Although some rural broommakers continued to peddle their brooms locally or in regional markets, most began to look to the northern cities, especially Boston and New York, as a reliable, expansive market for their goods. To some extent western Massachusetts farmers had been accustomed to trading with urban wholesalers since the seventeenth century: many inhabitants of the lower Connecticut Valley towns had regularly shipped foodstuffs down the Connecticut River from Springfield to Hartford and points south, and farmers in the northern hilltowns had been driving cattle east to Boston for years. In that respect brooms simply represented a new product on an old trade route.[13] But it was the expansion and enhancement of the transportation network in the early part of the nineteenth century—especially the construction and improvement of roads and the construction of short canals around the falls on the Connecticut River—that did most to facilitate trade, and by 1830 most of the local broommakers were sending the bulk of their production to the cities. Of the one hundred thousand brooms produced in Whately, for instance, two-thirds went to New York and the other third to Boston. With the completion of the Northampton–New Haven Canal in 1835 and the establishment of a direct rail link between Boston and the Hudson valley in 1841, rural broommakers in central and western Massachusetts had an even easier access to urban markets."[14]

The recollections of Charles Jones, a Deerfield farmer who was involved in the broommaking business as early as the 1830s, provide a useful description of the changing nature of broom distribution throughout the Northeast. In 1834 he took a load of brooms to Canada and sold them near the home of a man who had married a woman from Deerfield; though Jones had to travel a long way to sell his brooms, his destination was apparently determined not just by market prospects but at least in part by the more personal connection of community ties. But Jones later went in the other direction, both geographically and commercially, and took brooms south to the rail depots at Springfield and Palmer for shipment to urban wholesalers. According to Jones, "Nearly all the brooms manufactured in Deerfield found a market in New York City, and were generally sent to commission houses for sale." This increased involvement in urban trade caused local broommakers to become much more attentive to the fluctuations of the market; Jones noted that growers of broom corn often sold their crops to speculators well before harvest, and the price of broom corn and finished brooms became a common topic of conversation around the Deerfield tavern.[15]

To this point, perhaps, the story of broommaking might seem to be an almost perfect example of the general process of social change many historians identify as "modernization."[16] Increasing urbanization and improved transportation fostered an expanding commercial network that reached from city to countryside, and rural people became confronted with new economic realities and enmeshed in new economic relationships. Not only did rural producers raise their level of production, but they likewise developed new methods of distribution. Where once they had peddled their own goods and even engaged in barter exchange, they increasingly came to rely on more impersonal cash exchanges with urban middlemen. Even more important, the more they became involved with the world of modem commerce, the more they developed a "modern" commercial outlook and a greater sensitivity to the mechanisms of the market and the world beyond their immediate communities.

To be sure, some contemporary observers looked upon this trend with criticism and concern, arguing, as one New England farmer did, that "it is better that the farmer should produce what he needs for home consumption. . . . He may obtain more money from tobacco, hops or broom corn, than from breadstuffs but taking all things into consideration, will he be better off?"[17] Implicit in that question was the assumption, even the fear, that in their apparent rush to enter the marketplace, farmers would forsake or forget many of the most important attributes—especially family autonomy and self-sufficiency—that had defined rural culture in the past. Put differently, there was at least the suspicion that broom corn, like other cash crops, contained the seeds of destruction for some of the traditional values of farm life.

And yet too great an emphasis on the transforming power of the marketplace may obscure a more enduring adherence to tradition among the people who began to participate in it. Certainly further examination of the experience of rural broommakers suggests that something other than a predominant concern for economic expansion and profit governed their actions and attitudes. In order to appreciate fully the significance of market-oriented activity in rural society, it is useful to examine in some detail the context of the rural community. To this end the town of Hadley offers the best case study for broommaking. Hadley was the leading broommaking town in Massachusetts by the middle of the nineteenth century, and both the local literature and the local records—especially the federal manuscript census for 1850, when broommaking was at its height—allow us to get a sense of the place of broommaking within the context of the community. To some extent, of course, Hadley represents a unique case study because it was the center of broommaking activity, and it may not be altogether typical of other broommaking towns. On the other hand, precisely because Hadley was the center of broommaking, it provides a valuable insight into broommaking in its most highly developed form, if indeed such work could be described as "highly developed" at all. In the end, perhaps what the example of Hadley suggests most is the extent to which rural people were able to keep the business of broommaking compatible with the particular needs and general nature of a farm community.

Above all, the evidence clearly indicates that broommaking, unlike some other forms of household manufacture, did not become a highly centralized form of production. The production of shoes, cloth, and palm leaf hats, for instance, had increasingly moved from the household to the factory by 1850. Many rural merchants, who had formerly supplied unfinished materials on a "putting-out" basis to people working in their homes, began to open their own manufacturing operations and bring workers into a central workplace, where the labor process could be more easily regimented and regulated.[18] Broommaking, by comparison, had never been organized on a putting-out basis. The relative ease and low cost of growing broom corn and obtaining broommaking equipment meant that many broommakers could produce their own raw materials and own their own machinery without having to be continually dependent on a merchant. Even when Hadley was producing well over a half-million brooms a year, there was no broom factory, nor was there anyone who dominated the broommaking business in the town. The census reports on the town's products of industry listed forty-one broommaking enterprises in 1850, most of them fairly small-scale operations owned by a single individual or occasionally by two men who were related. The largest broommaking shop employed eleven hands and produced seventy thousand brooms, but none of the others employed more than six workers, and a dozen or so were one-man shops. Only seven of the broom shops produced more than thirty thousand brooms a year; the average annual output for all Hadley broommaking operations was between eighteen and nineteen thousand brooms.[19]

Moreover, broommaking did not appear to be a full-time calling for most of the owners of those shops. Thirty of the forty-one broom shops in Hadley were owned by men who listed their occupation as something other than "broommaker"—usually farmers, or in one case a laborer. For those men broommaking was apparently only a sideline business, a way to provide a decent supplement to a farmer's annual income. Only eleven broom-shop owners identified themselves primarily as broommakers—although John Shipman Jr., the owner of the town's biggest broom shop, seemed to have a slightly inflated view of his position and gave himself the pretentious title of "broommaster."[20]

And yet the very existence of "broommaker" as an occupational identity for those eleven broom-shop owners—and indeed, for the ninety-nine other Hadley residents identified as broommakers in the census records—is revealing in itself, for it points to the emergence of broommaking as an identifiable, or identifying, form of work. Hadley was by no means a town with a complex economy or a great deal of occupational variety. Like any other agrarian community, it had its share of local artisans and tradesmen, a few professionals, and around twenty laborers; taken together, however, those occupations engaged fewer than a hundred men. After the 287 farmers, the 110 broommakers in Hadley stood out as by far the largest occupational group in town.[21] We should not, of course, overstate the rigidity of the occupational categories listed by the census takers, nor should we assume that the choice between calling oneself "farmer" or "broommaker" was a permanent and restricting one. Still, it is important at least to note that the two callings did exist as separate categories. Many northern farmers engaged in a wide variety of economic activities and produced a wide variety of goods—not just grains and animal products, but maple sugar, potash, and the like—for market. Still, the production of these goods did not usually lead anyone to adopt a title other than the all-encompassing one of "farmer." Broommaking, on the other hand, proved to be different: it may have originated as a byproduct of farming, but by 1850 it was clear that broommaking had come to be recognized as a distinct form of labor.

In order to understand the significance of that identity of "broommaker" within the context of a farm town like Hadley, it is necessary to identify the broommakers. They were, for one thing, apparently all men. The gender-specific nature of broommaking is especially striking, in fact, because there was no obvious reason for it. There was nothing inherent in the nature of broommaking as a form of manual labor that would have made it unsuitable for women. By the middle of the nineteenth century women throughout New England were employed in various forms of production requiring manual labor, ranging from wage labor in mills and factories to outwork and piecework done in the home. But no women were listed as broommakers either in Hadley or in any other Massachusetts town. It is entirely possible and even probable that women were involved in broommaking to some extent, helping with the harvesting and processing of the brush or with the actual manufacture of the finished brooms. Within the context and traditions of the rural household the contribution of women to market production could often be taken for granted and therefore remain unrecognized, unreported, and unpaid. Still, the available records—local, state, and federal—strongly suggest that the broom shop remained a predominantly male province.[22]

Those males who worked as broommakers were, by and large, young and propertyless. The average age of the 110 broommakers in Hadley in 1850 was 26.9 years, and 95 of them were under thirty-five years of age. Their relative youth was also reflected in their family situations. The majority of broommakers were single men; only forty-six were listed as heads of their own households, and the average size of their families (3.7 related persons) was slightly below that of nonbroommaking families (4.3 related persons). Indeed, ten of the married broommakers did not live independently in their own houses but, like the sixty-four broommakers who were single, lived under the roof of their parents or some other older adult.[23] Perhaps the most important common trait among all broommakers, however, had to do with the ownership or control of property. As noted before, only eleven broommakers were listed as owners of broommaking shops. More to the point, only twenty-three broommakers—for the most part the handful of older ones between the ages of twenty-five and forty—owned real property of any sort, and the average value of their property was around $830, far below the average of just over $4,000 for landowning farmers, and even substantially below the average of just under $2,800 for landowning farmers in the same twenty-five to forty age bracket.[24] Admittedly a comparatively small amount of land would be adequate for growing enough corn to make thousands of brooms, and those few broommakers who owned land could hope to make a fairly stable and independent living out of their trade. Moreover, ownership alone was not the only means of access to land; it is possible that some broommakers rented enough land to allow them to become at least semi-independent producers.[25] Still, the available evidence, especially the census report listing the number of workers in each of the Hadley broom shops, suggests very strongly that those broommakers without land—without, in the most literal sense, the means of production—had to settle for being hired hands working in the shops of the more prosperous broommakers or, more often, of the farmers who ran broommaking operations on the side.[26]

And yet, just as it would be inaccurate to describe the broommaking process itself as a kind of nascent factory system, so too would it be misleading to suggest that broommakers represented an emerging rural proletariat. Most broommakers worked in a setting in which labor relations were defined largely by familial relations. Albert Hibbard, for instance, owned one of the largest broommaking operations in town, with a production of thirty thousand brooms in 1850. Hibbard was primarily a farmer rather than a broommaker, however, and he hired four hands, all single men in their late teens or early twenties, to run his broom shop for him. These young broommakers—a Frenchman, an Irishman, a Canadian, and a New Yorker—had no close relatives in Hadley, and they lived in Hibbard's household along with their employer, his wife, and three children. Josiah Jewett was likewise one of the leading broommakers in the town, but at the age of thirty-three he had no children old enough to work with him. He too hired four young men—all apparently local residents, or at least natives of Massachusetts—and, like Hibbard, he not only employed them in his shop but boarded them in his house. In fact, eighteen of the twenty-six broom-shop owners who employed two or more broommakers had hired hands living in their households.[27]

To some degree, then, many of the hired hands in the Hadley broom shops had a status not unlike that of apprentices and servants in seventeenth- and eighteenth-century New England, who lived in the home of their employers, took part of their pay in the form of room and board, and in general were considered to be as much household members as wage laborers. Some of the expectations and obligations still inherent in that status in the nineteenth century are suggested by an anecdote recorded by a local historian: "It was in this broom corn era that a good North Hadley deacon hired a farmer boy to work for six dollars a month and his board. The worker stayed a year, never spending or demanding money, and then called for his enormous wages of $75. The good deacon, driven to his wits end to amass such a sum, announced that it was the last time that he would ever be caught promising to pay such a sum in *cash*." In this case it is not so much the action of the young broommaker that is revealing, but the reaction of the deacon. A study of economic relationships in the nineteenth-century Connecticut Valley has demonstrated that the common practice of making non-cash payments endured well into the century; even though people kept accounts in dollars and cents, they quite often settled their debts by exchanging goods or labor or other favors, sometimes after having carried those debts on their account books for years.[28] No doubt the deacon's discomfort with the young man's demand for immediate payment of wages in cash stemmed largely from his difficulty in getting the money, but also partly from his surprise that the demand would even be made in the first place. The young broommaker's request seemed to be exceptional, inconsistent with the standards of extended credit and reciprocity that had held rural society together for years. Even in a world increasingly reliant on the impersonal exchange value of money, the value of personal relationships was still an important part of economic life at the local level.

In some cases the familial connections in the broommaking trade were much more pronounced, and broommaking was much more than just a source of income; it represented a kind of family tradition and, more importantly, a means of maintaining family ties over the generations. Consider, for instance, the family of Levi Dickinson, the Hadley farmer who started the whole broommaking business back in the 1790s. By the time of his death in 1843, his sons and grandsons were still heavily involved in broommaking. Dickinson's daughter Bethiah was married to John Shipman, one of the wealthiest farmers in Hadley, and their son, John Shipman Jr., not only owned the biggest broom operation in town but, as noted earlier, had become the self-styled "broom master" of Hadley. Levi Dickinson's own sons were by no means as wealthy as the Shipmans, but they too carried on the family's broommaking heritage. Harvey Dickinson was a broommaker by trade, as were his three sons, two of whom were still working for their father in their early thirties. Levi Dickinson's other son, Levi Dickinson Jr., was a farmer who did not own a great deal of land, and when he was in his sixties he had already deeded what land he did have to his oldest son Ebenezer, who followed in his father's calling as a farmer. Since the elder Dickinson had no property to offer his other two sons (Alfred, 23, and Levi P., 17), they, like a number of their kinsmen, worked as broommakers.[29]

Unfortunately, the available census records and vital records do not permit a positive family identification for all of the Hadley broommakers, so it remains impossible to know for certain how many families adopted the inheritance strategies suggested by this brief history of the Dickinson family. Still, the general composition of the group of broommakers within the Hadley population as a whole allows us at least to speculate on the significance of broommaking in intergenerational family relations. A demographic study of Hadley has indicated that ever since the late seventeenth century, Hadley farmers, like their counterparts in other old New England towns, were often unable to provide an adequate inheritance for all their sons by dividing land. Many sons had to leave home to look for land in the relatively new and unsettled towns on the frontier or look for work as laborers or tradesmen in the larger towns and cities. Throughout the history of early New England, families almost everywhere faced the same recurring paradox: migration was both a solution and a problem, creating opportunity for the individual while disrupting the unity of the family as a whole.[30] The broommaking business could not, of course, resolve this problem altogether, but it did at least provide an additional choice for some families in Hadley. Men who were farmers, and especially those who were involved in both farming and broommaking, could use broommaking as an alternative to dividing their lands, or at least as a way of postponing their sons' inheritances; that is, a father could designate one son to follow him in farming and, like Levi Dickinson Jr., look to broommaking as a means of providing a living for the other sons—and of keeping them close to home. If those sons were simply too young to be given land of their own, broommaking could be a useful interim occupation; more important, if the father had too many sons to too little land, broommaking might become a more long-term employment, perhaps even a permanent calling. Indeed, the significance of broommaking as a form of employment and inheritance may help explain the gender-specific nature of the trade. In general, the common profile of the Hadley broommaker—the young, unmarried farmer's son whose chances of obtaining a suitable inheritance in land were sometimes questionable—was precisely that of the kind of person in most agrarian communities who would be most likely to leave. Broommaking gave such men something to do, and therefore some reason to stay. Whatever the levels of production or profit provided by broommaking, that persistence alone would have been significant.

The point is not to idealize broommaking as a form of household manufacture, nor even to idealize the process of household manufacture itself. The point, simply, is to emphasize the importance of this form of production in reflecting and ultimately reinforcing the patterns of community and family life in an early nineteenth-century farm town. At a time when northern society was rapidly being transformed by an expanding capitalist economy, scarcely anyone could remain untouched by change; people in Hadley and in other rural communities throughout New England quite clearly began to participate more actively in market exchange and to develop more direct ties to urban commercial centers and the world beyond their immediate region. But this case study of broommaking also suggests the extent to which they could maintain a balance between economic opportunity and cultural continuity, keeping production organized on a small scale even as the level of output rose to remarkable heights. If, as James Henretta has argued, the preservation of the family as a productive unit remained a dominant part of the cultural values, the *mentalité*, of rural people well into the nineteenth century, then broommaking could serve that purpose reasonably well.[31] It did so, moreover, long after many other forms of household manufacture had given way to the centralizing processes of industrial capitalism.

To be sure, broommaking did not survive in the long run any better than other forms of household manufacture did. By most contemporary accounts, broommaking had reached its peak by the 1850s and 1860s, and it began to decline in Hadley and other Massachusetts towns throughout the postwar years. By the middle of the century farmers in the midwestern states, especially in the Ohio valley, had begun to grow broom corn, and according to most observers, they made good brooms. "The brooms made from the western brush were of handsome color . . . stronger and a better broom in every way," wrote one former Massachusetts broommaker. "No broom made from native brush could compete with them." The superiority of the western brooms was not lost on urban wholesalers. New York distributors, now linked to the midwestern states by an even more extensive transportation network, began to look to Ohio for brooms, and the old broommaking regions of Massachusetts and New York lost a substantial share of the market.[32]

Despite this new competition from the west, the business—and equally important, the process—of broommaking neither changed substantially nor died out suddenly. As late as 1875, Hadley was still by far the leading broommaking town in Massachusetts, with seventy-six people employed as broommakers, most of them apparently combining broommaking with farming. As one local historian put it, "From 1850 to 1875 there was scarcely a home in [the northern] part of the town that did not have one or more broom machines at work on the premises during the winter months." A decade later, in 1885, the number of Hadley men involved in the broommaking business had dropped to thirty, and by 1895 the number had fallen to eight.[33] But even in this period of decline the evidence is revealing, for it suggests that broommaking remained essentially what it had been throughout the first half of the nineteenth century—a household-centered form of production that was adapted to the seasonal rhythms of the farm. As it became increasingly evident that Hadley broommakers could not compete effectively in a national market, they did not take extreme steps to become better competitors. Rather, they clung to the old traditions of household manufacture, and when those failed, they gradually gave up an economic activity that had been part of their community for almost a century. In doing so they perhaps gave up part of their past as well as part of their future, but in a way they also underlined the continuity between their community's past and future: Hadley would be what it had always been—a farm town, not a factory town. In this broommaking community, at least, manufacture was only a means of supplementing farming as a way of life, not of supplanting it.

Notes

1. "Hadley Vol. 111," 13, Sylvester Judd Papers, Forbes Library, Northampton, Mass. See also Sylvester Judd, *History of Hadley, including the Early History of Hatfield, South Hadley, Amherst and Granby, Massachusetts*, 2nd ed. (Springfield, Mass.: H. R. Huntting, 1905), 360–61.
2. Among the most useful works dealing generally with northern agriculture in the early nineteenth century are Percy Wells Bidwell and John I. Falconer, *History of Agriculture in the Northern United States, 1620–1860* (Washington, D.C.: Carnegie Institution of Washington, 1925), esp. chaps. 11–25; Clarence H. Danhof, *Change in Agriculture: The Northern United States, 1820–1870* (Cambridge, Mass.: Harvard University Press, 1969); and Howard S. Russell, *A Long, Deep Furrow: Three Centuries of Farming in New England* (Hanover, N.H.: University Press of New England, 1976), esp. chaps. 24–38. See also Paul W. Gates, *The Farmer's Age: Agriculture, 1815–1860* (New York: Holt, Rinehart and Winston, 1960), esp. chap. 2. For the growth of market exchange, see George Rogers Taylor, *The Transportation Revolution, 1815–1860* (New York: Rinehart, 1951), and Rolla M. Tryon, *Household Manufactures in the United States, 1640–1860* (Chicago: University of Chicago Press, 1917; repr., New York: Johnson Reprint, 1966), esp. chaps. 4–8.
3. Alan Dawley, *Class and Community: The Industrial Revolution in Lynn* (Cambridge, Mass.: Harvard University Press, 1976); Jonathan Prude, *The Coming of Industrial Order: Town and Factory Life in Rural Massachusetts, 1810–1860* (Cambridge: Cambridge University Press, 1983).

4. Bidwell and Falconer, *History of Agriculture*, 252; *Plough and Anvil* 5 (1852): 241, as quoted in Danhof, *Change in Agriculture*, 144–45.
5. Prude, *Coming of Industrial Order*, 10; Christopher Clark, "The Household Economy, Market Exchange and the Rise of Capitalism in the Connecticut Valley, 1800–1860," *Journal of Social History* 13 (Winter 1979): 169–90; the quotations are at pages 182 and 176. See also James A. Henretta, "Families and Farms: *Mentalité* in Pre-Industrial America," *William and Mary Quarterly* 35 (January 1978): 3–33; and Michael Merrill, "Cash Is Good to Eat: Self-Sufficiency and Exchange in the Rural Economy of the United States," *Radical History Review* 3 (Winter 1977): 42–71.
6. Thomas Dublin has estimated that the number of palm leaf hatmakers was around 33,000 in the 1830s. (I am grateful to Professor Dublin for copies of two of his unpublished papers on hatmaking.) John Hayward, in *A Gazetteer of Massachusetts* (Boston, 1847), reported 13,311 women employed in hatmaking in 1845, but only 313 people employed in broommaking. As I have suggested below in the discussion of broommaking in Hadley, the actual number of people involved in broommaking on at least a part-time basis exceeded the number of people who worked full-time as broommakers and who listed their occupation as broommaking.
7. Louis McLane, *Documents Relative to Manufactures in the United States*, 2 vols. (Washington, D.C., 1833), 1:299. For information on early broommaking, see Charles Jones, "The Broom Corn Industry in the Counties of Franklin and Hampshire, and in the Town of Deerfield in Particular," *History and Proceedings of the Pocumtuck Valley Memorial Association, 1897–1904* (Deerfield, Mass., 1905), IV, 105–11; John Montague Smith, *History of the Town of Sunderland* (Greenfield, Mass., 1899), 182; J. H. Temple, *History of the Town of Whately, Mass.* (Boston, 1872), 178–79. For a remarkable and very detailed record of the seasonal nature of broommaking—and indeed of all aspects of work on a New England farm—see the Dennis Stebbins Farm Journal, 1838–1841, in the Stebbins Family Papers (Pocumtuck Valley Memorial Association, Deerfield, Mass.). In Stebbins's household, broommaking was done mostly during the winter and early spring months, from January through mid-April, and occasionally for short periods of a week or so in August, October, and November.
8. Temple, *History of Whately*, 178.
9. James Thomas, the first person to obtain a patent on a broommaking machine, was not from Massachusetts, in fact, but from West Chester, Pennsylvania. See U.S. Patent Office, Specification of Letters Patent No. 6717, 18 Spetember 1849. I am grateful to two specialists in rural Massachusetts life and material culture—Ritchie Garrison, Director of Education at Historic Deerfield, and Kent McCallum, Director of Crafts at Old Sturbridge Village—for sharing their knowledge of broommaking machines with me.
10. Charles Stanley Pease, ed., *History of Conway, 1767–1917* (Springfield, Mass., 1917), 53; Rodolphus Dickinson, *A Geographical and Statistical View of Massachusetts Proper* (Greenfield, Mass., 1813), 67. The 1820 manuscript Census of Manufactures for Massachusetts is on microfilm in the National Archives, Washington, D.C.
11. McLane, *Documents Relative to Manufactures*, 1:262–65, 272–75, 296–99.
12. Massachusetts census figures for 1844–45 showed 313 hands employed in broommaking, 278 of whom (88.9%) lived in Hampshire or Franklin counties. Of the 1,545,985 brooms produced in the state, 1,460,619 (94.5%) came from these two Connecticut Valley counties. For figures on broom production in these counties and in other parts of Massachusetts, see John G. Palfrey, *Statistics of the Condition and Products of Certain Branches of Industry in Massachusetts, for the Year Ending April 1, 1845* (Boston, 1846), 359; and Hayward, *Gazetteer*, 347–96.

13. For a discussion of trade between the Connecticut Valley and urban market centers in the seventeenth and eighteenth centuries, see Stephen C. Innes, *Labor in a New Land: Economy and Society in Seventeenth-Century Springfield* (Princeton: Princeton University Press, 1983); J. Ritchie Garrison, "Tradition and Change in the Agriculture of Deerfield, Massachusetts, 1760–1860," paper presented to the Historic Deerfield Colloquium on Recent Research in Western Massachusetts History, 1978; and Peter Bolles Hirtle, "Agrarian Economy in Flux: The Agricultural History of Deerfield, 1670–1760," paper prepared for the Historic Deerfield Summer Fellowship Program, 1973.
14. McLane, *Documents Relative to Manufactures*, 1:272–73; Taylor, *Transportation Revolution*, 38, 78.
15. Jones, "Broom Corn Industry," 105–7. Exactly how much money those rural broommakers made from their sales to urban distributors is difficult to calculate with precision. In the early 1830s one local observer estimated that it cost about nine cents to make a broom and at that time the retail price for finished brooms in the Boston market ranged from a low of fifteen to a high of twenty-five cents. Throughout the second quarter of the nineteenth century broom prices in Boston generally ranged from twelve to thirty cents, and the difference between the high and low prices for any given year could be substantial. See McLane, *Documents Relative to Manufactures*, 1:299; and Massachusetts Bureau of Statistics of Labor, *History of Wages and Prices in Massachusetts, 1752–1883* (Boston, 1885), 265.
16. The best statement of modernization theory as it has been applied to early nineteenth-century America is Richard D. Brown, *Modernization: The Transformation of American Life, 1600–1860* (New York: Hill and Wang, 1976).
17. Quoted in Danhof, *Change in Agriculture*, 23.
18. For examples of the centralization of outwork, see Dawley, *Class and Community*, esp. chap. 1; Prude, *Coming of Industrial Order*, esp. chap. 3; and Clark, "Household Economy."
19. The information on the Hadley broom shops is in the 1850 federal manuscript census, Schedule 5, Products of Industry. A bound volume of the manuscript census for Hadley is in the Forbes Library, Northampton, Mass.; the census is also on microfilm at the National Archives.
20. Occupational identification has been drawn from the list of Hadley households and the summary of Products of Industry in the 1850 manuscript census.
21. Ibid.
22. Hadley women were not identified by occupation in the federal census, and therefore I am reluctant to argue *categorically* that women did not work as broommakers; the absence of positive evidence in this case may be less a description of reality than an indication of a weakness—even a bias—inherent in the sources. There were, however, four women listed as broommakers in Illinois and six in New York in 1850, and those ten female broommakers may have been the exceptions that proved the rule. See U.S. Census Office, Seventh Census, 1850: *Statistical View of the United States* (Washington, D.C., 1854), 22. Moreover, the Massachusetts state census records *did* identify women by occupation, and yet I have found no evidence of women broommakers in Hadley in the reports for 1837, 1845, 1855, 1875, or 1895. There were a few women broommakers in other towns in the later part of the century, but again their numbers are so small as to seem exceptional. Relying on inference as much as evidence, then, I think it safe to conclude that broommaking was a trade that did not generally employ women, at least in a formal sense.
23. The age and family information is taken from the 1850 manuscript census. The age profile of Hadley broommakers is shown below:

Age range	No. broommakers (N = 110)
15–19	18 (16.4%)
20–24	30 (27.3%)
25–29	29 (26.4%)
30–34	18 (16.4%)
35–39	8 (7.3%)
40–49	6 (5.4%)
50 +	1 (0.9%)

24. The actual figures for real estate holdings are $831 for all landowning broommakers and $4,070 for landowning farmers. For broommakers and farmers in the 25-to-40 age bracket, the figures are $899 and $2,784, respectively. See the 1850 manuscript census.
25. I am grateful to Ritchie Garrison for reminding me of the importance of tenancy.
26. See the 1850 manuscript census, Products of Industry. The census figures show that the 41 Hadley broom shops employed 105 hands on a full-time basis and an additional 10 on a part-time basis. Assuming that the full-time broommakers and at least half of the part-time broommakers did indeed identify themselves as broommakers on the census of households, one can reasonably argue that the 99 broommakers who did not own and work in their own shops worked in one for someone else.
27. Ibid.
28. The anecdote is from Smith, *History of Sunderland*, 182. For a discussion of non-cash exchange, see Clark, "Household Economy," 173–75.
29. The material for the Dickinson family was compiled from the 1850 manuscript census and the genealogical index in Judd, *History of Hadley*.
30. Alan H. McArdle, "Population Growth, Out-Migration, and the Regulation of Community Size: Hadley, Massachusetts, 1660–1730," MA thesis, University of Massachusetts, 1975.
31. Henretta, "Families and Farms," 20–33.
32. Jones, "Broom Corn Industry," 110–11.
33. *Census of Massachusetts, 1875*, 2 vols. (Boston, 1876), 11, 410; Judd, *History of Hadley*, 457; W. B. Gay, ed., *Gazetteer of Hampshire County, Mass., 1654–1887* (Syracuse, N.Y., 1886), Part 11, 88–98; *Census of Massachusetts, 1895* (Boston, 1900), 4:571–73.

11

One of Hadley's best-known sons is certainly "Fighting Joe Hooker," born in 1814 to Mary Seymour and Joseph Hooker, in a gambrel-roofed house on the town common. (Hooker later lived in other houses on both Middle and West streets, but the birthplace was always the venerated site.) He attended Hopkins Academy, and then the U.S. Military Academy at West Point. After cutting his military teeth in Florida during the Seminole Wars, he served under Zachary Taylor and Winfield Scott during the Mexican-American War. Afterward Hooker stayed in the West, and tried his hand at farming in Sonoma County, California. But when the Civil War erupted, he eagerly sought a commission.

Hooker never returned to live in Hadley (he died in 1879, and is buried in Cincinnati, Ohio), but his presence has nevertheless loomed large in the community, which sent dozens of young men to fight alongside him in the war. In the spring of 1895, the Third Army Corps presented the town with a portrait of Hooker by Boston artist J. Harvey Young (1830–1918). That same season, these men—"war-scarred veterans" from his old regiments—gathered at his birthplace to remember him. A booklet titled Hadley: The Regicides, Indian and General History *was printed as a souvenir of the day; it recounts the story of the Angel of Hadley, and also describes the famed "palisade," placing Hooker in the long trajectory of the town's military history. In his essay, local artist Elbridge Kingsley also noted that the young men who witnessed the town's bicentennial in 1859, "with its unique Indian attack and gala dress parade," were (unbeknownst to them) about to take their own "turn at the serious business of war." Poet Clarence Hawkes, whose father had also served in the war, contributed two works, "Springtime in Old Hadley," and "How 'Fighting Joe Hooker' Took Lookout Mountain." Thousands of veterans, Hadley citizens, and guests assembled on the town common under an enormous tent to honor Hooker's memory (figure 11.1). His birthplace was destroyed by fire in April 1898; a boulder now marks the site where the house once stood. In 1903, a statue was erected in Boston to commemorate Hooker and the other Commonwealth men who served in the Civil War. Even today, his figure remains present on the town seal.*

Stephen Sears's essay does not tell us about Hooker's life in his boyhood homes, but it does help the contemporary community better understand its high-profile son in the context of the war that made him famous. We learn how his military skill has been assessed and re-assessed, and—perhaps most importantly—lay to rest local legends about some of Hooker's less-than-desirable legacies.

In Defense of Fighting Joe

Stephen W. Sears

MAJOR GENERAL JOSEPH HOOKER has long received a uniformly bad press from Civil War historians. "Fighting Joe" invariably lags toward the bottom of any ranking of the commanders of the Army of the Potomac, clumped together with John Pope and Ambrose Burnside. The old whispers that he was drunk at Chancellorsville, his one battle as army commander, are whispered anew. Alternatively, if it is allowed that in fact he was sober at Chancellorsville, it is said his fault was going teetotal upon assuming his new responsibilities; better for the army had he downed a few whiskeys when the fighting began in the Virginia Wilderness. As T. Harry Williams put it, "The sudden shutting off of his familiar stimulant was bad for Hooker. He depended on whiskey to brace his courage."[1]

FIGURE 11.1. *Celebration in honor of Joseph Hooker on the Hadley common, 1895. Courtesy of the Hadley Historical Society.*

But the historians' primary charge against Joe Hooker is that, drunk or sober, when he was confronted by Robert E. Lee at Chancellorsville he lost his nerve and thereby lost the battle. James McPherson describes the scene metaphorically: "Like a rabbit mesmerized by the gray fox, Hooker was frozen into immobility. . . ." These authorities point to firm documentation for their case—an admission of his loss of nerve by Hooker himself. In their acclaimed studies, Shelby Foote, Bruce Catton, and Kenneth P. Williams all quote the general's confession. Hooker's biographer, Walter Hebert, adopts the confession as a chapter title—"Hooker Loses Confidence in Hooker." A profile of Hooker in *American Heritage* trumpets, "He was close to winning the Civil War when he suffered an almost incredible failure of nerve." In a kind of final sanctification, Hooker's words are given voice in Ken Burns's 1990 television epic, "The Civil War."[2]

Is it any wonder, then, that Fighting Joe Hooker's military reputation has fallen into such low repute? What could be worse than an army commander losing his nerve in the midst of a battle? In fact, there *is* something worse—that general confessing his failing. For the historian seeking to document how the Union lost the Battle of Chancellorsville, here is the clear and simple answer, in the clear and simple words of the commanding general himself. And so in the books and the articles and the biographical studies—and on television—Joe Hooker has become fixed forever, as if in amber, as the general who lost his nerve.

It was not always thus. The revelation of Hooker's confession came nearly half a century after the occasion for it, May of 1863, and not all that many of his wartime comrades were still alive then to hear of it. Joe Hooker was always tremendously popular with his men—a popularity the equal of McClellan's—and he was well known and admired as the general who fed his troops as well as he led them. When he assumed command of the Army of the Potomac, in January 1863, Hooker was regarded, and deservedly, as the fightingest general in that army. On the Peninsula, in the Seven Days, at Second Bull Run and Antietam and Fredericksburg, he had proved himself a leader who showed no fear of going in with his men—he was wounded at Antietam—and who revealed no lack of decision in the heat of the fighting. Nor did the Chancellorsville defeat drive Hooker off the Civil War stage. In the Chattanooga campaign that fall he seized Lookout Mountain in spectacular fashion, and on the road to Atlanta the following spring his Twentieth Corps did more hard fighting for Sherman than any other outfit.[3]

Hooker remained popular and admired and respected after the war. Although crippled by strokes suffered in 1865 and 1867, he was active in veterans' affairs and visited the old battlefields and closely followed the early efforts at compiling histories of the war. He died, just shy of his sixty-fifth birthday, in 1879. A quarter century later, on Boston's Beacon Hill, an equestrian statue of Joseph Hooker, native son of Massachusetts, was unveiled with appropriate ceremony. Naysayers did not interrupt the proceedings.

Theodore A. Dodge, a fledgling historian of the war, was made uncomfortably aware of the admiration in which Hooker was held after he delivered a lecture on the Battle of Chancellorsville to a Boston audience in 1885. On that occasion, Dodge found not a few faults with Hooker's generalship at Chancellorsville—although he did not accuse him of drunkenness or of losing his nerve. Not long afterward, at a reunion of veterans of the Third Corps, Hooker's old outfit, Dodge found himself the object—indeed the victim—of an angry resolution: "Loyalty to the memory of our beloved commander, Major-Gen. Joseph Hooker, makes it a duty, on this occasion, to protest against unjust and uncalled-for criticisms on his military record as commander of the Army of the Potomac." In the words of poor Dodge, who was in attendance, "the bulk of the time devoted to talking on this occasion was used in denunciation of the wretch, in other words, myself," who had had the temerity to find fault with Fighting Joe.[4]

This is not to say that military historians of the late nineteenth century tiptoed around the subject of Chancellorsville. Theodore Dodge's attack was the sharpest delivered against Hooker, but certainly it was not the only one. After all, there was no gainsaying that he had been soundly defeated, despite having a two-to-one manpower edge over Lee, and that Jackson's surprise attack—Stonewall's last march—had victimized him in dramatic fashion. As general commanding, responsibility for the defeat was undeniably his. Therefore, undeniably, Hooker had been outgeneraled by Lee—in which category, of course, Hooker had plenty of company. Chancellorsville was General Lee's fifth campaign in less than a year, a brief span indeed to have taken the measure of four Union army commanders.

Although not recognized at the time—and not recognized by latter-day historians, either—Joe Hooker managed to have his say in the nineteenth-century debate over his generalship at Chancellorsville. He did so in an indirect way. Hooker wrote little after the war—there was no memoir, for example—and not a great deal during the war. Although he claimed that his report on Antietam (as printed in the *Official Records*) was written within two months of the battle, it was in fact only written fifteen years later. He filed no reports for Second Bull Run or Fredricksburg—and none for Chancellorsville. As to Chancellorsville, he liked to point out that his extended testimony before the congressional Joint

Committee on the Conduct of the War, in 1865, was to all intents and purposes his official report of the battle. Since his testimony, in today's parlance, was a "prepared statement," thirty-nine pages long, we can grant him his point.[5]

Hooker opened his second Chancellorsville campaign in 1876 with a letter to a Pennsylvania professor named Samuel Penniman Bates, who the year before had published a history of the Battle of Gettysburg. He "rejoiced to learn," said Hooker, that Professor Bates was "at present engaged in writing a history of the campaign of Chancellorsville," and he felt "extremely anxious that its narrative should be made up *impartially* to all concerned *and truthfully* as it concerns history." At the time, the only published study of Chancellorsville was the view from the Confederate side, by Jedediah Hotchkiss and William Allan—a book that Hooker volunteered to correct in detail for Bates's benefit. The general explained that he had "some manuscripts in my possession which I should like to lay before you before your work is completed." These dealt in particular with "the part Gen. Howard and his command played in the battle. . . ." As Professor Bates was soon to discover, mention of the name Oliver Otis Howard, who had commanded the Eleventh Corps at Chancellorsville, invariably caused General Hooker to see red.[6]

This letter was the first of fifty-six that Hooker wrote Bates over the course of the next three years, the last one written just three weeks before Hooker's death in 1879. Bates had responded eagerly to Hooker's overture, especially to his offer of documents. The *Official Records* volumes on Chancellorsville were a dozen years in the future, and so what the general was offering just then was a Civil War historian's dream come true. Having thus set the hook, the general reeled in his catch. He sent Bates long discourses defending his role in all the controverted points of the campaign. He traveled to the battlefield in company with him, a visit that Bates would later record for the readers of *Century* magazine's "Battles and Leaders of the Civil War" series. He read and carefully critiqued each of Bates's chapters as he finished them, making sure, among other things, that the professor was clear on Joe Hooker's acerbic views of such of his battlefield lieutenants as the Eleventh Corps' Otis Howard, the Sixth Corps' John Sedgwick, and the cavalry's George Stoneman.

While modern-day reviewers have characterized Bates's writing as turgid and discursive, his book is acknowledged to be "not uninformed." In point of fact, it offers the only clue we have to Joe Hooker's thinking and his decisions at several crucial points in the fighting. Hooker did not live to see the book into print—it was not published until 1882—but he seems to have been satisfied that his view of the Chancellorsville struggle would be represented. "So much *twaddle* has been written about this battle," he complained in one of his last letters to

Bates, but he remained hopeful: "A day of reckoning however is close at hand, and that is all that I want." Perhaps at last Fighting Joe Hooker's day of reckoning is upon us, but the path from then to now has been long and very rocky.[7]

What in due course would send Joe Hooker's military reputation plummeting was nothing more sinister than a footnote in John Bigelow Jr.'s *The Campaign of Chancellorsville*. Bigelow (as it has come to simply be known) fits the description of a weighty tome. Published in a limited edition of 1,000 copies by Yale University Press in 1910, it is an oversized, imposing volume containing 528 pages, 47 maps and plans, and the draping of Authority. The footnote, giving Major E. P. Halstead as source, appears in Bigelow's concluding chapter, titled "Comments," where he is describing what he terms "Hooker's irresolution in this campaign"; clearly Bigelow intended it to document that irresolution. The footnote relates an incident that took place "a couple of months" after Chancellorsville, during the march toward Gettysburg. The Army of the Potomac had just crossed the Potomac in pursuit of Lee, and army commander Hooker was riding with Abner Doubleday, who led a division in the First Corps, when Doubleday turned to him and asked, "Hooker, what was the matter with you at Chancellorsville? Some say you were injured by a shell, and others that you were drunk; now tell us what it was." Hooker answered, frankly and good-naturedly: "Doubleday, I was not hurt by a shell, and I was not drunk. For once I lost confidence in Hooker, and that is all there is to it."[8]

Since 1910, it is safe to say, every author (almost) writing about Chancellorsville, or about Joe Hooker, or about the change of command in the Army of the Potomac just before Gettysburg, or indeed writing any general military account of the period, or any study of the Union high command, has quoted or paraphrased or cited this exchange. These authors all appear to have done so without a second thought, so imposing is Bigelow's reputation.

Give it a second thought, however, and even on the face of it there is an odor to this incident. For example, Hooker is said to have replied that, no, he was not injured by a shell at Chancellorsville. Yet in fact he was quite seriously injured when a wooden pillar of the Chancellor house, against which he was leaning, was hit by a Confederate solid shot. In the weeks since the battle he had often spoken of this injury as a factor in his defeat, and for him now to deny it ever happened is not credible. His confession is even less credible. Joe Hooker, it is true, was likely to say all manner of surprising and outrageous things—but never in disparagement of himself. Quite the contrary. He had made sure it was widely known in these weeks that it was his lieutenants who had failed at Chancellorsville; he might have to accept the ultimate responsibility, but it was they who were really to blame for the lost campaign. For Joe Hooker to admit to a subordinate (and within hearing of that subordinate's aide hovering nearby) that he had lost his confidence, his nerve, in the midst of battle, is simply not believable.

Look closely at the retailer of this tale, E. P. Halstead, and it all quickly comes unraveled. Halstead had served on Doubleday's wartime staff, and in 1903—forty years after the alleged event—he included this conversation between Hooker and Doubleday in a letter describing the First Corps' role at Chancellorsville. Bigelow acquired the letter as research for his book. When the movements of Hooker's headquarters and of the First Corps' headquarters are tracked for this period, it is clear that they were dozens of miles apart, with never an opportunity for the two generals to meet like this. Indeed, Hooker and Doubleday were never near enough to meet at *any* time on the march north from the Rappahannock and before Hooker left the army command. For good measure, the rest of Halstead's letter is a grossly inaccurate account of the First Corps' actions at Chancellorsville.[9]

Halstead's tale is not all that uncommon for Civil War historiography of this period, the turn of the century—an elderly staff officer with at best a clouded recollection of some long-ago campfire speculation, or with at worst an urge to create a role for himself—in this case, a footnote—in the history of this war of the past. Of course the two principals were dead and unavailable to confirm or deny. Civil War bookshelves, alas, are crowded with memoirs and recollections of events that never happened, retailed by old Yanks and old Johnnies seeking a little sliver of notice in what had been for them the greatest experience of their lives.

With this slanderous cliché discounted, where does it leave us in evaluating Joe Hooker's generalship? It is useful to look first at what in the nineteenth century was termed the qualities for moral leadership. This was more than morality per se; it meant the whole of a man's character for leading in war. It needs to be understood, in this connection, that Joseph Hooker came into the Civil War, at least in the eyes of certain of his contemporaries, as something less than a gentleman. The antebellum army was a species of petty aristocracy, putting a high premium on social conformity, and with his rough edges Joe Hooker was no model of conformity.

His biographer, Walter Hebert, explains that during his posting in California in the 1850s "Idleness led Hooker along the usual path to the devil's workshop." He played cards for money, he drank, and he pursued female companionship in the manner of a middle-aged bachelor in the Victorian era—that is, he paid for his pleasure. It seems that civilian society was more tolerant of these habits than the military, and Hooker's raffish California reputation preceded him into the Civil War. General McClellan would write that in 1861 he gave a briefing on

Hooker to Mr. Lincoln: "I told him that in the Mexican War Hooker was looked upon as a good soldier but an unreliable man, & that his course in California had been such as to forfeit the respect of his comrades—that he was then a common drunkard & gambler."[10]

It is true enough that Hooker enjoyed a game of cards played for money, but that he was a common drunkard is another matter. There is good evidence that the reputation of a drinker that attached to Joe Hooker was more perceived than real. John Hay, Lincoln's wartime secretary, made a perceptive comment on the subject. In his diary Hay described dining one evening in Washington with a group that included the general. "Hooker drank very little," he wrote, "not more than the rest who were all abstemious, yet what little he drank made his cheek hot and red & his eye brighter. I can easily understand how the stories of his drunkenness have grown, if so little affects him as I have seen."

This would explain the contradictions in the contemporary evidence—Hooker *appearing* to have drunk to excess when in reality he drank no more (and probably less) than the average general, and was in no way impaired in the process. It also belies the imputation, made first by the vindictive General Darius Couch, that Hooker was an alcoholic who found his courage in a bottle and lost it if he stopped drinking. There are too many adamant and wholly reliable eyewitnesses to Hooker's sobriety—among them General George Meade, artilleryman Charles Wainwright, and intelligence chief George Sharpe—for anyone today to believe otherwise. Joe Hooker did not abuse alcohol, nor was he dependent on it.[11]

Nevertheless, the undercurrent of tales about Hooker's drinking, originating from his California days, persisted all the way through his war service, apparently unquenchable. Some who saw him lying comatose after his injury at Chancellorsville, for example, spread the gossip that he was dead drunk. Following the battle, cavalryman George Armstrong Custer made sure his old commander, General McClellan, knew what was behind the report of Hooker's wounding by a shell. "If anything," Custer wrote, "prevented him from succeeding, it was a wound he received from a projectile which requires a cork to be drawn before it is serviceable." Congressional investigators visiting the army could find no basis for such charges. The *New York Tribune* put its best correspondent, George Smalley, on the story. "I asked everybody likely to know," Smalley reported, "and not one witness could testify to having seen General Hooker the worse for whiskey." But the gossip was too deeply rooted to disappear.[12]

Another dimension of the general's moral character acted on the gossips like pure catnip. On January 31, 1863, soon after Hooker took command of the Army of the Potomac, artillerist Charles Wainwright entered in his diary, "I am asked on all sides here if he drinks. Though thrown in very close contact with him through six months, I never saw him when I thought him the worse for liquor." Then he added, "Indeed, I should say that his failing was more in the way of women than whiskey." Blue-blooded Charles Francis Adams Jr., grandson and great-grandson of presidents, is often quoted on this latter failing of Hooker's. During that winter of 1862–63, sniffed Captain Adams, "the headquarters of the Army of the Potomac was a place to which no self-respecting man liked to go, and no decent woman could go. It was a combination of bar-room and brothel." During this period in Washington, it was said, the general's carriage might be found of an evening drawn up outside one or another of the city's better-known brothels; indeed, a section of Washington's Second Ward thickly packed with brothels was known—and continued to be known for many years afterward—as Hooker's Division.[13]

In contrast to the tales of Hooker's drunkenness, there seems to be little doubt that the general patronized prostitutes, although Adams's contention that Army of the Potomac headquarters was little better than a brothel must be taken at a large discount. At age forty-eight and unmarried when he took command of the army, Joe Hooker apparently followed the practice of many bachelors of elevated station in the Victorian age, and he made no particular secret of it. The one myth in this connection is that the slang term for a prostitute derived from his name. In fact "hooker" long predated the Civil War, originating probably from streetwalkers "hooking" or snaring their clients.[14] This did not prevent insiders in Washington from winking and snickering at the nice conjunction between the general's name and the general's proclivity. The broad-minded dismissed the matter with a shrug. Hooker's enemies regarded it as evidence of his moral unfitness for high command.

One other burden Joe Hooker brought with him from his days in California was a mutually embittering relationship with Henry W. Halleck. For the general-in-chief of all the North's armies and the general commanding the largest of those armies to be at loggerheads was an awkward situation, to say the least; certainly it was one more burden President Lincoln had to bear. Halleck was characteristically guarded on the subject, saying only that Hooker was aware "that I know some things about his character and conduct in California, and, fearing that I may use that information against him, he seeks to ward off its effect by making it appear that I am his personal enemy." Hooker, characteristically, was not at all guarded about their dispute. During their days together in California, he explained, Halleck joined a law firm specializing in land claims, and Hooker, trying to protect the interests of acquaintances, charged Halleck to his face with "schemes of avarice and plunder. . . . Indeed I indulged in still harsher language. . . ." Whatever the truth of the matter—and Hooker's explanation is the more convincing of the two—it sounds like something Joe Hooker would say, and in a loud voice. He insisted Halleck carried a grudge against him right into the war. It was Halleck, he said, who had persuaded Lincoln to award command of the Army of the Potomac to Burnside in November 1862 rather than to him.[15]

When, two and a half months later, after the Fredericksburg disaster, Lincoln came to replace Burnside with Hooker, this time the president took the decision alone, without consulting General Halleck; he recognized Halleck's predisposition. Hooker's sole condition for accepting the appointment was his insistence on an arm's-length relationship with the general-in-chief—neither the Army of the Potomac "nor its commander expected justice at his hands," Hooker told the president. On all substantive matters he would deal only with Lincoln, and so it was until the finish of the Chancellorsville campaign. Halleck complained that he was the last person in Washington to know what was going on with the Army of the Potomac.[16]

Until Hooker retreated back across the Rappahannock, ending his Chancellorsville adventure, generally he was allowed to operate the Potomac army with a free hand. He could ignore the general-in-chief with impunity. Now, however, as Lee's army shifted northward and became an invading force, Mr. Lincoln began drawing in the reins on his army commander. The divide between Hooker and Halleck became a major factor in the growing crisis. "It was no use for me to make a request," Hooker said, "as that of itself would be sufficient cause for General Halleck to refuse it." The president sought to smooth the path between the two with a letter to Hooker marked "private." "If you and he would use the same frankness to one another, and to me, that I use to both of you," Lincoln wrote, "there would be no difficulty. I need and must have the professional skill of both, and yet these suspicions tend to deprive me of both. . . . Now, all I ask is that you will be in such mood that we can get into our action the best cordial judgment of yourself and General Halleck."[17]

It was to no avail, of course. Halleck, having regained the upper hand over his stubbornly independent subordinate, was not about to surrender it again. Neither he nor Hooker would blink, and in due course they clashed, disastrously for Hooker, over the garrison at Harper's Ferry. Hooker wanted the garrison for his army, Halleck refused him, Hooker filed his resignation in protest. It was accepted and Joe Hooker was gone—gone forever—from the army he had become so much a part of. Hooker noted bitterly that his successor, General Meade, was allowed to do as he wished with the Harper's Ferry garrison. In his valedictory to the Joint Committee on the Conduct of the War, Hooker leveled a broadside at

Henry Halleck. "If the general-in-chief had been in the rebel interest," he testified, "it would have been impossible for him . . . to have added to the embarrassment he caused me from the moment I took command of the army of the Potomac to the time I surrendered it."[18]

For historians persuaded by Bigelow's footnote that Joe Hooker had lost his nerve at Chancellorsville, it was but a short step to the conclusion that he welcomed the chance to relinquish army command in the face of the new test looming ahead. General Hooker, wrote T. Harry Williams, "was looking for an excuse to get rid of his command. He was afraid of Lee." But once the Bigelow footnote is deleted, as it were, the matter takes on a different cast.

It is acknowledged that Hooker's march north from the Rappahannock was carried out with considerable skill. It was Hooker who dispatched cavalry to the town of Gettysburg as the most likely point of concentration for the Confederates, and his moves shadowing Lee seem to have been taken with considerable confidence. This in spite of the fact that he was in constant friction with the general-in-chief, and was also the recipient of a warning from Mr. Lincoln: "I must tell you that I have some painful intimations that some of your corps and division commanders are not giving you their entire confidence." Indeed, it seems that the real purpose behind Hooker's resignation was merely to precipitate a showdown with Halleck. Joe Hooker's comment on the change of command, although written later, appears to be a true reflection of his feelings in that summer of 1863. The "wavering and vacillating" of some of his lieutenants did bother him, he admitted. "However," he wrote, "this would have been a source of no regret, could I have commanded, *as I wished to*, at Gettysburg, but the fates were against me."[19]

In contrast to the McClellan era, Lincoln's relationship with Hooker as army commander had been comfortable and open. The president was remarkably candid with his general when appointing him to the command, and Hooker responded with full reports of his intentions and with details of his plans. He also respected, and acted on, the president's suggestions. Whatever Joe Hooker's failings—and Lincoln was very much aware of them—this man would fight. He might be rash, he might intrigue for promotion, he might be suspect in his personal habits, but on his record he would fight. After Antietam, when McClellan was dragging his feet and Lincoln was casting about for a general to replace him, the president had observed to a visitor, "Now there's Joe Hooker—he can fight—I think that point is pretty well established—but whether he can 'keep tavern' for a large army is not so sure."[20]

It was the president's experience that fighting generals were in short supply, and at first, after Chancellorsville, Lincoln was willing to give Hooker the benefit of the doubt. He was not disposed, he said, to throw away a gun just because it misfired once. In any case, it would look bad to the country if the administration continued to relieve its generals after every battle. What finally changed the president's mind, as much as anything else, was the outspoken complaints against General Hooker by the Potomac army's high command. It had not sat well with these corps commanders when Hooker blamed some of their own—specifically Howard, Sedgwick, and Stoneman—for the Chancellorsville defeat. A generals' revolt had been a major factor in Burnside's overthrow after Fredericksburg; now, after Chancellorsville, the same fate befell Joe Hooker, ironically one of the originators of high-command discontent in this army.

When Lincoln warned Hooker about his dissident generals, he observed that the effect of such a revolt on the army would be "ruinous, if true." With a showdown battle sure to be fought any day, somewhere in Maryland or Pennsylvania, it was vital that there be harmony among the generals who had to direct the fighting. The dissidents made it clear to Lincoln that General Meade was their choice; Hooker had commended Meade as his best corps commander. With John Reynolds having taken himself out of contention for the high command, Meade's appointment was made without debate. Joe Hooker would have no second chance against Robert E. Lee; the fates, as he said, were against him.[21]

Amidst all the controversy that has swirled about this larger-than-life figure, all the gossip and debate about his moral character, it has been all too easy to overlook certain unique qualities of Joe Hooker's generalship. The first of these is how well Hooker was prepared for army command when compared to most of his fellow officers in the antebellum army. The primary training ground for the Civil War general had been the Mexican War. Much has been written of Lee's scouting missions on the march to Mexico City, of Jackson fighting his guns at Chapultepec, of McClellan's bravery under fire, and other such exploits. Yet beyond the indelible experience of serving under enemy fire, the tactical lessons of Mexico were mostly those of the smoothbore era. The age of rifled armaments—Springfields and Enfields and Parrott cannon—ushered in by the Civil War was something new under the sun for the American soldier.

What could be gained from the war with Mexico, however, was the experience of military administration—literally how to run a command, and how to do it efficiently. In this Joe Hooker's Mexican War experience was unexcelled. He served as chief of staff to no less than five generals. None was a professional; each relied on Major Hooker to run his command for him. This involved, in addition, leading troops in combat often enough to earn him three brevets for gallantry. When Joe Hooker met Lincoln for the first time, after First Bull Run, he blurted out, "I was at Bull Run the other day, Mr. President, and it is no vanity in me to say that I am a damned sight better general than any you had on that field." He may have spoken brashly, but he had the credentials to back up his brashness. And he did back it up.[22]

There is something refreshing about such candor, and indeed there is something refreshing about Joe Hooker. By all accounts, he was open and warm and disarmingly sincere in his personal relationships. "A gallant and chivalrous soldier," General Alpheus Williams said of him, "and most agreeable." To be sure, Hooker talked far too much and too indiscreetly and with too much brag, but what he said, upon examination, often sounds suspiciously like truth. His boast to Mr. Lincoln that he was a damned sight better general than any the Union had at First Bull Run is an example. Look at some of the Union names on that battlefield—McDowell, Heintzelman, Keyes, Hunter—and one is inclined to agree. When he observed that Ambrose Burnside had a brain the size of a hickory nut, he may not have been far off the mark. Hooker liked to boast, before Chancellorsville, that he had the finest army on the planet, and considering the sorry state of the army that he inherited from Burnside, and how he had restored it to life, there was truth there, too. In the midst of the Chancellorsville fight he issued an address to his army, saying, "our enemy must either ingloriously fly, or come out from behind his defenses and give us battle on our own ground, where certain destruction awaits him." This prediction would be much derided, yet at the time of its issue it was a perfectly accurate statement of the case—and, if the truth be acknowledged, "certain destruction" ought to have been Lee's fate.[23]

Joe Hooker was outspoken enough to wear his ambition on his sleeve. He sincerely believed that he was a better general than George McClellan (and he was), and that his fighting record rated him the command in McClellan's place. He had no doubt at all that he was a better general than Ambrose Burnside (and without a doubt he was), and he unblushingly campaigned for Burnside's spot. The Army of the Potomac, rooted and grown to maturity in Washington, was the most politicized of Civil War armies, which fact Hooker understood perfectly; to get ahead in that army, one had to have friends in high places. It was necessary and vital that he work at that. General Halleck, head of the army, was his enemy and the roadblock to his advancement, but Hooker hoped to neutralize Halleck by cultivating members of Congress and the two Cabinet members he regarded as the most influential—Secretary of War Stanton and Secretary of the Treasury Chase. Others might call this intrigue; Hooker called it pragmatism.

The one friend in high places who understood Hooker best was, of course, Abraham Lincoln. Lincoln's famous letter of January 26, 1863, handed to Hooker along with his appointment as Army of the Potomac commander, weighed the general's assets and liabilities in blunt but kindly fashion. After fifteen months of frustration trying to reach and reason with General McClellan, Mr. Lincoln, commander-in-chief, was determined that this general understand exactly what was expected of him. The letter's candor also owed much to the Lincoln–Hooker arrangement to shunt Halleck to the sideline in the forthcoming campaign; if Hooker insisted on dealing only with the president, it was best that he be clear on where he stood with the president. Hooker calmly accepted Lincoln's criticism that "you have taken counsel of your ambition" in undercutting Burnside, "in which you did a great wrong to the country," for he believed that accusation had been spread by Burnside himself as vengeance for losing the army command. Hooker was quoted as saying, "That is just such a letter as a father might write to his son," and it "ought to be printed in letters of gold." He was careful to preserve the letter, arranging for its publication in Professor Bates's book on Chancellorsville and in the *Official Records*.[24]

Hooker took hold of the army command like he had been born to it, and Lincoln had every reason to be pleased with his new general; it appeared that Hooker could after all "keep tavern" for a large army. Joe Hooker's talents as a military executive, talents honed in the Mexican War, seem to have come as a complete surprise to his contemporaries. In just two months he turned the Army of the Potomac around, to universal amazement. He cut the number of deserters on the rolls from more than 25,000 to less than 2,000. He introduced much-needed reforms in the daily running of the army, and saw to it that the men were well fed and well clad and well housed. This resulted in an enormous leap in morale. At the time of Hooker's appointment, Captain Henry Livermore Abbott, proper Bostonian, dismissed the new commander as "nothing more than a smart, driving, plucky Yankee, inordinately vain & . . . entirely unscrupulous." Six weeks later Abbott was writing, "I must give Hooker the credit of saying that this step is the very best for the army that could be taken." The *New York Times* editorialized that the Army of the Potomac "is about as much Hookerized as it was at one time McClellanized."

These administrative changes and reforms were so solidly grounded that in the aftermath of the Chancellorsville defeat, in May 1863, there was nothing like the virtual collapse of the army that had followed Burnside's defeat at Fredericksburg the previous December. A Massachusetts soldier summed it up by insisting, "The morale of the Army of the Potomac was better in June than it had been in January," and he recalled "nothing of that spirit of insubordination and despondency." To Joe Hooker's lasting credit, if he led the Potomac army to defeat at Chancellorsville, he left it strong enough to survive and win at Gettysburg. In that sense he might be better remembered as "Administrative Joe" than as "Fighting Joe." [25]

A second aspect of Hooker's generalship—one largely unappreciated by historians—was his dedicated effort to finding a new way to fight once he was in command and got his army to the battlefield. Throughout his fighting record, from Williamsburg on the Peninsula under McClellan to Fredericksburg under Burnside, Joe Hooker had been in the forefront of frontal attacks. At Williamsburg his division suffered almost 1,600 casualties in an unsupported frontal attack. In the Seven Days he defended against the enemy's frontal attacks. At Second Bull Run he led a frontal attack, on Pope's orders and under protest, and pronounced it "a useless slaughter." At Antietam he lost a third of his corps in a head-to-head slugging match with Stonewall Jackson. At Fredericksburg, in a fury at Burnside's tactics, he assaulted Marye's Heights, "lost as many men as my orders required me to lose," and suspended the attack. It was obvious that the rifled musket and the rifled cannon had made storming tactics tragically costly. There had to be, Joe Hooker thought, a better way.[26]

The particular problem Hooker faced in the Chancellorsville campaign was to mount an aggressive offensive, yet not throw his army against the entrenched enemy as Burnside had done—and, in fact, against an enemy far better entrenched in April than it had been at Fredericksburg in December. All Hooker's planning, all his maneuvering at Chancellorsville was designed, first, to force Lee out of his entrenchments, and second, to press on Lee the choice of either attacking the Federals or giving up the Rappahannock line and falling back on Richmond. And after three days of brilliant maneuvering, Hooker achieved exactly that position.

Then the familiar story, with everything going sour for Fighting Joe. There was more than ample justification for each of the charges he leveled against his lieutenants. Howard, Sedgwick, and Stoneman in particular were dismal failures on this battlefield. There were flukish failures of communications. Hooker made important tactical errors. Yet in spite of all these various failings and missteps, the battle was very winnable for the Union during that furious Sunday morning of fighting on May 3—until the moment that General Hooker was hurled unconscious to the front porch floor of the Chancellor house from the blow of a Confederate solid shot from one of Porter Alexander's rifled pieces firing from Hazel Grove.

Without Hooker's loss-of-nerve confession to explain his Chancellorsville defeat, this battlefront injury assumes major importance. It was 9:00 A.M. when Hooker went down. For three hours that morning he had been managing the contest like the Fighting Joe of past battles—personally posting his infantry and his guns, rushing reinforcements to threatened points, riding his lines to encourage his troops. He was in his element. Whatever else had gone wrong, one thing had gone right and exactly according to Hooker's original plan—it was the Confederates who were being forced to use storming tactics on this battlefield.

The night before, after Jackson's surprise flank attack on the Eleventh Corps, Hooker briefed Gouverneur Warren on how he planned to meet the enemy's renewed assault on May 3: "Genl. Hooker," Warren explained, "made his dispositions accordingly and intends to flank and destroy Jackson."[27] That remained his aim during the May 3 fighting—let the enemy fully commit his forces in attack, then counter with a flank assault on the Confederate left using his reserves. On the porch of the Chancellor house Hooker was too far forward for safety—Alexander had learned from prisoners that the house was Hooker's headquarters, and took it under fire deliberately—but it offered a commanding view of the field, and Joe Hooker was always a general who led from the front.

The morning had been an unrelenting struggle of attack and counterattack, tilting first to the Confederates, then to the Federals. At nine o'clock the tilt was Confederate, but to achieve that, Jeb Stuart—who had replaced the wounded Jackson in command of that wing of the Rebel army—had committed his last reserves. Hooker's reserves were still ample, and at the moment he was hit he was being handed a call for reinforcements to meet Stuart's charge. The solid shot hit the wooden porch pillar, split it lengthwise, and (in Hooker's words) hurled half of it "violently against me . . . which struck me in an erect position from my head to my feet." He lay unconscious for between thirty and forty minutes. At first it was assumed he had been killed. When he was found to be breathing, Dr. Jonathan Letterman, his medical director, expressed doubt that he would revive. When at last Hooker regained consciousness and tried to mount his horse to show himself and reassure the troops, he collapsed and vomited. In a daze, he was carried to the rear. "The blow which the General received seems to have knocked all the sense out of him," a staff man told his family. "For the remainder of the day he was wandering, and was unable to get any ideas into his head." General Abner Doubleday wrote that Hooker "suffered great pain and was in a comatose condition for most of the time. His mind was not clear, and they had to wake him up to communicate with him."[28]

These are the classic symptoms of severe concussion. For the rest of the day the commanding general drifted in and out of awareness; he probably suffered periods of amnesia. The question here is why Darius Couch, the senior general on the field, did not immediately take the command. The answer lies in the absence of Dan Butterfield from field headquarters. Butterfield, Hooker's chief of staff, was directing the army's left wing around Fredericksburg. In his place temporarily on the other wing, with Hooker at the Chancellor house, was James Van Alen. Brigadier General Van Alen was a Sunday soldier, a wealthy New York political appointee of no particular skills whom Halleck had recently palmed off on Hooker's headquarters. Van Alan had no idea what to do in this crisis, and apparently no one told him. Dr. Letterman, who was authority for the fact that Hooker was incapable of command and ought to be replaced, seems to have been reluctant to take any action without a decisive chief of staff to lead the way. General Couch was eventually called to the scene, but by then Hooker had regained consciousness and, superficially at least, appeared to be uninjured, and (as Couch put it) "I went about my own business."[29]

Hooker collapsed soon afterward, and it was at least half an hour before he was in a rational enough period to call Couch back again. In the more than an hour since Hooker was struck down, the battle had reached its crisis and then slid rapidly into the Confederates' hands. In that time, every call to headquarters for reinforcements from Union commanders on the firing lines had been meet by silence. The high command was struck mute. Even now there might still have been a chance for victory—Reynolds's First Corps and Meade's Fifth had hardly been engaged all that morning—but it would not be risked. Meade pleaded the case, but Hooker refused him.

Instead he turned command over to Couch, with orders to pull back to a new line to protect the army's Rappahannock crossings. What little of his mental faculties Hooker could still collect seemed now to be focused narrowly on one object—to save the army. His plan appeared to be in a shambles. His reasoning was clouded. Over the next days his mind began to clear, but even then he could think of nothing more than inviting an attack by Lee against his fortified lines. Then, after yet another communications failure, Sedgwick and the Sixth Corps retreated across the Rappahannock prematurely, and Hooker was done. He recrossed the river with the rest of the army. Joe Hooker's grand campaign, begun with such high hopes, ended in a cliché—not with a bang but with a whimper.

It was less than two months later that Potomac army commander Hooker met the same fate as his four predecessors. The question in Washington now became what to do with him. In contrast to the earlier four, Mr. Lincoln was active in supporting a fighting role for Fighting Joe Hooker. "I have not thrown Gen. Hooker away," he told Meade, and attempted to promote a corps command for Hooker in the Army of the Potomac. Meade managed to evade this possibility. "It would be very difficult for Hooker to be quiet under me or anyone else," Meade remarked in a private letter, and there was certainly truth to that. It is hard to imagine the irrepressible Joe Hooker meekly playing the subordinate in the army he once commanded.[30]

The solution was found when it was decided to send reinforcements to Rosecrans in the western theater in the form of the Eleventh and Twelfth Corps from the Army of the Potomac. These two corps had never been at home in the Potomac army—especially the Eleventh Corps, with unhappy experiences at both Chancellorsville and Gettysburg—and the army was glad to see them gone. And this offered the answer to the Joe Hooker problem—let him command the two orphaned corps. By early October of 1863 Hooker was established with his new command at Stevenson, Alabama.

The command structure in the West was soon reshaped, and Hooker found himself increasingly an outcast. Grant, put in overall command in the western theater, seemed to resent Fighting Joe being forced on him from Washington and hoped to be rid of him. General Grant, it was reported to Secretary of War Stanton, felt Hooker's "presence here is replete with both trouble and danger." Hooker's strong showing in taking Lookout Mountain during the Chattanooga campaign in November did not persuade Grant, who in his recollections was dismissive of Hooker's so-called "Battle Above the Clouds." "It is all poetry," Grant said contemptuously. Hooker said defiantly, "I find I am regarded with a great deal of jealousy by those filling high places here," but he believed that his soldiership, as he called it, would carry him through: "I have never yet seen the time that there was no place for a man willing to fight."[31]

In the spring of 1864, now under Sherman, Hooker marched on Atlanta in command of his two corps consolidated as the newly formed Twentieth Corps. He could take no comfort from having to report to William Tecumseh Sherman. Sherman, who had served with Hooker in the California days, wrote even before Chancellorsville: "I know Hooker well and tremble to think of his handling 100,000 men in the presence of Lee."[32] Presumably Sherman thought Chancellorsville confirmed his prediction. Like Grant, Sherman felt he had to tolerate Hooker because he was the president's choice. In any event, Hooker directed his corps effectively all during the advance to Atlanta's outskirts. Indeed, the Twentieth Corps did most of the fighting on this march and suffered by far the most casualties—over 5,000. These achievements only intensified Sherman's efforts to be rid of Fighting Joe.

His opportunity came suddenly in the battle for Atlanta. General James B. McPherson, commanding the Army of the Tennessee, was killed in action. Logic dictated that John A. Logan, who succeeded McPherson during the fighting as senior officer on the field, be named permanent commander of the Army of the Tennessee. Certainly Logan was qualified and had earned the position. Sherman would say that he rejected Logan as army commander because he was not a West Pointer, but there likely was a very different motive in the choice he did make. In naming Oliver Otis Howard as head of the Army of the Tennessee, Sherman surely knew how Joe Hooker would react.

Of all the corps commanders under Sherman, Hooker had the most seniority and the most experience—experience in, among other things, commanding an army. Hooker believed he was entitled to McPherson's command. To give it to Otis Howard, his former subordinate, the man he believed above all others was responsible for the Chancellorsville defeat, was an insult on Sherman's part, and a carefully calculated insult at that. Hooker's resignation was prompt. "Justice and self-respect alike require my removal from an army in which rank and service are ignored," he explained.[33]

So ended Fighting Joe Hooker's service in the Civil War. How might he be summed up? Of two things we can be sure—he was not a drunk, and he never lost his nerve in battle. Once these canards are out of the way, it is possible to paint him in more realistic colors. In that essential role of an officer—to take care of his men—he was paramount. No general on either side was better at that than Joe Hooker. No general in the Army of the Potomac had a better combat record. In every battle in which he was engaged—except one—his performance has to be rated at least "creditable" and at best "excellent." He was rough-edged and not much of a gentleman, and he talked far too much and far too loudly. He did not bother to disguise his ambition, and he did not suffer fools gladly.

As to the battle for which he will always be remembered, Joe Hooker is entitled to be heard. "You may like to know my opinion of the battle of Chancellorsville," he wrote Professor Bates. "I won greater success on many fields in the war, but nowhere did I deserve it half so much." Sitting in judgment after Chancellorsville, Mr. Lincoln said, "I have not thrown Gen. Hooker away." Nor should the historians of this war.[34]

Notes

1. T. Harry Williams, *Lincoln and His Generals* (New York: Knopf, 1952), 239. The most recent charge that Hooker was drunk at Chancellorsville is in Ernest B. Furgurson, *Chancellorsville 1863: The Souls of the Brave* (New York: Knopf, 1992), 285–87. Pope's command of the Army of the Potomac at Second Bull Run was unofficial but manifest.
2. James M. McPherson, *Battle Cry of Freedom: The Civil War Era* (New York: Oxford University Press, 1988), 645; Shelby Foote, *The Civil War: A Narrative* (New York: Random House, 1963), 2:315; Bruce Catton, *Glory Road: The Bloody Route from Fredericksburg to Gettysburg* (New York: Doubleday, 1952), 230; Kenneth P. Williams, *Lincoln Finds a General: A Military Study of the Civil War* (New York: Macmillan, 1949), 2:604; Walter H. Hebert, *Fighting Joe Hooker* (Indianapolis: Bobbs-Merrill, 1944), chap. 14; Gene Smith, "The Destruction of Fighting Joe Hooker," *American Heritage*, October 1993, 95–103; Ken Burns, *The Civil War* (PBS, 1990), episode 4.

3. Albert Castel, *Decision in the West: The Atlanta Campaign of 1864* (Lawrence: University Press of Kansas, 1992), 291.
4. Theodore A. Dodge, Lowell Lecture: "The Battle of Chancellorsville," *Southern Historical Society Papers*, 14:276–92; Dodge, *The Campaign of Chancellorsville*, 2nd ed. (Boston: Ticknor & Fields, 1886), 266–67.
5. Hooker testimony, *Report of the Joint Committee on the Conduct of the War*, vol. 1 (1865), 111–49.
6. Hooker to Bates, 16 February 1876, Samuel P. Bates Collection, Pennsylvania Historical and Museum Commission, Pennsylvania State Archives; Jedediah Hotchkiss and William Allan, *The Battle-Fields of Virginia: Chancellorsville* (New York: Van Nostrand, 1867).
7. Samuel P. Bates, "Hooker's Comments on Chancellorsville," *Battles and Leaders of the Civil War* (New York: Century, 1887–88), 3:215–23; Bates, *The Battle of Chancellorsville* (1882); Allan Nevins et. al., *Civil War Books: A Critical Bibliography* (Baton Rouge: Louisiana State University Press, 1967), 1:23; Hooker to Bates, 22 September 1879, Bates Collection.
8. John Bigelow Jr., *The Campaign of Chancellorsville: A Strategic and Tactical Study* (New Haven: Yale University Press, 1910), 477–78n.
9. E. P. Halstead, 19 April 1903, Bigelow Papers, Library of Congress.
10. Hebert, *Fighting Joe Hooker*, 38; George B. McClellan, memoirs draft, McClellan Papers, Library of Congress.
11. John Hay, *Inside Lincoln's White House: The Complete Civil War Diary of John Hay*, ed. Michael Burlingame and John R. Turner Ettlinger (Carbondale: Southern Illinois University Press, 1997), 80; Darius Couch in *Battles and Leaders*, 3:170; George G. Meade, *Life and Letters of George Gordon Meade* (New York: Scribner's, 1913), 1:365; Charles S. Wainwright, *A Diary of Battle: The Personal Journals of Colonel Charles S. Wainwright, 1861–1865*, ed. Allan Nevins (New York: Harcourt, Brace & World, 1963), 202, 214; George H. Sharpe memorandum, Joseph Hooker Papers, Huntington Library.
12. Robert G. Carter, *Four Brothers in Blue* (Washington, D.C.: Gibson Press, 1913), 270–72; George A. Custer to McClellan, 6 May 1863, McClellan Papers; George W. Smalley, *Anglo-American Memories* (New York: Putnam's, 1911), 158.
13. Wainwright, *Diary of Battle*, 162; Charles Francis Adams Jr., *Charles Francis Adams, 1835–1916: An Autobiography* (Boston: Houghton Mifflin, 1916), 161; E. N. Gilpin, 7 April 1911, Bigelow Papers; Margaret Leech, *Reveille in Washington, 1860–1865* (New York: Harper & Brothers, 1941), 264.
14. *The American Heritage Dictionary*, 3rd ed., 869.
15. Halleck to Sherman, 16 September 1864, William T. Sherman, *Memoirs* (New York: Library of America, 1990), 590; Hooker to Bates, 28 June 1878, Bates Collection.
16. Hooker testimony, *Report of Joint Committee*, vol. 1 (1865), 175, 112; Halleck to Stanton, 18 May 1863, *The War of the Rebellion: A Compilation of the Official Records of the Union and Confederate Armies* (Washington, D.C., 1880–1901), 25:2, 506 (hereafter cited as *OR*).
17. Hooker testimony, *Report of Joint Committee*, vol. 1 (1865), 175; Lincoln to Hooker, 16 June 1863, Abraham Lincoln, *The Collected Works of Abraham Lincoln*, ed. Roy P. Basler (New Brunswick: Rutgers University Press, 1953), 6:281.
18. Hooker testimony, *Report of Joint Committee*, vol. 1 (1865), 175.
19. Williams, *Lincoln and His Generals*, 259; *OR* 27:3, 349; Lincoln to Hooker, 14 May 1863, *OR* 25:2, 479; Hooker to Bates, 5 October 1878, Bates Collection.
20. T. Lyle Dickey, 20 October 1876, Michael Burlingame, ed. *An Oral History of Abraham Lincoln: John G. Nicolay's Interviews and Essays* (Carbondale: Southern Illinois University Press, 1996), 50.

21. Meade, *Life and Letters*, 1:385; Lincoln to Hooker, 14 May 1863, *OR* 25:2, 479.
22. Hebert, *Fighting Joe Hooker*, 25–33, 49.
23. Alpheus S. Williams, *From the Cannon's Mouth: The Civil War Letters of General Alpheus S. Williams*, ed. Milo M. Quaife (Detroit: Wayne State University Press, 1958), 265; Hooker to Bates, 3 January 1878, Bates Collection; Hooker address, 30 April 1863, *OR* 25:1, 171.
24. Lincoln to Hooker, 26 January 1863, Lincoln, *Collected Works*, 6:78–79; Hooker to Bates, 29 May 1878, Bates Collection; Anson G. Henry, 12 April 1863, Illinois State Historical Library.
25. Henry L. Abbott, *Fallen Leaves: The Civil War Letters of Major Henry Livermore Abbott*, ed. Robert Garth Scott (Kent: Kent State University Press, 1991), 165, 170; *New York Times*, 1 March 1863; Andrew E. Ford, *The Story of the Fifteenth Massachusetts Volunteer Infantry* (Clinton, Mass., 1898), 253.
26. Hooker testimony, *Report of Joint Committee*, vol. 1 (1865), 668.
27. Gouverneur K. Warren to Daniel Butterfield, 3 May 1863, Hooker Papers.
28. Hooker memorandum, 21 March 1877, courtesy Abraham Lincoln Book Shop; Jonathan Letterman, *Medical Recollections of the Army of the Potomac* (New York: Appleton, 1866), 137; William Candler, 7 May 1863, in Bigelow, *Chancellorsville*, 363n; Abner Doubleday memorandum, Doubleday Papers, New-York Historical Society.
29. Darius Couch in *Battles and Leaders*, 3:167.
30. Lincoln to Meade, 27 July 1863, Lincoln, *Collected Works*, 6:350; Meade, *Life and Letters*, 2:142.
31. Charles A. Dana to Stanton, 29 October 1863, *OR* 31:1, 73; John Russell Young, *Around the World with General Grant* (1879), 2:306; Hooker to Stanton, 25 February 1864, *OR* 32:2, 469; Hooker letter, quoted in Castel, *Decision in the West*, 97.
32. M. A. De Wolfe Howe, ed., *Home Letters of General Sherman* (New York: Scribner's, 1909), 250.
33. Hooker to George H. Thomas, 27 July 1864, *OR* 38:5, 273.
34. Hooker to Bates, 2 April 1877, Bates Collection; Lincoln to Meade, 27 July 1863, Lincoln, *Collected Works*, 6:350.

12

Contemporary residents of the Connecticut Valley know Hadley as a community rich in Polish heritage: pierogies, golumpke, and polka music abound. The 2000 U.S. census found that nearly a third of the present population (over 1,300 of some 4,800 residents) identify as Polish American. Yet surprisingly little scholarship has examined the story of the Polish community here, in part because the archival record of this comparatively recent chapter in the town's history has only just begun to be preserved in local collections. Apart from the records of the St. Isadore Society donated to the Historical Commission in 2002, very few materials are at present available in the public repositories historians look to for their research. The Pocumtuck Valley Memorial Association in Deerfield holds a collection of photographs that document Polish family farms in Hadley and elsewhere, and a small number of documents can be found among the collections of the Hadley Historical Society, but the kinds of family papers or organizational records that form the bread and butter of historical research are not yet preserved in area libraries. For that reason, the existing scholarship is largely grounded in oral history.

Though economists and social scientists began to notice the Polish migration in the early twentieth century, Hampshire College student Peter Hardin's 1975 thesis, "Poles and Puritans," was among the first "modern" efforts to document this story employing formal historical methods. A journalist in training at the time, Hardin drew on oral history techniques as well as research in public records to explore the first generations of immigrants and track their ability to become landowners. Two of the several chapters that make up Hardin's study are republished here, somewhat revised to transform them into a single essay. Five Hadley families shared their stories, observations, and insights; to respect his subjects' privacy, Hardin assigned pseudonyms to these narrators. His narrative stands largely as written, though many in Hadley today will recognize the stories of these long-standing members of the community.

Poles and Puritans

Peter Hardin

Mary Sucheski of Hadley recalled her uncle's immigration to western Massachusetts in 1888.[1] *"He came from Poland with no relatives," she said. "He didn't know anyone. He came to Ellis Isle, and he had to go into a room. They said, 'If someone comes to take you inside of ten days, you can leave. But if no one wants you, you have to go back.' There were many men sitting in the room. They fed them and they had cots to sleep on. Then a man came in and started looking at all of them. He walked around the room, looking at them; he passed my uncle twice. My uncle was praying inside. He said, 'Come on' to my uncle, he didn't understand English, but he understood and followed him. They got on a train, my uncle didn't know where they were going. The man paid ten dollars for him, for his board, I suppose. The train stopped at the South Deerfield station. There was a lady waiting for the train, with a white horse and buggy. The man introduced my uncle. He didn't understand, but he tilted his cap and they rode to Conway. It was the Allis dairy farm. He worked there.*

"He didn't go to church for three quarters of a month. Then one Sunday he got on his good clothes and just walked along. He came to South Deerfield center and went into the first church he came to. It was the Congregational Church of South Deerfield. When he went to that church, he had a prayer book in Polish. Their prayer book was in English. He took out his own and he never prayed so hard in his whole life."

Puritan dissenters from Hartford and Wethersfield, Connecticut, settled Hadley in 1659. On a peninsula jutting into the Connecticut River, they found a protected haven. The river offered a natural barrier on three sides against unexpected visitors, and the fields that farmers cleared along it became known as "the honey pot" for their productivity. Hadley made an ideal place to settle, and its subsequent long life as a prospering farming village testified to its favorable location and soils.

If those first Puritans could revisit Hadley today, they might recognize the fields that still stretch along the Connecticut River bottomlands, and the broad main streets drawn between the river's bends to the north and south. But they would also find a landscape transformed by commercial and residential development, and a population much different from Hadley's Anglo-Saxon founders.

A Better Life

Beginning in the late nineteenth century, Hadley was dramatically transformed by a wave of immigration from Eastern Europe. The transition began when farming was declining in Hadley and the nearby communities of Deerfield, Sunderland, Hatfield, and Northampton. Agents representing farmers from the depressed towns traveled to New York City to find cheap labor. They brought back hundreds of Polish immigrants who eventually settled, boosted the economy, purchased farm land, and took over. These immigrant pioneers and their children contributed to a little-known American success story.

Up until the 1860s and 1870s, Hadley's bottomlands, classed among the richest soils in Massachusetts,[2] supported diversified farming. Pork, beef, grain, fruit, and furs were marketed in New York, the South, and the West Indies.[3] Broom corn, first planted in 1797 by Levi Dickinson of Wethersfield, had supplied the raw material for Hadley's major industry, broom manufacturing.[4] Not long after the 1850s, however, farmers fell victim to competition and their own speculation, and after the Civil War, the western states outstripped Hadley as the nation's foremost producers. Hadley farmers turned to intensive cultivation of tobacco. Tobacco had been raised for private use since 1800, but after 1860 the town's growers stepped up their production rapidly. Hampshire County, which includes Hadley, increased tobacco production from 138,046 pounds in 1850 to 7,289,275 pounds in 1870.[5] Farmers speculated and overspeculated. When popular cigar style shifted from the light-colored wrappers grown in the Connecticut Valley to a darker leaf grown in the West, they suffered. In 1870, Hadley was overproducing tobacco and entering a tobacco slump that would last until 1890.[6]

At around the same time, farmers in nearby Sunderland introduced onion culture to the Connecticut Valley.[7] Hadley farmers soon realized that their land was well suited to raising onions, but the town did not have a large enough population to provide inexpensive labor. Its total population had been 2,301 at the time of the 1870 census, and it declined for the next twenty-five years, as young people heard the call of the West or left in search of education or better jobs.[8] A drop in the native-born population contributed most to the overall decline; the foreign-born population also decreased during the same period, though not as drastically (figure 12.1). Foreign labor consisted chiefly of French Canadians and Italians. In 1875, when Hadley's foreign-born population made up nearly one-fifth of its total population, immigrants were almost evenly divided between Canada and Ireland as their countries of birth.[9] The region's economy slumped. Property valuations in Hampshire County dropped about $6,000 per square

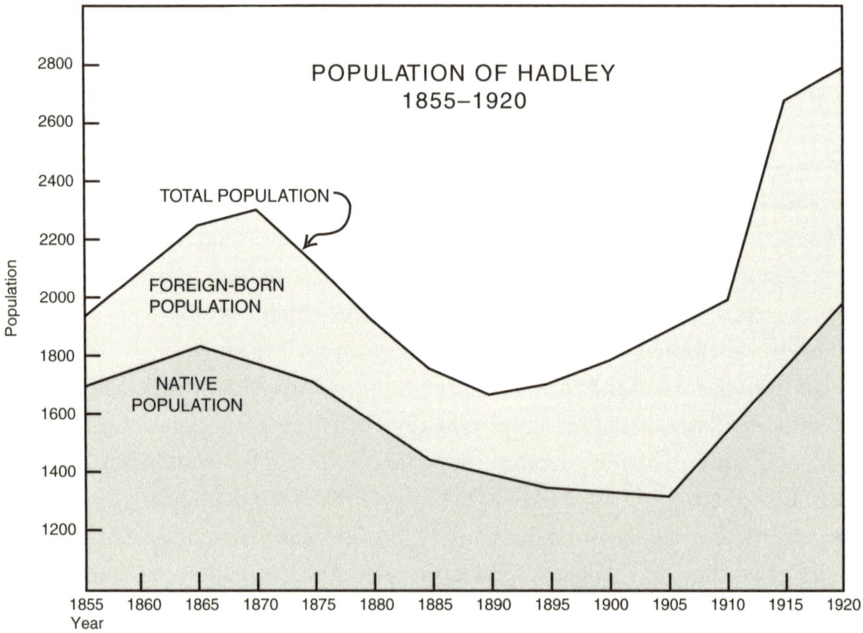

TABLE OF NATIVE/FOREIGN BREAKDOWN

1855	1860	1865	1870	1875	1880	1885	1890	1895	1990	1905	1910	1915	1920
1928		2246	2301	2124	1938	1747	1669	1704	1789	1895	1999	2666	
1693		1832		1712		1447		1354		1325		1743	

FIGURE 12.1. *Population of Hadley, 1885–1920.*

mile between 1870 and 1890. In neighboring Franklin County, the valuations dropped $2,000 per square mile, and in Hampden County, $3,500 per square mile.[10] The total value of real estate in Hadley plummeted from $1,094,000 in 1870 to $830,000 in 1890 (figure 12.2). During the same period, the value of assessed tangible personal estate dropped from $390,000 to $171,000.[11] The combination of depopulation and economic depression put area farmers in a desperate situation: they needed cheaper labor. In Deerfield, for example, farm laborers in 1880 were paid about $30 to $35 monthly, along with board; the average monthly wage in the nation as a whole was $19.[12]

Across the Atlantic, Polish peasants were also confronting difficult times. They had no nation of their own; Poland had been partitioned among Germany, Russia, and Austria in 1795. Nowhere in those countries was the social and economic outlook bright. In Austrian Poland, where peasants had more

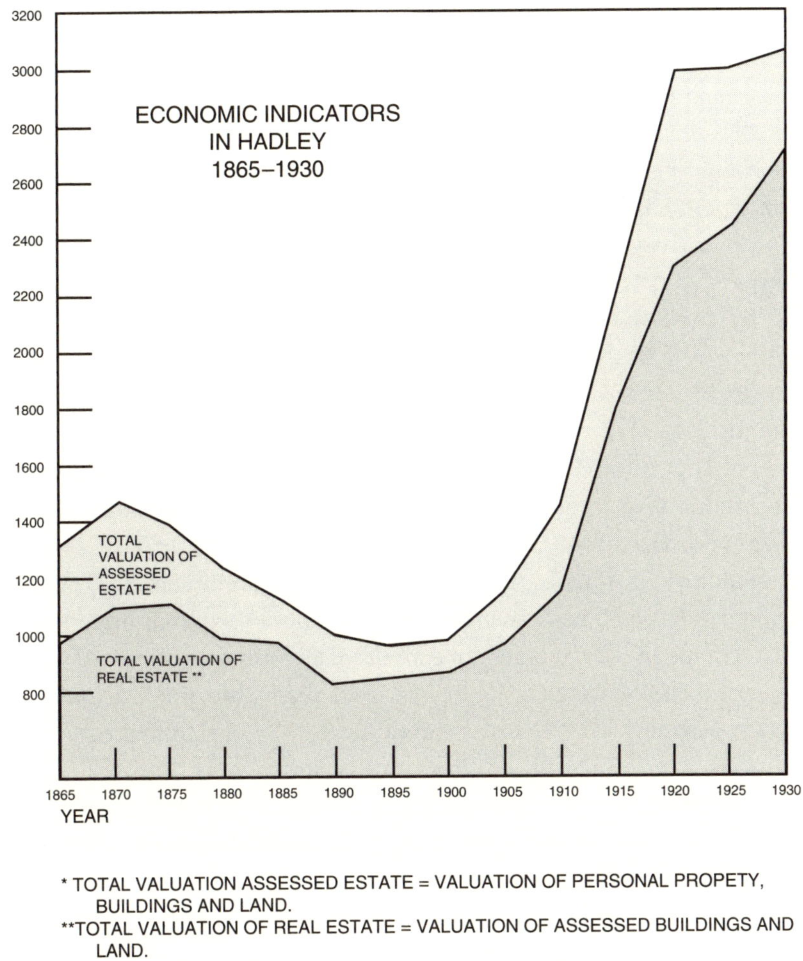

FIGURE 12.2. *Economic indicators in Hadley, 1865–1930.*

political freedom than their neighbors, a chronic depression raged between 1870 and 1914. Industrial development was slowed by the government in order to keep Galicia (the southern part of Austrian Poland) as the empire's breadbasket. The end of feudalism in 1848 had not brought relief for the peasantry and had given rise to excessive subdivision of land. This wrought havoc in a country where 80 percent of the people lived in farming villages. Peasant holdings in Galicia, for example, averaged seven acres in 1882; they averaged less than six in 1896.[13] When the peasant had so little land that he could no longer support his family, he sought wage work, only to find a low regional demand for farm labor and a scarcity of industrial jobs. Those who did find work suffered a drop in status when they were reduced to the position of day laborer without property.[14]

In German Poland, closer to 70 percent of the peasants lived in farming villages. Poles there were little better off economically, and they were politically and socially oppressed. Governmental authorities pursuing Bismarck's *Kulturkampf* policy attempted to suppress Polish national sentiment, to wipe out the Polish language and to teach only in German, and to dispossess Polish landowners. And in Russian Poland, special legislation had "Russianized" education by 1870, and religious persecution surfaced frequently. All of these conditions were further aggravated by overpopulation; the region's population doubled between 1850 and 1900.[15] Polish peasants faced a meager life, and many were on the lookout for new opportunities.

Tales of opportunity in America, whether exaggerated in steamship companies' promotions or recounted in letters from friends or family, were enticing. The peasants heard that in America jobs and land were available. They were hungry for land, and if America turned out to be a disappointment, they could return home to buy land with savings from their labor. Thousands made the leap, the first with no friends or family in America. Later immigrants joined growing colonies of their countrymen. By the 1880s the yearly rate of Polish emigration across the Atlantic was three times that of the 1870s (6,000 compared to 1,800); in the 1890s, it was about fifteen times greater; in the 1900s, twenty-four times greater; and in the remaining years before the World War I, twenty-six times greater. Almost all immigrants belonged to the lower classes, and unaccompanied men comprised the majority.[16]

Mary Sucheski's uncle was one of these men. His saga is typical of the Polish immigrants who first came to the Connecticut Valley. Labor agents from the valley traveled to New York City as early as 1885 to procure immigrants who would work cheaply for local farmers.[17] The agents sought to make quick money—their fee was the immigrant's first month's pay. In one incident, a labor broker in Northampton, the first such middleman to work locally, was reported to have bound the hands and feet of a "recalcitrant" Pole who sought freedom before his services were sold to a local farmer. The Pole, stashed in the rear of a wagon and covered with a blanket, was discovered by a police officer while the agent called on a friend. The policeman jailed him for the misdemeanor.[18]

Another well known middleman, Frances Clapp of South Deerfield, talked to a *Boston Globe* reporter in 1902 about Polish farm labor. He was businesslike in his assessment. "I have given the men to eat from ten to fifteen potatoes at a meal," Clapp was quoted as saying, "together with meat and bread. They do not care for pastry. They are fond of rye bread. They are rarely sick. They make good citizens." Clapp explained that the Poles were usually hired for an eight-month contract at $80 for the term, less the agent's fee of $10. They were paid at the end of the contract period because "there was a chance, too, that if they had money they might leave the farmer without help."[19] Clapp retired from the labor agent trade in 1895 after six years; workers began to secure employment for their families and friends, running Clapp out of business in the process.

That $80 salary was half the wage paid to Yankees. In the decade beginning in 1880, Poles in Deerfield earned $8 to $10 per month at first, and $16 to $18 after three to five years. Americans earned $16 to $25 per month.[20] Inexperience with modern farming techniques was one justification given for paying the Poles less.[21] Free room and board in Yankee homes made up in part for these low wages, but boarding conditions and the general treatment of Polish hired hands are not clear. When one Polish immigrant in Northampton found time to write letters home for fellow workers on Sunday afternoons, he complained that "they were treated by their employers like slaves, and had to sleep in the barn over a horse stable, on some straw or hay and a couple old horse blankets, with a fertilizer bag of hay for a pillow."[22] Yet apparently these men found their treatment and living conditions good enough to consider staying, and in letters home they invited others to join them. The women who came were quickly hired for domestic service. As a result of the growing Slavic immigration to the region, the population of Hadley began an upswing around 1895; the total native population continued to drop. Economic indicators revived.

The Poles' work habits impressed their employers. Early newspaper accounts lavished praise upon these immigrants, who were "industrious . . . and rarely . . . found idle."[23] They were "steady," "faithful," "non-complaining," "diligent," "untiring," and they showed "indefatigable industry." The Poles were willing to do labor the natives would not stoop to. Success in onion-raising hinges on using every possible inch of earth, which requires hand labor.[24] Onion seeds were sown directly in the field at three-inch intervals in rows spaced twelve inches apart. Weeding, by hand, was done three to five times during the summer. Onions were harvested, topped, and cleaned, all by hand. Tobacco production, which revived with the advent of cheap labor, a new import tariff, and a swing back to light-colored wrappers around 1905,[25] also demanded extensive hand labor.

News articles by Yankee writers chided fellow farmers for their laziness and declared that the Poles, in contrast, were "perfectly suited to the agricultural life."[26] But those who struck out on their own sometimes drew criticism. To better save money for buying land and a home, Polish immigrants often boarded together in large colonial houses while they worked as farm laborers or sharecroppers. Sometimes as many as four or five families lived in a single house, and by one report, as many as eight persons lived in one room.[27] Their crowding often drew censure, such as this remark in a local newspaper: "They herd together in a manner abhorrent to us."[28] Yet this austerity provided a way for individuals or families to move out of boarding homes, buy land, or pay a relative's passage to America.

A Family Business

Rick Sucheski lives in a large, comfortable early nineteenth-century farmhouse that once sheltered the family of a successful farmer of English descent. Over the red brick fireplace hangs a daguerreotype of a dark-haired and bearded man: his grandfather, Anthony Sucheski.

Anthony and his young son Michael emigrated to America about 1888, according to Rick Sucheski. They lived in Turners Falls, where Michael earned seventy-five cents a day sweeping up a factory. At sixteen, he turned to clearing wooded land owned by his brother in exchange for room and board, and he later toiled on an onion farm in Sunderland. After working for a North Amherst dairy farmer for several years, he saved enough to put down $1,500 toward the purchase of fifteen acres and a house in Hadley in 1905. Michael borrowed from a wealthy Yankee and paid the remaining balance by 1908. In the same year he bought an additional twenty-eight acres.

It took only three years' success at raising tobacco and onions for Michael Sucheski to begin lending money himself. Starting in 1911, just a few years after establishing his own farm, he entered a twenty-year period of moneylending—mainly to other Slavic farmers. It paid him an average 6 percent interest, and proved to be a profitable sideline. In time, he accumulated 120 acres that he deeded to a company comprised of his sons in 1935. Michael's success brought him acclaim. A *Boston Herald* reporter who interviewed him described him as a "wiry, dark-eyed, quick, smiling chap, with none of the look of the 'furriner' about him" and called him an "interesting pioneer . . . rated as a big man in the community."[29] He bought and sold local produce whenever he sensed he could profit, and his gross yearly income grew dramatically. In 1925 between twenty and forty people worked for him at various times during the season, casing, sorting, and sweating tobacco. Sucheski's rise from laborer to tenant to farm owner reflected a pattern common among immigrant farming families. Landowning Slavs surveyed in a 1935 study in Hadley had worked as hired men for an average of two to four years; in contrast, for non-Slavs in the Midwest the average was four to six years .[30]

Immigrants sometimes benefited from Yankee attitudes. The land that newcomers bought for the low price of $42 an acre in 1908 was available primarily because the natives thought little of it. Such land, overrun by brush and usually at a distance from the more expensive land by the river, was abundant in Hadley. Poles bought this land, cleared it, and discovered it was just as fertile as the lush bottomlands—one of their greatest contributions to the region's economy. Onion acreage in Hadley alone jumped from 677 acres to 4,850 acres between 1900 and 1920.[31] Land values began rising rapidly: in 1910 tobacco acreage cost $180 and onion acreage $150; in 1912, an acre of either cost $300, and in 1914, $500.[32]

The Poles also gained a reputation for punctual mortgage payments. "Locally Polish mortgages are regarded as excellent securities, and bankers invariably declare that the foreigners are, as a class, excellent people to do business with," stated a 1911 U.S. Immigration Commission report investigating Polish farmers in Sunderland.[33] Michael Sucheski's prompt payments epitomized this trait. He succeeded with significant help from his family, and large Polish-American families were common in the area. Contemporary writers described such scenes as a wife joining her husband in stoop labor while their newborn rested nearby in a carriage, or young children helping both parents weed onion fields. The 1920 U.S. census, the first to provide a breakdown of the town's population, showed that foreign-born white residents and those born of foreign or mixed parentage outnumbered residents of native white parentage by more than three to one (figure 12.3).[34]

Rick emulated his father's hard-driving business style. He earned a degree in management from a local business college. At fifty-nine, he has 125 acres of tobacco and onions, a full-time payroll of 18 employees, and demands that leave him little time to travel. "It's a risky crop, tobacco," he said. "It takes ninety days to grow it. It takes sixty days to cure it. And it takes less than a minute to ruin it. You know what I mean? You get a hail storm or something, one minute to ruin it." His perseverance and hard work recall the finest strengths of the preceding generation. Yet the strains and demands of farming suggest why many of his generation gave it up for a more secure life.

A Common Bond

Farming influenced each of the Polish-American families interviewed for this study. Their parents or grandparents came to the Connecticut Valley and worked

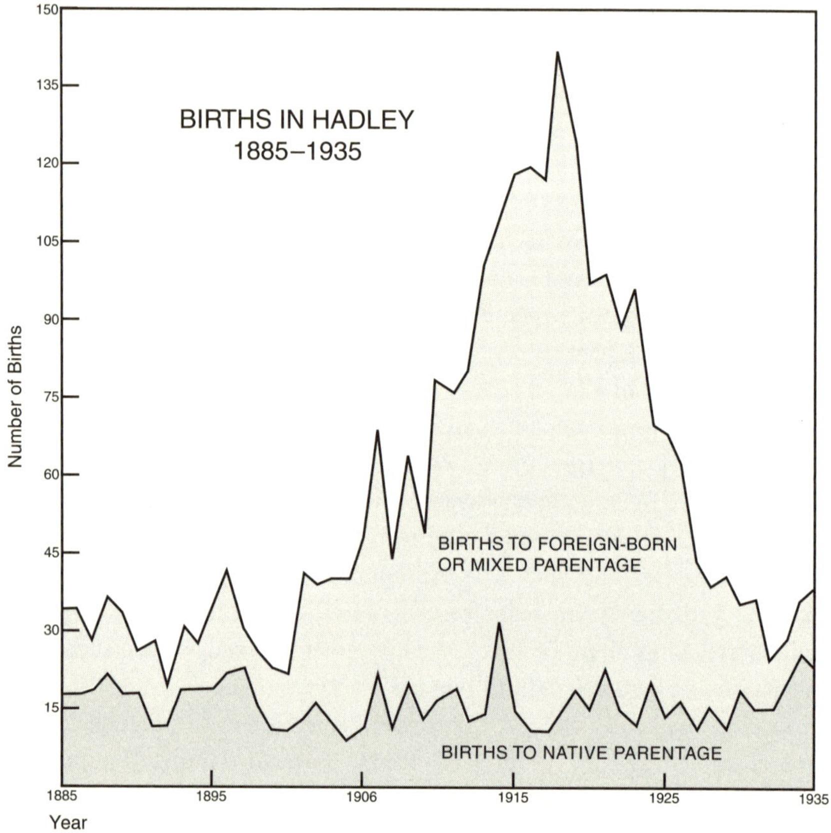

FIGURE 12.3. *Births in Hadey, 1885–1935.*

and saved to buy not only a home but also a small plot of land to farm. For all but one of the families, farming provided a natural route to self-sufficiency in the first generation. Although the newer generation often chose different vocations, each family maintains a personal tie to the agricultural life.

Grocer Stanley Jachulski raises five acres of asparagus behind his house. The only reason he doesn't farm for a living, he said, is that farming doesn't pay well enough. "There's no better feeling than to walk barefoot in sand, pick up dirt, see things grow. . . . That's a good life . . . once you get involved with farming, you can't help but love it." Another reason Stanley does not own a farm can be traced back to his father, Stanley Jachulski Sr., who came to America in 1897 with his own father, heading for factory work in Philadelphia. Later the family moved to Hatfield, and then to Hadley, where Stanley worked in feed stores and tobacco fields. By 1913, on his own, he discovered a bargain for a home and land. For only $5 down and an affortable mortgage he bought six acres on West Street. The seller then offered him a house across the street to go with the land, for $50 down and a comparable mortgage. Stanley accepted. To make a living, he managed a filling station and café on Russell Street, simultaneously farming a few acres. But poor health and the disastrous flood of 1936 combined to make times difficult. Stanley Jr. grew up working in his father's café and doing farm work for hire. While his pay for farm labor was typically low, a spirit of cooperation among farmers helped compensate. "In the old days," he said, "everybody would turn to [farming], it didn't make any difference whether it was her farm or your farm, or his farm, they worked just as hard as if it was their own."

Michael Bys, a professor in the Five Colleges, is descended from two generations of farmers and horticulturists. As Michael and his wife, Laura, reflect back on his ancestors and the old farmers they know, they think these Polish people chose Hadley, and farm work, rather than industry because they "always seemed to have this kind of tie with the land."

Joseph and Ann Stokosa left farming and horticulture behind for a more comfortable life. Joseph, the son of immigrants from Austrian Poland, was born on West Street in 1910. After his father's death and his own graduation from high school, Joseph worked on the West Street farm in summer and for an electric company in New Jersey in winter; in 1930 he decided to study business at a night college in Springfield because "there wasn't much future on the farm." His schooling led to a job in an office, and eventually he started his own business. His success enabled him to send three children to college.

Ann Stokosa's mother came to North Hadley from Eastern Europe because she had brothers living there and she had heard that the streets "were paved with gold. They really thought you could bend down and pick up gold." After her parents wed, they tried to buy a home on Main Street in Hatfield but were told that Poles were not wanted. They moved to Northampton instead, and Ann's father worked as a gardener. She graduated from college with a degree in sociology. Both Joseph and Ann have retained a love for nature and the outdoors. Their home looks out to backyard bird feeders and five acres of woods. "Being on the farm with open spaces everywhere," Joseph said, "I liked that, being able to walk around the house a little bit."

The Polish immigrants were favorably suited to agriculture, and they adapted readily to work profitable enough to enable them to save and begin independent farming. By 1906, three years before the heaviest five-year period of Polish land-buying,[35] Poles constituted 20 percent of the population and owned 5.3 percent of the land in Hadley, 5.7 percent of the taxable value in real estate, and

3.1 percent of the personal property.[36] By 1929 they constituted 60 percent of the population and owned 40.2 percent of the land.[37] Their success boosted Hadley's faltering economy: between 1850 and 1930, the town's total acres of cultivated land more than doubled, from 1,410 to 3,400.[38] Between 1885 and 1930, the value of assessed tangible personal estate nearly tripled, from $131,000 to $358,000; the total value of real estate rose from $830,000 in 1890 to $2,702,000 in 1930.[39] The hard-working Poles had made an indelible mark on Hadley's landscape.

As early as 1910, Northampton's daily newspaper criticized the Yankee farmer for "dawdling" and being "decadent," while praising the Poles for "their indomitable courage and industry . . . comparable only to the pioneer spirit of the early settlers," the Puritans.[40] Another writer, W. N. Morse, delivered this effusive tribute in 1910: "Our New England ancestors were pioneers in a wilderness of forests and Indians; the Poles have been pioneers in a wilderness of civilization, of economics, of a new language and strange customs. And much in the same measure that the early pioneers succeeded, and with many of the same tools—frugality, great manual toil, and many children—the sturdy new pioneers are coming into their own, an 'own' which is a possession not inherited, but earned."[41] That thread was picked up when a Boston newspaper wrote in 1924 that the Pole was "a modern pioneering Yankee, speaking consonants instead of Saxon vowels, and laboring in the smiling, open country instead of the wilderness."[42]

The Poles, who came to America seeking a better life for themselves and their families, had out-Yankeed the Yankees.

Notes

The material presented in this chapter is drawn from my 1975 Hampshire College thesis, "Poles and Puritans in Hadley, Massachusetts: An Historical Study of Hadley's Polish Population."

1. The names of all of those interviewed for this study have been changed to protect their privacy.
2. United States Immigration Commission, *Immigrants in Industries*, part 24, *Recent Immigrants in Agriculture*, vol. 2 (Washington, D.C.: Government Printing Office, 1911), 293.
3. Margaret Richards Pabst, *Agricultural Trends in the Connecticut Valley Region of Massachusetts, 1800–1900*, Smith College Studies in History 26 (Northampton, Mass.: Smith College, 1940), 10.
4. For more on broommaking in Hadley, see Gregory Nobles's essay in this volume.
5. Pabst, *Agricultural Trends*, 104.
6. Ibid., 105.
7. Edward Lucey, "The Immigration of Slavic Farmers to Hadley" (master's thesis, Massachusetts State College, 1936).

8. Lucey, "Immigration of Slavic Farmers," 20.
9. Pabst, *Agricultural Trends*, 88.
10. Ibid., 94.
11. George Westcott, *Massachusetts Assessors' Figures by Counties and Towns from 1865 to 1935 at Five Year Intervals* (Amherst: Massachusetts State College, 1937).
12. Lucey, "Immigration of Slavic Farmers," 20.
13. Paul Fox, *The Poles in America* (New York: Arno Press, 1970), 39. It has been estimated that the minimum acreage necessary to support a peasant family was about thirteen acres (ibid.).
14. Emily Balch, *Our Slavic Fellow Citizens* (New York: Charities Publication Committee, 1910), 49.
15. Victor R. Greene, "Pre–World War I Polish Emigration to the United States: Motives and Statistics," *Polish Review* 6, no. 3 (1961): 61.
16. Ibid., 46.
17. Lucey, "Immigration of Slavic Farmers," 18.
18. Ibid., 29.
19. *Boston Globe*, 29 June 1902.
20. All wage figures are from Balch, *Our Slavic Fellow Citizens*, 327.
21. Lucey, "Immigration of Slavic Farmers," 30.
22. *Daily Hampshire Gazette*, 2 May 1939.
23. *Daily Hampshire Gazette*, 1 January 1899.
24. Lucey, "Immigration of Slavic Farmers," 38.
25. Pabst, *Agricultural Trends*, 105.
26. *Daily Hampshire Gazette*, 1 May 1903.
27. Lucey, "Immigration of Slavic Farmers," 42; Balch, *Our Slavic Fellow Citizens*, 329. The average number of persons per room in Hadley increased from .54 in 1895 to .7 in 1915, according to Massachusetts Census figures.
28. *Daily Hampshire Gazette*, 4 May 1909.
29. *Boston Herald*, 4 May 1924.
30. Lucey, "Immigration of Slavic Farmers," 55; Lucey quotes the figures for the Midwest from W. J. Spellman, "The Agricultural Ladder," *American Economics Review* 31 (1918): 70. Lucey acknowledged that one could work as a hired man at an early age in the Midwest, while Slavs had to be at least twenty to emigrate.
31. Lucey, "Immigration of Slavic Farmers," 59.
32. Balch, *Our Slavic Fellow Citizens*, 328; *Boston Herald*, 16 April 1912; *Daily Hampshire Gazette*, 7 July 1914.
33. U.S. Immigration Commission, *Recent Immigrants in Agriculture*, 311.
34. United States Census, 1920.
35. Lucey, "Immigration of Slavic Farmers," 55.
36. Balch, *Our Slavic Fellow Citizens*, 329.
37. Lucey, "Immigration of Slavic Farmers," 37.
38. Ibid., 65.
39. Westcott, *Massachusetts Assessors' Figures.*
40. *Daily Hampshire Gazette*, 25 April 1910.
41. W. N. Morse, "Earning a Valley," *The Outlook* 96 (September 1910): 80.
42. *Boston Herald*, 24 May 1924.

13

Clarence Hawkes is somehow both the best and the least known of Hadley's most successful residents. At the mention of his name, almost everyone in the present-day community might respond "Ah yes, the blind poet," but few could offer much in addition to that.

When this collection of essays was first conceived, it was to include published and unpublished scholarship on Hadley's history, all of it already drafted in one form or another. But the transfer of Hawkes's papers from Northampton's Forbes Library to the Hadley Historical Society created an opportunity to glean much-needed insight into the career of this important literary figure that was not to be missed—if only a scholar could be convinced to take it on. Fortunately, Hadley counts among its residents James Freeman, a professor of English at the University of Massachusetts and a scholar known locally for his intellectual versatility and enthusiasm for local history. Jim embraced the charge with his usual vigor, and recovered for today's readers a sense of Hawkes's stature in his own time; his essay restores Hawkes to the context of post–Civil War nature writing, and to the world of literary criticism and public life well beyond the borders of the poet's home town.

Hawkes himself sustained an avid interest in local history. In fact, in at least one moment in time, he neatly wraps up several themes present in this volume: when Hadley celebrated its 250th anniversary in 1909, he designed a series of floats for the parade, and chose among his several topics "The Deeding of Indian Lands," "The Hadley Witch," and "The Angel of Hadley." As the present generation revisits its history at another anniversary moment, those same themes continue to preoccupy us, though in new ways, with new questions and assumptions.

America's Blind Naturalist

Clarence Hawkes and the World He Lived In

James A. Freeman

In 1943 United Press supplied its fourteen hundred papers with an article paying tribute to Clarence Hawkes (1869–1954), proof that the blind Hadley author's prose, poetry, and personal valor had touched the lives of uncounted people throughout the world (figure 13.1).[1] Born on a marginal farm, with little choice of vocation other than agriculture, he overcame two tragic boyhood accidents—losing part of his left leg at nine and his sight at thirteen—to become one of America's outstanding writers of nature books. These, as well as his poems, novels, and autobiographies, were made available in Braille and translated into French, Finnish, German, Danish, Chinese, and Japanese, an honor for any author. Robert Bartlett's *They Dared to Live* profiled him along with Helen Keller, Oliver Wendell Holmes, and Charles Steinmetz as a model of courageous achievement.[2]

Hawkes's talent struck everyone he touched. Helen Keller valued his friendship; Teddy Roosevelt and fellow naturalists admired his knowledge of animals; college presidents and state governors praised his achievements; Calvin Coolidge, soon to become governor of the state and president of the nation, kept Hawkes's picture on his desk; readers, ordinary or blind, American or foreign, thanked him because he inspired them; and Hadley neighbors appreciated his contributions to town life. His widely reviewed books were favorably compared with works by Rudyard Kipling and advertised alongside volumes by Robert Frost. In 1937 one commentator estimated that he had "won an audience of five million young people around the world."[3] Six years later the *Boston Sunday Post* calculated that his "newspaper and magazine articles, plus an occasional talk via radio," had reached at least one million more people.[4] His sixty-odd volumes may no longer be on family bookshelves, but they confirm his lifelong commitment to describing truthful encounters between people and the animated world. Even today, longtime residents of Hadley fondly recall his kindness to everyone, especially children, even when his reputation had spread so far.

A pessimist might have thought that Hawkes's effective life would end at age thirteen. Born during a blizzard in a western section of Goshen, Massachusetts, on December 16, 1869, he later reflected: "I have always been sorry that I was

FIGURE 13.1. *Clarence Hawkes. Courtesy of the Goodwin Memorial Library, Hadley, Mass.*

not born in June instead of December. In its serenity and beauty, instead of the storm and hardship of winter."[5] But he never held his unpromising entry into the world responsible for later setbacks. Rather, he made light of its harshness by calling to mind "a humble little cottage in Lithia, then called Road Island. This was not a very auspicious domicile in which to be born, but it was the best I could do under the circumstances. I was in something of a hurry at the time and did not have a chance to pick and choose, in the vernacular of airmen, I made what might be called a forced landing."[6] The lowly house was all that his father, Enos Smith Hawkes (1840–1894), could afford. Today tall trees have grown up to block the view young Clarence had of the deep valleys and distant hills in the area of Goshen, Ashfield, and Cummington, vistas that enriched his early days.

The boy needed such aesthetic benefits because his father had little money or property. The son of William Hawkes and Almira Smith, Enos was descended from John Hawks, one of Hadley's founders, and related to William Smith

Clark, third president of the Massachusetts Agricultural College (now the University of Massachusetts Amherst), as well as to William Cullen Bryant, the eminent poet of Cummington. Enos, however, inherited little. He and his brother William Smith Hawkes had gone west in the 1850s, a common destination for aspiring young people, but he obviously did not prosper. They enlisted in the Union army from Coloma, in Whiteside County, Illinois, on September 7, 1861. Enos served less than a year as a private in Company A, 34th Illinois Volunteer Infantry, until he was discharged for disability on August 19, 1862 at Battle Creek, Tennessee, for "disease of eyes."[7]

His time as "one of Uncle Sam's boys in blue in '61" was disastrous because (as his son put it, somewhat evasively) "hardtack had spoiled his digestion."[8] Enos's experience left him (again in his son's words) "a broken-down Civil War veteran."[9] He returned and occupied the house in Goshen on Loomis Road owned by relations, the Willcutt family, but commonly called the Allen house. The government may have helped him pay the rent: in March 1864 he began to receive a pension of $2.00 per month for "amaurosis," the occasional blindness that oddly prefigured his son's ailment.[10] Apparently the whole pension was not paid until two decades later, when the amount was recalculated; in 1884 he was again listed on the roll, this time at $24 per month, and at that time he also received arrears of $3525.00.[11]

His stay in Goshen from the early 1860s until 1879 made little impact on the tiny town, although an 1873 map clearly denominated the "E. Hawks" residence.[12] A compromised man, Enos "made the training of dogs and hunting almost his entire business for years."[13] He earned gratitude from his young son for teaching him "of the great out-of-doors world and the ways of all the furred and feathered folks of the New England Woods."[14] Hawkes's writings may covertly recall his father when they honor the courage and discipline of soldiers while at the same time lamenting war's waste and the overhunting of wildlife.

Hawkes's mother, Edlah Betsey Olive Bates Gurney (1849–1899), had, like Enos, been born in Ashfield, in Franklin County. They married in Ashfield on November 29, 1866, and spent young Clarence's early years in Goshen on Enos's "little rock-ribbed, sterile farm in the western part of the town."[15] The census of 1860 listed 439 inhabitants of the town, but that of 1870 counted only 368, a hint that the region lacked possibilities.[16] The boy's isolation was enlivened by visits to his beloved maternal grandmother, Mrs. Josiah Gurney (Emily Bates Jenkins, c. 1820–1877), in Ashfield, "an adjoining town made famous by Charles Eliot Norton and George William Curtis, and their Sanderson academy dinners." She awakened his appreciation "for birds and squirrels"; the opportunity to hear enlightening speakers sparked his early career as a lecturer.[17]

Even though young Clarence enthusiastically observed the countryside around the farms with his intense blue eyes, he differed little from his younger sister, Alice Edith (1872–1897), or three brothers, Enos Raymond (1875–?), Arthur Josiah (1877–1941), and the later-born Ernest William (1881–1957), known as "Kid." Soon fate made him special. Returning from Spruce Corner School in June 1879, when only nine, he jumped off a stone wall near their house, injuring his left foot. After weeks of infection, doctors came to the house on July 29. They began to operate before the anesthetic took effect, and he saw his own blood spurt onto the wallpaper; when he woke, he found his leg amputated below the knee.[18] The family moved in September from Goshen to the Gurney farm in Ashfield, where they lived with widowed grandfather Josiah (1806–1886).

Showing the determination that later distinguished him, Clarence managed to walk, first on crutches, then on a "peg leg," and tried to recapture a normal life. He boated, drove teams, snowshoed, pitched in baseball games, and even skated. For a brief four years, young Hawkes seemed to have regained some autonomy in his community. Then fate once more assaulted him. While hunting with his father near Spruce Corner in Ashfield at about noon on Tuesday, August 12, 1883, the thirteen-year-old Hawkes rested some fifteen rods away amid bushes, invisible to his father. When a woodcock swooped downward, Enos fired, lacerating his son's face with "mustard seed" shot. As Hawkes put it, "I looked for the last time with full vision upon Mother Earth and all her visible beauties."[19]

Clarence's immediate pain, shock, bleeding, faintness, and vomiting began two years of suffering. For six weeks after the mishap, he waited for his two broken fingers to heal and depended on ice packs to relieve the misery in his eyes. Sadly, he sensed that sight was fading: after only two weeks, a window at the foot of a stairs no longer lit them, and he had to count in order to descend.

The feisty lad now faced lifelong blindness. Doctors at home and at Boston's Eye and Ear Infirmary on Charles Street tried to restore his sight. The method now seems barbaric, yet at the time inserting needles into the injured eyeballs with no anesthetic was felt to be a possible cure. Interviewed four decades later by Bruce Barton, soon to be one of the giants of American advertising, Hawkes vividly recreated the horror of this odd regimen: "I do not like to dwell on the memory of the next two years. . . . There could be no anesthetic, for the object of the operation was to torture the eye so that it might, in a sort of frenzied self-defense, put forth new powers. . . . They strapped me to a table, put a rubber blanket under my head and tied my hands. Then there was brought into play a fiendish little machine which gripped the eye at every point where the muscles control it. . . . Imagine then a sharp lancet thrust slowly into the very center of the eyeball, down and down, until it must have reached the center of the brain."[20] When the physicians finally admitted that there was no hope, Hawkes felt almost relieved: at least the pain would stop. His mother did what she could to assuage his loss, reading to him from classic authors, tending his needs, and imprinting her devotion on his tenacious memory.

To a typical onlooker in the 1880s, Hawkes's first fifteen years had already provided all the independence he could expect. The local newspaper's report of his accident summed up the conventional response to a handicapped male in an agricultural setting: sightlessness "makes him certainly an object of commiseration."[21] His own father's plight had daily taught him the poignant effects of an injury. When Clarence lost his leg and his sight, no financial aid appeared. The family had already "spent about a thousand dollars for doctors" and had few resources for his future care.[22] Even the famous Helen Keller and her teacher, Annie M. Sullivan, depended on the kindness of strangers who launched an appeal for funds to place the two "in a position of permanent financial independence."[23] By any current standard, the insignificant boy from the country had no life ahead of him. As one reviewer later commented, "For most of us, the coming of blindness would mean the fall of the curtain, the end of the drama."[24]

Summoning his typical resolve, in the fall of 1885 he enrolled, although hesitantly, in Watertown's Perkins Institution for the Blind. Such a move took courage because, as Charles Winchell from Dalton, Massachusetts, who entered the school a decade later, observed, "very few people in western Massachusetts in those days knew much about Perkins."[25] Fortunately, the state paid his tuition. Even more fortunately, Hawkes, once the ultimate outdoor lad, thrived under the indoor routine. A headline writer for the *Boston Sunday Post* aptly called Perkins the "House of Joyous Darkness" for him.[26] His very first triumph—feeling the outline of a wooden puzzle piece that he recognized as Cuba—foretold his later fascination with faraway places. According to a report card for the academic year ending in June 1889, his lowest grade for Physics, Geometry, Arithmetic, History, and Language was 9 on a scale of 10. An encouraging note from the acting director said that he "ought to go to college."[27]

The education was so liberating that he stayed in the city for further lessons in music and oratory and, at the Emerson School, elocution, plus some lectures on law, apparently at Boston University. Perkins nurtured Hawkes's longstanding friendship with Helen Keller, who was in the class behind him and would make the school famous. A debilitating attack of grippe in the late spring of 1890 cut short his postgraduate program. At twenty-one, he moved back to his family, now residing in Cummington because the Ashfield farm had been sold in the spring of 1885.

Hawkes needed all the resources he could muster when he began the tough job of supporting himself. He reasoned that his neighbors might enjoy respite from the harsh routine of backcountry life by attending lectures like those available at Norton's Sanderson Academy in Ashfield and at Chautauqua, New York. He could speak about American literature. According to his own recollections, the years from 1891 to 1895, "knocking about lecturing," required enormous effort, physical and emotional.[28] He had to brave rain and whiteout sleet storms, small audiences, and meager pay, yet he lived up to his commitments. One fatiguing address earned him $1.65. But reviews of his talks predicted a lifetime of admiration. His address on "the chief American poets" at Ashfield's Congregational chapel "was a fine literary treat . . . finely rendered." As usual, the performance had a moral purpose. He accepted the normal linkage of church venues, "high" culture, entertainment, and ethical improvement. Hawkes "closed with an exhortation to the young to do with their might whatever they had to do."[29]

During the spring of 1892, the family moved from Cummington to Hadley, where he spent the remainder of his productive life. He obviously felt he had reached a nurturing haven. Ancestor John Hawks had helped found the town in 1659. His beloved sister, Alice, graduated from Hadley's Hopkins Academy in the class of 1895, having sung soprano in the Choral Club and won a prize for elocution, little suspecting that she would die two short years later.[30] "My home," Hawkes fondly explained, "faces upon the broadest and most beautiful street in the world, which is flanked by four rows of enormous elms."[31] Its location, on a mile-long common spanning a loop in the Connecticut River, allowed him and a friend to launch a skiff from the upstream landing (now known as the Dike) and enjoy a leisurely float, fishing or sensing "the most beautiful seven miles of river scenery" that included, in his day as in ours, "green, fertile meadows, with the twin mountains of Holyoke and Tom dreaming in the distance."[32]

Inspired by literary giants he encountered at school (notably his Cummington relative William Cullen Bryant) as well as by nature, Hawkes readied his own verse for publication. At Perkins he had edited the school newspaper, *The Echo*, and printed his first poem in it. Now, despite numerous rejections, he continued "bombarding newspapers and magazines with poems," so many that "in 1895 it was said that I had more poems printed in leading weeklies and magazines than any other poet in America."[33] To publish a collection of poems, however, he had to guarantee three hundred subscribers. With characteristic courage, during a blisteringly hot August he hired five boys to drive to far-flung dwellings in the Hampshire hills and collect enough pledges so that the first of five collections, *Pebbles and Shells* (1895), could appear.

Like most of Hawkes's poetry, it employed the predictable metrical forms, sentimental content, and plain diction familiar to Victorian ears. The volume earned a reputation, and so he could more easily follow it with four others: *Three Little Folks: Verses for Children* (1896), *Idyls of Old New England* (1897), *Songs for Columbia's Heroes: War Poems for 1898* (1898), and *The Hope of the World* (two editions, 1900). He kept his name before the public in subsequent years by printing separate poems in newspapers and magazines. These compositions, totaling perhaps two thousand,[34] found their way into anthologies and earned him his customary epithet, "the blind poet of Hadley."

Although finances were still limited, he married Bessie Wilder Bell (1869–1958) on Monday morning, October 30, 1899.[35] She was the artistic daughter of Samuel Reuben Bell (1839–1920), a tobacco dealer, and Sarah A. Wilder Bell (c. 1843–1913).[36] Bessie probably studied at Hopkins Academy; Brooklyn's famed Pratt Institute admitted her in September 1893 so she could take courses in "Instrumental Perspective" and "Drawing—figure from life."[37] She also studied in New York City with Bruce Crane, a popular landscape artist who specialized in bucolic scenes empty of people but glowing with autumnal hues.

Their marriage was rich with cooperative efforts. They would take jaunts to scenic spots so she could paint and he could revel in nature. She illustrated *Three Little Folks, Idyls of Old New England*, and *The Hope of the World* with appealing line drawings. At home, she enjoyed gardening. Together they often sat on their porch, welcoming passersby, especially children, some of whom, now grown and living in the area, still warmly remember them. He dubbed their place Bird Acre in honor of the "woodpeckers, nut-hatches and chickadees" that he and Bessie began to feed as soon as they moved in.[38] The two appreciated each tree around the house: "Next to the birds, the trees are my best nature friends at Bird Acre."[39]

Most important, Bessie encouraged Hawkes, support he noted in his interviews and book dedications. After three decades together, he tenderly called her a "generous" woman: "my eyes, my right hand and my constant helper [who] has furnished much of the light of my life. I gladly give her credit for much of my achievements."[40] Five years later, in his dedication to *The Master of Millshaven*, he called her "My Dear Wife after whose courageous life, I have modeled the heroine of this book." (This noble character, Evelyn Henderson, daughter of a heartless tycoon, performs good deeds among the poor and eventually converts her father to philanthropy.)

Although he was still a young man living in a small town in the state's west, Hawkes soon made himself known to a larger audience. In 1900 the prestigious Boston Authors' Club elected him to membership. His associates there were older and more famous. The president, Julia Ward Howe (1819–1910), who had nominated him, was the author of the famous "Battle Hymn of the Republic." She advocated pacifism, votes for women, and Mother's Day, all topics that resonated with Hawkes. Howe, the mother-in-law of Michael Anagnos, who directed Perkins from 1885 to 1890, read to the school's students once a week. She recalled Hawkes from those sessions, and he later wrote that the two remained friends "for about twenty years."[41]

Hawkes continued to earn respect. After the death of his mother in 1899, he began to specialize in the nature works that made his considerable reputation. He initially published short sketches in publications like *Woman's Home Companion*, *Outing Magazine*, and *Overland Monthly*. These early vignettes predicted the longer works to follow. They looked directly at natural processes, including pain and death, even when they ran under the heading "For Boys and Girls." A typical example: one chilly night a farmer wounds a grouse, who suffers agony as it burrows in snow or hides in branches to evade a predatory fox and a hungry owl.[42]

Always a quick learner, Hawkes moved on from such modest compositions to create more than fifty full-length studies of animals, beginning with *Master Frisky* (1902), about a dog. Then, like Noah's ark, his books transported frogs, beavers, birds, bears, moose, wolves, bison, "bronchos," reindeer, Shetland ponies, circus elephants, foxes, cow ponies, circus horses, and turtles from their habitats to the eager imaginations of uncounted youngsters. His menagerie lived, as he proudly observed, in discrete sections of a wide universe: "Alaska, Arizona, Wyoming, upon the great central plains, in Canada, in Finland, and on the Malay Peninsula, not to mention north of the Arctic circle in Eskimo land."[43]

With buoyant enthusiasm, he carefully researched and interviewed to get his details correct. Uncle William Hawkes, who served as his secretary, had early regaled him with tales of the West as it was when he and his brother Enos explored it; later he would continue to interview travelers, and he checked out armloads of books from nearby libraries: Jones in Amherst, Goodwin in Hadley, and Forbes in Northampton. His brother Ernest William Hawkes became an authority on the native peoples of Alaska, perhaps inspiring such works as *Igloo Stories*. Along with unvarnished facts, he welcomed Mark Twain–like tall tales: a 1901 letter from the Ashfield town historian Frederick G. Howes informed him of a lightning flash that "knocked Payson sensible," of an Uncle Eli, who was told that if drafted for the Civil War he "should hire him a prostitute," of a day when "the thermometer was 121 degrees below zero," and of "one cow that was 17/16 Jersey."[44]

Almost immediately, editors of anthologies began to include Hawkes's writings. Like Dante, who imagined that famous pagan poets welcomed him among their company, Hawkes must have felt that the nationally distributed collections rewarded his decades of diligent composition. One needs to take a deep breath before naming his colleagues, living and dead, in these compilations. Being grouped with luminaries from Shakespeare to Amy Lowell and offered to such large audiences certainly compensated him for those early, small Chautauqua groups in chilly churches or hot barns.

He forged personal as well as professional bonds with some of the authors in the anthologies. His scrapbooks contain dozens of fan letters. He would send out a composition or book and regularly receive grateful thanks from notables. Hugh Lofting, for example, wrote from his Connecticut home to say that his daughter was enjoying Hawkes's novel *Wanted a Mother*. Perhaps with some embarrassment, Lofting admitted that his own Doctor Doolittle books were never intended as "nature stories. . . . They are, as you will see, purely fantastic with just enough seriousness to make them plausible."[45]

Hawkes's many appreciative fans picked up what they wanted from his works. Edgar Rice Burroughs, creator of Tarzan, read Hawkes.[46] By 1921 scientific journals were mentioning his contributions.[47] The anthropologist Grenville Goodwin, who died in 1940 at the age of thirty-three, was an expert on the Apaches. He had ingested the mystique of the undomesticated during his early teens, when "he was devouring a steady diet of boys' books by the likes of Ernest Thompson Seton and Clarence Hawkes—romantic adventures with animals and native heroes set in the Far North and the Wild West, articulating a classic frontier paradigm of rugged self-reliance and outdoorsmanship."[48]

First known for his poetry, then for these wildlife accounts, Hawkes also won esteem for other genres. As early as 1905, an article with a picture of him in his Hadley study applauded him: "Clarence Hawkes is essentially a writer of nature studies, though he is equally brilliant in fiction. Though blind, Mr. Hawkes sees with the eyes of an imagination that suggests soul memories of the years ago."[49] A 1915 ad for books in the *New York Times* paired his autobiographical *Hitting the Dark Trail* with Robert Frost's *North of Boston* and *A Boy's Will*.[50]

Popularity led to academic recognition from four colleges. He received the only honorary degree, a Master of Arts, given at William Smith's sixth commencement in Geneva, New York, on June 11, 1917. Hawkes moved the audience by telling a fable about a prince who "met with an accident, which made him unfit for the conquest of arms, but then he became a jester and by his wit, goodness and kindness he accomplished more than he could have accomplished by the sword."[51] With the First World War's emphasis on manly vigor, such a parable rightly recalled the other virtues that sustained civilization. Syracuse University conferred a Master of Letters on him on July 11, 1917.[52] Amherst

College awarded an honorary Master of Arts in 1919. The gracious presentation said, "To a neighbor who has triumphed over heavy hindrances, who has read with his hands when his eyes failed him, who has taught little children the ways of Nature and older children the lessons of beauty and courage—to a neighbor who has won merited fame abroad we extend the hand of fellowship at home."[53] Finally, American International College in Springfield, Massachusetts, awarded him an honorary Doctor of Letters on June 7, 1938.[54]

Recognition continued throughout Hawkes's life. For example, on the sixtieth anniversary of his blindness, *Nature Magazine* quoted a eulogy by his late friend William Temple Hornaday (1854–1937), first director of the Bronx Zoo, author and crusader to save American bison, Alaskan fur seals, and birds whose plumes adorned women's hats. Hawkes was "the born Nature-lover, the woodsman, the chronicler, and the painter of mental pictures, who for a brief few years looked into the pulsing heart of Nature, focused his mental camera upon her during a few brilliant days, and then suddenly, with a stroke of lightning the world became black. . . . With marvelous fidelity, he paints what he has seen and yet remembers."[55]

Hawkes died from heart failure a month past his 84th birthday, at 8:30 A.M. on January 19, 1954, at Northampton's Cooley Dickinson Hospital. Bessie survived until a heart attack took her in her 88th year on January 28, 1958. Although their physical hearts failed, their spiritual hearts were always strong, inspiring others to strive and seek and not to yield. Today they rest together with the first settlers of their town in the peaceful Old Hadley Cemetery, between the newly clean Connecticut River and fields still plowed in narrow medieval strips, a survival of the past that may be unique on earth today. They always did enjoy continuity, human and natural.

Poetry

As the famous naturalist Dallas Lore Sharp wrote, "None of Mr. Hawkes's books need a commentary and affidavits. His purpose is plain, his story simple, his language clear."[56] His poems were public communication, not modernist self-indulgence. In both technique and subject matter, they looked backward. He candidly announced his standards: "I am something of a reactionary all along the line. I do not care especially for free verse. I have always considered it a lazy man's way of writing poetry. When a poem is not metrical, has no color or sense, why should we label it poetry? . . . Perhaps I am a back number, but I much prefer Tennyson and the Brownings to Swinburne and Ella Wheeler Wilcox."[57]

Unlike the hermetic utterances that learned authors like Ezra Pound and T. S. Eliot and Wallace Stevens delivered to a new generation of readers in the early twentieth century, Hawkes's words expressed universal impressions, artfully phrased, yet determinedly accessible, all in the manner of popular nineteenth-century verse. He proudly strode up the mountain of poetry in the company of acknowledged models such as William Cullen Bryant, Henry Wadsworth Longfellow, and John Greenleaf Whittier. Most of his poetry is (in the phrase of critic Kenneth Burke), "equipment for living,"[58] because it describes encounters with the physical world and then explains the consequences of such contacts. It continually finds (as does Hawkes's character Old Ben in *Stories of the Good Green Wood*, who cites Shakespeare's Duke from *As You Like It*) "books in runnin' brooks, sermons in stones, an' good in everything."[59] The speakers, their settings, the subject matter, and the poetic techniques sum up a century of vibrant populist verse.

Repeatedly, especially in the five early collections, Hawkes's speakers promulgate the Rousseauian–Wordsworthian respect for common people. Many narrators talk in unlettered dialect but are the authority figures. The first page of *Idyls of Old New England* uses *nater* for *nature*, *ain't*, *'ud* for *would*, *wa'n't* for *weren't*, *yer* for *your*. These colloquialisms further the notion that plain speaking better conveys honest emotion. The narrator of "Ma's Posy Beds" admits,

> Somehow I like the good ole kinds
> O' posies full as well,
> (Instead o' those with Latin names
> That nobody can spell,)
> Like mirigold an' asterziz
> An' calliopsis fair . . .[60]

Even when the verse concerns a celebrity like Hadley's Civil War general Joseph B. Hooker and a grand triumph like the capture of Lookout Mountain, the language remains simple:

> Know you the tale of a battle won
> Some thirty years ago,
> On a mountain top, when the Autumn sun
> In the west was sinking low?[61]

One of Hawkes's most famous poems imagines a black southerner named Ole Moses as he recalls "How Massa Linkum Came" to Richmond after the Civil War. A preacher prays with the President in front of the crowd,

An' den dey broke into a shout
Dat mought hab woke John Brown,
An' cheered until I t'ink de noise
Would bring de heabens down.

Far from demeaning this engaged speaker, the unlearned lines communicate his reverence for our iconic hero and further the optimistic wish that the war was worth the losses. Lincoln's son enjoyed the poem.[62]

The speakers in *Three Little Folks*, his second volume, are children. Perhaps like his own brothers and sister, they share their "sweet and fanciful stories" with the poet, "the old man who lives down in the village." He writes their experiences "in a book," a plot device Hawkes would later use in his novels.[63] "A Merry-Go-Round" (made from cart wheels), "Sliding Down Stairs" (on Papa's chair, which shatters), "What the Brook Told Me," and "Playing House" present a uniformly positive panorama of rural life. As one reviewer noted, the language fits the young speakers and "does not utter as the voice of childhood those mysterious thoughts which are as a rule the readings of the overtones and undertones of older years into the plain song of simple life."[64]

When narrators address the reader in received standard English, they emanate the same earnestness. Two stanzas from *The Hope of the World* call attention to earthly decay and suggest a pious remedy:

Is this sad wall, of dark and crumbling stones,
That time hath eaten like a dead man's bones,
The bulwark of old Rome who ruled the world
And builded empire from a hundred thrones?

. . . .

O let Christ's spirit through the world awake,
Let hands reach down and hands degenerate take,
Let shoulders strong bear burdens for the weak,
Let love abide e'en for the whole world's sake.[65]

A literary analyst might call attention to the unobtrusive technical devices: the AABA rhyme scheme popularized by Edward FitzGerald's epigrammatic *Rubáiyát of Omar Khayyám* (1859); the first stanza's *erotesis* (rhetorical question); the adjective "sad" transferred from object to viewer; the *prosopopoeia* (personification) of time; the *recordatio* (summing up past events) in stanza 1, lines 3–4; the *anaphora* (repetition) of "let"; the aureate diction of "O" and "e'en"; the *synecdoche* using "hands" and "shoulders" to stand for whole; the parallel structure of stanza 2; the *invocatio* (prayer form) of stanza 2; the whole sequence as both an *apocarteresis* (leaving one hope while turning to another) and a *philophronesis* (attempt to stop God's wrath by humble repentance). But such misplaced learning, although common in high schools and colleges of Hawkes's day, contradicts the demotic spirit of his diction.

As with speaker, so with setting and subject. Hawkes places us in a tactile world in which common objects like hayfields or starry nights teach us our place in the physical, social, and spiritual realms; they assert a conviction that all nature is a system of signs which, rightly understood, can improve us. This belief unites mystics from every culture.

> I love ter think we humans grow toward God
> Jest like the lily rises from the sod,—
> That friendship with the fields an' mother earth
> Give ter the human soul a wondrous worth.[66]

Sometimes the object appears only as a springboard for moral decoding:

> Don't let no hole git in yer moral fence,
> But keep it jest above Temptation's nose,
> For if one little peccadillo goes
> Ter tother side a score will follow hence.[67]

In other poems the speaker emphasizes a phenomenon in order to discover its lasting importance. Several poems take as their subject the sinking of the battleship *Maine* in Havana harbor on February 15, 1898. No matter what the cause, Spanish treachery or accident, chaos affected everyone.

> My God! That flash, that flame, that deaf'ning roar
> That fills the vaulted heavens o'er and o'er!
> That sudden shock that turn the peaceful sea
> Into an Aetna's dire ferocity.[68]

Despite the lurid possibilities of the incident, which "yellow" newspapers exploited, Hawkes quickly goes past the emotions it inflamed to extract an ethical meaning.

> Remember the *Maine*, but not with bitter hate
> Against the land that may have done her wrong,
> For God will judge although He tarry long,
> His arm is sure, His justice is not late.[69]

Peace will come after the literal explosion of the ship and the metaphoric outburst of war to insure "man's ire, / The Rage of war, the venom battle brings, / Melt like miasmic mists, when morning flings / Her beams afar."[70] The lesson of his meditations on the blast reflects the missionary zeal of his era: "Let liberty and justice be your aim, / In darksome lands let truth's bright beacon shine."[71]

In short, the palpable universe, with its frogs and waterfalls and passing seasons, pleases on two levels, the instinctive, sensory plane and the educated, moral plane. Everything terrestrial exists for our delight and our edification; the supreme artist created all so we might both feel and understand and, inevitably, bond. Hawkes upholds a democratic philosophy by demeaning cities, college snobs, and wealth while elevating sunshine and flowers and birds, humble chores like plowing a field or making maple syrup, as well as stern ancestors and their heart-felt religion: "It wuz a rugged gospel / That inspired our noblest deeds."[72] His Christmas and Easter poems reiterate the possibility of universal fellowship.

We can only guess how much Hawkes's many readers treasured these verses. One of them, Clara Clough Lenroot, recalled the hard life her mother lived in the 1860s on a farm near Osceola, Wisconsin, close to the St. Croix River. When she died, Lenroot, who had recited Bryant and Longfellow on her own two-mile walk to school, found the most appropriate tribute for her departed parent in the words Hawkes wrote in praise of his own mother, in his poem "Tired Hands."[73]

Nature Writings

Shortly after Hawkes's mother died in 1899, he shifted his attention from poetry to narratives about animals. Throwing himself into this new interest, he became something of a cultural revolutionary by boldly reconciling four apparently incompatible ideas about nature: that it was almost divine, that it provided an escape from complexity for men who didn't want to grow up, that it was demonic, and that it was trivial.

Following Romantics like William Wordsworth, some authors whom Hawkes respected tried to replace conventional Christian theology with a heightened reverence for the universe. Salvation from anxiety and instruction for action, they claimed, could come from the nonhuman world. They espoused the hope that retreat to physical nature might open in them a vision of infinity. As Ralph Waldo Emerson famously said, "Standing on the bare ground,—my head bathed in the blithe air, and uplifted into infinite space,—all mean egotism vanishes. I become a transparent eyeball; I am nothing; I see all; the currents of the Universal Being circulate through me; I am part and parcel of God."[74] Hawkes and his fictional speakers often sounded like disciples of Romanticism. One pair of affirmations typify his belief. He begins *Notes of a Naturalist*, "There's a balm in Mother Nature, / For earth's heartache and its pain," and then writes, "The seeing eye is not an acquired faculty, but a gift of God vouchsafed only to the child of Nature. . . . This special vision is a spiritual quality."[75] Less mystically, the idyllic poems of William Cullen Bryant assumed that people who communed with seasons, creatures, and plants could access some indwelling spirit. His famous "Thanatopsis" begins, "To him who in the love of Nature holds / Communion with her visible forms, she speaks / A various language."[76] All of us, the theory ran, can appreciate the enchanting exterior of nature and perhaps her inner significances.

Hawkes's attention to nature seems so visceral that no one would accuse it of being a mere retreat from adult complexity. When Hawkes spotlighted people, he seldom made them conform to the older escapist pattern of many American narratives, in which one or two males flee to a wilderness, mainly so that they can indulge their self-centered fantasies. Washington Irving's henpecked Rip Van Winkle set the pattern for James Fenimore Cooper's Leatherstocking and Chingachgook, Herman Melville's two young sailors who jump from a stern New England ship onto a South Pacific island in *Typee*, and Mark Twain's Jim and Huckleberry Finn, who (in Huck's words), "got to light out for the Territory ahead of the rest, because Aunt Sally she's going to adopt me and sivilize me."[77]

Hawkes bravely diverged from this flight pattern. He eagerly entwined himself with an authentic natural world to augment his relation with all animated life, not separate himself from any part of it. When he does depict a mentor-pupil encounter, he emphasizes the vital knowledge that connects both the older generation and the younger to an eternal system. In *Big Brother*, for example, the aptly named hired man Uncle Solomon teaches both the farm owner and his son to recognize the tracks of a marauding bear, attract him by leaving a dead sheep in the open, and finally shoot him from a skillfully constructed blind. Personally, Hawkes used his knowledge of the physical universe to bond with other people. He committed to memory around eighty separate birdcalls, using records sent by Cornell University and the New York Foundation for the Blind.[78] Intrigued by this closeness to birds, Thornton Burgess wrote him a technical letter asking the exact kind of grebe—horned, Holboell's or Western—he had noticed in Hadley. Burgess promised to read Hawkes's reply over radio stations in Boston and Springfield.[79]

A third group of popular writers communicated a savage world of competitive animals, one that frightened the mind of observers and endangered their bodies. They destroyed the benign concept of mutualism that assumed all species could coexist in harmony. Nineteenth-century naturalists accepted Isaac Newton's proof that the cosmos ran according to mechanical laws independent of human desires. So too animals obeyed instinct. Edgar Allan Poe's grotesque story "The

Murders in the Rue Morgue" (1841) described a runaway orangutan who brutally slaughters two elderly women in Paris. Just before Hawkes's birth, Charles Darwin's *Origin of Species* (1859) showed how an inexorable biological imperative killed off inefficient species and preserved only those that outmuscled their competitors. Even Karl Marx's belief that all group life demanded a fight between the rich and the poor added to impatience with the Romantics' spiritually uplifting vision and the escapists' fictions about wilderness as sanctuary. Sometimes animals were oddly useful to human beings. In Herman Melville's *Moby Dick* (1851), the great white whale symbolized the world's cryptic evil and explained the monomania of Captain Ahab. Theodore Dreiser, also, assumed the only lesson one learns from creatures is that you brawl or die. His novel *The Financier* (1912) begins as a young man watches a squid and a lobster fight to their deaths. This lethal spectacle energized him to become a millionaire, seizing control of Chicago's rail system and exploiting the women in his life.

Two final popular authors pondered the possibly destructive links between human and animal life, contradicting the impartial vision Hawkes was to communicate. H. G. Wells's disturbing *The Island of Doctor Moreau* (1896) wondered whether science might turn beasts into semihuman beings. Its conclusion: animals may temporarily resemble us, but they will inevitably obey their lust for blood and revert to feral predators. The most relentless exponent of the savage wildlife theory, Jack London (1876–1916), assumed that domesticated animals will quickly revert to savagery (*The Call of the Wild*, 1903) and that humans do not differ from beasts: he names one protagonist, who quotes Shakespeare but does not hesitate to kill, Wolf Larson (*The Sea Wolf*, 1904).

A fourth group of best-selling authors, including Hawkes's contemporaries Beatrix Potter (1866–1943) and Thornton Burgess (1874–1965), trivialized and sentimentalized the first two powerful beliefs in nature as spiritual salvation or as physical escape while ignoring the notion of perpetual hostility. Their beasts were humorists, innocuous playthings that frolicked and chattered in a world with little transcendent meaning. In Burgess's *The Adventures of Jerry Muskrat* (1914), the inhabitants of the Smiling Pool and Laughing Brook have "conventions" at the Big Rock, all speaking the same language and agreeing to work together to avoid traps set by the farmer's boy. Most unsettling, the illustrator dressed them in surreal, English-gentleman costumes—top hats, frock coats, and umbrellas or walking sticks for Grandfather Frog, Ol' Mistah Buzzard, and Spotty the Turtle. These Disneyfied creatures reassured their audiences that the world is human-centered, benign, sexless, and predictable. The recognizable antics of the wee beings proclaimed that people already know everything about the natural world—it mirrors human society—and thus they need not explore it.

Almost any observer could have predicted that Hawkes would write truthfully about the outdoors and thus often contradict fashion. "I had been born and bred a child of Nature," he recalled. "There was no sound or scent of hers, no song, or sound of woe, that I did not know."[80] From his first rambles in the woods with his father, from his earliest guidance by his mother and by grandma Gurney, he felt that all living things possess an identity: they sing a unique song, indent a distinctive footprint, sprout differently shaped leaves, or live in artfully adapted dwellings. His memory of phenomena provided the basis for a lifetime of clear observation: "In some mysterious manner," he said, "the sensitive plates exposed in my youth secured perfect pictures of each passing season and of a multitude of the varying aspects of nature."[81]

Hawkes's encyclopedic reading augmented his capacious memory, providing him with narratives from two millennia in which four-footed or two-winged creatures reveal truths about human lives. From the Greek slave Aesop, whose turtle always outraces the hare, through medieval cycles like that of Reynard the fox, who constantly tricks Isengrim the arrogant wolf, to Uncle Remus's Brer Bear, Brer Fox, and Brer Rabbit, the menagerie had amused and instructed generations. Hawkes's early stories understandably glanced backward to earlier models like Aesop. Old Ben Wilson, who instructs the young narrator in *Stories of the Good Green Wood*, retells a fable of "how 'twas the rabbit lost his tail" to the waddling-but-persistent turtle. Likewise, "A Night with Ruff Grouse" quickly established the danger faced by the wounded old partridge by invoking the ancient title for a relentless adversary: "Ruff's feathers stood up with fright and his eyes grew big with terror: it was Sir Reynard, and he was after him."[82] The popular dialect fables of Uncle Remus probably encouraged Hawkes's evocations of characters like Old Ben.

Hawkes repeatedly demonstrated that raccoons, plovers, weasels, and circus ponies have distinctive traits that should be appreciated. They are not humans; they are animals who live interesting lives in a beautiful yet dangerous world. His realistic biographies admit that they fight for survival, clothed in fur or feathers, not spats, but also show that they love their offspring, enjoy good weather, exhibit curiosity, can be loyal to deserving partners, and may remember their past actions. A few times in his books, a beast resembles a person, as when polar bear cubs "wrestle like two boys."[83] Usually, though, his first concern is to accurately depict the life cycle of his subject without imposing on it the pattern of human development or emotions. A fellow naturalist, Gene

Stratton Porter, author of the admired frontier novel *Girl of the Limberlost*, accurately observed: "How Mr. Hawkes does it, I do not know, but he does describe nature sympathetically and accurately. His animals are not humanized. He has the wisdom to recognize that the processes of nature are distinctly cold-blooded."[84] He allows us to see how a sled dog lies on his back after a long day's haul and chews off the ice that has congealed on his paws; he marvels that "a young robin requires 14 feet of earthworms per day";[85] he informs us that the half-digested moss taken from a slain reindeer's belly, mixed with berries, provides hunters in Lapland with a tasty meal;[86] he takes us on a tour of a beaver's lakeside dwelling, noting the materials, dimensions, and reasons for the design.[87]

Hawkes transports us to the green woods or snow-swept tundra so often forgotten by an unobservant, urban human. Realistic truths replace irrelevant cuteness or lurid savagery. Further, they invite readers to appreciate a *plenum*, a universe filled with fascinating activity. The speaker of *Big Brother* reminds readers that in the wild, animals have passed, are passing, and will continue to pass whether or not anyone observes them:

> There were many tracks in the snow on this winter afternoon that interested Red Fox.
>
> There was the two by two of the red squirrel, and also the two by two of the weasel. These two tracks were identical, save for the fact that if one looked sharply he might have discerned where the hair on the weasel's belly had brushed the snow between jumps. The T shaped track of the rabbit was unmistakable, with the shank always pointing in the direction the rabbit is traveling. The scraggly tracks of the partridge were for all the world like the footprints that the barn fowls make in the farmyard. There was no mistaking the lace-like track of the wood mouse, and the clumsy trail of the skunk was like no other trail; often his pudgy belly fairly dragging in the snow.[88]

The narrators in his books often examine one animal but then shift focus to include others, always aware that innumerable creatures inhabit our globe. A year-old walrus, minutely described in *Igloo Stories*, lives in a frozen environment that also houses "the sea-cow and the sea leopard," along with gulls, little auks, White Arctic geese, blue foxes, polar bears, and killer whales.[89]

Hawkes's stories maturely accept nature both as inspiring to the human soul and as potentially lethal. They reject binary extremes that force a reader to decide whether the world will comfort or crush people. On the one hand, they confirm a Romantic inclusiveness by sponsoring the benefits of contact with creatures. He fixes his inner eye on the features anyone can observe, all the while implying that such clear vision will promote in the audience feelings of at-homeness in the world. Coming close to genuine animals, people inevitably benefit, and readers who experienced unmediated contact with the wilderness would feel patronized by characters like Benjamin Bunny, Peter Rabbit, and Jimmy Skunk. As the narrator in *Dapples of the Circus* says: "In these days of machines, when so much is artificial, what better playmate could children have than one of these little horses? Learning to care for him and drive him under all conditions, develops character as almost nothing else will."[90]

On the other hand, Hawkes admitted that even the most deserving humans could expect little direct help from animated nature. In *King of the Flying Sledge*, set in frozen Lapland, when Olga, daughter of old Oscar and husband of Hans, lies dying from childbirth, her father passively murmurs, "We must have faith; God is good."[91] Hans, however, sets out by sledge to fetch a doctor. On the trail he marvels at the Northern Lights. True, the "orange, crimson, blue, yellow" sky revealed (in the words of Psalm 19) God's glory and handiwork, but they did little for his needy wife and child:

> Just as though the Creator was setting off some mighty fireworks, or pyrotechnic display, to awe the antlike creatures who crawled to and fro on Mother Earth and called themselves lords of creation.
>
> This was the thought of Hans as he gazed reverently over his shoulder. How insignificant and puny we were, after all, when face to face with the workings of nature!
>
> How little the elements, the wind, fire, and water, considered man when they went mad and did the work of nature![92]

Hawkes's vision of nature as simultaneously healing and destructive might have offended contemporaries who mentioned most facts of reproduction and survival only indirectly. He calmly recorded births and deaths; for instance, *Wood and Water Friends* has a familiar introductory note: "This is God's world that we live in. With His hands He fashioned it; the woods and the waters. He made it for an inspiration and delight. So let us be mindful of its beauty and its wonder and hold them in our hearts as a sacred precious thing that shall make us rich as Kings and fill our souls with peace and understanding."[93] But such a soothing piety coexists with Darwinian objectivity: in the forest, "no creature ever dies of old age" (29); despite other writers' fantasies about animal parliaments, "life is a battle" (203); all obey "that instinct of self-preservation" (259) prompting them to flee or kill. In this one book Hawkes mentions the deaths, usually violent, of a sparrow, a woodchuck, a ferret, baby woodpeckers, baby robins, a snake, a hawk, a weasel, a hunting dog, a frog, a baby fox, otters, fish, a muskrat, a baby jay, a mink, and a bittern.

Hawkers forced his audiences to accept their involvement in the natural world. One of his *Notes of a Naturalist* sounds an ominous warning based on his lifelong study: "It is the fact that the wild kindred war so continually on one another. The larger on the smaller, the stronger on the weaker. Life here in the ancient woods is a continual struggle. I suppose that his law helps the species, for only the strongest and wisest survive, but I fear that in the immediate future a great plague is coming on the world because of the folly of man."[94] His credibility made such a jeremiad powerful. Having escaped the "Nature Faker fuss" (as he called it) of the century's first decades, he battled for authenticity, a mission he outlined in *The Light That Did Not Fail* and *My Country.*

Novels

Each of Hawkes's four novels reinforced the message in his poetry and nature books: we are inextricably connected to both the social and the animal world whether or not we admit the bond. *Wanted a Mother* (1922), *Doctor Thinkright* (1934), *The Master of Millshaven* (1936), and *Uncle Billy, the Curious Cobbler* (1939) all asserted that self-destructive narcissists could be converted to joyful members of a larger society by means of a dramatic encounter. This experience of being morally "inverted" or "turned bottom side up" (as the spunky heroine of *Wanted a Mother* puts it)[95] recalls two of the oldest Christian success tales, those of St. Paul and St. Augustine. Saul the Jesus-hater was transformed into Paul the missionary after his unhorsing on the Damascus road. Three hundred and fifty years later, the spiritually tormented Augustine sat weeping under a fig tree in the garden of his cottage in Milan. Miraculously, he heard a child's voice chanting, "Pick up and read!" The biblical text he chose changed his identity from libertine to truth seeker. Hawkes used Victorian narrative tactics to encourage readers that it is possible to transform oneself into a better person if one heeds the benign signs in nature, in human character, and in literature.

Wanted a Mother presents a threesome of actors familiar from widely read nineteenth-century fiction. The eight-year-old orphan Eleanor Abbott leaves the Ashton poor-farm to live with her reluctant Aunt Lucretia and timid Uncle Nathan, her late mother's sister and brother. Eleanor has both the beauty—blond curls and big brown eyes—and the feisty truthfulness that moved the popular audiences of the time. All she craves is someone to love her. Like her literary predecessors, however, she finds that the people nearest to her cannot supply affection.[96] The cold Lucretia humiliates her niece because Eleanor's mother had married the man she loved. Nathan, although he is kindly, can do little to mollify Lucretia's cruelty. He bonds with Eleanor only when the two are out of Lucretia's sight. Whenever Eleanor feels downcast, she gains comfort from an old dog and from writing about her misery in "a book of secret thoughts."

Hawkes taps into the deep well of Victorian pathos when he recounts the aunt's glaring eyes, snapping voice, and rejecting attitude (25).[97] The wicked stepmother motif, found in a wide range of narratives, from the peasant fairy tales of the brothers Grimm to middle-class fiction, makes her plight almost archetypal. Eleanor persists in her quest for affection despite the rebuffs: "The frightened waif went to attack the very formidable castle in which abode the icy heart of her bitter, unforgiving Aunt" (25).

Lucretia converts because she snoops in Eleanor's secret book and realizes the truth of the accusations the child has penned against her. Like Augustine's biblical text, the journal forces her to confront her incivilities. Other tales told of people who also kept thought journals, most notably Mark Twain's Pudd'nhead Wilson, but they were not invested with this special power to change character. Readers could parallel Eleanor's improving words with those of another fictional orphan. Robert Browning's sunny Pippa, "that ragged little girl," walks through a northern Italian town on her one day off from the silk mill. She sings a song that transforms murderers and adulterers when they accidentally hear it, a refrain that Hawkes quoted to cheer people up during the war-anxious 1940s.[98] *Wanted a Mother* ends when Lucretia fully accepts little Eleanor, makes new clothes for her, willingly cooks meals, and invites Eleanor's friend from the poorfarm to become a live-in hired man. Thanks to the child's writings, Lucretia learns "to bottle up a lot of [sunshine]" in her heart (98).[99]

Similar renovations occur in *Doctor Thinkright.* Here the kindly old physician lives up to his allegorical name. With perception, Thinkright restores wounded hearts. A hypochondriac woman learns to put others first when the doctor adopts a spunky orphan and demands that she care for him. The stony heart of the miser Caleb Flint melts when the doctor maneuvers him into buying Christmas gifts for poor children and playing Santa Claus. A hypocritical factory owner, who chides the doctor for not attending church, reforms after being forced to visit people he has wronged—a poor washerwoman whose husband he had fired, a clerk who embezzled money to pay a high mortgage, a former worker in his unsanitary mill now dying of tuberculosis. In a strong subplot, the doctor becomes part of the lives of the town prostitute and a young alcoholic, whose lives also improve.

The optimistic Thinkright closely resembles Hawkes himself. The doctor has had "a life full of sorry,"[100] although in public "his face was like the great sun showing above the eastern hilltops" (29). Similarly, "he had always loved children" (30), carries a cane, and has a brother in California (Hawkes's youngest brother, Ernest, had earned a PhD at the University of Pennsylvania in 1915 and, after various teaching jobs, moved in 1919 to Glendale, California). One of Thinkright's maxims is especially touching to those who know Hawkes's history: "We are all blind to our own sins. It is only other people who see them" (25). The medical theory of counterirritants that pained Hawkes in Boston as a newly blind teenager may resurface when the matron of the orphan asylum balks at releasing a mischievous lad to the complaining spinster: "Children are a sort of bombshell in a home where they are strangers" (33); Dr. Thinkright agrees, insisting, "You see, the child is medicine. It is to be a heroic dose, something so much worse than her ailments that she will forget them" (34). Hawkes lightens the seriousness of such shock therapy when little Tommy humorously dresses as a physician in oversize clothes and takes Edith's temperature with a "thermonica" (59–62). Like Eleanor, the old therapist himself derives comfort from "a little notebook" (16) of wise words. Each conversion the doctor effects alleviates "heart trouble." As he explains to pale Edith Grayson, the imaginary invalid who illustrates her name when speaking with a "colorless voice" (19): "The trouble with your heart is that it is supremely selfish. That is what makes you ill. You have not generosity enough to think of others, so you always and forever think of yourself" (23).

Sometimes the mechanism for redemption is a child, like Tommy. George Eliot had already mapped out that plot in *Silas Marner* (1861), in which the misanthropic weaver Silas takes in the foundling Eppie and learns love from her. Other times, as with greedy Flint, Hawkes uses the precedents of Augustine's two life-altering encounters, with a book and with disembodied voices. Hawkes has Flint speak like a second Scrooge from Dickens's *Christmas Carol*: "I don't ever think of anyone specially on Christmas, and no one thinks of me. It's mostly humbug" (75). Flint reads Dickens's novel and a current newspaper report of his generosity and explodes with anger, but then he overhears a conversation among strangers that accuses him of stinginess. These assaults on his self-possession lead him to gaze into a mirror and, renewed, practice saying "Merry Christmas."

The Master of Millshaven revisits the subject of reformation from dark selfishness to positive social awareness.[101] Published in 1936, with the Depression apparently confirming Marxist fears that exploitative capitalism would collapse, Hawkes's novel eased anxieties by being set in the 1890s. The "master," a middle-aged man, was, like Lucretia in *Wanted a Mother*, once disappointed in love. He now pursues wealth at all costs, controlling mills, the police, banks, and newspapers in the three-tiered town of Millshaven. There, factories and poor workers mingle on the flats; the clerks and tradespeople live on the next higher terrace, and the "aristocrats" on the top. The master's daughter, Evelyn, his foil, denies genetics and generously works with the poor. Cullen Hayward, the male hero and Evelyn's love interest, sounds like a younger and more practical Dr. Thinkright. Blinded accidentally by a friend, he loves the country (as did William Cullen Bryant), but he becomes a lawyer in the city. There he combats a heartless plan by the master to further demean the lowly—building another factory on a playground.

Uncle Billy, the Curious Cobbler completes the quartet of conversion novels. Its title character had lost his wife and child two decades before in the West but now treats an entire eastern town as his family. He mends both soles and souls, having "discovered the appalling fact that every one is lonesome."[102] His good works benefit a wide range of victims. He donates money anonymously so the grade-school teacher, Miss Browning, can pay for an operation to cure her young brother's deformed leg; he instills such conscience into three mischievous students who had disrupted her class that they heartily apologize to her and become friends to her "cripple brother" (24); he reforms a gang of juvenile delinquents "from Tinpot Alley" (53) by inviting them to dinner and to a football game; he educates the cynical businessman Hiram Pepper so he can appreciate nature and generosity.

Uncle Billy draws strength to perform these charitable deeds from the same beliefs that motivated Hawkes. Both accepted Wordsworth's idea that the child is closest to perfection and loses vital links to the universe as it ages. Pondering a pair of "battered little shoes," Uncle Billy muses: "They are miles nearer Heaven than we grownups. Sometimes, I think, the longer we live the further off we get from heaven" (15). Many of Hawkes's adult characters must consciously recall this fact if they are to function altruistically. The miserly, no-nonsense Hiram almost accidentally reads one of Thomas Hood's poems ("I'm farther off from heaven than when I was a boy") and begins to renew himself. Significantly, like the miser Flint in *Doctor Thinkright*, Hiram next "caught a glance of his face in a looking glass" (97–98), an obvious but efficient way for readers to feel that the words have forced him to confront his true identity. The first token of Hiram's reformation is his approval of repairs to a tenement he owns. Later he reads the scene from Mark Twain's novel in which Tom Sawyer observes his own funeral, an optimistic proof we can reverse the loss usually associated with living too long.

A related idea that sustained both Uncle Billy and Hawkes was that injuries might be repaired. In the novel, children who can afford a hospital operation will escape from the life of a cripple. Hawkes employs the Rousseau-like notion that the four boys have been corrupted by society. They destroy Uncle Billy's melons, but that vandalism in his garden does not end their connection to the public; rather, it initiates their rehabilitation because, with proper guidance, even rogues may regain their earlier innocence. Their present state cries for improvement: one lives in a saloon, another has been forced to sell newspapers on the street since his earliest years. Uncle Billy invites them to dinner, compels them to confront their real identity when he calls each by his Christian name rather than his nickname, allows them to describe their upbringings, and sets in motion their personal confessions, contrition, and redemptions.

Hawkes shared with Uncle Billy a third conviction, one about the value of tradition. The novel ends with a lavish Christmas dinner for five hundred poor children. Domestic and public meals cement relationships. The original supper at Uncle Billy's prompted the rascals who ruined his melon patch to slick down their hair, douse themselves with cologne, and try to observe proper etiquette at table; the Christmas feast brings together the town's abjectly poor (not just "the respectable poor" who do not "really need our love and pity" [159]), the three school cut-ups (who hand out invitations), Hiram (who pays for the event after "he had read Dickens' Christmas Carol the night before, and had been shocked to see how much like old Scrooge he had become" [148]), and Uncle Billy (who retells the Nativity story and moves everyone's emotions). The name of the banquet building, Foresters Hall, and the presence of a gigantic Christmas evergreen hint that all people can most easily mingle when they recall nature. The hall becomes a *temenos*, a sacred space, which for a brief moment exhibits the best reciprocal virtues of society purged of invidious distinctions based on wealth or physical condition. Hawkes's lifelong involvement in other shared activities—sporting events, politics, and Hadley's 250th anniversary ceremonies—here finds its most potent symbol.

These four novels offered a uniquely American solution to social and spiritual problems. They foresaw a happy ending to the struggle of social contraries that wastes energy and distracts people from bonding.

Reputation

For such a talented celebrity, one mystery remains: why is Hawkes not famous in our day? He suffered so many cruel subtractions in his early years that he seemed doomed to a life of tragic passivity, but he triumphed, displaying the strength that inspires legends. In 1927 a popular biographical encyclopedia published an eight-page excerpt from *Hitting the Dark Trail*, along with entries on other of "the World's Famous Men" like Thomas Henry Huxley, Leo Tolstoy, and Oscar Wilde.[103] By 1931, everyone agreed that "Clarence Hawkes probably is the most widely known native of the Hampshire hills in the field of literature."[104] Fraternal groups like the Sons of Union Veterans of the Civil War, the Knights of Pythias, and the Lions Club regularly honored him.[105]

Yet folk memory has separated Hawkes from the company of penniless Ben Franklin, rural Abe Lincoln, and isolated Helen Keller. Today we must work to recapture the larger-than-life status Hawkes enjoyed in his own era. The passing of Hawkes's reputation may have been caused by several modernist habits. To begin, accessible poetry like his no longer impresses audiences. Hawkes's predictable rhymes, humane sentiment, and generality contradict current expectations of idiosyncratic verse forms, sophisticated irony, private symbolism, anguished confession, and discontinuity. Next, the representation of nature now demands high-definition, big-screen, surround-sound films of animal adventures, or exciting memoirs of exotic field trips, or philosophical hymns to the outdoors, or glossy children's booklets, or cartoon simplifications. This deluge of high-tech multisensory offerings has edged out even well made writing such as Hawkes's. In addition, the quest for social justice that Hawkes felt would best be served by a conservative Yankee leader like Calvin Coolidge can be questioned as nativism or paternalism. His admiration for Coolidge or Warren G. Harding or even Herbert Hoover now makes it seem as if time-bound wishful thinking rather than political acumen governed his preferences.

Although tastes have changed, we still can admire the qualities that allowed Hawkes to produce so much. His perseverance, pluck, and patience, far from being abstractions, actualized his tremendous potentials for creativity and kindness. His feats of memory alone would impress anyone, especially in his day, when even trained orators and preachers spoke with the help of texts. His poetry urged the conservation of time-tested virtues and decent sensations. His nature books fleshed out with imagination the facts of nonhuman life that, properly understood, would benefit all creatures. His novels offered an alternative view of a world temporarily damaged by rapacious businesses, selfish hearts, and gloating materialism. These strong truths deserve to live again in the hearts of people near and far from Hadley.

Notes

1. Two rewritings of the press release: "Six Decades in Darkness," *Daily Hampshire Gazette*, 14 August 1943, 6; Frank G. Jason, "Clarence Hawkes, Blind Poet, Celebrates 60 Years of Bringing Courage to Sightless," *Boston Sunday Post*, 22 August 1943. The president of Amherst College, Stanley King, congratulated Hawkes after the UP release: "No one takes a warmer pride in your accomplishment than the College, which is proud to count you as

her foster son. Each generation of college students at Amherst has known you, and the young men who have played on our athletic teams have thought of you as perhaps their most consistent friend." Letter from Stanley King to Hawkes, 8 September 1943, Amherst College Archives.

2. Robert Bartlett, *They Dared to Live* (New York: YMCA, 1937).
3. "Clarence Hawkes Is Included among 35 Who 'Dared to Live,' " *Daily Hampshire Gazette,* 10 November 1937, 4.
4. Jason, "Clarence Hawkes."
5. Clarence Hawkes, *Notes of a Naturalist: Jottings in Field and Forest* (Boston: Christopher, 1938), 46–47.
6. "Clarence Hawkes Speaks at Goshen," *Daily Hampshire Gazette,* 15 August 1931, 1. The doctor who had to trudge uphill through the whiteout snow may have been Thomas Gilfillan. According to Stephen M. Howes, former chair of the Cummington Historical Commission, Gilfillan might have started from the house he occupied from 1856 to around 1874 on Cummington's Main Street—ironically, next door to the house later occupied by the Hawkes family from 1885 to 1892. He would have headed up the steep slope. Leaving behind his exhausted horse, the determined doctor was helped by a "kind farmer" (perhaps Howes's own great-grandfather, Jesse Willcutt, who had lived since 1857 in the last house in Swift River on the route to the Hawkes place). Stephen M. Howes, interview by author, 21 December 2006. Hawkes describes the winter birth in *The Light That Did Not Fail* (Boston: Chapman & Grimes, 1935), 12–17; the kindly physician may reappear as Dr. Thinkright in Hawkes's novel of that name.
7. Illinois Civil War Records, ilsos.gov/genealogy/CivilWarController (accessed 25 June 2008). Hawkes's name appears in the record as Hawks.
8. Clarence Hawkes, *Hitting the Dark Trail: Starshine through Thirty Years of Night* (New York: Henry Holt, 1915), 17.
9. Hawkes, *The Light That Did Not Fail,* 30.
10. Date of award: Imogene Hawks Lane, *John Hawks: A Founder of Hadley, Massachusetts* (Baltimore: Gateway Press, 1989), 390; amount of award: *List of Pensioners on the Roll, January 1, 1883,* 2 vols. (Baltimore: Genealogical Publishing, 1883; repr., 1970), 1:354.
11. "Ashfield," *Greenfield Gazette and Courier,* 23 June 1884.
12. "Chesterfield and Goshen," *County Atlas of Hampshire, Massachusetts, from Actual Surveys under the Direction of F. W. Beers* (New York: F. W. Beers, 1873), 14–15.
13. "We are happy to report," *Hampshire Gazette and Northampton Courier,* 28 August 1883, 2.
14. Hawkes, *The Light That Did Not Fail,* 80. For some reason, Hawkes does not mention that his father had secured three patents, one for a game protector, a second for a painting machine, and a third for a scrubbing machine. Lane, *John Hawks,* 390.
15. Hawkes, *Hitting the Dark Trail,* 14.
16. Anne Sabo Warner, *A Bicentennial History of Goshen, Massachusetts, 1781–1980* (Goshen, Mass.: Historical Commission, 1980), 188, 373.
17. Hawkes, *Hitting the Dark Trail,* 14–15. Typically, Hawkes followed up the connection with Norton. The respected Harvard professor of fine arts, translator of Dante, and former editor of the *North American Review, Atlantic Monthly,* and *The Nation* convened famous lecture dinners in August from 1879 until 1903 at the academy building. More than 140 speeches from such luminaries as G. Stanley Hall, president of Clark University, Charles Dudley Warner, editor of the *Hartford Courant,* author William Dean Howells, Booker T. Washington, president of Tuskegee Institute, and James Russell Lowell enriched auditors' minds; see Betty and Edward Gulick, *Charles Eliot Norton and the Sanderson Dinners, 1879–1903* (Ashfield, Mass.: Ashfield Historical Society, 1990). Eliot's objections to Amer-

ican culture as puerile and crass as well as his opposition to U.S. empire-building in Cuba may not have convinced the grown-up Hawkes, who was consistently patriotic, but the sharing of ideas appealed to him early and late. Eliot praised Hawkes because his writing did not "minister to the popular taste for gossip" (letter from Charles Eliot Norton to Hawkes, 6 April 1895, Hawkes Manuscript Letters, Hadley Historical Society, Hadley, Mass. [hereafter cited as Hawkes Manuscript Letters] 1:6). Later Eliot ordered two of Hawkes's books (letter from Charles Eliot Norton to Hawkes, 20 October 1906, Hawkes Manuscript Letters, 1:66).

18. Hawkes, *Hitting the Dark Trail*, 27.
19. "Hadley's Blind Poet," *Daily Hampshire Gazette*, 13 February 1906, 8, cols. 5–8, quoting the *New York Sun*. Perhaps his father's mental condition contributed to the careless shooting. In November 1882, Enos had traveled to High Point, North Carolina, to attend a dog show. There he "went crazy" ("Berkshire County," *Springfield [Mass.] Daily Republican*, 20 November 1882, 6). The incident was widely reported. An intriguing notice in the Greenfield paper read: "E. S. Hawkes, who went to North Carolina to attend a field trial of dogs about election time and was reported from southern sources to have gone insane, has returned home, and makes a long statement concerning his experiences in the South. His story will appear in these columns next week" ("Ashfield," *Greenfield Gazette and Courier*, 11 December 1882). Unfortunately, no follow-up story appeared. Reporters offered two different reasons for Enos's breakdown: "While there is insanity in his family, Hawks's present condition is attributed to a severe attack of vertigo from which he suffered while visiting a married sister at Florence recently" ("Berkshire County," *Springfield Daily Republican*, 20 November 1882, 6). The only corroborating evidence for this claim is that fact that Enos's paternal grandmother, Abigail "Nabby" Marsh (c. 1772–1842), did end her days "at the Worcester Insane Hospital." ("Died," *Greenfield Gazette and Courier*, 29 November 1842, 3. Personal communication, Shirley Majewski, Pocumtuck Valley Memorial Association Library, Deerfield, Mass., February 2007.) Another explanation came out eleven days after the first notice of his homecoming: "E. S. Hawks of Ashfield has returned home and appears to be much improved, but still tells some remarkable stories of being pursued and of his dogs being killed, because he was a republican and from the North" ("Berkshire County," *Springfield Daily Republican*, 23 Nov 1882, 6).

    I offer still another possible cause for Enos's psychological disorder that is based on his being a cousin of William Smith Clark (1826–1886), mentioned earlier as the third president of Massachusetts Agricultural College. The flamboyant Amherst politician, teacher, and traveler to Germany and Japan, as well as companion and perhaps lover of Emily Dickinson, had urged friends and relatives to buy stock in western gold, silver, and coal mines. By the spring of 1882, the scheme had collapsed, ruining many and leaving Clark in disgrace. Although Enos (as the Springfield newspaper account of 20 November 1882 described him) was "quite poor and has a wife and four children," he may have anticipated the lump sum pension, borrowed against it to invest in Clark's scheme, and lost all, exacerbating his poverty and his psychological problems.
20. Bruce Barton, "God Took My Eyes That My Soul Might See," *American Magazine* 102 (July 1926): 80, 82. Reprinted as "Here Is a Remarkable Story That Answers All Those Who Have Any Quarrel with Their Circumstances," *Boston Sunday Post*, 23 November 1930, Color-Feature section, 2. Reprinted in Hawkes, *My Country: The America I Knew* (Boston: Chapman & Grimes, 1940), 149–70, along with appreciative letters responding to it.
21. "Serious If Not Fatal Accident at Spruce Corner, Ashfield," *Daily Hampshire Gazette*, 21 August 1883, 2.

22. "Notable Men," *Daily Hampshire Gazette*, 13 October 1908, 10.
23. "In Regard to Helen Keller," *The Critic* 27 (17 April 1897): 792.
24. Review of *Hitting the Dark Trail, The Bookman* 51 (December 1916): supplement 36.
25. William T. Heisler, "An Interview with Perkins' Past," *The Lantern* 47, no. 2 (March 1978): 12. The purposeful schedule at Perkins resembled such earlier routines as those suggested by Thomas More's *Utopia*, printed by Ben Franklin, parodied in Gilbert and Sullivan's *Gondoliers*, and adhered to by young Jimmy Gatz, the upwardly mobile hero of F. Scott Fitzgerald's *The Great Gatsby*. From the school's founding, students rose at 5 A.M., assembled at 6 in the chapel, and ate breakfast at 8, after which the boys walked and the girls did housework. Two hours of school lessons began at 9, followed at 11 by community singing. After a half-hour recess, pupils returned to class from 11:30 to 1 P.M. Then dinner and recess, followed by work from 2 to 6, supper from 6 to 7, then another hour of singing followed by an hour allotted to "reading newspapers, and history" (*Fifth Annual Report of the Trustees of the New-England Institution for the Education of the Blind* [Boston: Press of the Boston Courier, 1837], 7–8). The academic courses mirrored those of other schools, with the addition of mechanical aids such as "Eaton's wooden ciphering-boards"—devices with squares marked out by brass strips so students could place numerals in the proper position (*Fifty-Sixth Annual Report of the Trustees of the Perkins Institution and Massachusetts School for the Blind for the Year Ending September 30, 1877* [Boston: Rand, Avery, 1878], 68). A similar wood, leather, and metal device that guided Hawkes's handwriting now rests in the Goodwin Memorial Library, Hadley, Mass. I appreciate the information about Perkins supplied by Jan Seymour-Ford, a research librarian at the school.
26. Barton, "Here Is a Remarkable Story," 2.
27. Quoted in Paul M. Kelly, "Adversity as No Obstacle: The Life and Times of Poet and Naturalist, Clarence Hawkes" (master's thesis, Westfield State College, 1992), 11.
28. Hawkes, *Hitting the Dark Trail*, 107.
29. "Ashfield," *Greenfield Gazette and Courier*, 23 January 1892, 5.
30. *Hopkins Academy, 1667–1895* (Springfield, Mass.: Henry R. Johnson, n.d.), 16.
31. Hawkes, *Hitting the Dark Trail*, 125.
32. Clarence Hawkes, *Notes of a Naturalist*, 57–58.
33. "Fifty Years of Blindness No Great Handicap to Hadley's Famed Poet," *Holyoke Daily Transcript*, 12 August 1933.
34. "Dr. Hawkes, Blind, Near 80; Poet and Sports Authority," *Springfield Sunday Republican*, 11 December 1949.
35. The wedding took place in her parents' home at 51 (now 107) West Street, a few yards south of Route 9, directly opposite Hawkes's own house. Built about 1760, the large white structure housed the Smith family until 1870. Then Bessie's father Samuel bought it from his aunts, Ruth (wife of Ephraim Smith) and Maria (wife of Elijah Smith), who had lived there since their father-in-law, Seth, died in 1828. This house, Hawkes's home, and the double row of trees that march resolutely north and south along the beautiful common still stand, witnesses to New England tradition.
36. 1869 Birth Records and 1899 marriage certificate, Hadley Town Hall. Hawkes specially thanks "My brave little mother-in-law" who "did much of my reading" (*Hitting the Dark Trail*, 128).
37. Pratt information kindly supplied by Paul Schlotthauer, archivist at the Pratt Institute.
38. "Clarence Hawkes Is 66 Years Old Today," *Daily Hampshire Gazette*, 16 December 1935, 1.
39. Clarence Hawkes, *The Service Man's Friend* (Boston: Chapman & Grimes, 1944), 28.
40. "Clarence Hawkes Speaks at Goshen," *Daily Hampshire Gazette*, 15 August 1931, 2.

41. Hawkes, *The Service Man's Friend*, 51. Howe may have introduced Hawkes to the vice president of the Authors' Club, Thomas Wentworth Higginson (1823–1911). Hawkes's restatement of Abolitionist beliefs in his graduation speech from Perkins would have been congenial to Higginson, who had led black soldiers during the Civil War, and Hawkes's verses might have impressed him—he co-edited Emily Dickinson's poems. Or his cousin, Henry Lee Higginson, a trustee and member of Perkins' corporation, may have noticed the young writer. Other members were also familiar with him. Mabel Loomis Todd (1856–1932), friend of Higginson and the other editor of Dickinson, and her husband, David Peck Todd (1855–1939), an astronomy professor at Amherst College, knew him. The year before, Mabel had recognized his talents and wondered in an appreciative letter whether he would like to speak under the auspices of the Amherst Historical Society before an audience of "fifty or sixty," a welcome change from rustic buildings and few auditors (letter from Mabel Loomis Todd to Hawkes, 27 December 1899, Hawkes Manuscript Letters, 1:40). The Boston group included authors whose interests coincided with Hawkes's. Arthur Gilman (1837–1909) distinguished himself as a genealogist, a historian of Rome and the American people, and an editor of Chaucer. His plan to provide a college education for women may have influenced Hawkes's later campaign to form female conservation groups. The patriotic words of "America, the Beautiful," written by fellow member Katharine Lee Bates (1869–1929), consoled Hawkes in Hadley during World War II (*The Service Man's Friend*, 50). Finally, John Townsend Trowbridge (1827–1916) wrote books for boys that stressed adventure and clean living, two staples of Hawkes's own works.
42. Clarence Hawkes, "A Night with Ruff Grouse," *Woman's Home Companion* 31 (November 1904): 49.
43. "Fifty Years of Blindness No Great Handicap to Hadley's Famed Poet."
44. Copy of letter from Frederick G. Howes to Hawkes, 3 December 1901, Ashfield Historical Society, Ashfield, Mass., accession number 4307e.
45. Letter from Hugh Lofting, 26 December 1923, Hawkes Manuscript Letters, 1:173.
46. See www.erbzine.com/dan/h1.html for a list of Hawkes books owned by Burroughs (accessed 30 June 2008).
47. Howard Clark Brown, "A Survey of the Naturalistic Periodical Literature of America," *American Midland Naturalist* 7, no. 3 (May 1921): 75–76.
48. Grenville Goodwin, "Excerpts from the *Apache Diaries*," *Journal of the Southwest* 43, nos. 1 and 2 (Spring/Summer 2000): 4.
49. "With *The Overland Monthly* Contributors," *The Overland Monthly* 46 (October 1905): 366.
50. Advertisement for Henry Holt & Company, *New York Times*, 9 October 1915, 12.
51. "Master's Degree Conferred upon Clarence Hawkes," *Daily Hampshire Gazette*, 14 June 1917, 2. Linda Benedict of the Hobart–William Smith Library kindly sent me a commencement program that lists the twenty-one graduates, only two of whom had majored in English. Latin, French, and History were more popular.
52. The Syracuse archives contain Hawkes's 1947 request for a duplicate certificate; the 1942 fire at Northampton's Forbes Library had destroyed the original plus "six honorary diplomas which I had . . . received from different American Colleges" (typescript letter from Hawkes to Chancellor Graham of Syracuse, 22 September 1947; information promptly supplied by Mary O'Brien, Archives and Records Management, Syracuse University Library). "Amherst Alumni Dine," *New York Times*, 19 June 1919, 11.
53. George F. Whicher, "The Victory Commencement," *Amherst Graduates' Quarterly* 8, no. 4 (August 1919): 122.

54. "Principals at A.I.C. Commencement," *AIC Yellowjacket*, 8 June 1938. Information generously furnished by Katherine DeLiso, Shea Memorial Library, American International College. Just as Hawkes retained data from (as Bartlett's A.I.C. citation put it) "maps, atlases, geographies and natural histories," so he held on to friends. The A.I.C. commencement program noted that Professor Dallas Lore Sharp Jr. (1900–1970) awarded the BA degrees. Three decades before the ceremony, his father, Dallas Lore Sharp Sr. (1870–1929), the Boston naturalist who, like Hawkes, provided a powerful voice for the ideals of conservation and preservation, had begun a fond correspondence with Hawkes. Sharp's first letter set the tone for their mutually respectful relationship: "Every genuine nature-lover appreciates your work, and every lover of courage, patience and the gentleness that makes men great sympathizes with you and admires you profoundly" (letter from Dallas Lore Sharp, 6 May 1906, Hawkes Manuscript Letters, 1:63). The two reconfirmed their friendship when the Sharps visited the Hawkeses in Hadley, a trip that in 1915 required nine hours each way from Boston. But the amity he felt "would have made twice the journey infinitely worth taking" (letter from Dallas Lore Sharp to Hawkes, 5 July 1915, Hawkes Manuscript Letters, 1:107). On another visit that fall, Sharp jocularly promised to bring his sons (probably including Dallas Jr.), "if you can give us boys bunks on the floor" (letter from Dallas Lore Sharp, 29 September 1915, Hawkes Manuscript Letters, 1:112).
55. "Clarence Hawkes." *Nature Magazine* 37, no. 2 (February 1944): 104. Hawkes fondly refers to "one of his [Hornaday's] famous books" in Hawkes, *Big Brother: The Story of a Trick Bear* (Springfield, Mass.: Milton Bradley, 1930), 90.
56. Dallas Lore Sharp, "Introduction," in Hawkes, *Hitting the Dark Trail*, xi.
57. Hawkes, *The Light That Did Not Fail*, 130–31.
58. Kenneth Burke, *The Philosophy of Literary Form* (New York: Vintage, 1957), 353.
59. Clarence Hawkes, *Stories of the Good Green Wood* (New York: Thomas Y. Crowell, 1904), 48; also quoted in *Notes of a Naturalist*, 13.
60. Clarence Hawkes, "Ma's Posy Beds," in *Idyls of Old New England* (Northampton, Mass.: Picturesque Publishing, 1897), 57.
61. Clarence Hawkes, "How 'Fighting Joe Hooker' Took Lookout Mountain," in *Pebbles and Shells* (Northampton, Mass.: Picturesque Publishing, 1895), 69.
62. Clarence Hawkes, "How Massa Linkum Came," in *Pebbles and Shells*, 79. Robert T. Lincoln appreciatively wrote Hawkes on 28 June 1895: "Permit me also to congratulate you at the bravery and cheerfulness with which you bear your heavy burden" (Hawkes, *The Light That Did Not Fail*, 108). Hawkes tells how he learned the facts about Lincoln's visit in *My Country*, 63. Radio stations broadcast the verse.
63. Clarence Hawkes, *Three Little Folks: Verses for Children* (Northampton, Mass.: Picturesque Publishing, 1896), 13–14.
64. Review of *Three Little Folks* appended to Clarence Hawkes, *Songs for Columbia's Heroes* (Springfield, Mass.: New England Publishing, 1898), 20.
65. Clarence Hawkes, *The Hope of the World* (Springfield, Mass.: New England Publishing, 1900), 29–30.
66. Clarence Hawkes, "Human Flowers," *Idyls of Old New England*, 29.
67. Clarence Hawkes, "Keep Up Yer Fences," ibid., 99.
68. Clarence Hawkes, "The Fate of the *Maine*," *Songs for Columbia's Heroes*, 37.
69. Clarence Hawkes, "Remember the *Maine*," ibid., 44.
70. Clarence Hawkes, "The Coming of Peace," ibid., 72.
71. Clarence Hawkes, "Columbia and Britannia," ibid., 73.

72. Clarence Hawkes, "The Ole Meetin-House," *Idyls of Old New England*, 76.
73. Clara Clough Lenroot, *Long, Long Ago* (Appleton, Wis.: Badger Printing, 1929), 30.
74. Ralph Waldo Emerson, "Nature," in Sculley Bradley and Richmond Croom Beatty, eds., *The American Tradition in Literature*, vol. 1, 3rd ed. (New York: W. W. Norton, 1967), 1066–67.
75. Hawkes, *Notes of a Naturalist*, 8, 11.
76. William Cullen Bryant, "Thanatopsis," in *The American Tradition in Literature*, 473–74.
77. Mark Twain, *The Adventures of Huckleberry Finn* (1885), ed. Sculley Bradley, Richmond Croom Beatty, and E. Hudson Long, 2nd ed. (New York: W. W. Norton, 1977), 229.
78. Edwin Way Teale, "Birding by Ear," *Audubon* 50 (November 1948): 352.
79. Letter from Thornton Burgess, 25 February 1930, Hawkes Manuscript Letters, 1:199.
80. Hawkes, *Hitting the Dark Trail*, 56.
81. "Afield with a Blind Naturalist," *The Outing Magazine* 51 (December 1907): 347. These accurate images preserved Hawkes from any accusation of being, in John Burroughs's phrase, a "Natural History Münchausen." Burroughs's seminal article, "Real and Sham Natural History," appeared in *The Atlantic Monthly* 91 (March 1903): 298–309. It points to errors in the work of Ernest Thompson Seton while praising the accuracy of Hawkes's friend Dallas Lore Sharp. Ralph H. Lutts gives an illuminating history of the controversy in *The Nature Fakers: Wildlife, Science and Sentiment* (Charlottesville: University of Virginia Press, 2001).
82. Hawkes, *Stories of the Good Green Wood*, 9, 49.
83. Clarence Hawkes, *Igloo Stories: Six Tales of Eskimo Land* (Boston: Christopher, 1937), 96, 99.
84. Quoted in Hawkes, *The Light That Did Not Fail*, 123. Also in Hawkes, *My Country*, 86.
85. Hawkes, *The Service Man's Friend*, 48.
86. Clarence Hawkes, *King of the Flying Sledge: The Biography of a Reindeer* (New York: Henry Holt, 1915), 10.
87. Clarence Hawkes, *Shaggycoat: The Biography of a Beaver* (Philadelphia, G. W. Jacobs, 1906), passim.
88. Hawkes, *Big Brother*, 12.
89. Hawkes, *Igloo Stories*, 45–46.
90. Clarence Hawkes, *Dapples of the Circus* (Boston: Lothrop, Lee & Shepard, 1923), 18–19.
91. Hawkes, *King of the Flying Sledge*, 19.
92. Ibid., 27–28.
93. Clarence Hawkes, *Wood and Water Friends* (New York: Thomas Y. Crowell, 1917), xii. Subsequent quotes in this paragraph are cited by page number in the text.
94. Hawkes, *Notes of Naturalist*, 77–78.
95. Clarence Hawkes, *Wanted a Mother* (Philadelphia: G. W. Jacobs, 1922), 250. Subsequent quotes are cited by page number in the text.
96. Eleanor sums up a century of worthy but abandoned children. The best-known waifs: Charles Dickens's Oliver Twist (1839), David Copperfield (1850), and Pip of *Great Expectations* (1861); Charlotte Bronte's Jane Eyre (1847), Wilkie Collins's Madonna Grice of *Hide and Seek* (1854), George Eliot's Esther Lyon of *Felix Holt, the Radical* (1866), and Ouida's Musa of *In Maremma* (1882).
97. The cold language and three characters may owe something to two popular works by the Brownings that Hawkes probably knew. In 1864 Elizabeth Barrett Browning told of another unloved charge, Aurora Leigh, who, after her parents die in Italy, must return to England as the ward of her father's hostile sister. Although the aunt had loved her brother,

she hated the Tuscan mother and thus dislikes Aurora: "She stood upon the steps to welcome me, / Calm, in black garb. I clung about her neck,— / Young babes, who catch at every shred of wool."

98. Robert Browning, "Pippa Passes. A Drama," in *Bells and Pomegranates* (1841); quoted in Hawkes, *The Service Man's Friend*, 19.
99. The sunshine phrase now seems mawkish, but in its day American ears probably accepted it without criticism. "Aura Lee," the tender love ballad composed by W. W. Fosdick and sung by Union soldiers since 1861, has these lines: "Yet if thy blue eyes I see, / Gloom will soon depart; / For to me, sweet Aura Lee / Is sunshine through the heart." The popular radio program *Vic and Sade*, which from 1932 until 1947 chronicled with affection and humor the trivial events of small-town life in Illinois, mentioned the well-known phrase with a hint of parody. Once husband Vic returned home in a "jolly" mood. He explains to his wife that a reporter from their local newspaper asked about his trip "down South" to Kentucky, Indiana, and Ohio, so Vic handed in fifteen pages of description. "I feel good," he boasts, "because my soul is a buttercup which has caught the liquid sunshine in its golden chalice" ("Vic's Geographical Trip," 1939).
100. Hawkes, *Dr. Thinkright*, 15. Subsequent quotes are cited by page number in the text.
101. Clarence Hawkes, *The Master of Millshaven* (Boston: Chapman & Grimes, 1936).
102. Clarence Hawkes, *Uncle Billy, the Curious Cobbler* (Boston: Chapman & Grimes, 1939), 15. Subsequent quotes are cited by page number in the text.
103. *University Library of Autobiography, including All the Great Autobiographies and the Autobiographical Data Left by the World's Famous Men and Women*, vol. 15 (n.p.: National Alumni, 1927), 345–53.
104. "A Son of Goshen," *Daily Hampshire Gazette*, 9 July 1931, 8.
105 . "Clarence Hawkes Honored," *Daily Hampshire Gazette*, 25 July 1936, 8; "Clarence Hawkes Given Three Degrees by the Knights of Pythias," *Daily Hampshire Gazette*, 14 December 1937, 6; "Clarence Hawkes Made an Honorary Member of the Northampton Lions Club," *Daily Hampshire Gazette*, 10 February 1937, 12.

14

To the list of prominent citizens who once called Hadley home one must also add Roger Sessions, one of the premier composers of the twentieth century. In this essay, musicologist Andrea Olmstead traces the outlines of Sessions's long career and begins to suggest ways in which the choices he made musically reflect his unique sense of his family's illustrious history in the region.

Most Hadley residents today know more about Sessions's ancestors than about Sessions himself, largely because the family is so prominently represented, not only by the c. 1713 Porter House (the oldest extant house in town, near the center of the town common), but also the Porter-Phelps-Huntington House, a museum founded by James Lincoln Huntington in the mid-twentieth century. Like most historic house museums, the latter site tends to emphasize earlier eras over later ones, and most visitors leave having learned much about the first generations to occupy the site, and less about the house's years as a summer retreat and its transformation from family dwelling to house museum. But those decades, too, were both crucial and fascinating. To be sure, as historian Bruce Laurie points out in his book Beyond Garrison: Antislavery and Social Reform, *the Huntington family was deeply enmeshed in a wide range of reform movements of the nineteenth century—social justice activism that was grounded in an alive and acute sense of social responsibility. In the first half of the nineteenth century in particular, Huntingtons were among Hadley's most prominent citizens, but they were also influential in far larger circles. Frederic Dan Huntington (1819–1904)—the grandson of Elizabeth Porter Phelps, whose gift of silver to the First Church is the subject of Karen Parsons's essay in this volume—was born and died in Hadley, but is best known as an Episcopal bishop in New York State. His daughter Arria Huntington (1848–1921), who also lived most of life in New York State, advocated on behalf of homeless women and women in prison; she also spearheaded efforts to pass New York's first child labor laws. Catharine Huntington (Arria's niece and Roger's cousin) was a well-known actress and prominent activist. Among the documents of the Porter-Phelps-Huntington family on deposit at Amherst College is the eloquent and moving appeal she made when she was arrested for protesting the execution of anarchists Sacco and Vanzetti. "I am an American citizen by inheritance," she wrote. "The name of my family appears on the Declaration of Independence. When the liberties which my ancestors established are endangered as they have been in Boston during these recent horrible weeks, I consider it my particular duty to protest."*

This entwined sense of inheritance and obligation influenced many members of this large family, and it is the backdrop against which Roger Sessions must be understood.

As American music in the early twentieth century rediscovered its roots, Sessions—always confident of his own patrimony—pursued other avenues of artistic exploration and expression. The results include some of the most impressive achievements in twentieth-century sound.

"Like one of the trees"

Roger Sessions and Hadley

Andrea Olmstead

Driving along the Connecticut River on Route 47 in Hadley, one is led by signs to a local historic site, the Porter-Phelps-Huntington House Museum, also known as Forty Acres. During the summer months, visitors can take a guided tour of the house, built in 1752, and the possessions of six generations of families who lived there. With its antique furniture and portraits of ancestors who entered the clergy, taught at Harvard, or fought in the Revolution, the house radiates continuity with the past. One of its best known former residents, the Reverend Frederic Dan Huntington, the Episcopalian bishop of central New York, had a daughter named Ruth who grew up and met her future husband—her second cousin, Archibald Sessions—at Forty Acres. Their son Roger (1896–1985) would become one of the foremost composers of the twentieth century, and the house and the heritage it represents are notable for both their presence and their absence in his work.

Sessions said of his ancestral home: "Forty Acres is haunted, you know. Very strange things have happened there. There's even a secret passage. I love it very much, and I feel like one of the trees there."[1] It is "a wonderful old place, a beautiful place," he mused, "but these things can have various implications. I'm very attached to it myself, in a way, but I have a kind of horror of it, too."[2] The house and the family behind it would shape Sessions in ways both great and small. In part because of his family's New England tradition and preoccupation with ancestry, Sessions did not feel it necessary to prove himself "American" in style, as did such contemporaries as the Brooklyn-born composer Aaron Copland, whose works, including *Appalachian Spring, Lincoln Portrait*, and *Fanfare for the Common Man*, helped define America musically. Sessions said: "I come from an old family and that is *undoubtedly* part of my life, because I realized that with that background I always had a basic sense of social security; I mean a security in American society. Anything I did and put my whole self into must have something American about it. I don't believe in being self-conscious about these things; then the music becomes essentially contrived."[3] Sessions was conflicted about his heritage: on the one hand, he took pride in it, but on the other, he was deeply suspicious of the excessive nationalism that at times suffused American culture and society in the first half of the twentieth century.

Roger Sessions's reputation today rests on his nine symphonies, three piano sonatas, four concertos, two quartets and a string quintet, two operas, and four orchestral works with voices.[4] Among modernist American composers he rivals Charles Ives, Aaron Copland, and Elliott Carter in stature, and his influence as a teacher compares favorably with that of Arnold Schoenberg, Paul Hindemith, and Nadia Boulanger. The times in which Sessions lived produced many extraordinary composers: Béla Bartók, Edgard Varèse, Paul Hindemith, Carter, and John Cage, to name only a few. Among Sessions's most immediate American contemporaries, the composers whose music can appropriately be compared with his are Virgil Thomson (born in the same year, 1896; died in 1989), Aaron Copland (1900–1990), Elliott Carter (b. 1908), and Samuel Barber (1910–1981). Sessions avoided the extreme simplicity of Thomson, the homespun quality of Copland, and the carefully wrought rhythmic schemes of Carter; he was closer to the voice-dominated and text-tied music of Barber. Sessions's own "style" (he would have objected to the term) relies on independent contrapuntal lines weaving a dense web of voices that moves over a fast underlying pulse, all brilliantly and colorfully orchestrated. The music is dissonant, yet melodic, long-breathed, yet quick-pulsed, and follows a logical and often traditional formal scheme. His achievement was acknowledged in the many honors bestowed on him, including election to the American Academy of Arts and Letters (1953) and the American Academy of Arts and Sciences (1961), the Brandeis Creative Arts Award (1958), the Gold Medal of the American Academy of Arts and Letters (1961), and a MacDowell Medal (1968). He received fourteen honorary doctorates. Perhaps most significantly, he was awarded the Pulitzer Prize not once but twice: a career award in 1974 and another for his Concerto for Orchestra in 1982.

Recognized as the leading American symphonist of the twentieth century, Sessions is considered one of the primary representatives of high modernism. He was also widely known as a teacher. In both his teaching and his writing he upheld high ideals, stressing craftsmanship and, by example, integrity of purpose. During the course of a fifty-six-year teaching career, Sessions profoundly influenced many important students, most notably Milton Babbitt.[5] He also wrote several influential books. Observing that much "nonsense has been written about music," he cautiously offered two eminently reasonable texts. His six 1949 Juilliard lectures were published as *The Musical Experience of Composer, Performer, Listener*, which his family called the "fascinating little book," after a reviewer's description.[6] In 1968/69 Sessions delivered the Charles Eliot Norton Lectures at Harvard, and these resulted in another book, *Questions about Music*, also refreshingly free of technical jargon.[7] *Roger Sessions on Music: Collected Essays* contains articles written over a forty-year period.[8] He called *Harmonic Practice* "that goddamn book" because writing it took time away from composition; it is widely used as a theory textbook.[9]

In the length of his creative life and the pattern of his compositional career Sessions is highly unusual in music history. His compositional life spanned seventy-five years, encompassing most of the twentieth century: his first piece was composed in 1910, and he was still writing near his death in 1985. This longevity can be rivaled only by Heinrich Schütz, Richard Strauss, Igor Stravinsky, and Elliott Carter. Few composers have experienced the acceleration of output the late-blooming Sessions enjoyed. Remarkably, the bulk of his forty-two works were written after 1950, when he was fifty-four. His most productive period was between the ages of sixty and eighty-five, the year he won the second Pulitzer Prize.

Although long revered by students, musicians, and other composers, Sessions has not yet been accepted by the public. This is in part because his music was, to quote Alfredo Casella, "born difficult." Recordings were slow in coming: not until 1996 were all nine symphonies available, while of the ten vocal works and operas only one (*When Lilacs Last in the Dooryard Bloom'd*) is commercially recorded. His lofty personality, New England upbringing, and idealism would not allow him to engineer—much less pay for—performances or recordings. Sessions, who was strongly influenced by Romain Rolland's novel *Jean-Christophe* (it won the Nobel Prize in 1915), also felt it was usual for genius to be ignored, and his passivity doubtless hindered his career.

Roger Huntington Sessions was born in Brooklyn, New York, on December 28, 1896, the third of Ruth and Archibald Sessions's four children. (Although for most of his life he used Huntington, his mother's maiden name, as his middle name, after her death he dropped it.)[10] Ruth left Archibald in 1900, when Sessions was three, a circumstance he said "didn't simplify life for [us] children."[11] Ruth had already been bringing the children with her from Brooklyn to Phelps Farm every summer, and now her mother, Hannah Sargent Huntington, bought her the Henshaw house at 109 Elm Street in Northampton. For twenty years she ran it as a Smith College dormitory; it is still known as Sessions House. Sessions lived there, with sojourns at boarding schools and college and more summers at Phelps Farm, until the fall of 1921.

Both parents had musical backgrounds. Ruth had studied piano at the Leipzig Conservatory in the early 1880s, and Archibald sang in Theodore Thomas's chorus in New York. Nevertheless, in 1910 they were doubtless amazed to be told by their resolute thirteen-year-old, home from the Kent School (a boarding school in Connecticut), that he had already written an opera and was determined to become a composer. Archibald actively supported Roger's ambitions. Sessions entered Harvard at fourteen and graduated with a bachelor of arts degree in 1915. He received a bachelor of music degree from Yale (1917), where he studied with Horatio Parker. His most influential composition teacher was Ernest Bloch, whom Sessions sought out in New York in 1919. Sessions taught at Smith College from 1917 to 1921, when he became Bloch's assistant at the Cleveland Institute of Music (a position he held until 1925). In 1920 he married a Smith student, Barbara Foster (1899–1980).

Sessions returned to Hadley from Cleveland in June 1923 when he conducted his first important piece, *The Black Maskers* Incidental Music, based on a play by the ultramodern Russian Symbolist playwright Leonid Andreyeff. It was produced at Smith College and directed by Samuel Eliot Jr. Sessions worked on the music from February 11, 1923, through the day of the dress rehearsal, June 9. He and Yale musician Carl Buchman stayed at Forty Acres and Phelps House. Although the entire work took four months to compose, Romualdo's Song was written in one night at Forty Acres and the Dirge in a single day.[12] Sessions wrote three numbers at Forty Acres, and Buchman copied out the orchestral parts. Worried about the number of musicians, Sessions wrote his wife, Barbara, "Oh—will you call up Aaron [Copland] on Tuesday or Wednesday + ask him whether he has heard from Miss Kidder and wire me if he has? Bixler can't come— + so that leaves us very short on cellos. He promised to write to Miss Kidder yesterday."[13] Next to arrive was Barbara, who quickly summed up the situation—they would not finish in time for the performance—and sent out "an S.O.S. call to New Haven for Quincy [Porter]." Porter joined Sessions the day before the final rehearsal, and he brought along Hope LeRoy Baumgartner, a Yale instructor. The four worked on the parts, which were finished "in the nick of time."

Rehearsals were prepared by Smith faculty member Crucita Moore, and Leland Hall trained the student performers; the orchestra included a number of other faculty members as well as Porter. An overture written by Miriam Stevenson (class of 1923) was performed for the production. Eliot, the director, remembered, "The expense was so great (each torch had to have its own dimmer, operated by someone who could watch when a B[lack] M[asker] put it out and a servant relighted it) that the class of '23 was in debt for quite a while."[14]

The production took place June 14–16, 1923. Because Smith College had no place to stage dramatics, it was held at the downtown Academy of Music, "so named because in 1892–93, when it was built, many descendants of Jonathan Edwards's parishioners were still leery of the word Theater."[15] The production involved 115 students, all seniors, plus an orchestra of 40 players. The kettle-drum player, Katharine Abbot Wilder, would later recall the chemical smoke from the burning castle coming backstage during rehearsals. (During the performance the orchestra sat under the set, stage right. The smoke was just as bad there.) She was nervous about keeping the drums in tune amid such modern sounds, but the composer/conductor told her it would not be too bad if the drums were a bit off. Fifty years later, she recalled the thrill of hearing the composer say, "Well done." Whenever a major orchestra did the *Black Maskers* Suite, Wilder took pride that she had played in the premiere.[16] Caroline (Bedell) Thomas, a cellist, recalled that at first she hated the wild modern music, and would rush to Music Hall and play Bach to wash it out. As rehearsals progressed, she grew to appreciate the challenging music.[17]

Sessions wrote in the Forty Acres diary that "the [first] performance was by all odds the least [good] of the three, and quite unsatisfactory in many ways. The music was so placed as not to be well heard, the orchestra players missed various cues, and the play ended before the conflagration music was half finished." "The Saturday performance," he noted, "was by far the best of the three. The orchestra missed fewer cues; Sam Eliot arranged matters so that the prelude to Scene IV, in some ways my favorite number of the nine, was better heard; and the conflagration music came out at such a tempo that for the first time it was heard in its entirety. Barbara and I stayed for the banquet afterwards, and were driven home by two of the Black Maskers."[18]

The production attracted a number of Sessions's friends to Forty Acres. On Wednesday the Swiss couple Jean and Denise Binet, his colleagues from the Cleveland Institute of Music, had their first glimpse of the New England countryside, and they were shown all the details and told all the stories about Forty Acres and Phelps Farm. On Thursday, the day of the first performance, "the Misses White of Heath, not to mention 'Uncle Archie' [Sessions's father]" came to Phelps Farm. More guests arrived the next day, including Sessions's former teacher, Ernest Bloch, the director of the Cleveland Institute. The group visited the hilltop cabin where two of Sessions's aunts, Arria and Molly, lived and signed their guestbook: under the column for residence Bloch put "Somewhere on the Planet Earth"; under "remarks" Binet copied Bloch, writing "(married too)."[19] Barbara Foster's family, Sessions's in-laws, joined the group, sister Eleanor having arrived via motorcycle. Bloch's friend from Cleveland, Isabel Swift, also came. A party was held for all the guests in the north parlor of Phelps House.

Supper was a picnic near Phelps Farm; the evening entertainment was held in the Long Room at Forty Acres, with Bloch giving "a graphic account of the various intrigues attending the [1910] performances of *Macbeth* in Paris." After some of the guests, including Bloch and Isabel Swift, had gone, the remaining party "vegetated, slept, talked of Harvard (a great descent from earlier conversations!), and felt a pleasant sense of relaxation." Sessions departed for the Cleveland Institute's summer school, cousin Catharine Huntington, herself a noted actress, left for Provincetown, and Barbara went to her hometown, Claremont, New Hampshire. Sessions concluded his diary entry: "This is not the place, exactly, to speak of the decisive experience which this has been for myself. But no setting could have been more perfect for a decisive experience of any kind."[20]

FIGURE 14.1. *Roger Sessions in the 1920s. Courtesy of the Irving S. Gilmore Music Library, Yale University.*

Roger and Barbara moved to Europe in 1925 and remained there until 1933, supported by two Guggenheim Fellowships (in Paris and Florence), a three-year Rome Prize, and a Carnegie grant (in Berlin). Thus Sessions had a front-row seat to observe the rise of fascism in both Italy and Germany, experiences that sharpened his left-leaning political sensibilities. For example, in August 1927 a Boston newspaper reported that Sessions (perhaps motivated in part by Bloch and by Catharine, who was deeply engaged in the protest movement) was the only American abroad to write to Massachusetts governor A. T. Fuller about his refusal to pardon Sacco and Vanzetti. The cable read: "AS MASSACHUSETTS CITIZEN MUST PROTEST ENERGETICALLY SACCO-VANZETTI EXECUTION. ONLY CLEMENCY CAN REDEEM YOU AND MASSACHUSETTS IN EYES OF POSTERITY."[21]

During the years 1928 to 1931 his close friend Aaron Copland—by this time a rising star in the musical world—gave three seasons of Copland-Sessions Concerts in New York, Paris, and London. The series presented music solely by the younger generation of Americans and Europeans, including works by both Copland and Sessions. Since he was living in Europe, Sessions participated very little; Copland did most of the organizing. These concerts helped establish both composers in the public's mind.

Already fluent in French, German, and Italian, Sessions learned Russian during this period, writing to Igor Stravinsky, Nicolas Slonimsky, and Serge Koussevitzky in their own language. He also befriended a number of Europeans who later came to the United States: Ernst Krenek, Artur Schnabel, Otto Klemperer, Darius Milhaud, and Arnold Schoenberg. One of his closest relationships in the 1960s was with Luigi Dallapiccola, the most important Italian composer of the mid-twentieth century. In the 1930s Sessions was sometimes viewed in this country more as a European composer than an American.

After the couple's return from Europe, Sessions divorced Barbara in 1936 in order to marry Elizabeth Franck (1906–1982), whom he had met while teaching summer school at the University of California at Berkeley in 1935. They had two children, John (b. 1938), who made his home in Northampton, and Elizabeth (b. 1940), of Santa Fe. Sessions's twenty-three-year teaching career at Princeton had begun in 1935. He taught at the University of California at Berkeley from 1945 to 1953, when he returned to Princeton, where he remained until he was retired in 1965. Appointed Bloch Professor at Berkeley, 1966–67, he also gave the Charles Eliot Norton lectures at Harvard in 1968–69. He accepted a post at the Juilliard School of Music in 1965, and taught there until 1983.

Excluding juvenilia, Sessions's forty-two pieces can be divided into five creative periods, delineated sometimes by his moves within the United States and often by large, frequently vocal, works. Nothing from the juvenilia or his work with Horatio Parker at Yale or Bloch in New York is published except the suite version (1928) of the 1923 *The Black Maskers* incidental music. This somewhat expressionistic work, written under the sway of Stravinsky's influence, remains the composer's best-known piece.

The first period of Sessions's career—the years between 1924 and 1935, when he and Barbara were living mainly in Europe—was relatively unproductive. Only three large works were written in this period: the First Symphony (1927), the Piano Sonata (1930), and the Violin Concerto (1935). The Concerto took eight years to complete and marked a turning point. Its technical difficulty, seen as insurmountable by the debut performer slated to premiere it, gave the Concerto an unwarranted reputation as unplayable that temporarily damaged Sessions's career. Sessions's habit of procrastination and his slow pace of composition frustrated his early supporters, including Copland and Serge Koussevitzky. Koussevitzky presented the premiere of the First Symphony with the Boston Symphony Orchestra in 1927, the only Sessions performance the influential conductor ever gave. The tonal First Symphony could be called Neoclassical, and it also shows Stravinsky's influence. Sessions's own stylistic traits, however, are clearly in evidence: long phrases, dense polyphonic accompaniments, dissonance, colorful orchestration, and highly contrapuntal and rhythmically complex textures.

Important pieces from the time following his return to the United States and remarriage include the String Quartet No. 1 (1936), the Duo for Violin and Piano (1942), and the Second Symphony and Second Piano Sonata (both 1946). The largest and most impressive work of the period is his one-act, thirteen-scene opera based on Hoffman Reynolds Hays's translation of Bertolt Brecht's first-class radio play, *The Trial of Lucullus* (1947), an antiwar story about the Roman general.[22]

The Trial of Lucullus launched the next period of Sessions's career, years that would culminate in his magnum opus, *Montezuma* (1963). The story, Sessions felt, was similar to that of *The Trial of Lucullus*: both illustrate the "futility of conquest." Both can be viewed as Sessions's political commentary on war, including the Cold War. During the 1950s Sessions worked on other major pieces, but he kept returning to the Sicilian Antonio Borgese's libretto about Mexico's conquest. After Borgese's death in 1952, Sessions reduced it from four acts to three. The composition of *Montezuma* took twenty-eight years to complete, including and underlining this entire third creative period. A large, colorful orchestra dominates the opera, whose music is the composer's most passionate. The two most memorable moments—the meeting of Cortez and Montezuma and the human sacrifice—are relayed in tableaux, the stage picture and the lush, vivid music entirely responsible for their effect. As an opera composer and in his works for the voice, Sessions was Verdian rather than Wagnerian, in that the voice is always paramount despite the almost Wagnerian orchestration. Premiered in 1964 in Berlin and sung in German, *Montezuma* was not given an American premiere until 1976 by the Opera Company of Boston, or a New York premiere until 1982 at the Juilliard School.

At the beginning of the 1950s, Sessions partially adopted the twelve-tone method (Arnold Schoenberg's method of composing with twelve notes related only one to another) in part inspired by a growing friendship with Schoenberg. Unlike Schoenberg, however, Sessions used six-note scales with an added tone. This adoption came a few years after the death of his domineering mother, who had been quite critical of Sessions and his siblings. Ruth's criticism had made Sessions so self-conscious that for a long time he was inhibited from writing much music. Her death in 1946 seemed to free him compositionally: his productivity increased, as noted above. He continually downplayed the twelve-tone method, however; he never wrote about it and once remarked, "The music is God; the twelve-tone system is just a parish priest."[23]

His String Quartet No. 2 (1951) inclined toward twelve-tone methods, and in the next work, the Sonata for Violin (1953), Sessions unconsciously incorporated some of them. The large-scale *Idyll of Theocritus* for soprano and orchestra (1954), however, demonstrated that Sessions's twelve-tone approach was not as rigid as that employed by Dallapiccola, to whom the work is dedicated, or as Schoenberg's. The *Idyll* uses two refrains and graphic musical climaxes to tell its love story. The Piano Concerto (1955), Third Symphony (1957), String Quintet (1958), Fourth Symphony (1958), and Divertimento for Orchestra (1960) flowed from Sessions's pen in what was for him rapid succession, and each met with critical success.

After *Montezuma* came Sessions's fourth and most prolific period. He produced *Psalm 140* for soprano and orchestra (1963), Symphony No. 5 (1964), the Third Piano Sonata (1965), the Sixth (1966), Seventh (1967), and Eighth (1968) symphonies, and a Rhapsody for Orchestra (1970). The latter three symphonies might be viewed as a trilogy dealing with Sessions's reactions to the Vietnam War—anger and, finally, resignation, among others. Sessions himself thought of them this way.[24]

Again a large vocal work delineated the beginning of a new era in Sessions's music. His last decade of composition was inaugurated by what admirers regard as his masterpiece, the cantata *When Lilacs Last in the Dooryard Bloom'd* (1970). During this period Sessions also wrote a Double Concerto, for violin and cello (1971), a Concertino for Chamber Orchestra (1972), Three Choruses on Biblical

Texts, with orchestra (1972), Symphony No. 9 (1978), and the Concerto for Orchestra (1981). The pace of composition had slowed. Nevertheless, at age eighty, Sessions optimistically began a third opera, *The Emperor's New Clothes*, to a libretto by Andrew Porter. Though left incomplete, it would have been a comedy that paralleled *Falstaff*, the opera of another octogenarian, Giuseppe Verdi.

Despite Sessions's deep immersion in international music circles, his personal sense of "social security" was grounded in his family's heritage and the constant presence of Forty Acres and Phelps Farm. He expressed his attachment to Forty Acres by comparing himself to a tree there, and this analogy was more than metaphorical. Strength, consistency, and assuredness are reflected in his person and his music. A student described Sessions at a festival at Oberlin College in 1961: "Sessions always seems to remain his own calm, quietly amused, integral self. His manner does not change from living room to seminar room to cafeteria to conductor's podium to speaker's rostrum in front of an audience of 2000. Thus, in his quiet way he was boring, informative, infuriating, lovable, cerebral, incompetent, inspiring, brilliant—we didn't know what to make of him."[25]

In a conversation in the 1970s, when Sessions was seventy-seven, he described Forty Acres and his background in a story that suggests how the composer thought about his family's heritage:

> We have an old, old family house in Hadley, Massachusetts, right on the Connecticut River. It's a wonderful old house. One of my ancestors was one of the founders of Hadley. In 1752 Moses Porter decided it was safe to build a house outside the town stockade. Sometimes [the town] was subject to attack by the Indians, even by the French from Canada. Porter was a captain in the [colonial militia].
>
> I remember my grandfather [Frederic Dan Huntington]. He died when I was seven. He became bishop of Central New York. First he was a Unitarian minister. He became a professor of Christian [Morals] at Harvard. Then he got bored, so to speak, with the Unitarian church, and joined the Episcopal church and became a minister in Boston, and then became bishop of Central New York. . . .
>
> He married a wonderful lady from Boston [Hannah Sargent]. I always told people I had a grandmother complex. She was descended from a man who was a general in the revolutionary war [Major General Benjamin Lincoln, her great-grandfather, who was Washington's secretary of war.][26]

In this straightforward account, Sessions mentions the elements people usually note about their family's history—its longevity, the presence of prominent citizens on the family tree, and the people he remembered best. More telling, perhaps, is an anecdote that Sessions liked to tell about his ancestry. It literally began with the novelist's opening cliché: It was a dark and stormy night. A letter from Sessions to a friend and a diary kept by two of the other participants reveal why this particular night during the years of World War I was so memorable. At 4 P.M. on August 9, 1917, violinist Quincy Porter and pianist Bruce Simonds gave one of their series of concerts of French and Belgian music at Amherst College. These concerts were to raise money for the Red Cross; at a dollar a ticket they made $91.38 that evening.[27] Afterwards, twenty-year-old Sessions and the two performers had a "wild time" at a dinner and musicale at the home of Martha Dickinson Bianchi, Emily Dickinson's niece, who lived in The Evergreens, Austin Dickinson's house, next to the Dickinson homestead. Around 11:00 P.M. they "tore [them]selves away" from Amherst to leave for Forty Acres and Phelps House. Sessions drove a cart pulled by the family horse, Rex, with only one seat to accommodate "the three geniuses."[28] The skittish horse preferred to walk downhill and proceeded at a snail's pace.

Rex also disliked thunderstorms, which soon enveloped the trio. "Drove by ghostly barns," Porter wrote, "illuminated by flashes of lightening.—Strange flowing sound in the distance—nearer and nearer—covered up violin case by putting it in the bottom of the buggy and stretching feet over it."[29] They then "drove furiously over the narrow road, boughs swishing past our faces; pitch blackness, except for the dim lantern on the buggy." Sessions, who could not see with water streaming over his glasses, "disappeared into the darkness with the violin" to leave it for the night at the cabin his maiden aunts—Arria and Molly Huntington—occupied at the top of Huntington Road, "lonely and surrounded by woods." Sessions's older sister, Hannah, answered the door. The aunts insisted on entertaining them—it was by now midnight—so the trio tied up Rex and, soaked to the skin, "plunged through a tunnel of sopped bushes" (they were wearing summer concert attire and white pants) and reached the bungalow, which had no running water or electricity. The "storm raged outside in picturesque confusion, and we stood and dripped until dry enough to sit down."[30] All three signed the aunts' guestbook: Simonds gave the date with time (12m[idnight]—1a.m.), and wrote in the "remarks" column, "Macbeth Act I, Sc. I," and Sessions noted "Après moi, le deluge." Porter wrote "Noah's Ark"; six years later, when he returned during the *Black Maskers* production, he commented, "Better weather this time."[31]

Hannah Sessions got dressed and talked with them, but Arria, in nightclothes, conversed "from behind a screen [which was only proper for a Victorian lady] on the subject of genealogy."[32] Arria had been born in 1848 and Molly in 1862, and the older aunt had written a book about her family history.[33] The conversation between Quincy Porter and this "1848 aunt" concerned whether their common ancestor was Hezekiah Porter, six generations back, or Eleazar Porter, five generations back. They concluded that the relative was Eleazar, and therefore that the two musicians were fifth, rather than sixth, cousins.

The three men decided to venture forth at 1:00 A.M. They led Rex through the mud, but a blinding flash sent them dashing for cover in a nearby shed, where they stayed for twenty minutes. They started once again, Sessions "having discarded coat and necktie and clad in shirt, white flannels, best low shoes, and straw hat, leading the horse, Quincy similarly clad carrying the lantern, and Bruce sitting in the wagon, and all three of us singing at the top of our lungs like larks—of the genus *polonius bacchanalis*."[34] "Oceans of mud, and no cessation in the torrent. Steep down-hill," Porter recalled. They discovered one of the workhorses loose, seeking shelter from the rain by the barn door of Forty Acres.[35] "Sharp lightening and thunder, put in at a shed after flash which dazzled us for three seconds, giving us splendid after-images." They arrived at Phelps Farm at about 1:40. "R[oger] bade B[ruce] go into the house and assure the family that we were alive, saying 'Hello' reassuringly as he opened the door: which B. did, but found the lower house deserted, and only after climbing the stairs, heard Mrs. S. say drowsily 'Roge, is that you?' Anticlimax. John appeared in pajamas. No one had worried, thought of us in Amherst."[36] Sessions's mother, Ruth, and his younger brother, John, also wanted to hear their exploits, which were recounted. The three finally got to bed around 3:00 A.M.

Sessions liked to relate this anecdote (much abridged from its presentation here and minus both Mme. Bianchi and the weather conditions) in part because his aunt's late-night discourse on genealogy demonstrated what he saw as snobbish behavior that made him ambivalent about his heritage. "So I mean, this is a dangerous subject, that's all," Sessions remarked later.[37] "That kind of snobbish interest in family ancestors," he insisted, "is oppressive, stifling, and dreadful. There's an awful lot of Huntington family pride in [his cousin James Lincoln Huntington's book *Forty Acres*], and that always bored me very much."[38] This conflict may have caused his "kind of horror" of his ancestral home. While influenced by his liberal relatives politically, he also was thoroughly rebellious. He took comfort in his sense of Americanness bestowed by such a family, but he disliked the nativism or nationalism that conversations like Arria's might imply.

Given his vocal disdain for pedigrees that can too easily slip toward prejudice, it is ironic that Sessions was viewed by critics as a Puritan New Englander. "I've run across that in my career, because my music was supposed to be very New England and so forth and austere. Of course, it's just the opposite. I don't think anybody who has ever known me has thought I was conspicuously austere."[39] While those who knew Sessions would agree that as a person he was not especially austere, one can still understand, from listening to much of the music, the view that it is harsh and strict and speaks with an Old Testament fervor. The Three Choruses on Biblical Texts is a good example. The work was commissioned by Amherst College in commemoration of the sesquicentennial anniversary of its founding; Sessions chose the text.[40]

In the 1930s and 1940s, Sessions, who did not believe in cultivating "Americanism" in music any more than in society, culture, or politics, found himself at odds with his colleague Aaron Copland. As a second-generation American, Copland reflected in his music an enthusiastic and self-conscious use of distinctive American styles that Sessions never embraced. Early in his career Copland was influenced by American jazz, and later by traditional forms such as folk music and hymns. Unlike Copland, Sessions avoided both programmatic pieces (*Billy the Kid*, *Rodeo*) and a consciously sought American flavor in his melodies.

Sessions's Americanness showed, however, in more subtle ways. For instance, his masterful *When Lilacs Last in the Dooryard Bloom'd*, scored for soprano, contralto, and baritone soloists, mixed chorus, and orchestra, dedicated to the memory of Martin Luther King Jr. and Robert F. Kennedy (who were both assassinated while Sessions was working on the piece), was based on Walt Whitman's poem on the death of Abraham Lincoln (who, like King, was killed in April, when lilacs are in blossom). The lines Sessions chose as his text were

> When lilacs last in the door-yard bloom'd,
> And the great star early droop'd in the western sky in the night,
> I mourn'd—and yet shall mourn with ever-returning spring.
>
> O ever-returning spring! trinity sure to me you bring;
> Lilac blooming perennial, and drooping star in the west,
> And thought of him I love.

These verses, together with the dedication, honored simultaneously four great figures in American history: Lincoln, Whitman, King, and Kennedy. Indeed, many of Sessions's works, especially symphonies, can be seen as memorials to the dead. That Sessions was influenced by American political figures can be seen in other dedications as well. His 1946 Symphony No. 2 was dedicated to Franklin D. Roosevelt, and the third movement of the 1965 Third Piano Sonata was dedicated to the memory of John F. Kennedy. Again, both presidents had died during the composition of these works.

Sessions could wear his heritage lightly; he had nothing to prove about his

"Americanness." "Anything I did and put my whole self into must have something American about it," he would later observe. His family's liberal politics did shape him, but a conservative thread also ran through the family, giving him something to react against: his aunts clearly took pride in their ancestry, and his father and siblings became Republicans, as opposed to Sessions's Democratic (even Socialist) leanings. That he had come from an old family, with such visible remnants as Forty Acres to remind him of it, provided Sessions with a sense of stability. Feeling "like one of the trees," he was rooted in Hadley and could afford to adopt an "internationalist" mantle. In a century dominated by two seemingly opposed factions—those of Stravinsky and Schoenberg—Sessions transcended the zeitgeist by absorbing the lessons of each camp (while remaining on lifelong friendly terms with each of its protagonists) and sticking faithfully to his own direction. By identifying with the long line of European composers while maintaining an internal sense of national identity, Sessions merged the two.

When Sessions died, on March 16, 1985, his daughter-in-law Giovina Sessions and his niece Jane Ann Byrne had a bronze plaque made, and in the summer of 1985 the two of them buried Sessions's ashes in his ancestor's graveyard, the Old Hadley Cemetery. The plaque would have given Sessions two reasons to quibble. First, though Sessions had long before stopped using the middle name he was given at baptism, Huntington, his family restored the initial H on his headstone, reasserting his place in the family history. Second, when they sought to establish his birth date, the two consulted an untrustworthy source: Ruth Sessions's autobiography.[41] There Ruth gave as December 27, 1896, as the date of Session's birth, instead of the correct date, the 28th. Their last decision, however, seems supremely appropriate—the addition of the single word "Composer."[42]

A personality such as Sessions's, committed to high artistic achievement, could not accommodate public taste or prevailing musical fashion if they contradicted his inner dictates. His uncompromising approach to composition and allegiance to the highest ideals account for the caliber of his intensely individual music. Continually subjected to criticism that his music was too hard to play, ultimately Sessions found that both the capabilities of performers and the willingness of audiences to accept difficult works had caught up with him. He had to wait patiently for years, in some cases decades, for his music to receive accurate performances and recognition, but he remained undaunted. Success to him meant only achieving his ideals, not attaining household recognition.

Like Bach, Mahler, Schubert, and many other composers, Sessions did not live to see his music universally prized. Fortunately, he possessed the endurance, the patience, and the hard-earned self-confidence to believe in the future and recognize that his music would endure for generations to come. After his death, the *New Yorker*'s music critic, Andrew Porter, wrote of him, "For music, he embodied what is finest in American thought, character, and genius. In nine symphonies, in concertos, two operas, and many other works, he gave it utterance. He was one of the country's—and the world's—great men."[43]

Notes

Much of the material presented here is drawn from my book *Roger Sessions: A Biography* (New York: Routledge, 2008).

1. Andrea Olmstead, *Conversations with Roger Sessions* (Boston: Northeastern University Press, 1987), 150. Architectural historians have found no secret passageway at the site; perhaps Sessions confused the secret passage at Sessions House in Northampton, where he grew up, with Forty Acres.
2. Roger Sessions, interview by Frank Rounds, 13 March 1962, Columbia University Oral History Collection, 8.
3. Roger Sessions, interview by author, 12 April 1975, New York.
4. Although he is considered primarily a symphonic composer, Sessions may eventually be equally regarded for his vocal music; he wrote almost as much music for voices as for symphony orchestra. Several factors, including the fact that only one of his ten vocal works is commercially recorded, contribute to this somewhat lopsided appraisal of his output.
5. Sessions's other students include Edward T. Cone, Peter Maxwell Davies, Mark DeVoto, David Del Tredici, David Diamond, John Eaton, Lehman Engel, John Harbison, Vivian Fine, Miriam Gideon, Andrew Imbrie, Earl Kim, Leon Kirchner, Ursula Mamlok, Donald Martino, Conlon Nancarrow, Dika Newlin, Frederic Rzewski, Eric Salzman, Harold Schiffman, Paul Turok, Hugo Weisgall, and Ellen Taaffe Zwilich, as well as younger composers such as Larry Bell, Joel Feigin, Kenneth Frazelle, Tod Machover, and George Tsontakis.
6. Roger Sessions, *The Musical Experience of Composer, Performer, Listener* (Princeton: Princeton University Press, 1950; repr., New York: Atheneum, 1962).
7. Roger Sessions, *Questions about Music* (Cambridge, Mass.: Harvard University Press, 1970; repr., New York: W. W. Norton, 1971).
8. *Roger Sessions on Music: Collected Essays*, ed. Edward T. Cone (Princeton: Princeton University Press, 1979).
9. Roger Sessions, *Harmonic Practice* (New York: Harcourt, Brace & World, 1951).
10. Roger Huntington Sessions is the name listed on his baptismal certificate; on his birth certificate his middle name is given as Pitkin, a family name from a still earlier generation. At the baptism his aunt Arria, much to the surprise of Sessions's parents, renamed the baby Roger Huntington.
11. Andrea Olmstead, *Roger Sessions and His Music* (Ann Arbor, Mich.: UMI Research Press, 1985), 10.
12. Because Romualdo's Song was not altered for the subsequent Orchestral Suite, it is the earliest catalogued work by Sessions.
13. Roger Sessions to Barbara Sessions, "Sat 11.20, Batavia NY," June 1923, Roger Sessions Collection, box 1, Library of Congress (hereafter cited as Roger Sessions Collection).
14. Samuel Eliot Jr., letter to the author, 17 November 1978.

15. Ibid.
16. Katharine Abbot Wilder, "A Memorable Experience of My College Years," typescript, circa 1974, Smith College Archives, Northampton, Mass.
17. Letter from Caroline (Bedell) Thomas to Kathleen M. and Stephen L. O'Connor, 16 January 1989, Smith College Archives.
18. Sessions's entry, 19–20 June 1923, in James L. Huntington's Forty Acres guest diary, box 80B, p. 19, Porter-Phelps-Huntington Family Papers, owned by the Porter-Phelps-Huntington Foundation, on deposit at the Amherst College Archives and Special Collections, Amherst, Mass.
19. Guestbook, 16 June 1923, Roger Sessions Collection, box 4, folder 12.
20. Sessions's entry, 19–20 June 1923, in James L. Huntington's Forty Acres guest diary.
21. *Boston Evening Transcript*, 8 August 1927, cited in Andrea Olmstead, *The Correspondence of Roger Sessions* (Boston: Northeastern University Press, 1992), 85 n. 1.
22. Written unusually quickly for a student production at Berkeley, this effective, dramatic, and lyrical opera has been produced only three other times (at Princeton, Northwestern, and Juilliard). The opera is neither published nor recorded; copyright problems with the Brecht estate prevent one of Sessions's greatest works from being more widely disseminated.
23. Olmstead, *Conversations*, 38.
24. Ibid., 40.
25. Paul Alan Levi, "Roger Sessions: A Personal Account," unpublished paper, 1974, quoted in Andrea Olmstead, "Roger Sessions: A Personal Portrait," *Tempo* 127 (December 1978): 14.
26. Olmstead, *Conversations*, 149–50.
27. The concert program was Lekeu's G-major sonata, (L. Couperin-)Kreisler's violin arrangement, Magnard's *Movement lent—calme* (the second U.S. performance), Ravel's *Ondine*, d'Indy's *Laufenburg*, and the Franck A-major sonata.
28. Joint diary/scrapbook of the Red Cross tour kept by Quincy Porter and Bruce Simonds (Simonds writing in the third person), Porter Papers, mss 15, series IX, folder 31, 1, p. 127, Yale University Music Archives.
29. Porter-Simonds diary, 127.
30. Ibid., 127–28.
31. Guestbook, Roger Sessions Collection, box 4, folder 12.
32. Sessions to George Bartlett, 12 August 1917, in Sarah Chapin, ed., *The Tin Box Collection: Letters of Roger Sessions and His Family and Friends* (Concord, Mass.: privately printed, 1992), 150. The Porter-Simonds diary says it was a curtain (128).
33. Arria S. Huntington, *Under a Colonial Roof-tree: Fireside Chronicles of Early New England* (Boston: Houghton Mifflin, 1891).
34. Sessions to George Bartlett, 12 August 1917, Chapin, *Tin Box Collection*, 150.
35. The barn is now the Hadley Farm Museum in Hadley.
36. Porter-Simonds diary, 129.
37. Sessions, interview by Frank Rounds, 4.
38. James Lincoln Huntington, *Forty Acres: The Story of the Bishop Huntington House* (New York: Hastings House, 1949); Olmstead, *Conversations*, 55–56.
39. Olmstead, *Conversations*, 155–56.
40. Henry G. Mishin, Roger Sessions in *The Genesis of a Commission: Roger Sessions, Three Choruses on Biblical Texts* ([Amherst, Mass]: published by the Friends of Amherst College Music on the Occasion of the Amherst College Sesquicentennial Celebration, 1974).
41. Ruth Sessions, *Sixty-Odd: A Personal History* (Brattleboro, Vt.: Steven Daye Press, 1936).
42. His geographical placement in the cemetery is also accurate, seen chronologically. On the

left of his grave is the white marble cross marking his sister Mary's remains with her dates (December 15–27, 1891), and even closer, on the immediate right and with the same-sized bronze plaque, is his younger brother John's grave with his dates (1899–1948). Sessions's parents, Ruth and Archibald, also cremated, are both buried in the Old Hadley Cemetery near these graves; oddly, however, there are no markers bearing their names. Sessions's aunt Arria and his grandparents Frederic Dan and Hannah Huntington are close by and clearly marked.

43. Andrew Porter, "Musical Events," *New Yorker*, 8 April 1985, 9.

15

Land preservation has been an issue of rising concern to the town of Hadley over the course of the twentieth century and now in the early years of the twenty-first. With Northampton and Amherst expanding on either side, pressure to develop Hadley's farmland has grown steadily more acute. In this essay, Ethan Carr tracks efforts to preserve what is arguably Hadley's best-known asset: the Holyoke Range. Placing that story in larger regional and national contexts, Carr's narrative rises and falls as much as the range itself. His account ends in 2000, but questions surrounding the preservation of the town's historic and scenic landscape persist; Save the Mountain, together with community groups like Hadley Neighbors for Sensible Development and area land trusts such as the Kestrel Trust and the Valley Land Fund, have continued to raise public awareness on matters of conservation and help protect landscapes, waterways, and wildlife habitats. But issues surrounding both development and preservation will continue to challenge the community in the years to come, and will surely be a story that historians of twenty-first-century Hadley will continue to tell.

Preserving Mt. Holyoke

Ethan Carr

Mt. Holyoke has been a cynosure of tourism and scenic sensibility in the Connecticut River Valley since the early nineteenth century. An early "mountain house" resort was established on its summit in the 1820s, and the existing Summit House was built in 1851.[1] The first version of the inclined railroad up to the hotel was built a few years later. By that time Mt. Holyoke was a major destination on the itinerary of American picturesque tourism, known for its views of the winding Connecticut and the intervale meadows and agricultural fields that extended along it. The views from the mountain were made famous by dozens of artists and engravers, most notably Thomas Cole, whose 1836 painting, *View from Mount Holyoke, Northampton, Massachusetts, after a Thunderstorm—The Oxbow*, is perhaps the best known single image of Connecticut River Valley scenery.

In the twentieth century the preservation of the 1851 hotel and the fate of the mountain landscape around it became linked. Threats to each inspired measures to protect both; historic and scenic preservation went hand in hand on Mt. Holyoke. The most serious threat to both the Summit House and the landscape around it came during the decades following World War II. At that time many mountain houses in the Northeast fell into disrepair or were destroyed, and the Commonwealth of Massachusetts, which acquired the old hotel in 1940, seemed content to watch it fall into complete disrepair. In the meantime the landscape around Mt. Holyoke was being threatened by traprock quarries that supplied gravel to busy road contractors. But as the postwar interest in "outdoor recreation" swelled into the "backpack boom" of the 1960s and 1970s, the mountains were more visited than ever. The Mt. Holyoke Range became part of ambitious "national recreation area" schemes that called for extensive acquisition and management of land. These early efforts to preserve the landscape, however, at first did not consider the value of the historic hotel and the unique inclined railroad that led up to it. Such vestiges of nineteenth-century tourism did not easily find a place in postwar models for managing "natural" landscapes and only gradually were recognized as significant "historic resources" in their own right.

In the end, expansive national recreation area plans were not successful in preserving the Summit House or the surrounding Mt. Holyoke Range. Local residents and advocacy groups, joined by state and local government, provided the impetus and vision necessary to save both the historic structure and eventually much of the landscape around it. The partnership approach that began in the 1970s has developed in recent decades to include a wide range of participants and strategies. The long and significant history of preserving the cultural landscape of Mt. Holyoke continues, and continues to provide insights into how the people of the Connecticut River Valley, and by extension of the nation as a whole, have tried to understand, represent, and preserve their relationship to their environment.

Early Preservation Efforts

The changes that the twentieth century brought to Mt. Holyoke extended and altered aspects of earlier ideas and imagery of the region. Appreciation of the Connecticut River Valley landscape had been guided since the late eighteenth century by the notion of an "American arcadia."[2] The compositions of nineteenth-century painters and engravers, as numerous historians have suggested, reflected the larger balance of a landscape composed of rich agricultural lands framed by forested hillsides and rock ledges. But this delicate balance of land uses shifted in the second half of the nineteenth century, when regional manufacturing increased and the relative economic importance of farming declined. New England industrial towns grew quickly, even as much farmland was abandoned, creating a stronger and in some ways more hostile contrast between what was increasingly seen as "Man and Nature." In his 1864 book of that title, George Perkins Marsh observed that what had seemed an arcadia was also a society with an insatiable appetite for natural resources. The harmonious balance famously rendered by Cole had been shifted, probably disastrously, by the relentless advance of modernization. By the 1870s a movement to salvage and regenerate the nation's remaining forests indicated a broad desire for forest conservation, which in itself belied the pastoral ideal of a benign human presence in the landscape.[3] By the end of the century, the arcadian prospect from Mt. Holyoke had become more difficult to apprehend. As much of agricultural New England reforested through succession, the reality of mill towns and industry contrasted a threatened nature with the spreading effects of industrialization and population growth.

Shifting perceptions of landscape inevitably guided how Mt. Holyoke was seen and managed in the twentieth century. Mountain houses (epitomized by the 1823 Catskill Mountain House, the 1851 Mt. Holyoke Summit House, and the 1853 Tip Top House on Mt. Washington) had been a popular sensation, linked to the contemporary, thriving market in Hudson River School imagery. Changing tastes and patterns in public recreation eroded the popularity of both phenomena in the twentieth century. In the years immediately before and after World War I, motor vehicles rapidly eclipsed trains, river launches, and even dramatic inclined and cog railways (like the one that had ascended Mt. Holyoke since 1854) as the preferred means of accessing and enjoying scenery. The new form of transportation directly affected the profitability of many older resorts. Visiting scenic areas by rail and steam launch, nineteenth-century tourists were the paying customers of railroad and hotel entrepreneurs who often provided livery services and handled other logistics of getting their clients to their hotels. Automotive tourists not only moved themselves but also showed a tendency to care for themselves as well, either by camping or by finding less expensive and more convenient (roadside) accommodations. Their machines allowed the pleasure of visiting mountaintops as part of a scenic drive, and their mobility soon spelled difficulties for businesses that depended on a more captive group of patrons who were more likely to stay in one hotel for a prolonged period.

Automotive tourists, in fact, were not really customers at all. They were the "public," in the same sense that the people who used urban public parks in the nineteenth century had been. Automobiles encouraged expanding the concept of the public park—a reservation supported with public funds and administered by a park commission—to regional, state, and national levels by giving the general public (defined, of course, mainly as the middle class) more affordable and pervasive mobility. Once more distant scenic areas were more accessible, they could be transformed into public places in this specific sense. Hundreds of county, state, and national parks were established in the early twentieth century, and almost all were developed (or redeveloped) for improved automobile access with scenic drives, picnic areas, campgrounds, and new "rustic" lodges and museums. While the dozens of mountain houses built on northeastern mountaintops in the nineteenth century declined, new regional and state parks flourished and were visited by millions of (mainly automotive) tourists in the early twentieth century.[4]

Massachusetts was a particularly important center for developing new types of twentieth-century regional landscape reservations. Mt. Greylock State Reservation, the first of its type in the commonwealth, was established in 1898. Wachusett State Reservation followed the next year.[5] In 1900, landscape architect Charles Eliot began the campaign to pass state legislation that established the Trustees of Reservations in 1901, an unprecedented private land trust that facilitated the preservation of threatened areas. That same year, Eliot and other advocates again convinced the state legislature to take another step in land preservation by creating the Metropolitan District Commission. This regional park commission acquired and developed a system of what Eliot called "scenic reservations" in the Boston suburbs.[6]

In the Connecticut River Valley as well, concerned citizens had organized to preserve threatened scenery by 1900. That year, Christopher Clarke, a successful businessman and music promoter in Northampton, organized a campaign to have Mt. Tom established as a state reservation. Clarke was born in 1827, and in 1851 had been responsible for bringing Swedish soprano Jenny Lind to Northampton for a concert (she visited the Summit House on the same trip). His prodigious efforts to organize support for public ownership of scenic areas around Northampton bore fruit in 1903 and 1906, when Mt. Tom and Mt. Sugarloaf, respectively, were brought into the state reservation system.[7]

Clarke next turned his attention to Mt. Holyoke. John Dwight, owner of the Summit House, died in 1903, and his heirs put the old hotel (the original 1851 structure plus a large addition made ten years earlier) and its surrounding 256 acres up for sale in 1905. After three years on the market, it was evident that the business was not considered a lucrative opportunity. Neither had the state or county governments moved to acquire the property to expand the state's underfinanced and fledgling reservation system. In 1908 Clarke joined a group of like-minded businessmen and preservationists to form a corporation, the Mount Holyoke Company, to acquire the Summit House property in order to prevent the destruction of the hotel and its surrounding forest. They also intended to modernize the resort for twentieth-century tourism. John Dwight's heirs contributed to this largely altruistic enterprise by accepting $25,000 of the company's stock as payment, a sum considered a fraction of the property's actual value.

From the outset, the company's owners, most of whom Clarke had personally recruited, were clear that their goal was (according to the *Daily Hampshire Gazette*) to "preserve the mountain with its natural beauties and furnish attractive accommodations for those wishing to visit it." They were also clear about what this would require: the construction of an expensive road to the summit for automobile access. The "antique cable railway," which in various forms had hauled guests up the side of the mountain since 1853, would "probably be removed," and a garage and a stable would be located on top of the mountain. Besides issuing stock to the Dwight heirs, the company sold an additional $23,000 in stock in 1908 and immediately set about the construction of the new road.[8]

The inclined railroad continued to be operated as part of the hotel business (except for the 1908 season when the owners closed it), but the Mount Holyoke Company's investment priorities clearly lay with improving access by road. Although the new summit road featured a maximum grade of 10 percent, the company's directors nevertheless felt it was still too steep and winding, and they rebuilt the entire road the following summer. In 1910 the road from Hockanum Ferry to the Half-Way House (the starting point for the inclined railroad) was also rebuilt and macadamized.[9] From the beginning, Clarke and the Mount Holyoke Company's directors also shared the not unrelated vision of eventually making Mt. Holyoke a truly "public reservation" by having the state of Massachusetts assume ownership. Clarke died in 1915, but not before launching the next phase in the campaign to preserve Mt. Holyoke. In 1914 the state legislature had created a State Forest Commission empowered to buy cutover logging lands and establish forest reservations. Clarke quickly convinced the new commission that Mt. Holyoke should become such a reservation. He then lobbied the legislature to buy out the Mount Holyoke Company for $50,000, considerably less than the company had already invested in the property. Clarke did not emphasize the property's forest resources in his appeal but instead focused on its potential for public recreation, including the "fine new automobile road."[10] The next year Frank W. Rane, a state forester, prepared a glowing report on the potential of Mt. Holyoke as a public park, noting that it was "not merely a forestry" issue but a question of "preserving for all time to the state a beautiful spot." Rane recommended acquiring the property and dedicating it to Christopher Clarke. He also noted, however, that both Hadley and South Hadley were opposed to having the property removed from the tax rolls and that the nearby reservation at Mt. Tom made another park seem unnecessary to many.[11] Indeed, the state legislature quickly rejected the proposal.

With Clarke now gone and the state in no mood to buy out the Mount Holyoke Company, its owners convened to decide how to proceed. The company had never made money, but the goal of preserving the property remained. None of the stockholders was more committed to that goal than Joseph Allen Skinner, a wealthy silk manufacturer from Holyoke who had already served as the first president of the company between 1908 and 1910. In December 1916 he bought out his fellow stockholders for $50,000 and became the sole owner of Mt. Holyoke and its hotel. In the coming decades Skinner served as a worthy curator of the property. On the one hand he continued to explore the possibilities of state acquisition; on the other he invested generously in improvements. Following the advice of foresters, he logged stands of blighted chestnut (while they still had commercial value) and planted thousands of white pines in their place. The hotel was modernized with plumbing and electrical service, new rooms, and improved management. In 1927 the inclined railroad was converted from steam to electric power and the automobile road was improved and straightened as well. Skinner seemed determined that the Summit House would survive the transition to the twentieth century even as other northeastern mountain houses were headed into decline and disappearing.[12]

Skinner also never gave up Clarke's idea of seeing the property pass into public ownership and management. In 1919 the Massachusetts State Forest Commission was reorganized as the Department of Conservation, indicating a broader approach to land preservation by the state. By 1929 the department had acquired 100,000 acres of forests as well as some important automotive tourist destinations, such as the Mohawk Trail and Windsor state forests. Most of these state lands, however, remained largely undeveloped for recreation until 1933, when Franklin D. Roosevelt's creation of the Civilian Conservation Corps (CCC) launched the entire nation on an unprecedented era of state and national park making. FDR's "tree army" initially stressed forestry and natural resource management, but the ability of crews of young men to build roads, overlooks, lakes, bathhouses, and other recreational facilities soon became clear. In Massachusetts, as in most states, CCC construction established a legacy of recreational facilities that even today defines the core of the state park system.[13]

But while the CCC made improvements at nearby Mt. Tom and Mt. Sugarloaf, Mt. Holyoke remained in private hands through the 1930s and therefore missed an important period of federal largesse in park development. This was due in part, ironically, to Joseph Skinner's extraordinary efforts to keep the Summit House economically viable and in good condition. During this time Massachusetts was eagerly identifying properties for acquisition as state parks, since the CCC and other federal programs would pay for their development. In 1934 a proposal to acquire Mt. Holyoke began to work its way through the state legislature. The legislation called for a new park covering 800 acres of the Mt. Holyoke Range (including Skinner's property) as a memorial to Calvin Coolidge (although local newspapers recalled that it was the venerable Christopher Clarke who had first envisioned such a preserve twenty-five years earlier).[14] The plan was backed by the Department of Conservation, the agency coordinating most CCC and other park developments in the state. By 1936 the Department of Conservation and the Massachusetts State Planning Board were collaborating with the National Park Service to produce a statewide park and parkway plan that included recommendations for many acquisitions.[15] That year the Massachusetts legislature also authorized funds for the purchase of 500,000 acres of new forests to be identified by the Department of Conservation and the State Planning Board and then developed with federal funds and CCC labor. The proposal for an 800-acre park on the Mt. Holyoke Range soon made it to the floor of the legislature and began to be seriously debated. Many of the old arguments, such as loss of tax revenue, resurfaced. But clearly there was a more favorable reception of the idea than Clarke and Skinner had received earlier.[16]

But while the Department of Conservation was in favor of a new Mt. Holyoke park, the agency recoiled at the idea of maintaining and operating the Summit House, which it saw not so much as a historic resource as merely an eighty-five-year-old wooden hotel that would almost certainly require an enormous budget to maintain. Conservation Commissioner Ernest J. Dean made these concerns clear in 1937 when he enthusiastically endorsed buying the land but insisted that the "acquisition of a hotel and its operation is not . . . to be considered as a proper function of this department." State ownership would mean demolishing most of the hotel and ending its commercial operation. While perhaps the oldest (1851) portion of the hotel would be preserved for its historical interest, even this would depend on supplemental appropriations. The "disposal of [the] hotel on [the] summit," reported the *Springfield Union*, was Commissioner Dean's "only problem" with establishing the new park.[17] This attitude would only harden and continue even into the post–World War II era. The management of natural resources reached new levels of professionalism during the New Deal, typically in reorganized state departments of "conservation" or "natural resources." But these agencies typically emphasized the acquisition of land, the management of natural resources, and planning for public "outdoor recreation." Historic buildings in an otherwise "natural" setting often simply did not fit into state or federal land management plans or budgets.

Sentiment in favor of making Mt. Holyoke a park ran high at a series of public meetings in 1936 and 1937. Commissioner Dean confessed that he "had never been so swamped with letters" in favor of a park proposal, and he gave the plan his nominal support. A large delegation of western Massachusetts citizens representing mainly business interests and civic groups traveled to Boston to lobby for the purchase. In fact, the only "real opposition," according to the *Springfield Union*, was from a small group of "Hadley farmers," some of whom apparently owned wood lots on the mountain. But although Commissioner Dean and the Department of Conservation could have prioritized the purchase of Mt. Holyoke at this time, they did not. In a report to the legislature in 1937 Dean specified that he considered acquisition desirable only if "a satisfactory solution can be determined upon regarding . . . the hotel situated on the summit of the mountain." That December Skinner even lowered his asking price to $30,000. But money had never been the issue. Commissioner Dean responded again by saying that his agency would not recommend purchase until the legislature made additional appropriations specifically for the maintenance and operation of the hotel.[18]

The hurricane that devastated so much of New England in September 1938 almost solved the problem. The large 1894 addition to the Summit House was so badly damaged that Skinner decided to demolish it, with the knowledge of course that the state had already promised to tear down at least that portion of the building if they ever took over the property.[19] After razing three-quarters of his hotel Skinner offered the state the entire parcel as a gift. In June 1940 the state accepted the gift which, on Skinner's request, was to be named Joseph Allen Skinner State Park.

A dedication ceremony was held in September, with Skinner and many other figures who played prominently in the history of the Summit House in attendance to hear Governor Leverett Saltonstall speak on the "solemn duty of conservation." Raymond J. Kenney, the new conservation commissioner, announced that he hoped the CCC would be able to develop the park and build a stone museum on the summit. His parks director, Edgar L. Gillett, specified that although "plans had been drawn up" for such a stone structure to replace the Summit House, they had been changed in response to "public sentiment."

The old hotel, he said, would not be razed. It remained unclear, however, what plans if any the state had for the future of the structure.[20] In any case, Congress discontinued the CCC early in 1942 before a new camp could be established to begin work at Skinner State Park.

A Park at Last

Mt. Holyoke was finally a public park, but World War II, followed by the cold war years, kept park budgets meager in Massachusetts, as in the rest of the country. David Graci, the most important historian of Mt. Holyoke, refers to the next forty years as a period of steady decline for the Summit House, during which it experienced "yet another threat to its very existence . . . neglect."[21] In 1942 the electric motor for the inclined railroad burned out, never to operate again, and during the war the number of visitors fell. But the postwar years saw an almost immediate spike in visitation to Mt. Holyoke, a phenomenon familiar to state and national park managers all over the country. In 1934 Skinner had reported about 3,000 visitors, increasing to 5,200 in 1936. In 1947 the number was well over twice that, and every year set a new record: more than 12,000 in 1953 and beyond 13,000 in 1954.[22] Low park budgets continued during these years, nevertheless. Under a reduced maintenance budget the Department of Conservation, as it had feared, could do little except watch the Summit House deteriorate.

The one thing state park managers were willing to do was make road improvements and enlarge parking areas, which were needed improvements since the inclined railroad was now inoperable. But rather than attempt to restore rail service up the mountain, in 1947 A. K. Sloper, the new conservation commissioner, announced that the tramway would be demolished and sold for scrap. "It has been the policy of this department," he explained, "to remove . . . any structure which is no longer usable, especially if the expenditure of state funds is required annually for its maintenance."[23] The inclined railroad subsequently became the center of a long struggle between local preservationists and the state of Massachusetts over what place and role, if any, historic structures should have in the new state park.

The response to Sloper's plans indicated that the Summit House had a fiercely loyal constituency, including the Pioneer Valley Association, a Northampton civic group that represented hundreds of local businesses and other commercial interests. One businessman, Roger Johnson, had grown up in Hockanum, where his father, Clifton Johnson, had been a renowned author, painter, and photographer. The younger Johnson, acting on behalf of the Pioneer Valley Association, organized a public relations and lobbying campaign to persuade the state legislature to repair the Mt. Holyoke railroad rather than demolish it. In a furious response to Sloper, widely reported in area newspapers, Johnson pointed out that the railroad was in better condition than had been suggested and that it was the only responsible means for alleviating the "dangerous" traffic situation at the Summit House. The "only covered funicular in the world," the tramway also was beloved by the majority of park visitors who were awaiting its repair. "It is ridiculous for you to conclude," Johnson insisted, "that because it needs a few minor repairs it should be torn down."[24]

Newspapers soon reported on the "battle" to save the historic cable railroad, but Johnson suffered a setback that winter when heavy snow caused a portion of the shed covering the length of the tracks to collapse. Undeterred, Johnson managed to secure (he thought) a $20,000 appropriation from the state legislature in 1949 for repairs to begin the next year. But in what would prove to be a pattern, apparent success in the legislature never resulted in the Department of Conservation receiving or using the funds as intended. By 1951, the Summit House's centennial year, still no work had been done. Upgrades to the road and parking facilities, however, continued. Over the next several years as Johnson built public support and assembled estimates for the work, the Department of Conservation continued to delay. In 1953, when the estimated cost of repairs had swollen to $70,000, the directors of the Pioneer Valley Association gave up their campaign. The Department of Conservation redirected the funds that Johnson had already secured for the railroad to make additional improvements to the summit road and parking areas. The remains of the unique, covered tramway were intentionally burned by the state in 1965.[25]

By the mid-1950s, concern had shifted to the preservation of the Summit House itself, which according to newspaper reports was a "shambles" because "not a nickel had been spent" by the state on its upkeep despite continued record numbers of visitors (15,000 in 1955).[26] Then in 1956, remarkably, state senators Ralph A. Mahar and Maurice A. Donahue filed a joint bill requesting $850,000 for the restoration of the Summit House and the inclined railroad. Francis W. Sargent, the new commissioner of the Department of Natural Resources (formerly the Department of Conservation), took on the project as one of his first priorities. Boston architect Andrew H. Hepburn of Perry, Shaw, Hepburn, Kehoe & Dean, a central figure in the restoration of Colonial Williamsburg, was retained to develop the proposal and scope of work. For the next two years he worked on what proved to be an elaborate proposal for the complete redevelopment of Mt. Holyoke. The plan called for a new restaurant that would "preserve the historic value" of the Summit House by encapsulating the old lobby and the

Jenny Lind Room within a larger structure. The inclined railroad, defunct and abandoned, would be completely rebuilt in a new, modernized form. After years of total neglect, the state had now proposed an almost fantastic redevelopment scheme that would replace one landmark with what they hoped would be another. By 1957 newspapers reported that the "historic prospect house [was] again making headlines" as the ambitious proposal caught the public's imagination. Most remarkable of all, the state legislature passed a "measure" apparently authorizing the $850,000 expenditure, which Governor Foster Furcolo signed that August.[27] Just a few years earlier, Roger Johnson had been denied even the modest funding necessary to repair the tramway.

The Boston architects went to work in earnest and the next summer presented an elegant, modernistic design for a large restaurant with a circular observation terrace and windows looking out on the valley. Presented as a model to the Department of Natural Resources and the public, it featured a second level above the restaurant with a public area, offices, and smaller circular terrace directly above the restaurant terrace. The building could best be described as an example of contemporary modernism adapted to a more "rustic" setting, mainly through horizontal massing and extensive stone cladding. The parts of the old hotel that had been incorporated were not immediately discernable from the exterior; but a new tramway led directly into the structure's public lobby—a unique arrangement that Hepburn revived for its particular "historical value."[28] The total cost of the building and railroad was now estimated to be one million dollars.

But almost immediately it became clear that the funding was in trouble. The measure passed a year earlier had only authorized a bond sale, which now was unlikely to be made because of the high cost of the building. To make matters worse, $50,000 that had been appropriated for desperately needed repairs to the Summit House had been spent on architects' fees. The entire unlikely proposal evaporated as quickly as it had surfaced.[29]

A New Preservation Battle

The entire movement to preserve Mt. Holyoke was about to take an entirely new turn, in any case. The increased numbers of visitors to the mountain in the postwar era reflected the popularity of new kinds of outdoor leisure activities, such as hiking, pursued by a new generation of the public that would soon begin to express its own concerns and values. And while the fate of the Summit House continued to trouble many, there were other threats to the Mt. Holyoke Range taking shape that had the potential for destroying more than just one building. In 1954, for example, the B&M Construction Company opened a gravel quarry off Route 47. Other traprock quarries soon sprang up on the range.[30] At the same time, the Metacomet-Monadnock (M&M) Trail was being surveyed and constructed by hikers.[31] The boom in backpacking—and the resulting public awareness of threatened landscape scenery—soon came into conflict with the intensifying need for the crushed traprock that could be profitably blasted out of the ledges of the Mt. Holyoke Range.

By 1960, newspaper articles on Mt. Holyoke included characterizations of the B&M quarry's activities as "Man's Assault on Nature" and the "Giant Scar . . . Being Hacked" into the mountains.[32] The source of these polemics (accompanied by convincing photographs) was the South Hadley Conservation Society, a new group of preservationists headed by Richard L. Johnson, who was ably assisted by his cousin Roger Johnson, the former champion of the inclined railroad. Johnson's new preservation battle, however, was to save the entire landscape of the Mt. Holyoke Range from quarries, residential development, indiscriminate logging, or any other activity that promised to scar the view of the mountains from the surrounding valley. The remedy, according to the South Hadley Conservation Society, would be finding the means to put a much larger area of the Mt. Holyoke Range into public ownership. To accomplish this, in 1961 the organization involved two important partners: Charles Foster, commissioner of the Department of Natural Resources, and Ronald Lee, regional director of the National Park Service. The initial strategy was to seek funding from the state legislature to create a vastly expanded state reservation. The Park Service was brought in for technical assistance. The Mt. Holyoke Range might not be of "national park caliber," explained Foster, but the Park Service had been "interested for years" (at least since 1936) in Mt. Holyoke and had "considerable information" useful for planning such an ambitious park.[33]

The solution, Commissioner Foster felt, was not to "remove a single eyesore" but to prevent anything like it from happening again. To help accomplish this, the new partners produced a brochure, *The Case of the Holyoke Range . . . and a Proposal*, while simultaneously introducing state legislation that would authorize the Department of Natural Resources to acquire 10,000 acres of the range. "With the accelerated pace of land consumption," they argued, "there is danger that this beautiful region can be despoiled and robbed of the very qualities which have made it so desirable." Public ownership of the Mt. Holyoke Range would provide for public recreation, preserve vital watersheds, and guarantee that this "historic and picturesque natural resource" would continue to be an "outstanding feature . . . of the Connecticut Valley."[34] Foster stressed that the proposal was the result of "local action" in response mainly to the traprock quarries that appeared in the 1950s. He also cited a study by the Outdoor Recreation Resources Review Commission (appointed by President Eisenhower in 1960) that suggested the Connecticut River Valley was underserved in terms of recreational facilities, including parkland, campgrounds, and picnic areas.[35]

The entire public relations and legislative effort had been carefully planned by an experienced group, but it nevertheless immediately encountered serious political difficulties. Town governments were angered that they had not been involved in the planning process. In Hadley, Hockanum, and Belchertown, public meetings became forums for angry denunciations of the park legislation, particularly the provisions that would have allowed private property to be acquired through condemnation. Even the usually supportive *Daily Hampshire Gazette* editorialized that the "Hadley selectmen" had a point: the proposed bill included overly broad language regarding acquisition of land by eminent domain. Commissioner Foster found himself "denying rumors" that his department planned to take private homes and farmland for the creation of the new state park. Letters to the editor included heated polemics and accusations that the plan was being "carried out with strategy and secrecy" to subvert the rights of private property. The South Hadley Conservation Society and Commissioner Foster quickly offered to amend the proposed legislation and modify the eminent domain provisions, but the damage had been done.[36] By introducing the legislation simultaneously with the brochure, they had created a strong sense that town governments and individual property owners had been excluded from the planning process in an unacceptable manner. The bill failed in the state legislature.

In the meantime, another effort in large-scale landscape management in Massachusetts was playing out quite differently. The Cape Cod National Seashore, established in 1961, was a successful and unprecedented example of landscape preservation. The National Park Service had been attempting to establish "national seashores" since 1939, when Cape Hatteras National Seashore was first conceived. The acquisition of land for Cape Hatteras, however, dragged on for decades because the federal agency could not purchase property directly for the purpose of establishing a new park, and so relied on donations of land from the state of North Carolina. The state could either purchase land or receive it as a gift and then turn it over to the federal government for park purposes. But in the case of Cape Cod, Congress provided appropriations for direct federal acquisition of land for the creation of a new park, the first time any national park legislation contained such provisions. In what became known as the "Cape Cod Model," the legislation also prevented the condemnation of private land in any municipality that cooperated by implementing zoning ordinances that met standards set by the Department of the Interior. The Park Service, local officials, and private property owners developed mutually acceptable approaches to preservation at Cape Cod, and in so doing implemented a new prototype of federal park management.

This was a busy period in recreation planning, particularly at the Department of the Interior. In 1962, following the advice of the Outdoor Recreation Resources Review Commission, Secretary of the Interior Stewart Udall created the Bureau of Recreation. This new agency took over many of the Park Service's recreation planning responsibilities and also administered the funds for public land acquisition generated through the 1963 Land and Water Conservation Fund Act.[37] Other national seashores followed, as well as national recreation areas and other ambitious and innovative federal park planning initiatives. The 1964 Ozark National Scenic Riverway, for example, incorporated two state parks and 80,000 acres of public land stretching along 140 miles of rivers and streams.[38]

It was in this context of federal activism and large-scale planning for outdoor recreation that in 1965 Senator Abraham Ribicoff of Connecticut introduced legislation in Congress to produce a study of a proposed Connecticut River National Recreation Area. The Bureau of Outdoor Recreation went to work in 1966 and over the next two years produced *New England Heritage: The Connecticut River National Recreation Area Study*, an ambitious investigation of the potential of a new federal park along a 400-mile corridor from the source of the river near the Canadian border to the Long Island Sound. The planners felt the potential was good, and therefore recommended establishing a 56,700-acre national recreation area in four New England states. Other elements of the proposal included the creation of two new state parks in Connecticut, an expansion of the Mt. Tom state reservation by 3,000 acres, a new recreation area at Turners Falls, the creation of a "Rogers' Rangers Historic Riverway" in New Hampshire and Vermont, and a "scenic automotive tourway" along the length of the entire corridor. The federal portions of the new park would be concentrated in three "units": the Gateway Unit (23,500 acres) at the mouth of the river; the Mt. Holyoke Unit (12,000 acres), covering the Mt. Holyoke Range; and the Coos Scenic River Unit (21,200 acres) along the river corridor in New Hampshire and Vermont. In all three units, a combination of land acquisition, easements, and restrictive zoning would be used to preserve landscapes and to offer better opportunities for outdoor recreation. Perhaps because of its previous history in the area, the National Park Service was charged specifically with planning the Mt. Holyoke Unit.[39]

In January 1969, House Representative Silvio O. Conte of Massachusetts introduced legislation in Congress to implement the Bureau of Recreation's suggestions for the Connecticut River Valley. Senator Ribicoff introduced a similar bill in the Senate that spring. But the 1968 Bureau of Recreation report, by the planners' own admission, had been quickly prepared by a group of professional researchers and planners with little involvement from the many communities to be affected by the plan. The proposal emphasized recreational uses and public access, and many critics soon argued that preservation of natural resources should have been a higher priority. Other residents feared that the emphasis on recreation would mean an influx of urban populations into their relatively rural communities. The Connecticut River National Recreation Area was also proposed for a far more densely populated, urbanized area than other recreation areas had been, and therefore would require more extensive condemnation of private property.

For all these reasons, political opposition to the plan appeared immediately. The Vermont and New Hampshire congressional delegations, ever wary of federal intervention, never supported the legislation, ending any further involvement by those states. In 1970 Senator Ribicoff introduced another piece of legislation to implement the Connecticut portion of the recreation plan on its own. After a contentious two-year period in which different configurations for the Gateway Unit were repeatedly revised, local opposition finally ended any federal role in the Connecticut project. Planning for the preservation of the Connecticut River estuary was taken up at state and local levels, successfully resulting in state legislation in 1973.[40]

In Massachusetts as well, the 1968 federal plan precipitated widespread public opposition. The proposed 12,000-acre Mt. Holyoke Unit included the village of Hockanum, the Northampton meadows along the river, and the entire range itself. Eighty-five percent of the proposed park was privately owned land; yet those property owners had not been involved in planning process and neither had the municipalities that would be seriously affected by such a development. At a public meeting in Northampton requested by Senator Edward Kennedy, the Bureau of Recreation received a litany of complaints, especially regarding the potential loss of tax revenues, the taking of private farms and woodlots, and the lack of community participation in the process. As a result, the next year when the Park Service began preparing a "master plan" for the Mt. Holyoke Unit, it did so in partnership with a newly appointed Citizen Advisory Committee. Committee members were appointed by the state commissioner of natural resources and represented each of the towns affected, as well as a number of civic and commercial groups. The committee was chaired by State Representative John Olver.

The Park Service planners, led by David Kimball, at first presented plans to the committee that continued to stress outdoor recreation and public access, in line with the 1968 recommendations. The reaction of the committee, as well as the public at many meetings in 1970, made it abundantly clear that the emphasis would need to shift to "preservation," with far fewer numbers of visitors desired or accommodated. By 1971 the Park Service and Olver's citizen committee had worked out a plan that anticipated 3,400 visitors a day, down from 16,000 originally planned for in 1970. The proposed park now covered 12,400 acres, only 1,100 acres of which would be zoned or developed for active use; 10,900 acres would be zoned for "preservation and conservation" and would remain undeveloped. Other aspects of the plan included access to swimming, beaches, and boating along the river, and a new tramway to the top of Mt. Holyoke, eliminating access to the Summit House by private car. About 400 acres in Hockanum and Granby would remain in private hands, subject to local zoning.[41]

Although local complaints continued to be heard in public meetings, the process had been relatively open, produced specific recommendations, and reached at least a limited consensus among the often fractious towns that surround the Mt. Holyoke Range. The citizen advisory committee had worked closely with the Park Service planners, and Senator Kennedy, who introduced legislation in 1971 to implement the plan, had been involved as well. State Representative Olver led a local campaign to emphasize how earlier concerns about the creation of a federal park had been addressed.[42] But the legislation for the park, rechristened the Mt. Holyoke Unit of the Connecticut Historic Riverway, nevertheless languished in Congress and continued to be a contentious issue locally. In the end, the 1971 park plan was tied to the fate of the Connecticut Gateway Unit that Senator Ribicoff was sponsoring at the same time. When the latter effort was abandoned in 1972, the Massachusetts advocates were on their own. Whittled down to just the Mt. Holyoke Unit, the Connecticut Historic Riverway proposal was no longer of "national park caliber," as the Park Service had characterized the 1961 state park proposal. By the end of 1972, seven years of federal efforts to establish a national recreation area in the Connecticut River Valley had effectively come to an unsuccessful end.[43]

Continuing Preservation Efforts

In a familiar pattern, state agencies and officials now attempted to implement their own version of what had proven to be overly ambitious federal recreation planning. In 1973 Commissioner Arthur Brownell of the Department of Natural Resources organized a revised effort to acquire 5,175 acres of the Mt. Holyoke Range, mostly at higher elevations. The state would also assist local towns is drafting protective zoning ordinances for another 15,000 acres. The plan emphasized cooperation with town governments and property owners and flexibility in methods of preservation, including acquisition, easements, revenue sharing, tax incentives, and conservation zoning. Response to public concerns raised over the previous eight years helped reshape the planning process. The proposal specified that a citizen advisory committee would continue to play an influential role, that only "passive recreation" would be allowed on the range, and that the Summit House would be "improved and made a historical feature" of the new park.[44]

A spate of newspaper reports on the public meetings organized by Commissioner Brownell, however, revealed that the new state plan was only slightly less controversial in surrounding towns than the federal plans had been. One headline, "Holyoke Range Park Is Praised in Amherst, Criticized in Hadley," perhaps sums up much of the general public reaction.[45] While Granby and South Hadley appeared to have mixed feelings, Amherst and Hadley were at loggerheads, strongly for and against any park proposal. Perhaps anticipating difficulties in the state legislature, Brownell then worked with John Olver to devise a new legislative package later that year that linked the fate of the Mt. Holyoke Range to that of the Boston Harbor Islands. In an attempt to enlist powerful eastern Massachusetts politicians to the cause, Olver's new legislation proposed a "Bicentennial Corporation" that would be funded to acquire both the western mountain range and the eastern islands. The corporation would be run by an appointed board, and would not be allowed to condemn land in any town without prior approval of its selectmen. Otherwise, the legislation reflected the same goals and arrangements as Commissioner Brownell's proposal. But again the legislation was doomed, defeated by the lack of unity among local governments around Mt. Holyoke (Hadley continued to oppose the plan) and a parsimonious legislature that chose not to see what the acquisition of the Mt. Holyoke Range and the Boston Harbor Islands had to do with celebrating the nation's bicentennial.[46]

In the meantime, the Summit House, all but forgotten in these grand "recreation area" schemes, continued to deteriorate. In 1967 (two years after the state burned the inclined railroad) the barn near the Half-Way House also burned, taking with it a trove of objects, photographs, guest registers, and furnishings from the old hotel, all of which had been stored there for safekeeping. By the late 1960s, the condition of the Summit House itself was a scandal; it was described as a "shell of its former glory" or simply "falling apart."[47]

In 1963 the State of New York's Department of Environmental Conservation had intentionally burned the grandest summit house of all, the 1823 Catskill

Mountain House. The reason given for that destruction was that it had fallen into a dangerous and irreparable condition. The Mt. Holyoke Summit House, perhaps now the most significant of the remaining mountain hotels, seemed destined for the same fate. All it would take was a few more years of neglect and the Department of Natural Resources might free itself of the old hotel that it had never wanted in the first place. As plan after plan for the wider preservation of the Mt. Holyoke Range failed, the precarious and abysmal condition of the Summit House in the mid-1970s seemed to symbolize the fate of the landscape around it.

By 1975, however, the state legislature had finally appropriated funds for the acquisition of 5,200 acres of land and easements on the ridge of the Mt. Holyoke Range. Acquiring these forested, higher-elevation areas apparently caused less controversy, and this more limited expansion of Skinner State Park was finally approved. Commissioner Bette Woody, of what was now known as the Department of Environmental Management, also decided that the moment of truth had arrived for the dilapidated Summit House. At a public hearing in South Hadley, she sought opinions and suggestions for the management of the hotel, which was, she insisted, "structurally unsound" and at a point of deterioration that could make restoration prohibitively expensive. At the meeting were the twenty-five members of the newly appointed Summit House Task Force, a group of local residents, historians, and other interested individuals whom Commissioner Woody had asked to consider alternatives for the Summit House. Three of Woody's proposed alternatives involved the demolition of the building and its replacement with an observation platform or some other more easily maintained structure; only one alternative entailed restoration of the hotel. Woody made it clear that the "real commitment" of her agency was to the "preservation and conservation of the Holyoke Range" and that no part of the $2.4 million that had been appropriated for land acquisitions could be used for restoring the Summit House.

But if public sentiment over various park proposals had been divided over the years, the old hotel had a way of bringing people together. Commissioner Woody discovered near-unanimity among the 150 people present in favor of restoring the Summit House, as well as considerable anger that the state had let it deteriorate for so long. By the end of the month, Henri Forget, chairman of the Summit House Task Force, made it clear at a public meeting in Hadley that the task force members—and most of the public they had met with—strongly favored restoration. From the beginning the Summit House Task Force sought to find funding sources and creative suggestions for reuse of the building; demolition was never considered a desirable alternative.[48] One of the most successful efforts to build support for the Summit House at this time came from Gwendolyn Clancey, one of the task force members, who produced a film about the hotel's history. In the fall of 1976 the film was shown all over the region, usually picking up coverage by local newspapers when it was.[49] The task force also solicited suggestions for new uses for the building and ways to fund its restoration at a series of public meetings. The grassroots campaign had an effect. That fall the state hired Maximilian Ferro, an architectural consultant, to study in detail the structural and economic feasibility of restoring the Summit House. Ferro's report was issued in January 1977 and recommended restoring the existing structure to its historic use as a small hotel and restaurant. Guests would park at the Half-Way House and proceed to the Summit House by horse-drawn carriage or sleigh.[50]

Public support for some kind of restoration was strong and relatively unified. But the Department of Environmental Management still remained ambivalent about the entire idea of having a hotel and restaurant in what agency officials increasingly characterized as an "overused" and ecologically sensitive area. By the end of the year, Bob Yaro, the Department of Environmental Management's chief planner, criticized Ferro's proposal because he considered such a business inconsistent with "the needs of the park as a recreation area and the frail ecology at the mountaintop."[51] With natural resource managers at the Department of Environmental Conservation openly ambivalent about the desirability of keeping the Summit House at all, the situation once again threatened to end in stalemate and inaction.

And then, remarkably, the state legislature surprised everyone, including the Summit House Task Force, and appropriated $600,000 for fiscal year 1979 to restore the Summit House and cover the cost of a new "visitor center" for the expanded Skinner State Park. The news was enough to reactivate the citizen advisory committee, now known as the Holyoke Range Advisory Committee (the group originally created in response to the federal recreation plans of the late 1960s), which had been inactive for years.[52] The architectural firm Alderman & MacNeish, of West Springfield, was selected in 1980 to design the new visitor center and the Summit House restoration. The goal of the plans for the hotel, according to Mark Sirulnik, the project architect, was to restore the hotel to its "former splendor" circa 1890, and even to rebuild a covered tramway up the hillside from the Half-Way House. As engineering and architectural studies proceeded, the state was also acquiring land and easements along the Mt. Holyoke Range. When the restoration of the Summit House began in 1982, 2,500 acres of additional protected land had already been obtained.[53] The preservation of both the mountain landscape and the mountain house proceeded together, the fate of each apparently linked to the other.

In 1981, the Holyoke Range Advisory Committee formed a nonprofit organization, eventually renamed the Friends of the Mt. Holyoke Range. This institutional stability for citizen involvement and advocacy was a by-product of the long preservation struggle.[54] Extensive restoration of the Summit House proceeded over the next six summers, as John Sadlow of the Department of Environmental Management supervised an in-house restoration crew that did most of the work. Completed in 1988, the building now serves essentially as a visitor center and house museum, still featuring the "grandest cultivated view in the world."[55] Other uses, including a restaurant, continue occasionally to be discussed but are unlikely ever to be feasible when needed sewer, water, and transportation improvements are considered.

The Summit House restoration, done in the context of expanded land preservation by the state and the increasingly active and organized citizen involvement in the management of the park, symbolizes an optimistic conclusion to the long and difficult history of preserving Mt. Holyoke in the twentieth century. Of course, threats to the natural and cultural heritage of Mt. Holyoke continue to occur. In 1999, for example, a subdivision was planned for the former B&M traprock quarry. This was the site, ironically, that had originally activated the South Hadley Conservation Society in 1960 and had initiated an era of ambitious federal and state plans intended to prevent precisely this type of development. But in 1999, after the long and difficult history of proposed preservation plans for Mt. Holyoke, something else happened: citizens created a new organization, Save the Mountain, which formed a partnership with conservation groups, civic organizations, and state and local governments to stop the development. In 2000, as a result of the advocacy and fund-raising of Save the Mountain, a private donation was used by state government to acquire most of the quarry site through eminent domain. The town government of Hadley gave its full approval.[56] The right partners had come together in a cooperative way to achieve the further preservation of the Mt. Holyoke Range, something no federal recreation plan ever managed to achieve.

The very presence of the restored Summit House today embodies this evolution in the meaning and process of "preservation" in the twentieth century. An unlikely survivor of an earlier era of tourism, its significance has continuously been altered in response to changing ideals for the management of the Mt. Holyoke Range and, in a larger sense, the balance of "man and nature" in the region. So visible from many of the communities below, the restored Summit

House persists, despite all the vicissitudes of its history, as an active symbol of the mutual engagement of the people and the landscape of the Connecticut River Valley.

Notes

1. The Mt. Holyoke Summit House has also been known in the past as Prospect House and the Mt. Holyoke Hotel. It is referred to consistently here as the Summit House for the sake of clarity.
2. See Martha J. Hoppin, "Arcadian Vales: The Connecticut Valley in Art," in *Arcadian Vales: Views of the Connecticut River Valley*, exhibition catalog (Springfield, Mass: George Walter Vincent Smith Art Museum, 1982).
3. The publication of George Perkins Marsh's *Man and Nature* (1864, second edition 1874), the success of J. Sterling Morton's suggestion for Arbor Day celebrations in the 1870s, and the establishment of the American Forestry Association in 1875, among other events and publications, all indicated a growing awareness for the need of some kind of protection for the rapidly disappearing trees of North America. See Hans Huth, *Nature and the American: Three Centuries of Changing Attitudes* (1957), new ed. (Lincoln: University of Nebraska Press, 1990), 168–77.
4. In the Connecticut River Valley and elsewhere, trolley companies and railroads did often remain important sponsors of resort development in the early twentieth century (as was the case on Mt. Tom, where the Holyoke Street Railway financed the reconstruction of the Mt. Tom Mountain House in 1901). The trend toward automobile tourism, however, coincided with the decline of most of the mountain houses. The last Mt. Tom Summit House was demolished in 1938. The Eyrie House built on Mt. Nonotuck in 1861 burned in 1901 and was not rebuilt. The mountain house on Mt. Sugarloaf (the first built in 1864) was destroyed by the 1930s. For a history of Connecticut River Valley mountain houses, see David Graci, *Mt. Holyoke: An Enduring Prospect* (Holyoke, Mass.: Calem Publishing, 1985). For an account of the dozens of mountain houses built on northeast mountain tops beginning in the 1820s, see Laura and Guy Waterman, *Forest and Crag: A History of Hiking, Trail Blazing, and Adventure in the Northeast Mountains* (Boston: Appalachian Mountain Club, 1989).
5. Shary Page Berg, *The Civilian Conservation Corps: Shaping the Parks and Forests of Massachusetts* (government report, Commonwealth of Massachusetts, Department of Environmental Management, 1999), 5.
6. Gordon Abbott, Jr., *Saving Special Places: A Centennial History of the Trustees of Reservations, Pioneer of the Land Trust Movement* (Ipswich, Mass.: The Ipswich Press, 1993), 15–21.
7. Graci, *Mt. Holyoke*, 61–64. Both reservations remained under county administration, however, with privately owned and operated summit houses.
8. "Christopher Clarke Gets Mt. Holyoke Preserved," *Daily Hampshire Gazette*, 23 March 1908. Unless otherwise noted, all of the articles from Massachusetts newspapers cited in this chapter may be consulted in the archives of Historic Northampton, Northampton, Mass.
9. Graci, *Mt. Holyoke*, 70–74.
10. "Mt. Holyoke as a State Reservation," *Daily Hampshire Gazette*, 18 February 1915.
11. "Reservation Plans for Mt. Holyoke," *Daily Hampshire Gazette*, 1 February 1916.

12. "Railway to Top of Mt. Holyoke Is Electrified," *Springfield Union*, 15 June 1926; Graci, *Mt. Holyoke*, 74–76.
13. See Berg, *Civilian Conservation Corps.*
14. Newspaper reports are unclear on the exact origin of this proposal, but by 1934 the Department of Conservation was actively planning for state park expansions, with the National Park Service officials administering the CCC state park program. The Coolidge memorial park, however, seems to have been local in inspiration. "Memorial Plan Arouses Interest in Northampton," *Springfield Republican*, 7 November 1934.
15. In 1936 Congress passed the Park, Parkway, and Recreational Study Act, which empowered the National Park Service to actively collaborate with state park departments (which it had been doing on a more limited basis since 1933) in planning state park systems and developing them with CCC labor. The result, in Massachusetts, was the *Park, Parkway, and Recreational-Area Study* (government report, Massachusetts State Planning Board in Cooperation with the Department of the Interior, National Park Service, 1941).
16. "Debate Buying Mt. Holyoke," *Daily Hampshire Gazette*, 12 December 1936.
17. "Would Have State Buy Mt. Holyoke Range," *Springfield Union*, 15 January 1937.
18. Dean was also reported (after the fact, in the *Springfield Daily Republican*) to have said that western Massachusetts had enough recreational lands for its population, while the denser population in the east was underserved. His reluctance to acquire and manage the Summit House, however, is the reason frequently mentioned in newspaper reports in 1937. "Public Hearing on Mt. Holyoke Plan Wednesday," *Springfield Union*, 20 February 1937; "Large Group Asks for Purchase of Mt. Holyoke," *Springfield Union*, 23 April 1937; "Dean Report on Taking of Mt. Holyoke," *Daily Hampshire Gazette*, 6 December 1937; "Mountain Given to State by J. A. Skinner," *Springfield Daily Republican*, 20 June 1940.
19. "Mt. Holyoke Summit House Must Be Torn Down for Most Part," *Daily Hampshire Gazette*, 29 September 1938.
20. "Mt. Holyoke Now Expected to Have a New Summit House," *Daily Hampshire Gazette*, 7 September 1940; "Tablet Unveiled at Mt. Holyoke," *Daily Hampshire Gazette*, 16 September 1940; "Old Summit House Not to Be Razed," *Daily Hampshire Gazette*, 16 September 1940; "State Accepts Skinner's Gift of Mt. Holyoke," *Springfield Union*, 20 June 1940; Graci, *Mt. Holyoke*, 80–81.
21. Graci, *Mt. Holyoke*, 81.
22. "Debate Buying Mt. Holyoke," *Daily Hampshire Gazette*, 12 December 1936; "Century Old Prospect House Visited by 12,540 So Far This Year," *Daily Hampshire Gazette*, 16 October 1953; "Record Number of Visitors View Valley," *Daily Hampshire Gazette*, 1 December 1954.
23. A. K. Sloper to Roger Johnson, 21 May 1947.
24. Roger Johnson to A. K. Sloper, 31 May 1947; Roger Johnson to A. K. Sloper, 12 June 1947.
25. "Johnson Denies Mt. Holyoke Railway Sliding Down Slope," *Springfield Union*, 13 June 1947; "Battle Is Going On to Save Mt. Holyoke Cable Railway," *Springfield Union*, 19 June 1947; "$20,000 Sought to Repair Railway on Mt. Holyoke," *Springfield Daily News*, 10 January 1949; "Historic Mt. Holyoke Tramway Will Probably be Torn Down," undated clipping [1953], Mt. Holyoke College Archives, South Hadley, Mass.; "State Bureau Burns Ruined Cable Line," *Holyoke Transcript-Telegram*, 18 February 65; Graci, *Mt. Holyoke*, 84.
26. "Once Famous Mt. Holyoke Summit House Now a Shambles," *Springfield Daily News*, 13 August 1958.
27. "Bill Is Filed for Improving Skinner State Park," *Daily Hampshire Gazette*, 7 September 1956; "Historic Prospect House Again Making Headlines," *Daily Hampshire Gazette*, 13 March 1957; "Hadley Park Bill Signed by Furcolo," *Daily Hampshire Gazette*, 16 August 1957.

28. Although the architects' model apparently was not preserved, photographs of it were published by the newspapers. "Historical Nature Preserved in Famous Architects' Plans," *Daily Hampshire Gazette*, 20 August 1958.
29. "$50,000 for Summit House Was Used to Make a Model," *Springfield Daily News*, 15 August 1958; "Summit House Funds—Coming or Not?" *Springfield Daily News*, 20 August 1958.
30. The Town of Hadley passed an ordinance in 1956 preventing this land use in the future, but the B&M's operations were not affected.
31. The trail was surveyed by Professor Walter M. Banfield of the University of Massachusetts Amherst in the late 1950s. See the "Mt. Holyoke Range Historical Timeline" maintained by Robb Strycharz for the Friends of Mt. Holyoke at www.chronos-historical.org/mtholyoke. The timeline is an excellent source for local history, and includes many historical documents, maps, and press clippings.
32. "Mt. Holyoke Summit House," *Springfield Republican*, 21 August 1960.
33. Charles H. W. Foster to Robert E. Barrett, 25 May 1961, papers of Charles Johnson, private collection.
34. The South Hadley Conservation Society, the Massachusetts Department of Natural Resources, and the U.S. Department of the Interior, National Park Service, *The Case of the Holyoke Range . . . and a Proposal*, brochure, 1962, 20–21.
35. "Mt. Holyoke Range Proposal Given Impetus by Brochure," *Daily Hampshire Gazette*, 28 February 1962.
36. "Hadley Selectmen Have a Point," *Daily Hampshire Gazette*, 9 March 1962; "Other Side of the Mountain," *Springfield Union*, 15 March 1962; "Homes, Farms Not Needed in Plans for Park," *Springfield Union*, 15 March 1962.
37. Edwin M. Fitch and John F. Shanklin, *The Bureau of Outdoor Recreation* (New York: Praeger, 1970), 79–80, 89.
38. Barry Mackintosh, *National Parks: Shaping the System* (Washington, D.C.: GPO, 1991), 72–75.
39. Department of the Interior, Bureau of Outdoor Recreation, *New England Heritage: The Connecticut River National Recreation Area Study* (Washington, D.C.: GPO, 1968); Gregory G. Curtis, "Connecticut Historic Riverway: A Case Study of Acceptance and Rejection of a National Recreation Area" (PhD diss., University of Connecticut, 1974), 9, 19, 34–47.
40. Curtis, "Connecticut Historic Riverway," 48–63; 70–74; 105–39.
41. Robert A. Shanley, "Attitudes and Interactions of Citizens Advisory Groups and Governmental Officials in the Water Resources Planning Process," unpublished report, University of Massachusetts Amherst, 1976, Jones Library Special Collections (hereafter cited as JLSC), 67–72; Curtis, "Connecticut Historic Riverway," 78–85.
42. *The Mt. Holyoke Unit of the Proposed Connecticut Historic Riverway: A Report of the Massachusetts Citizens Advisory Committee, John W. Olver, Chairman*, brochure, 1971, JLSC.
43. Curtis, "Connecticut Historic Riverway," 139.
44. Massachusetts Department of Natural Resources, *A Plan for the Protection of the Holyoke Range*, government report, 1973.
45. "Holyoke Range Park Is Praised in Amherst, Criticized in Hadley," *Amherst Record*, 10 June 1973, JLSC.
46. Curtis, "Connecticut Historic Riverway," 139–45.
47. "Halfway House at Skinner State Park," *Springfield Union*, 6 February 1967; "Summit House Still Draws Visitors," *Holyoke Transcript-Telegram*, 9 August 1966; "Park Shows Valley's Nature—and Man's," *Springfield Union*, 29 July 1969.

48. Mac Gress also served as chairman of the task force. "Foundations Weak, But Support for Summit House Strong," *Amherst Record Weekend*, 4–5 October 1975; "Summit House Fans Seek Quick Action," *Daily Hampshire Gazette*, 1 October 1975; "Restoration Sought for Summit House," *Daily Hampshire Gazette*, 24 October 1975; Graci, *Mt. Holyoke*, 89–90.
49. For example, "Movie Aims at Saving Hadley Summit House," *Greenfield Recorder*, 23 October 1976.
50. Maximilian L. Ferro, "Historic and Economic Assessment, Summit House," unpublished report, Department of Environmental Management, 1977.
51. "Summit House: Debate Over Its Future Continues," *Daily Hampshire Gazette*, 10 December 1977.
52. "Holyoke Range Committee Is Back," *Daily Hampshire Gazette*, 18 September 1978; Graci, *Mt. Holyoke*, 91. John Olver probably was the moving force behind the appropriation.
53. Graci, *Mt. Holyoke*, 92–93.
54. "Group Is Forming to Assist Holyoke Range Development," *Daily Hampshire Gazette*, 24 August 1981.
55. The total cost of the restoration was about one million dollars. This figure was kept down by the Department of Environmental Management through the use of in-house restoration crews. "Summit House Renovations," *Daily Hampshire Gazette*, 22 September 1988.
56. See Save the Mountain's comprehensive documentation of this entire issue at www.savemtholyokerange.com/arch.html.

CONTRIBUTORS

MARTIN ANTONETTI is the curator of rare books in the Mortimer Rare Book Room at Smith College, and he also teaches courses in the history of the book and in contemporary artist's books for Smith's Art Department. He has written and lectured on many aspects of these fields, including fine printing, the evolution of letterforms, bookbinding, and book collecting. Before coming to Smith College he was librarian of the Grolier Club in New York City, the country's premiere organization for bibliophiles. He is also on the faculty of the University of Virginia's Rare Book School and is currently vice president for publications of the American Printing History Association. He received his library degree from Columbia University, where he specialized in bibliography and special collections librarianship.

LYNNE Z. BASSETT is an award-winning independent scholar and museum consultant, specializing in New England's historic costume and textiles. She is a former curator of textiles and fine arts at Old Sturbridge Village and curator of collections at Historic Northampton. Her interest in the early clothing of the Connecticut River Valley extends from her experience as a researcher for the Wadsworth Atheneum's 1985 exhibition *The Great River: Art & Society of the Connecticut Valley, 1635–1820*.

ETHAN CARR was an assistant professor of Landscape Architecture at the University of Massachusetts Amherst when he undertook the research presented in his chapter. He is now a professor at the University of Virginia, where he teaches courses in landscape history, landscape architectural theory, and historic preservation, as well as design studios. Carr earned both his BA and MA in History of Art and Archaeology at Columbia University, and his MLA at the Harvard University Graduate School of Design. He has also worked extensively with the National Park Service as a historical landscape architect. He is the author of *Wilderness by Design: Landscape Architecture and the National Park Service*, which received an American Society of Landscape Architecture award for research. While a resident of the Pioneer

Valley, Carr also put his scholarly expertise to work on behalf of the Town of Hadley, collaborating on a University of Massachusetts Public Service Endowment Grant to study the town common and Great Meadow, research that culminated in a report that helped residents draw attention to the historical significance of that landscape, which was subsequently listed among the Commonwealth's most endangered places.

ELIZABETH S. CHILTON received her PhD from the University of Massachusetts Amherst in 1996; she was an assistant and then associate professor at Harvard University from 1996 to 2001 and is currently an associate professor and chair of the Department of Anthropology at the University of Massachusetts Amherst. Her research specialties include North American Indians, the archaeology of eastern North America, hunter-gatherers, the origins of agriculture, archaeological ceramics, geoarchaeology, and cultural resource management.

CHRISTOPHER DONTA received his PhD from Bryn Mawr College in 1993 and is Senior Project Archaeologist at UMass Archaeological Services and an adjunct faculty member in the Department of Anthropology at the University of Massachusetts Amherst. He has conducted over 190 archaeological projects in New England, as well as archaeological research in the Southwest and Alaska, ranging from Paleo-Indian sites to the historic period.

JAMES A. FREEMAN is a professor in the English Department at the University of Massachusetts Amherst. A graduate of Amherst College and the University of Minnesota (PhD, 1968) his areas of specialty include British literature of the early nineteenth century, the Bible, and an array of subjects in popular culture, including American radio, Joan of Arc, and the material culture of gravestones in the United States, Europe, and Asia. His publications include "The Protestant Cemetery in Florence and Anglo-American Attitudes toward Italy" (*Markers: Annual Journal of the Association for Gravestone Studies*, 1993), "Milton's Roman Connection: Giovanni Salzilli" (*Milton Studies*, 1984), and "The Roof Was Fretted Gold" (*Comparative Literature*, 1975).

PETER HARDIN was raised in Indiana and New York City. At Hampshire College, he discovered a passion for researching history that would last through a career in journalism. He ultimately became Washington correspondent for the Richmond *Times-Dispatch*, where some of his favorite projects involved original historical research. Hardin lives in Takoma Park, Maryland, with his wife, Karen MacPherson, and their two children

Siobhan M. Hart is a graduate of the Department of Anthropology at the University of Massachusetts Amherst. Her research focuses on New England Native history and archaeology with an emphasis on the relationships between archaeology and contemporary issues and politics. She co-directed the 2006 UMass Archaeological Field School excavations in Deerfield, Massachusetts. This work contributed to her dissertation, which explored the intersections of archaeology and various stakeholder communities in the middle Connecticut River Valley.

J. Edward Hood is Vice President for Museum Program at Old Sturbridge Village. He received a master's degree in anthropology from the University of Massachusetts Amherst, specializing in the archaeology of historic New England, and has been a practicing archaeologist and architectural historian in New England since 1985. His past research projects and publications include the historical landscape of Deerfield, Massachusetts, and the material lives of Native Americans and African Americans in nineteenth-century New England.

Bridget M. Marshall is a University of Massachusetts Amherst graduate and an assistant professor in the humanities at the University of Massachusetts Lowell, where her teaching and research interests include Gothic novels, American literature, and popular culture. Her studies of witchcraft trials in Massachusetts stem from an internship undertaken for Historic Northampton during her doctoral studies, when she created the permanent online exhibit *The Goody Parsons Witchcraft Case: A Journey to 17th-Century Northampton.*

Marla R. Miller is a historian of early American women and work at the University of Massachusetts Amherst, where she directs the Public History Program. Hadley became her adopted hometown during the course of her graduate studies, and after completing her doctorate at the University of North Carolina in 1997 she made the community her home. Her first book, *The Needle's Eye: Women and Work in the Age of Revolution*, a study of the clothing trades in the Connecticut River Valley, and Hampshire County in particular, is one product of her long immersion in the community's history, but over the years she has also been pleased to serve on the Hadley Historical Commission, the town's Cemetery Commission, the board of directors of the Porter-Phelps-Huntington Foundation, and the publications committee for the 350th anniversary celebration.

ALICE NASH is an associate professor of history at the University of Massachusetts Amherst. Her research interests center on the impact of colonization on the indigenous peoples of northeastern North America, with a particular interest in family and gender relations. Her publications include "Antic Deportments and Indian Postures: Embodiment in Anglo-Indian New England," in *"A Centre of Wonders": The Body in Early America*, edited by Janet Moore Lindman and Michele Lise Tarter; and "'None of the women were abused': Indigenous Contexts for the Treatment of Women Captives in the Northeast," in *Sex without Consent: Rape and Sexual Coercion in America*, edited by Merril Smith. Her first book, on family, gender, and religion in Wabanaki history, 1600–1763, will be published by the University of Massachusetts Press.

GREGORY H. NOBLES is a professor of history and director of the honors program at the Georgia Institute of Technology in Atlanta. A grant from the Early American Industries Association supported research for an earlier version of his chapter, which was presented at the annual meeting of the Organization of American Historians in 1983. Professor Nobles's other publications on the Connecticut Valley region include *Divisions Throughout the Whole: Politics and Society in Hampshire County, Massachusetts, 1740–1775*; "The Rise of Merchants in Rural Market Towns: A Case Study of Eighteenth-Century Northampton, Massachusetts" (*Journal of Social History*, 1990); and "Shays's Neighbors: The Context of Rebellion in Pelham, Massachusetts," in *In Debt to Shays: The Bicentennial of an Agrarian Rebellion*, edited by Robert A. Gross.

BRIAN W. OGILVIE is an associate professor of history at the University of Massachusetts Amherst. His most recent book, *The Science of Describing: Natural History in Renaissance Europe*, examines the origins of modern botany and zoology in the sixteenth and early seventeenth centuries. He has received fellowships from the National Endowment for the Humanities, the Columbia University Institute for Scholars, the Woodrow Wilson Foundation, the National Science Foundation, the Max Planck Institute for the History of Science, the Folger Shakespeare Library, and the Learned Culture of Seventeenth-Century Europe. Currently planning a book-length essay on natural theology and the argument from design, he is interested in Renaissance culture, the philosophy of history, the history of witchcraft belief and persecution, and the history of religion.

ANDREA OLMSTEAD was the Christopher Hogwood Research Fellow at the Handel & Haydn Society from 2005 to 2007. She has taught Music History at the Juilliard School, the Boston Conservatory, and the New England Conservatory. The author of three books on Roger Sessions and of *Juilliard: A History*, Olmstead has written numerous articles, reviews, and program and CD liner notes, and has given pre-concert talks for the Boston Symphony Orchestra and the Handel & Haydn Society, among others. Also a record producer, she has produced seven CDs of music by Larry Bell. Her book *Roger Sessions: A Biography* was published in 2008.

KAREN PARSONS is the Jennie Loomis Family Instructor in History at the Loomis Chaffee School in Windsor, Connecticut. She is a graduate of the Winterthur Program in American Material Culture at the University of Delaware, and has served as curator of the Hadley Historical Society and guest curator at the Porter-Phelps-Huntington House Museum.

RITA REINKE has worked in New England archaeology for twenty years, focusing on eighteenth- and nineteenth-century rural landscapes. She earned her master's degree in anthropology from the University of Massachusetts Amherst.

STEPHEN W. SEARS is the author or editor of a dozen books on the Civil War, including *Controversies & Commanders: Dispatches from the Army of the Potomac*, from which his chapter is taken. His most recent book is *Gettysburg*. He is a fellow of the Society of American Historians.

LAUREL THATCHER ULRICH is Phillips Professor of Early American History and director of the Charles Warren Center for Studies in American History at Harvard University. Formerly a professor of American history at the University of New Hampshire, she is the author of *Well-Behaved Women Seldom Make History*; *The Age of Homespun: Objects and Stories in the Creation of an American Myth*; *Good Wives: Image and Reality in the Lives of Women in Early New England, 1650–1750*; and numerous articles and essays on early American history. She won the Pulitzer Prize for History in 1991 for *A Midwife's Tale: The Life of Martha Ballard Based on Her Diary, 1785–1812*. She received her BA from the University of Utah in 1960, her MA from Simmons College in 1971, and her PhD from the University of New Hampshire in 1980. During her tenure as a MacArthur Fellow, she assisted in the film production of a PBS documentary based on her book *A Midwife's Tale*. Her work is also featured on an award-winning website, DoHistory.org.

Douglas C. Wilson, who died in 2008, worked for nearly thirty years as a writer, editor, and publications director at his alma mater, Amherst College. His anthology, *Passages of Time: Narratives in the History of Amherst College*, was published in 2007. He also spent thirteen years reporting news for the *Providence Journal*, first in Rhode Island and then as the paper's Washington correspondent and bureau chief. Wilson held a master's degree from the Fletcher School of Law and Diplomacy at Tufts University.

INDEX